Gods in the World

RELIGION, CULTURE, AND PUBLIC LIFE

RELIGION, CULTURE, AND PUBLIC LIFE

Series Editor: Matthew Engelke

The Religion, Culture, and Public Life series is devoted to the study of religion in relation to social, cultural, and political dynamics, both contemporary and historical. It features work by scholars from a variety of disciplinary and methodological perspectives, including religious studies, anthropology, history, philosophy, political science, and sociology. The series is committed to deepening our critical understandings of the empirical and conceptual dimensions of religious thought and practice, as well as such related topics as secularism, pluralism, and political theology. The Religion, Culture, and Public Life series is sponsored by Columbia University's Institute for Religion, Culture, and Public Life.

Prophetic Maharaja: Loss, Sovereignty, and the Sikh Tradition in Colonial South Asia, Rajbir Singh Judge

Moral Atmospheres: Islam and Media in a Pakistani Marketplace, Timothy P. A. Cooper

Karma and Grace: Religious Difference in Millennial Sri Lanka, Neena Mahadev

Samson Occom: Radical Hospitality in the Native Northeast, Ryan Carr

Perilous Intimacies: Debating Hindu-Muslim Friendship After Empire, SherAli Tareen

Baptizing Burma: Religious Change in the Last Buddhist Kingdom, Alexandra Kaloyanides

Gods in the World

Placemaking and Healing in the Himalayas

AFTAB S. JASSAL

Columbia University Press
New York

Publication of this book was made possible in part by funding from the Institute for Religion, Culture, and Public Life at Columbia University.

Columbia University Press
Publishers Since 1893
New York   Chichester, West Sussex

Copyright © 2024 Columbia University Press
All rights reserved

Library of Congress Cataloging-in-Publication Data
Names: Jassal, Aftab, author.
Title: Gods in the world : placemaking and healing in the Himalayas / Aftab Jassal.
Description: New York : Columbia University Press, 2024. | Series: Religion, culture, and public life | Includes bibliographical references and index.
Identifiers: LCCN 2024013473 (print) | LCCN 2024013474 (ebook) | ISBN 9780231214964 (hardback) | ISBN 9780231214971 (trade paperback) | ISBN 9780231560559 (ebook)
Subjects: LCSH: Hinduism—India—Garhwal (Region)—Rituals. | Nagaraja (Hindu deity)—Cult—India—Garhwal (Region) | Healing—India—Garhwal (Region)—Folklore. | Folk songs, Garhwali. | Spiritual healing—Hinduism. | Dalits—India—Garhwal (Region) | Social justice—Religious aspects—Hinduism.
Classification: LCC BL1161.H56 J37 2024 (print) | LCC BL1161.H56 (ebook) | DDC 294.5/38095451—dc23/eng/20240506

Cover images: View of the Himalayas and Jhakar Saim temple.
Photographs courtesy of the author.

Contents

Acknowledgments vii
Note on Transliteration xi
Prelude: The Healing Room xiii

Introduction: Textures of Divine Presence   1
1. Making "Dev-bhumi," the Land of the Gods   26
2. Affliction and Healing   52
3. Political Divinities in the Village Square   75
4. Undoing Love: Ghost Affliction and Patrilocal Marriage   97
5. Out of Place: Lives of Oracles and Priests   127
6. Playing in the Rain: Scenes from a Himalayan Pilgrimage   154
Epilogue: Beyond Belief   184

Indian-Language Words with Diacritics 191
Notes 197
Bibliography 225
Index 235

Acknowledgments

I thank the many friends, teachers, colleagues, and students whose voices and hands have shaped this book. This ethnography would not have been possible without the wisdom and generosity of the religious practitioners with whom I work in Uttarakhand, India. If this work captures even a small fraction of their beauty and power, it expresses my gratitude for their kindness and hospitality. I also thank Dinesh Bhajalwan, Vikrant Chandola, Subhadra Joshi, P. K. Tamta, and their families for their generous guidance and hospitality as I traversed unfamiliar mountainscapes in Uttarakhand. I am indebted to the Arya and Bisht families for their friendship and care. I am grateful for the work of exceptional scholars and artists based in Uttarakhand—Govind Chatak, Maheshwar P. Joshi, Lalit Keshwan, Shivprasad Naithani, Shivanand Nautiyal, Jugal Kishore Petshali, Data Ram Purohit, Chander Singh Rahi, and others. Their English- and Indian-language writings have informed generations of students, including myself.

My admiration for Joyce Flueckiger as an ethnographer, advisor, and friend knows no bounds. The humanity, lucidity, and rigor she brings to the study of religion in South Asia is inspiring, as is her warmth, dedication, and care as a mentor. Laurie Patton's luminous scholarship and ability to honor and navigate dharmic complexity continue to motivate my academic work. I thank her for teaching me how to teach and for her wise counsel in times of difficulty. I am thankful to Paul Courtright, sage and healer, for his generosity of spirit, outstanding pedagogy, and wide-ranging contributions to Hindu studies. V. Narayana Rao's pioneering work and dazzling lectures at Emory transformed how I think about text, performance, and society in India. Being his student is an immense joy in my life. In my early twenties, my journey as an anthropologist of religion began with David Shulman, and our wondrous conversations in Jerusalem remain a part of my being. As a person, poet, intellectual, and activist, he continues to inspire me.

Lucinda Ramberg's insightful suggestions breathed new life into the text, and I am grateful for her inspiring scholarship and ethical commitments. I also thank Frederick Smith and William Sax for their extraordinary scholarship and the enthusiasm and support they have shown to junior scholars, including me. As a graduate student, I also benefited from working with Gyanendra Pandey and Vincent Cornell and reading Sanskrit with Nadine Berardi and John Dunne.

My manuscript reviewers provided deep, careful, and generous readings of my work, which greatly improved the book. As models of scholarly engagement, intellectual rigor, and compassionate critique, they helped clarify and develop the book's arguments in a myriad of ways. At Columbia, I am immensely grateful to Matthew Engelke, editor of the *Religion, Culture, and Public Life* book series, my editor, Wendy Lochner, and the editorial board at Columbia University Press for supporting this project. Working with Wendy has been a great privilege, and I thank her for believing in the book and steering it to publication in the smoothest, most joyful way possible. I was honored to participate in a book workshop organized by the Institute for Religion, Culture, and Public Life (IRCPL) with Rachel McDermott, Jack Hawley, and Matthew Engelke, whose incisive commentary and encouragement were invaluable in the final revisions. My thanks to Justine Esta Ellis at IRCPL and Lowell Frye, Leslie Kriesel, Chang Jae Lee, Alyssa Napier, Will Oemler, and others at CUP, and Ben Kolstad at KGL for all their hard work throughout the production process.

Among my wonderful colleagues and students in the Anthropology Department at the University of California, San Diego, I am particularly thankful to Nancy Postero, Tom Csordas, and Steve Parish. Steve offered illuminating responses to an early draft of the book. My graduate school colleagues at Emory University, in the South Asia Initiative at UCSD, the Department of Religious Studies at Colgate University, and the Thompson Writing Program at Duke University have also been superb interlocutors over the years. I thank Harshita Kamath for organizing a conference at Emory in honor of Joyce Flueckiger in 2021, where I had the opportunity to present an early draft of chapter 6. My thanks to Paul Sheppard for his meticulous research assistance on the manuscript. Rahul Tiwari created the map of Uttarakhand.

Many friends and colleagues have walked with me through life's tribulations. They have engaged my work and provided critical feedback at academic conferences, seminars, workshops, and informal gatherings in India, the United States, and other parts of the world; some have been partners in music. I am especially thankful to Amaar Abbas, Amy Allocco, Brenda Baletti, Tarik Benmahrnia, Vinny Bhagat, Prashant Bharadwaj, Monica Camacho, Amy Cimini (and Dusty), Claire Edington, Francisco Eme, Haluk Erzurumlu, Khaled Farrag, Keolu Fox, Todd Henry and Daeryuk Shin, Carter Higgins, Yeshwant Holkar, Aijaz Hussain, Shai Meir, Rishika Mehrishi, Townsend Middleton, Amit Miller, Alaa Muhanna, Nidal Muhanna (and his family in Peki'in), Didi Oshrat, Dan Navon, Brian Pennington, Jitender (Rinku) Singh, Russell Sticklor, Mohan and Nayana Trivedi (and family), Miri Urman, Peter Valdina, Kalindi Vora, and Luke Whitmore for their friendship. Lifelong friends Ashhar Farooqui and Neha Dixit, musicians and filmmakers who live and work in Uttarakhand, have inspired me for many years. I'm excited for our collaborations, including on some of the visuals that appear in this book and a series of short films. We've been working and dreaming together for decades, and it's incredible to be on this journey with them. The love and support of Meher, Manju, Krishan, and Sidhant means the world to me. I thank my grandparents, my Nani ji and especially my Nana ji, whose library of philosophical and literary treasures drew me into the study of Indian religions as a teenager.

Finally, to my father, Raminder. The world is magical because I revel in his brilliance, artistry, grace, and humor every day. To my mother, Smita, for giving me music and literature. Her passion for art, learning, and exploration fills my world with light. To my brother, Nirvikar, for a lifetime of joy, laughter, and affection. And to Saiba, in white, red, and black. Without her, I'd be cold and silent, adrift in space. Instead, she is here. My warmth, vayu, (e)arth, and rasa.

Note on Transliteration

For ease of access, I have italicized but not employed diacritics for Indian-language terms that appear in the book. For interested readers, I have included a list of many words and phrases with diacritical marks at the end of the book.

Map of Uttarakhand. Shaded and unshaded areas in this figure represent the regions of Garhwal and Kumaon, respectively, which make up the state of Uttarakhand, India.

Prelude

The Healing Room

On a sunny June morning, Sohan, an oracle, sat down on a woven mat and cushion in his healing room to prepare for a day of work ahead.[1] In the Himalayan region of Garhwal, in the north Indian state of Uttarakhand, oracles like Sohan are called *bakkyas*—literally, "ones who speak."[2] Individuals suffering from illness or distress visit oracles to receive a diagnosis, treatment, or advice, which oracles provide by ritually embodying local gods and goddesses. Many oracles in the region hail from Dalit (caste-oppressed) backgrounds, and unlike Sohan, many are women.

A powerful local deity spoke and acted through Sohan, but it was not necessary for a visitor or "client" to have a prior relationship with this deity to seek healing. All were welcome, but this did not mean the healing room was always a pleasant or safe space. Here, deity, oracle, and client came together in intense, emotionally charged interactions, which often felt more like heated negotiations between family members rather than interactions between humans and nonhumans. In this site of flux, deep, life-changing, and sometimes painful relationships between humans and divinities were forged.

The walls of the healing room were mostly bare except for one directly in front of Sohan, which held posters of various divinities as well as hanging brass bells, votive offerings presented by clients. Garlands of money covered some of the posters, evidence of client appreciation for prayers answered. Shiny red and gold streamers crisscrossed the ceiling, creating a thatched canopy above. On a raised ceremonial altar in front of Sohan, an oil lamp burned, producing an ambient glow, alongside a number metal trays laden with fresh flowers, fruit, burning incense, sacred ash, plastic containers filled with "holy water" collected from a nearby tributary of the River Ganga, Shiva-*lingas* (aniconic images of the god Shiva), tin plates engraved with sacred incantations (*mantras*), geometrical ritual diagrams (*yantras*), and numerous images and statuettes of deities.

A wiry man in his forties, Sohan had a wispy beard and sunken eyes. Outside the healing room, he was quiet and nervous, a sharp contrast from his interactions with clients, where he embodied the authority and intensity of the deity. When the first client entered the room and the healing session began, Sohan turned to face the ceremonial altar. In this position, he had his back to his client, which was unusual for oracles. Sohan keeping his back to his clients did not, however, take away from the intimacy and intensity of their interactions. On the contrary, as the day progressed, I saw how Sohan facing away from his clients seemed to make them more comfortable and candid about their conflicts and difficulties. Like a Roman Catholic confessional box, the sense of separation produced its opposite, a paradoxical intimacy.

While Sohan faced the back corner of the room, his brother-in-law Billu, whose home we were in, sat on his haunches directly behind clients, ready to spring into action to facilitate the activities of the healing room. I was invited to sit in another corner of the room from where I could observe without disrupting the flow of events. Billu had a crucial role to play as translator. Even though the deity was present during the ritual, at times, he could not be directly accessed by clients. Upon entering trance and then at various other points in the ritual, the deity's words, spoken through Sohan, were unintelligible. The deity sometimes spoke in a "divine language" that was beyond the grasp of ordinary humans, Billu explained. Only Billu, through years of painstaking effort and experience, could translate what the deity was saying. Even when the deity was speaking in the local dialect, his intonation was broken, strained, and punctuated by deep breaths and strange sounds. As facilitator and interpreter, Billu was indispensable to the work of the healing room.

In fact, the healing room was a space of multiple translations: through his body, Sohan also "translated" the presence and agency of the deity into human form, language, and activity. In the process, Sohan was ontologically transformed into something more, someone else. Further, in these ritual contexts, deities themselves *also* act as translators, often mediating between human beings and other, more removed divinities, such as Shiva or Nirakar, who are sometimes described as transcendent beings possessing neither form nor attribute.[3]

My eyes wandered around the healing room and settled on a prominently displayed poster on the wall. At first, I had barely noticed it because compared to the other objects and images that surrounded us, this mass-produced example of "calendar art," readily available in newsstands and roadside stalls, seemed unremarkable. The poster depicted a ritual diagram (yantra) made up of a series of nested triangles, squares, and circles. At the center of the poster was a red dot, surrounded by concentric shapes that grew larger and more encompassing as one's eyes traveled from the center of the poster to its periphery. Along the border of the poster were twelve goddesses, each with her own distinctive attributes and moods. Despite their differences, the goddesses were all clothed in red, mirroring the red circle at the center. The geometric forms linked an inner space of dense interconnectivity and power, suggested by the red dot, to the familiar, phenomenal world of name and form represented by the goddesses. As my eyes traveled from center to periphery, I felt the effect of a geometric, progressive unfolding, one intended to bring the twelve goddesses into the healing room and into the world.

Pointing to the poster, Billu said, "This is the deity's power [*shakti*]. Everything is shakti. God is one. All the deities in Garhwal are one, even though they have different names." I understood Billu as saying that, although people worship many deities—each for their own particular powers, desires, attributes, and moods—ultimately, they were all partial forms of an all-encompassing, formless Absolute. Just as the nested shapes of the yantra framed each other, the poster shaped interactions between oracles and clients, enacting a chain of human and nonhuman intermediaries, including oracles, that connect the human-social world to a hidden, powerful realm.

Sohan's first client of the day was Ramesh, a heavyset young man. He seemed worried as he walked into the healing room, bowed, and folded his hands in greeting. Ramesh was from a neighboring village, and he used to seek healing quite regularly in the past. Ramesh sat down, and Sohan, with his back to him, began rocking back and forth, calling on his deity to become present in/on his body.

Sohan—or rather, the deity—then began mumbling in a high-pitched, questioning voice, which grew louder, though his words remained indecipherable—an otherworldly stream of clicks, pops, flutters, and chirps. Over time, strings of phonemes that bore a closer resemblance to ordinary human language began to crystallize within this sonic morass, but I still struggled to follow him. As I watched the oracle tremble with power, I became aware of how our perceptions, memories, and narrations skim the surface of what we call "experience." Yet, the deity's presence, their closeness, realness, and interiority demanded a leap of faith beyond our everyday assumptions.[4]

Once the trembling subsided and it was clear that the deity was present, Ramesh blurted out: "I am trying to find success in life, but all my attempts are being stymied."

The deity stopped talking, turned around, and held Ramesh by the arm. After a few moments, he spoke, now in a clear voice: "You are in pain; you have borrowed money from your family members, and you have also borrowed money from people outside of your home...."

Ramesh was clearly taken aback.

Billu translated: "The *devata* [deity] is saying that you are unhappy because you have taken money from people."

"No, no, my lord, it's nothing like that...." Ramesh protested weakly.

The deity repeated his accusation, which was also a diagnosis: "You have taken money! Isn't this true? You are even ready to run away from your home out of fear." If this were true—and from Ramesh's reaction, I inferred that it was—I wondered how the oracle could have known this. Were Ramesh's financial dealings well known through the village grapevine? Was this something Ramesh himself had confessed in a previous interaction with the oracle? Or was this something that the oracle had intuited in the moment?

The deity spoke: "Everything will turn out fine. Do not fear.... But you have forgotten God's [*bhagavan*'s] name...."

"I am taking your name right now![5] I am here ... what more can I do?!" Ramesh's voice soared. Perhaps realizing that this might not be the best way to pacify the deity, Ramesh softened his tone, "Lord, only you can fulfill my aspirations; I plead with you, help me," he said, with hands folded.

The deity's speech once again became indecipherable, so Billu clarified: "The deity is saying that an *ashta-bali* [a multiday sacrificial ritual] needs to be performed. Many things [devotional practices] need to be done, but they are not being done." The deity accused Ramesh of failing to perform ritual worship for various local deities.

Ramesh agreed. "As soon as my desire is fulfilled, I will perform the sacrificial ritual; I will bring you a bell [as a votive offering], or whatever you want...."

The deity continued, "You do not hold back your generosity, but things become impossible when you accrue debt."

To begin the process of repairing relations with the deities, Billu advised Ramesh to present an edible offering made of flour (called a *rot*) and 21 rupees.

The mention of money seemed to agitate Ramesh. "But lord," he said, "I have no money coming in from anywhere! Who will help me?!"

The oracle responded in a stream of angry, indecipherable speech. Billu translated: "The deity is saying that until someone calls him, he does not go to their place [*sthan*]. Never."

The deity added, "Even if you call me, I will not come. I enjoy being where I am.... But when my anger arises, I cause great difficulty. And *then* I go into people's homes!"

This surprising back and forth illustrated a general truth about deities in the region: that they can be experienced as benevolent, healing presences but also as afflictive beings capable of causing immense harm. Ramesh was being warned that deities for whom "place" had *not* been made were liable to produce affliction and misfortune. I made a mental note to ask Billu about this cryptic statement about "place" later.

The deity then named numerous deities who were unhappy with Ramesh. At this point, Ramesh, who had been silent for some time, again objected: "But lord, until *I* am helped, how can I do anything? Sometimes I feel so sick, I want to throw up. This is my situation . . ." he choked. With tears in his eyes, he whispered, "Deity, my faith [*vishvas*] has been broken."

The deity nodded somberly. "There is disquiet among both two-legged and four-legged creatures in your place. Even the deities won't help you. . . . Have you propitiated the "water beings" yet?"

Ramesh shook his head. The deity responded: "Then how do you expect your situation to improve? Even the goddess of your home is angry. . . ."

Ramesh hung his head in silence.

Sensing that the session was winding down, Billu began preparing a healing mixture of ash from the ceremonial altar, sanctified grains of uncooked rice, and dried flower petals, among other things, for Ramesh to take home with him. Billu wrapped these in a sheet of paper torn from a school notebook and tied it with string. Ramesh accepted the packet, touched it to his forehead, and put it in his pocket. Ramesh knew the mixture was a material manifestation of the deity's power and was intended to protect and nourish him.

Before leaving, Ramesh made one final plea: "Deity, if you help me, I will present you with an offering of a bell (*ghanta*) . . . whatever you want."

"I don't ask anything from you, only what you are able to do," the deity snapped, protesting the crude transactionalism of Ramesh's framing. In his protestations, the deity made clear that he did not see their relationship as a one-to-one exchange. Even though deities *were* desirous of material gifts, such "exchanges" were important in so far as they were constitutive of long-term relationships of trust and mutual care. For the deity, what was important was for Ramesh to acknowledge and commit to their ongoing relationality.

Before Ramesh left, the deity reiterated this message of mutual obligation: "If even one of the things I have said turns out to be false, you can hold me to account. . . ." By now, other clients had begun to line up outside the healing room.

As the healing room bustled with the arrival of new clients, new and old crises, and divine advice that was sometimes harsh, sometimes conciliatory, the memory of Ramesh's charged interaction with the oracle stayed with me, not because it was unusual but because it exemplified the intimacies among deities, oracles, and human beings. I was struck and a little frightened by the way the deity and Ramesh had accused one another of not living up to their respective obligations. Unlike the guarded social norms of respect in the region, particularly toward elders, relationships between devotees and deities were often strangely egalitarian and expressive. As one of my interlocutors put it, "We only argue with those with whom we are close."[6]

Then, there was also the nuanced relationship between the oracle and deity that made healing possible. After his day of work was over, I asked Sohan what it felt like to embody and channel the deity. He described it "like a fisherman pulling in fish from a river (*nadi*). You don't see what's there [in your net], but you feel the 'pressure' [Eng.], so you pull it toward you. And then you ask, 'What are you? Who are you?' And then it tells you: 'I am so and so; I want this or that.'" In Sohan's description, the fish gives itself to you, but the human actors in the healing room must pull the deity in and communicate with them. Sohan's description offered a beautiful account of learning to sense differently, an expertise nurtured over time. To know not only when but also how to pull deities into the world.

Gods in the World

Introduction

Textures of Divine Presence

The Diagnosis

One autumn night, I was hanging out in a temple courtyard in Garhwal. I was attending a full-moon religious ceremony, and even though it was late, everything was brightly illuminated, thanks to the numerous fires people had lit to stay warm. The air was smoky, moonlight pierced through the hazy sky, and the smell of conifers wafted around us.

A man approached me. He was older, perhaps in his sixties. Because younger people were usually shy to talk to strangers, during festivals, I often found myself in the company of elders, many of whom were curious, jovial, and eager to talk to "outsiders."[1] He asked what I was doing at this event. I replied that I was interested in learning about how Pahari *log* (people "of the mountains," as those who live in this part of the Himalayas often refer to themselves) interact with local deities. My interlocutor responded that he came from a lineage of oracles—he possessed the ability to "see" the inner thoughts and life situations of others. He had been born with this ability, he said, and even though he had not become a professional oracle, "it flowed in his veins." He told me that he knew my "real reason" for being at the festival. "I will tell you the dream that brought you here," he said.

He placed two fingers on my wrist, felt my pulse, and closed his eyes in deep, concentrated silence. Then, he said, "You dreamed of a snake that was dismembered. It was cut into two, maybe three, pieces."

I had no memory of such a dream, and when I shook my head to say no, he seemed skeptical.

He closed his eyes again and said: "You dreamed of a snake that was cut into several pieces. Or maybe it was some other animal—a goat, perhaps?"

I said I hadn't. He didn't try again but insisted that I had had some version of the dream he was describing. I could see he was losing patience, so to avoid offending him, I said that perhaps I had forgotten my dream. As he released my wrist, he said he was certain I had forgotten. Having cleared up the matter (sort of), he warmed up to me, introduced me to his companions, and invited me to his home. We spent many hours talking about oracular healing that night.

Though I had no recollection of the dream-image the oracle had described, the image of a dismembered snake and our unsettling exchange impressed me. I knew that snakes were sacred in this part of the world—there were many serpent deities (*nag devata*) that were commonly worshiped—and, as such, the image of an injured snake was disturbing. When serpents and serpent deities are harmed or wronged, they can inflict *nagadosh*—literally, the "fault of the serpent," or "serpent affliction"—on those who harm them. Nagadosh can take the form of a virulent illness or deadly misfortune. I began worrying that the oracle was suggesting that I had knowingly or unknowingly harmed a serpent. The dream could mean that *I* was suffering from a supernatural affliction, like others who had attended the festival. If he was diagnosing me, I realized, he was also suggesting that I was not merely an observer or researcher but also someone in need of healing. I wondered what it would take to piece the snake back together, to re-member, suture, or heal it/me.

These different possibilities raise some profound and perhaps unanswerable questions about what it means to research people's relationships with their deities and experiences of illness, misfortune, and healing as an anthropologist. By suggesting that I, too, was suffering and in need of healing, the oracle implicated me in my research: no mere "observer," I was now an involved participant in oracular and healing rituals.[2] In implicating me, the oracle also made it clear that it was not possible to be a secular, nonbelieving (that is, neutral and objective) researcher engaged in studying the relationship among divinities, humans, and wellbeing. I was not immune to, nor situated outside of, the processes I was observing. It was not enough to simply "understand" how people related to their deities; I also had to *feel* the deities' presence and *be affected* by them.[3] His reading of my dream, whether real or not, was designed to make place for deities in my life. What I would learn through the course of my research is that "making place" for deities is not a simple or straightforward process. Not only is it a two-way, reciprocal process, but like human relationships, it requires care, labor, attention, and sustaining many ups and downs.

"But how do gods become real in the experiences of people and communities?" Robert Orsi's question offers a powerful starting point for considering the modes of attention, care, and reparative labor performed by ritual practitioners in the north Indian state of Uttarakhand to maintain harmonious relations with their deities who exert immense power over their lives.[4] Divinities—that is, gods, goddesses, ancestors, ghosts, and other nonhuman actors—do not merely exist in a supernatural realm, but they are also present in and of the world. Some ancient beings are familiar to people from Sanskrit- and vernacular-language traditions, such as the Mahabharata, Puranas, or various regional oral epics. Others are newer to the supernatural realm, recently deceased ancestors or historical figures.

Scholars of Hindu traditions have noted how divine "presence" includes attributes, or manifestations of god, such as name, form, behavior, and place. For example, Philip Lutgendorf, writing about the centrality of "play" (*lila*) in Vishnu-centered theologies, quotes a phrase that came up repeatedly in the Ramayana exposition performances that he recorded in north India: "The Lord has four fundamental aspects [*vigrah*]: name, form, acts, and abode [*nam, rup, lila*, and *dham*]—catch hold of any one of these and you'll be saved!"[5] Diana Eck, discussing iconic images (*murtis*) of deities, notes that the noun *vigrah* "comes from a verbal root (*vi+grh*) that means 'to grasp, to catch hold of.' The *vigrah* is that form that enables the mind to catch hold of the nature of God."[6] Building on these understandings, I suggest that the concept of "place," *sthan* or *than*, is a primary means through which worshipers "catch hold" of, or come to know, deities in Uttarakhand. Making place for a god is generative of "presence"—a lived (and living), multisensory experience of a deity in the world.[7]

Deities in Uttarakhand are regularly made present in ritual contexts involving "possession," or divine embodiment, in which deities are embodied by human mediums. In embodied form, deities intervene in matters intimate and domestic as well as collective and political—from healing healthcare concerns to easing familial tensions to solving village disputes. Their worshipers call on them not only in times of joy but also for assistance and advice during times of difficulty. Pahari (lit., "of the mountains") families include both human and divine members, and their narratives and ritual practices enact such kin relations. Deities share intimate, familial bonds with their worshipers and are a part of their kin networks as *kul devatas*, or lineage deities.[8] For instance, the gods

Nirakar, Nagaraja, and Saim Devata are sometimes referred to as the "maternal uncles" (*mama*) of lesser gods, while certain goddesses, such as Nanda Devi, are regarded as mothers, daughters, or daughters-in-law of certain communities.

Gods in the World explores the affective, moral, and political stakes of human-divine relations in Uttarakhand, what happens when those relationships are disturbed, and how people heal and repair those fissures. Divinities are experienced as familiar and remote and as immanent and transcendent. Like human relationships, relations between humans and divinities in Uttarakhand can also be intense and fraught. Human and nonhuman actors both make demands on each other; they argue, negotiate, and fight. Human devotees not only make demands on deities in the form of prayers or wishes, but deities, too, make demands of their devotees. Divinities, like humans, have their own pressing desires and distinctive personalities; they require care.[9] Yet, they are powerful, more powerful than humans, and in South Asian contexts, power is not only creative but also dangerous and destructive.[10] As such, interactions between deities and humans can have critical, life-and-death consequences.

In a world "where the divine and mundane are not sharply delineated,"[11] humans and deities are entangled in intimate, complex relationships that have far-reaching effects. Deities and various other nonhuman actors in Uttarakhand *intervene* in the lives of people in meaningful ways. In addition to these nonhumans being known through their sensory effects—such as "seeing" (*darshan*) a deity during temple worship—nonhuman agency is apprehended through its tangible effects on everyday life, on particular social and political categories and crises. Thus, the presence of a deity cannot be divorced from the material effects through which that deity is known.[12] As Matthew Engelke writes, "Materiality is the stuff through which 'the religious' is manifest and gets defined in the first place: how God, or the gods, or the spirits, or one's ancestors can be recognized as being present and/or *represented*."[13] *Gods in the World* shows how nonhumans do not inhabit a realm outside, or beyond, the mundane; on the contrary, the gods and goddesses of Uttarakhand are very much *in* the world.

Gods of Place

This book centers on one consistent and powerful demand that deities make of their worshipers: *in exchange for curing human suffering, divinities often demand that a "place" be made for them.* But what exactly does it mean to "make place" for a god? And how does this act become integral to maintaining human-divine relations?

Deities in Uttarakhand are connected to particular places, such as villages, temples, forests, rivers, or mountains. Here, *place* constitutes both a material location—which reveals and contains divine presence—as well as a metaphorical sense of belonging. When deities are "out of place," either materially or metaphorically, they can produce human illness, misfortune, or suffering. Thus, devotees spend significant amounts of time, energy, and resources keeping their deities emplaced and content. Making place for a deity is a manifestation of devotion, and practices of *placemaking* include divine embodiment, oracular healing, ritualized performances of narrative song, temple worship, and translocal pilgrimage, among others. In other words, these placemaking practices, which we will see unfold in the course of the book, are efforts to maintain or repair relations with deities.[14] *Gods in the World* argues that placemaking is a critical technology of healing that transforms social reality.

While doing ethnographic research, I came to appreciate how placemaking practices help alleviate the suffering of Hindu devotees in Uttarakhand. A male oracle (*bakkya*) of the popular deity Bhairavnath told me how Pramod, a young man from a nearby village, had come to him with physical maladies that were not responding to medical treatment, including chronic body aches and loss of vision. For months, Pramod's health had been deteriorating, to the point that he was bedridden and unable to provide for his family. On one of Pramod's visits to the oracle, the deity Bhairavnath had diagnosed the underlying cause of Pramod's physical infirmities: his problems stemmed from his excessive drinking.

The deity also revealed that, one night, Pramod and his wife had had an intense argument, with harsh words spoken on both sides. That night, a protector deity from Pramod's wife's natal village had entered their home and afflicted Pramod. The angry protector deity had manifested in Pramod's body as a form of *dosh*—literally, a "fault," "blemish," or "affliction"—causing him the physical distress he was now experiencing.[15]

The god Bhairavnath advised Pramod that a cure would require him to "make place" for the protector deity both in his heart and his home. Pramod was told to ritually invite the deity from his wife's village to reside in his home. He would then have to worship this deity alongside the other deities worshiped in his family. Implicit in this cure was also a warning to Pramod: he needed to be mindful of how he treated his wife, or else he was vulnerable to incurring the wrath of her protector spirits. However, by being given "place," the afflicting deity would no longer trouble Pramod but offer him health and prosperity instead.[16]

I often heard accounts like this—of the intimate connections between affliction, placemaking, and healing—during my research. The story reveals popular etiologies of ill-health in the region, namely, that deities, when angered or dissatisfied, can manifest as afflictive presences and "attach" themselves to persons, animals, and places, bringing disease and misfortune. In this case, the deity intervened on behalf of Pramod's wife to provoke a change in Pramod's behavior. For Pramod to be healthy again, the afflicting deity had to be made peaceful (*shant*) and benevolent. Pramod did this by offering the deity "place," which transformed Pramod's home into a legitimate dwelling place for the protector deity from, significantly, his wife's village. The deity thus became a benefactor as opposed to a source of harm and misfortune. While in this story, the protector deity was given place in Pramod's home, deities might also desire that place be made for them in other ways, such as in the form of a physical temple constructed by the person, family, or village that is afflicted, which also serves to increase the deity's fame and prestige.

Gods in the World describes how, through rituals and everyday practices, devotees make place for divinities in many ways and at different scales, including not only in/on their own bodies but also in homes, villages, and temples. Even the state of Uttarakhand itself comes to be known as an "abode of the gods" (*dev bhumi*) (see chapter 1). In moving through different sites and scales of presence, the book shows how deities exist in multiple forms and how different iterations of a deity do not necessarily cohere to produce one stable entity; rather, a divinity's form and activity in relation to their worshipers changes in accordance with the specific kind of placemaking at work.

Practices of Placemaking

In the example above, it was through ritual work, particularly the expert practices of an oracle, that Pramod's suffering was alleviated. During the ritual, the god Bhairavnath appeared and "spoke" through the oracle to Pramod to reveal the truth of what was afflicting him. In Uttarakhand, rituals of divine embodiment are seen as critical placemaking practices that allow deities to appear in/on human bodies as flesh-and-blood incarnations (avatars). In addition to practices of divine embodiment, *Gods in the World* also explores the oral narratives (*gathas*)[17]—performed to the accompaniment of music and dance—through which deities are known, made present, and experienced in the lives of their devotees.

In addition to oracular healing rituals, such as the one Pramod experienced, deities are also made present in family rituals conducted in domestic spaces, village festivals, temple settings, and translocal pilgrimage. While connected and overlapping, there are differences in the ways divinities are encountered in each of these settings. For example, some Pahari deities—such as Bhairavnath, who helped diagnose and cure Pramod—are made present in rituals conducted by oracles called *bakkyas*. In these rituals of divination and healing, the deities "speak" (*bak bolana*); that is, they diagnose maladies and prescribe remedies.

Another ritual performance tradition in which deities are made present is called *jagar*.[18] In jagar, deities "speak" *and* "dance" (*nach*).[19] *Nach* refers to how the deity "comes over" their human medium, which is synonymous with divine embodiment or "possession." During the jagar ritual, the "dancing" god enters into dialogue with their devotees, advising the sponsors of the ritual and addressing their interpersonal and material difficulties. The term *jagar* is derived from the Sanskrit root *jagr*, which literally means to be awake, watchful, or attentive. The word *jagar* suggests an all-night vigil where people stay awake into the night in the performance of worship; however, the term has less to do with participants in jagar ceremonies staying awake than it does with awakening the deity/s. In other words, in jagar, the god/dess or ancestor being invoked is "awakened" to their worshipers through storytelling, music, and "dance."[20] Like the healing rituals conducted by oracles, jagar ceremonies also occur in intimate domestic spaces and involve divine embodiment: as part of their awakening, the deity is invited to embody her/himself through a human medium, called a *pasva* (beast), *ghora* (horse), or *dangariya* (small horse).

However, while rituals of divination and healing are performed to alleviate illness or misfortune, jagars are performed during times of unforeseen crisis and as part of cyclical festivals or commemorations. They are officiated not by oracles but by ritual specialists called *jagaris, jagariyas, dhamis,* or *gurus*.[21] Jagars and the deities invoked in them can serve a variety of functions. For instance, they enable deities to cure illnesses, receive offerings, exorcise ghosts and malevolent spirits, ensure a good harvest, and give advice in times of difficulty (chapter 4).[22]

In Uttarakhand, deities are also encountered in large temple settings and during pilgrimages. In these sites, deities are met as temple icons and as other material forms, including stones, trees, or mountains.[23] In temples, caste-privileged priests mediate contact and exchange between deity and devotee, unlike in jagar or bakkya rituals, which are most often officiated by priests belonging to socioeconomically marginalized communities. As we will see, sometimes pilgrimages in the region can also involve divine embodiment, leading to tensions among different communities of Hindu devotees—those who are more and less comfortable with these rituals. Yet, for devotees, the performance of temple worship and jagar can also be extensions of the same practices of placemaking for the god. Devotees believe that by undertaking pilgrimages to important temple sites and performing worship there, deities will reward them by granting their desires and removing obstacles in their path. As the god grants their devotees' wishes, their devotees vow to sponsor jagar ceremonies in their home villages and/or make other kinds of offerings as expressions of their devotion and gratitude.

Pahari gods, on their part, are not necessarily circumscribed to specific ritual contexts; a number of Pahari deities are found across different sites of presence. For instance, the god Nagaraja (lit., the "serpent king")—whose devotees commonly identify him as a form of the pan-Indian god Krishna—is equally at home in jagar rituals as he is in prestigious regional temples, such as Sem Mukhem.[24] A large segment of the population reveres Nagaraja as the "chosen deity" (*isht-dev*) of the region of Garhwal—one of the two large regions that make up the state of Uttarakhand—and almost every village in Garhwal hosts a shrine dedicated to the god.

The place, or sthan, occupied by a deity—whether in the body of a human medium, during a village festival, or in a temple site—does, however, shape their identity, activities, and how they are experienced by their devotees. Other scholars have similarly observed powerful, mutually constitutive connections among place, person, and divinity in South Asia.[25] For example, Diane Mines demonstrates how local temple organizations in Tamil Nadu use different processional routes to "make" the village in multiple ways. As such, Mines describes how bodily movement makes space/place. In relation to these practices, she points out that as early as the first century BCE, Tamil poetry connected person and place not only metaphorically but also metonymically so that a "man's land is like the man himself."[26]

The efficacy of placemaking in Uttarakhand also hinges on powerful, intrinsic links—both metaphoric and metonymic—between person, place, and divinity. In one sense, to make place for a deity is to make room for that deity in one's life; here, a worshiper's willingness or ability to "make place" signifies their entrance into a long-term, reciprocal relationship with a deity. In another sense, offerings of place also index a deity's fame, prestige, and power—an important reason why some devotees invest so much of their time and money into temple-building projects. At still another level, by acting on a deity's (literal/material) place, one transforms not only the deity but also the range and affective tenor of relations between deity and worshiper, such as, for example, in the case of Pramod, turning a deity's afflictive presence into a benevolent, protective force.[27]

In focusing on placemaking practices, I draw on but also depart from other theorists of space and place. While many of these works explore how geographic *spaces* become transformed into social places suffused with meaning,[28] by contrast, I examine placemaking as a practice that *enables personally and collectively transformative interactions between human and nonhuman actors.*[29] Placemaking can involve opening space for a divinity to enter and inhabit a particular site, containing or keeping a divinity "in place," and transporting a divinity from one location to another.

"Opening space" for a divinity entails creating a field—a base and a theater[30]—for human-divine interaction. Meanwhile, the act of keeping a divinity "in place" establishes limits on that divinity and the scope for human-divine contact, which can be beneficial but also dangerous to humans. Containing presence in this way ameliorates the negative effects of a divinity's power that, in "excess" (*ugra*), causes various forms of personal and collective harm.[31] Another benefit of keeping deities "in place" has to do with managing the fluctuating intensities of presence, to make a deity's power (*shakti*) continuously—and safely—available to humans. As my Pahari interlocutors often told me, deities are "like the wind" (*hava*); they are unpredictable, coming and going as they please.[32] Thirdly, "transport" refers to moving a deity from one place to another, which people do for a number of reasons, such as to find a more suitable dwelling place for a deity, closer or farther away from human habitation, depending on the need.[33] This book extends these notions of transport to also consider how practices of divine embodiment and translocal pilgrimage (chapter 6) are also ways of transporting and extending the power and scope of deities.

Sites of divine presence, then, include "the body, the home, the homeland, and the cosmos."[34] These are all formations of place that constitute significant points of contact between humans and nonhumans in Uttarakhand. How or in what way can the *body* be thought of as a place that a deity inhabits? As Thomas Tweed writes, "Bodies are organic-cultural sites that interconnect with other spaces."[35] In this view, the body as subject does not merely move through space and inhabit place but is itself an "organic-cultural *site*"—a place, as it were. Here, Tweed echoes Nancy Munn's theory of the body as a "mobile spatial field," an essentially chronotopic understanding of the body.[36] Developing Munn's idea I show how deities enter and inhabit the body-sthans of human mediums in rituals of divine embodiment through speech and dance. As such, I understand divine embodiment, or "possession," as the localization of divine presence within and through human bodies.[37] However, while a body-sthan constitutes the primary locus of divine presence in the context of possession, it represents a different order of sthan than, say, a built structure like a temple. During rituals of divine embodiment, the body of a human medium is merely a temporary and transitional place of dwelling on a deity's way to and from other, more permanent places, such as worshipers' homes and temples. Processes of placemaking can thus also link a deity's presence across multiple sites. An analytic of placemaking also helps connect diverse forms of religious practice—such as divine embodiment, temple worship, translocal pilgrimage, and ritualized storytelling—to one another. This gesture refuses the separation between these practices imposed by, for example, caste-privileged temple priests to delegitimize the practices of oracles and jagar priests who belong to socioeconomically marginalized communities.

Gods in the World shows that divine embodiment in Uttarakhand is not only confined to the domestic sphere or relegated to the margins of society, nor is it associated solely with women and so-called low caste communities.[38] Rather, it is a ubiquitous feature of Pahari religion, central to the public sphere, and an important part of the religious repertoire of landed elites and caste-privileged men (see chapter 3).[39]

In recent years, anthropologists of religion working in South Asia have critiqued the tendency to see possession solely as a symbolic medium for the subversion of dominant social and political orders, particularly by marginalized groups. Some of these scholars have drawn our attention to the hegemonic aspects of possession rituals. For instance, Isabelle Clark Decès (previously Nabokov) describes the ways the (female) individual is psychologically fragmented and "split apart" to account for her personal experience and, at the same time, reproduce her received role within the dominant culture.[40] From this perspective, possession is "a normative and legitimated activity" that is "an integral part of a self-regulating system of social control."[41] Moreover, as William Sax observes, in Uttarakhand, possession is an important means for contesting social prestige, and political benefits accrue from the performance of certain kinds of possession.[42] Possession can be both an act of social subversion as well as social confirmation.[43]

In its analysis of rituals of divine embodiment, *Gods in the World* foregrounds the agency of nonhuman social actors to move beyond analyses of possession that read it as merely a symbolic expression of other, "more real" psychological and social conflicts.[44] In a similar vein, Joyce Flueckiger, writing about the Gangamma tradition of Tirupati, proposes a framework that includes "description of a world in which the goddess is accepted as an active agent in/on/through the human body, and in which such agency is not bracketed as not 'really' true or relevant in an ethnographer's search for understanding family and institutional structures, power and gender dynamics, agency, and so forth."[45]

As Flueckiger argues, a rigorous sociopolitical analysis does not preclude seeing nonhuman entities as ontologically real and active agents in the world.[46] Approached in this way, Pahari ritual performances emerge as relations in which human and nonhuman agents act to further their own, often competing, interests. While deities interact with other salient social and political forces, relationships between deities and humans cannot be reduced to questions of human power relations alone, such as contestations within or between different caste or class groups. *Gods in the World* attends to the complexity of relations between deities and humans by recognizing deities' own power and presence as legitimate social actors within Pahari communities. It follows how divinities both shape and are shaped by social, ecological, and historical realities.

The Politics and Precarity of Placemaking

The centrality of placemaking practices for people in Uttarakhand is also related to the fact that, in the region's fragile ecological environment, "place" is not a given but is contested and fraught. As we will see in chapter 1, the concept of placemaking is central to promoting Uttarakhand as a destination for religious tourism, an effort that intersects with a push to develop the region while clashing with longstanding environmental activism that has called for greater protection of fragile ecosystems.[47] Divine desires for place thus also resonate with human desires for material stability in a precarious and unstable political and geographical landscape.

The central Himalayan region of Uttarakhand has a total land area of approximately 53,500 square kilometers, 93 percent of which is mountainous and over 65 percent forested. High Himalayan peaks and glaciers dominate the northern regions of the state, some of which are inaccessible for much of the year. Many of the river systems of South Asia, including rivers significant to Hindu cultural history, the Ganga and Yamuna, originate in this Indo-Tibetan region.

The state of Uttarakhand is a relatively new addition to the Indian nation-state. In November 2000, Uttarakhand was carved out of the northern districts of Uttar Pradesh, the most populous state in India, after a long struggle for political autonomy. One of the driving forces for the creation of this new state was the widespread desire among its inhabitants for greater economic development and governmental representation. Supporters of the statehood movement argued that statehood would stem the large flow of outmigration to other parts of India. However, since statehood, more than a third of Uttarakhand's rural population has migrated out of the state. State formation appears to have accelerated, rather than decreased, outmigration, which many had hoped would improve the economic lives of Uttarakhand's inhabitants.[48] Rates of rural unemployment remain high, especially in the mountainous rural districts where 70 percent of the population resides.[49]

Meanwhile, development projects have made inhabitants of the region more, not less, vulnerable to ecological disasters. In the last decade or so, new buildings, roads, tunnels, and hydropower projects along the river valleys of the Ganga and Brahmaputra have been built close to active landslide zones in the Himachal, Uttarakhand, Arunachal, and Sikkim Himalayas.[50] These projects are thought to be largely responsible for the aggravated flash floods, storms, and landslides that now regularly destroy people's livelihoods and dwellings. For example, on February 7, 2021, near the Nanda Devi National Park, a UNESCO World Heritage site, more than seventy people were killed after a hanging glacier separated from a mountain and plunged into the Rishiganga river basin, causing massive flooding and landslides that destroyed two hydroelectric dams. Prior to the disaster, scientists had warned government officials that the combination of global warming and massive dam projects was exposing the region's delicate ecosystem to great danger. Contra this advice, the government of India, in recent years, has built five hundred miles of highway in the mountains of Uttarakhand to improve access to Hindu temples in the high Himalayas, overriding the advice of many scientific experts.[51] In previous disasters, such as the 2013 flash floods and landslides that caused the deaths of over ten thousand people in the state and caused estimated economic losses of over Rs. 3000 crores (USD 360 million),[52] similar patterns emerged. In the aftermath of the 2013 disaster, several news reports claimed—contrary to arguments made by state officials—that the floods were not the result of a natural calamity but, rather, had been exacerbated by rampant stone crushing and strip mining that has occurred along the banks of the Ganges in Uttarakhand in the last decade.[53]

Environmental activists in the region, some of whom articulate their demands in Hindu idioms, have long warned against these forms of development. In other words, both the push for religious tourism *and* greater environmental protection are articulated in Hindu idioms. Many different actors mobilize Hindu traditions and myths to argue for maintaining the sanctity and purity of the landscape, while others mobilize this language to argue for the need for further touristic development. For example, in 2011, two years before the floods of 2013, Swami Nigamanand, a Hindu religious leader, died at the Himalayan Institute of Medical Sciences in Dehradun after keeping an indefinite fast to protest the extractive development occurring in the state. A right-wing Hindu organization, the Vishwa Hindu Parishad (VHP), actively opposed the building of the Tehri dam.[54] In 2017, the high court of Uttarakhand conferred legal personality on the Ganges River, recognizing the river as not only a natural resource but also a divine being.[55]

Contemporary environmental efforts in Uttarakhand over the protection of lands and place build on grassroots movements that rose to prominence in the 1970s and 1980s. The most well-known of these is the Chipko movement, which was led by Pahari women who acted in defense of traditional forest rights and agitated against state and commercial encroachment in the 1970s.[56] As part of Chipko agitations, local women famously tied sacred threads around trees and recited passages from the Bhagavad Gita. In the 1980s and onward, local environmentalists, such as Dhoom Singh Negi, Sunderlal Bahugana, and others, expanded on the efforts of the Chipko movement to resist rampant strip mining, road building, and the construction of large dams, such as the Tehri Dam.

The book stages these ecological transformations alongside tense political developments underway regionally and nationally in contemporary India, including efforts to transform Uttarakhand into a national religious pilgrimage destination, known and marketed as *dev bhumi* (lit., "land of the gods")—as well as the broader "Hindu-ization" of contemporary Indian public life due to the ascent of right-wing Hindu political forces. For example, in October 2017, Prime Minister Narendra Modi visited Kedarnath, one of Uttarakhand's most well-known pilgrimage destinations, and declared, "Through the work we are doing in Kedarnath, we want to show how an ideal *"tirth kshetra"* [pilgrimage site] should be."[57] For many commentators, a serving prime minister's visit to a Hindu religious site and claiming it as a political victory directly contravened India's secular constitution.[58] Since then, the notion of Uttarakhand as *dev bhumi* has repeatedly been used to bolster the popularity and legitimacy of the ruling Hindu nationalist BJP government.

Today, political, commercial, and religious actors continue to promote Uttarakhand as a Hindu pilgrimage destination and as a sacred geography, thanks in part to the alignment between Hindu gods and goddesses in the region and their locations in various sacred places. Many of the tourists who regularly flock to Uttarakhand's pilgrimage destinations—often doubling the population of those regions during peak tourist season—do so to visit newly created pilgrimage sites, such as the temple sites of Sem Mukhem and Danda Nagaraja (see chapter 1), or the Chhota Char Dham temple circuit.[59]

While scholars and observers have paid significant attention to "placemaking" as a political project, in which environmental activists and prodevelopment figures are pitted against each other, there has been considerably less attention given to how ordinary people in the region are affected by and respond to ecological imbalances and how these imbalances are understood as manifestations of disturbed human-divine relations (chapter 2). *Gods in the World* highlights the stakes of placemaking by drawing attention to the everyday and longstanding labor of Pahari people in maintaining harmonious relationships with their land and surroundings. This daily work of maintenance is neither *for* nor *against* development; rather, it brings an altogether different frame into view. "Place" serves not as a backdrop but rather as the *foreground* of human-deity negotiations. The everyday labor of placemaking, beyond moments of emergency or disaster, centers precarity as a condition of human existence marked by a lack of material and psychological security. In so doing, placemaking reminds people in the region that the spaces and places of human—and divine—habitation cannot, and should not, be taken for granted. It reminds people that place must constantly be made and remade because it can easily slip away.

Further, by attending to the local, everyday frictions that arise around practices of making place for gods in Uttarakhand, *Gods in the World* shows how contestations to Hindutva and Brahminical Hindu authority are alive and well in this part of the Himalayas. These contestations take place on the bodies of divinities as well as through the appropriation or delegitimization of specific places and practices. Despite these highly publicized efforts to draw Uttarakhand and its Hindu communities into the BJP's (caste-privileged) vision of religious nationalism, we see that these efforts are not without resistance or the existence of alternative religious imaginaries.

Caste in Uttarakhand

The politicization of caste and religion in contemporary India, which includes the reclamation of holy places, is taking place in highly fraught and unstable local and regional contexts. While there have been robust critiques of Brahminical Hinduism from secular, liberal intellectual and political voices in recent years, *Gods in the World* offers an understanding of how Hinduism is also contested from *within*—that is, from communities that also consider themselves Hindu but have very different ways of relating to their gods and the world around them than what many traditional and modern elites deem appropriate. At stake in these contestations are the politics of social difference, particularly caste.

The English-language term *caste* generally denotes two loosely related concepts: *varna* and *jati*. Varna (lit., "color") refers to the four social groups into which Hindu society is organized, namely, Brahmins, Kshatriyas, Vaishyas, and Shudras, in descending order of ritual purity, as first theorized in ancient texts such as the Rig Veda and *dharma-sutra* and *-shastra* literature. Jati (lit., "species") is a much more complex, socio-politically relevant concept that refers to "multitudinous endogamous hereditary groups that regulate reproduction and set the terms of interaction in actual social life."[60] While only four varnas exist, thousands of competing jatis, whose relative status changes over time and varies regionally, populate South Asian social worlds.

The majority of Hindus in Uttarakhand are categorized as Brahmin (22–25 percent of the population), Rajput/Thakur (Kshatriya) (35 percent), or Scheduled Caste (SC) (19 percent).[61] Several decades ago, Gerald Berreman observed that, in Uttarakhand, both Brahmins and Rajputs owned land, and religious and cultural differences between these two groups were not as pronounced as in other parts of north India.[62] Brahmins and Rajputs both wield great social, political, and economic influence in Uttarakhand.[63]

While many SC groups in postcolonial India prefer the name Dalit, which means "crushed" or "oppressed,"[64] in the past, they were called untouchables, the most "impure" according to the varna framework. Although "untouchability" (*chua-chut*) has been prohibited under Indian constitutional law, historically, and into the present day, discriminatory practices against Dalits include "restrictions on commensality, marriage, and social proximity," including "restrictions on use of common wells and vessels; exclusion from common schools or access to education; debarment from owning land; forced obligations to perform polluting or otherwise demeaning menial tasks; and unpaid labor."[65] Dalit people are also expected to perform "everyday displays of superiority and deference"[66] toward people of so-called "upper-caste" backgrounds.[67] Dalits experience greater discrimination in villages where they constitute a minority compared with Dalit-majority villages.[68]

However, considerable regional variability also exists in the relative socioeconomic status of Dalit jatis across Uttarakhand. In Uttarakhand, the Dalit community is comprised of numerous jatis, such as Auji, Bera, Bajgi, Bhil, Bhul, Chamar, Darji, Dholi, Kolta, Lohar, Mistri, Tamta, Ordh, and others. In popular discourse, these jatis perform so-called traditional occupations, such as carpentry, masonry, metalwork, tailoring, tanning, and so forth. There are gradations within these occupations; some Dalit jatis are thought to possess lower status than others because they are associated with more stigmatizing occupations.[69] For example, as Ramnarayan Rawat argues in his history of the Chamar community in Uttar Pradesh, in the nineteenth and twentieth centuries, the Chamar community's essentialization as "leather workers" enabled their criminalization and subjugation by both colonial and Hindu elites.[70] However, the relationship between a Dalit jati and their supposedly "traditional" occupation is dynamic, contextual, and complex.

In Uttarakhand today, even though only a small fraction of Dalits are engaged in the "traditional" occupations associated with their jatis,[71] occupational essentialism, often reflected in people's surnames, continues to be employed as a tool of socioeconomic control and disenfranchisement by caste-privileged communities. To counter such stereotyping, over the past several decades, many Pahari Dalits (as Dalits in other parts of India) have chosen to adopt jati-neutral surnames—that is, names that are not specific to any one jati—such as Lal, Das, Ram, Arya, and Shilpakar. Adopting jati-neutral names, I was told, could also emphasize Dalit unity and "downplay old divisions within the [wider Dalit] community." By alluding to politically competitive relations between Dalit castes and subcastes, this comment serves as a reminder that "Dalit," like other identities, should not be viewed as a homogeneous, internally undifferentiated category.[72]

The politicization and assertion of Dalit identity in Uttarakhand, which was part of the state of Uttar Pradesh until 2000, also has a long and complex history. Until the early twentieth century, the derogatory term *Dom* was employed as an umbrella term for "all artisans and service-providing castes," that is, all non-Brahmin and -Rajput castes. Beginning in 1905, the jati of "copper smiths" organized themselves as the Tamta Sudhar Sabha to resist casteism and secure political rights. A few years later, after expanding to include all other "artisan" (*shilpakar*) jatis in Uttarakhand, this organization was renamed as the Shilpakar Sabha.[73] In 1924, the fact that so-called Doms were not allowed to use palanquins—that is, *dola-palkis*—in wedding processions sparked off a series of mass protests against caste oppression in Uttarakhand, "marking an awakening among Dalits."[74]

Due to the work of organizations led by both Dalit and non-Dalit activists and leaders, like the Shilpakar Sabha, the Ambedkar Mahasabha, and the Hindu "reformist" Arya Samaj, the identity marker Shilpakar came to replace the stigmatized term *Dom* on census forms, albeit for very different political reasons.[75] Hindu reformist organizations, led by caste-privileged Hindus, such as the Arya Samaj, sought to "purify" (*shuddhi*) members of the "impure" castes,[76] marking them integral members of the Hindu community to "decrease the possibility that they would convert to minority religions to seek social advance."[77] Citing J.M. Sebring,[78] Stefan Fiol observes, "In the 1920s and 1930s the activities of Arya Samaj reformers in Almora and other areas of Uttarakhand also contributed to the so-called Brahmanization of many Shilpakar artisans, which led to an elevation or at least a blurring of status."[79] Meanwhile, Dalit leaders such as Munshi Ram "sought to reject lower-caste status markers (such as the consumption of beef) and adopt upper-caste status markers (such as wearing the sacred thread and reciting Sanskrit).... They conducted a series of 'purification' rituals in which Shilpkars received the sacred thread (*janeo*)."[80]

Around this period, the term *Harijan* (lit., "people of God") was also introduced as an alternative appellation by caste-privileged Hindu reformers and political leaders, such as M. K. Gandhi. While the terms *Shilpakar* and *Harijan* are regularly employed in government documents, newspaper articles, and polite conversation, many of my younger Dalit interlocutors see these terms as condescending, especially the latter. In the minds of many, the word *Harijan* evokes an "outsider" perception of Dalits as people who are "chained to caste Hinduism as voiceless victims of violence and injustice."[81]

After India achieved independence, Pahari Shilpakar communities were designated as SCs, which made them eligible for affirmative action programs and other forms of governmental support.[82] During fieldwork, many of my interlocutors self-identified simply as "SC," a terse, neutral signifier. While it is true that "changes in categorization ... have done little to alleviate caste stigma in the central Himalayas,"[83] these shifts must be seen as part of a larger effort to "obliterate the humiliating and ignoble social identities ascribed to [Dalits] by caste Hindu society."[84] Instead, Dalit assertion has included the invention of new social identities "endowed with dignity and self-respect."[85]

This ethnography foregrounds ritual specialists who belong to Dalit communities in Uttarakhand, with whom I spent the majority of my time in the field. In numerous Hindu religious contexts, both within and outside Uttarakhand, both male and female-identifying Dalit ritual specialists mediate between Hindu deities and their devotees, a religious role comparable to that of Brahmin priests in temple settings.[86] The knowledge and expertise of Dalit ritual specialists, including their expertise as professional musicians, are not only greatly valued by other Dalits but also by caste-privileged communities, who retain their services for a wide array of religious activities in their homes, villages, and temples. Yet, while many lay Rajputs and Brahmins accept the authority and expertise of Dalit religious experts, Brahmin temple priests are generally ambivalent or even hostile toward them (see chapters 1, 5, and 6).[87] Some of this hostility—targeted at both Dalits and Muslims—has sharpened due to the presence of virulent Hindu nationalism in the region.[88]

While barring Dalits from Hindu temples is illegal under Indian jurisprudence, Dalit ritual specialists and lay persons spoke to me at length—usually in hushed tones—about how they were made to feel unwelcome at temple sites because of the negative attitudes of Brahmin priests. One of my Dalit interlocutors recounted how, as a child, he witnessed his parents being reprimanded by Rajput members of his village for simply walking past a temple while a ritual service was taking place inside. His parents were told that the "shadows" (*chhaya*) they had cast as they had walked past had "polluted" the ritual. As punishment, they were forbidden from moving around in the vicinity of the temple. Much of *Gods in the World* analyzes how Dalit religious experts grapple with these contradictions in their everyday lives and ritual work. On the one hand, they "perform critical social roles by communicating with divinities through sacred rituals and facilitating social dancing at festivals," but on the other hand, they "live in highly impoverished and stigmatized communities."[89]

As with Dalit people elsewhere, ongoing forms of caste oppression led some of my Dalit interlocutors away from performing ritual worship for Hindu deities in favor of converting to other religions or joining socially egalitarian, anticaste "spiritual" organizations such as the Sant Nirankari Mission or Radha Soami Satsang Beas (RSSB).[90] While "Dalit emancipation" can be achieved through the "rejection of Hinduism,"[91] "conversion" does not always necessitate a "complete rupture with past affiliations, followed by unequivocal adhesion to new ones."[92] Among others, a growing, popular movement in Uttarakhand for Pahari Dalits is the Sant Nirankari Mission, which is connected to Sikhism and the north Indian *sant* (lit., "saint") devotional tradition, including the teachings of the Dalit saint Ravidas.[93] As the political scientist Ronki Ram argues, Dalit involvement with the Sant Nirankari Mission and similar organizations can represent a form of "Dalit homecoming as well as a radical mode of Dalit social protest."[94]

An Ethnographer in the World

I first began traveling to Uttarakhand for extended periods when I was a high school student in New Delhi. Every May and June, when the summer heat in the north Indian plains became unbearable, a few friends and I would board a bus at the Inter State Bus Terminal (ISBT) and arrive in Uttarakhand eight to twelve hours later. We would then spend weeks traveling through Himalayan mountains and forests. Because we were living on shoestring budgets, we invariably ran out of money at some point and would end up sleeping for free in rest houses (*dharamashala*) connected to temples, or sometimes, a kind stranger would offer us shelter in their home.

When I began my dissertation fieldwork in Uttarakhand more than a decade later, I heard a story that reminded me of my own experiences as a teenager seeking refuge in the mountains. The story, one of the first I recorded, was about the god Krishna dreaming about Garhwal: exhausted from the ravages of warfare and kingship, he fell in love with Garhwal's natural beauty and decided to reside there; he asked the ruler of this land, Gangu Ramola, for a sthan to inhabit, a place to call his own (chapters 1 and 2).

I could relate. While in Garhwal, my friends and I had no desire to go back to the regimented, humdrum existence that awaited us at home. I felt suffocated by Delhi, the rigors of the Indian educational system, and the seemingly impossible pressures to succeed. In my first year as a college student, a family friend who managed an adventure tourism company offered me a job helping to organize trekking expeditions for groups like the Boy Scouts of America or well-off computer engineers from Bangalore. This experience gave me the opportunity to work closely with local Pahari porters, cooks, and guides, some of whom invited me to their villages where I was introduced to the languages, oral traditions, religious practices, and gods and goddesses of Uttarakhand. These travels and the people I encountered ignited a desire to live and work in Uttarakhand and an abiding interest in the anthropology of religion, more broadly.

As a graduate student and since, my fieldwork was made possible by a number of the friendships I developed during my visits to the region in high school and university. Vikrant Chandola, whose family was from Garhwal and who was my music teacher in school, was instrumental in my research. His father, Uma Shankar Chandola, a respected classical Hindustani musician, put me in touch with many of my interlocutors in Garhwal, who, in turn, introduced me to storytellers, musicians, and rituals specialists across the region. For many months during my dissertation research, I lived in Vikrant's ancestral home in Garhwal, where his uncle, a renowned poet and painter, had resided. After Vikrant's uncle's passing, his house had been left uninhabited. Vikrant's cousin sister, also a musician, opened the house for me, and that became my home base for many months. She and her husband invited me to several jagar performances, and during one such event in 2010, I met the jagar performer Ram Lal, who became a close interlocutor and teacher. Ram Lal was a gifted storyteller and musician; he was blind, had a phenomenal memory, and possessed an encyclopedic knowledge of Pahari ritual performance traditions. He not only performed the stories and songs as he had learned them from his teacher but also performed versions of these songs that he had learned from other performers. He compared multiple versions of the "same" story, thought deeply about what the stories meant, and had brilliant insights into his own and others' performance methods.

Early in my fieldwork, I had to make two important methodological decisions (to the extent that I had control over them): whether to stay in one place or move periodically from village to village, and whether to work with ritual specialists or lay practitioners. My experiences with ritual specialists like Ram and others had thus far been very positive, so I decided to let their knowledge and expertise guide my research. The fact that jagar performers were, for the most part, itinerant performers who moved around constantly, going wherever they were invited to perform, resolved the first methodological question for me:[95] since I was working with different jagar performers, I, too, had to travel extensively. Since these performers often worked late into the night and then napped for a few hours in the open air before heading home, I rarely remained in any one place for too long; working with itinerant performers made me an itinerant ethnographer.

Getting from one village, town, or district to another sometimes required hours of walking on narrow, unpaved mountain trails or long rides in crowded jeep taxis and on ramshackle, irregular local buses. The geography of Garhwal presented particular challenges to my ethnographic fieldwork. Distances that appeared numerically insignificant, such as twenty or thirty kilometers, took hours or an entire day to complete because of the extreme altitudes and jagged landscapes. The unreliable, unpleasant, and occasionally downright frightening experiences of traversing the Himalayas in rickety GMVN (Garhwal Mandal Vikas Nigam) buses were offset by majestic views of the Himalayas and the warm hospitality that greeted me at my destinations.

The staccato rhythms of my fieldwork, exhausting as they were, resembled what jagar performers go through on an everyday basis, as well as the restlessness of deities' search for place. It seemed fitting that I, too, became an ethnographer of no fixed abode, trailing gods through their many emergences, transformations, and vanishings at dawn. At the conclusion of each jagar, as the performers packed up their drums, I wondered where the deity would appear next, where they were going, and, by extension, where I was going. Surprisingly, over time, the claustrophobic, frenetic theaters of much of jagaris' everyday lives—dusty bus stands, temple fairs, and small, incense-filled domestic spaces—began to feel spacious to me.

While many of my interlocutors were aware of and distinguished between two major classes of researchers: "foreign" and "native" Pahari scholars, the fact that I was neither was unusual at the time. Since I came and went with the musicians and performers who were all Dalit, in Rajput and Brahmin-majority villages, I was unable to stay for long with the families for whom these rituals were being performed. During these visits, the performers did not eat with the sponsors of the jagars, but sponsors often invited me to eat with them. I chose to remain outside and eat and drink with the performers. This choice came at a cost, and it adversely affected my relationships with caste-privileged villagers as well as with Brahmin priests.[96]

Many of my Pahari interlocutors initially read me as "upper-caste" due to my obvious socioeconomic and educational privileges. But when they heard my first name, which is Persian in origin and associated with Muslim communities, they were puzzled. The mystery deepened when my middle name was added to the mix, which evokes Sikh or Rajput heritage, while my last name is Sikh.

When questions were asked about my family background, as they regularly were, my interlocutors learned that my father was Sikh (and fond of Urdu/Persian poetry, which partially explained my first name), while my mother was a Hindu, Brahmin woman from Uttar Pradesh, Uttarakhand's neighboring state. I had grown up intimately familiar with both Sikh and Hindu traditions.

Sometimes, these connections facilitated positive relations between me and my Pahari Brahmin and Rajput interlocutors, even though, at other times, they were wary of my proximity to Dalit people. While I possessed certain linguistic and sociocultural competencies that made me legible to my interlocutors, other things—such as the fact that I had grown up in a "big city," studied at elite schools and universities, and was an economically privileged NRI (Nonresident Indian)—also set me apart from them.

Unexpectedly, for my Dalit interlocutors, the Sikh part of my identity became a source of connection between us. Even though casteism is prevalent in Sikh communities, many of my Dalit interlocutors related to Sikhism as anticaste. While my Dalit interlocutors spoke guardedly around caste-privileged Hindus, my "mixed" background and status as someone outside of traditional Pahari Hindu social hierarchies enabled us to communicate more freely.

The nature of my fieldwork was also invariably gendered. Because the jagaris and other religious specialists with whom I interacted during my fieldwork were mostly male (although some of the oracles with whom I worked were female[97]), my contact with Pahari women was, in any case, limited. Beyond this, having sustained interactions with Pahari women—specifically, those not related to ritual performers themselves—was difficult to do in a socially appropriate way. While nonkin men and women in Uttarakhand are known to interact more freely than in other parts of rural north India, as an outsider, I was rarely allowed to interact with women in the absence of men. Often, in these situations, when I engaged a woman in conversation, a husband, brother, or some other male relative would answer for her. This, however, changed when I began spending time with women while they engaged in agricultural labor (see chapter 4). Much of the physically demanding agricultural work in Uttarakhand is carried out by women, so spending long days with women while they worked in the fields allowed me to speak with and learn from them. During this time, I was introduced to the experiences of Pahari women in the ritual performances I was studying, which profoundly transformed my understanding of those traditions.

Gods in the World moves through six chapters that explore the ways humans and divinities make place for each other. Each chapter focuses on a moment of crisis, such as an illness or political discord, that illuminates how devotees relate to, experience, and come to know divinities and how they, in turn, intervene in the lives of their devotees. Each chapter follows the relation between supernatural and human actors from public to increasingly more intimate spaces, in progressively narrowing scales of place that localize the materiality of divine presence, with far-reaching ontological, aesthetic, and sociopolitical ramifications. For example, chapter 1 focuses on the making of the region of Garhwal as the "land of the gods" through building infrastructure and temples; chapter 2 examines narratives of affliction to show how placemaking is a key technology of healing; chapter 3 describes how local gods intervene in matters of collective importance, and how the village is made into a site of divine presence; chapter 4 is about jagar rituals that are performed for ghost-afflicted married women who have to learn to embrace the deities of their marital home and leave behind their natal kin; chapter 5 looks at the lives of oracles and jagar priests and how their relations with deities became reciprocal, mutually beneficial, and long-term; chapter 6 examines a pilgrimage tradition that shows how regional identity is constituted through the movement of embodied deities through place.

Chapter 1, titled "Making Dev-bhumi, the Land of the Gods," focuses on temples as sthans that shape how deities are known and experienced. This chapter examines how prestigious, regionally significant temples in the region of Garhwal—specifically, Danda Nagaraja temple in Pauri District and Sem Mukhem temple in Tehri District—are imbricated in social and geopolitical processes of placemaking for the deity Nagaraja, who is identified as a form of the pan-Indian god Krishna. I turn to these increasingly popular temples to show how placemaking becomes a process that is not only about the worship of Nagaraja, or deity-devotee relations, but also about making Uttarakhand into a national pilgrimage destination (as the "land of the gods"), state discourses on development, and histories of migration and conquest. Contestations of sthan become allegories about political control and the "Hindu-ization" of Uttarakhand. While there have been many significant critiques by intellectuals and scholars of ongoing, often state-sponsored efforts to Hindu-ize landscapes and places, and the social and political violence that often inheres as a result, this chapter attends to how these efforts to Hindu-ize the region have also been sharply contested, for example, by differently positioned devotees of the same god. As a result, we see how resistances to Hindu nationalist narratives and projects of placemaking also emerge from within communities that consider themselves Hindu.

Chapter 2 is titled "Affliction and Healing." While in the first chapter, contestations of sthan allegorize political and religious control of Uttarakhand, in the second chapter, the god Nagaraja's desire for and capture of sthan articulates with human experiences of affliction and healing. In this chapter, I listen to oral narratives of the god Nagaraja, the "serpent king," as they are performed in jagar, as well as powerful forms of indigenous commentary that complicate these narrative traditions. The narratives tell us how the god Krishna, after the end of the Mahabharata war, came into conflict with a local Garhwali ruler named Gangu Ramola, who thwarted Krishna's desire for sthan. For denying Krishna sthan,

Gangu Ramola became afflicted with *nagadosh*, or "serpent affliction," a destructive, disguised manifestation of the god that almost destroys Gangu and his kingdom. These narratives recount how nagadosh is resolved and Nagaraja is made *shant*—that is, peaceful and benevolent—through offerings of sthan.

The narratives and commentaries in this chapter articulate deep-rooted intuitions regarding the broader relationship between person, place, and divinity in Uttarakhand. They describe divinities' desire for sthan in relation to people's everyday experiences of affliction and healing. For instance, we learn that personal "healing" is achieved by repairing relationships between humans and divinities, which indelibly shape human existence. Moreover, in local understandings, healing is never a straightforward, linear process; instead, it proceeds in fits and starts and spirals as different forms of "affliction" act upon and through one another to produce healing. As such, affliction and healing are not seen to constitute an oppositional binary; rather, they are recursive, iterative movements in a process of relational and existential transformation.

In chapter 3, "Political Divinities in the Village Square," I turn my attention to how the village is made into a site of divine presence and how this form of place-making affects both deities and humans. Through close ethnographic attention to a multiday performance of the Mahabharata epic that takes place annually in village grounds (*maidan*) across the Garhwal region, we see the ways local deities intervene in and are affected by matters of collective importance as well as how fraught and unpredictable human-divine relations can be. During one such Mahabharata performance, I describe how an embodied deity instigated a village crisis by demanding an expensive tax or tribute, which led to a contentious public exchange and airing of grievances by village inhabitants, revealing how notions of divine authority and agency are threaded through everyday concerns about local governance in the region. In the end, the crisis was resolved through acts of politicking by both human and divine actors, demonstrating how public rituals of divine embodiment in village *maidans* become sites of negotiation between competing divine and human interests.

Chapter 4, "Undoing Love: Ghost Affliction and Patrilocal Marriage," delves into how nonhuman actors intervene in and are a key part of kinship structures in Uttarakhand. Young women in Uttarakhand who make the fraught transition from natal to affinal home at the time of marriage are said to become particularly vulnerable to bodily attack and affliction by ghosts—that is, *chhal* and *bhut*—who wander restlessly in the wilderness beyond the boundaries of human settlement. Drawing on feminist anthropological scholarship on kinship and affliction in South Asia, I argue that ghost affliction and its treatment in jagar are ways for individuals and families to grapple with the physical, emotional, relational, and ontological ruptures and dislocations inherent in practices of patrilocal kinship. While an exorcism performed for a ghost-afflicted woman seeks to extricate her from her "past self" and natal kin in order to facilitate her absorption into her marital home, women themselves experienced and narrativized ghost affliction as one of many hardships they endure in patrilocal marriage, thereby interpreting ghost affliction as a form of structural, rather than individualized, violence. Whereas preceding chapters theorize the ways human beings make place for divinities, this chapter emphasizes the ways place is made for human beings, particularly young brides, and the spectral beings who enter and inhabit their persons as afflictive presences.

Chapter 5, "Out of Place: Lives of Oracles and Priests," is about the tumultuous lives of jagar priests and oracles, ritual experts who preside over and mediate interactions between deities and devotees. The lives of socially marginalized Dalit ritual experts are shot through with the contradictions of caste-based violence, deprivation, the struggles of migration, and experiences of loss and suffering, including homelessness, unemployment, familial conflict, cycles of substance dependence, and bouts of "madness." My interlocutors described these experiences as different ways of being *out of place*: of feeling marginalized, lost, sick, or unmoored. They described being called to serve the gods as priests and oracles following periods of intense turbulence as finding their way home.

This chapter tracks how ritual experts find their way "home," both literally and figuratively; it is about how they learn to listen to gods, which endows their lives with purpose and meaning. Their stories emphasize not just human agency but how human and divine connections can be harnessed to experience fulfillment and healing for both gods and practitioners. At the same time, they also show how being *in* place is never settled; particularly for those who occupy positions on the margins, "place" must be constantly made and remade.

The last chapter, "Playing in the Rain: Scenes from a Himalayan Pilgrimage," is about pilgrimage practices in the region of Kumaon and the ways deities move through place (and time). In July and August, during the monsoon season, deities from across Kumaon travel back to what is referred to as their "childhood home," a temple called Jhakar Saim. On this pilgrimage journey, accompanied by devotees and jagar priests, local divinities are embodied by their human mediums as playful, childlike, and feminized presences. During this pilgrimage, deities—who in other contexts are known and experienced as formidable, demanding figures—live out the experiences of their female devotees. "As the world becomes female," in the words of Joyce Flueckiger,[98] deities sing, dance, and celebrate their return to Jhakar Saim, and they shed tears of sorrow when it comes time to leave. The deities' emotional journey of homecoming during the rainy season is significant because it softens otherwise rigid (social and ontological) boundaries between divergent contexts of religious knowledge, practice, and authority, such as the performance of jagar in domestic settings, on the one hand, and Brahminical temple worship, on the other. However, these movements toward greater integration are not without their limits. For instance, during the pilgrimage, Dalit priests come face-to-face with their Brahmin counterparts in carefully choreographed yet potentially volatile public interactions. These moments bring into relief fundamental disjunctures between Brahminical and non-Brahminical epistemologies and ontologies, revealing how religious authority is contested through pilgrimage practices involving moments of both articulation and fissure.

Finally, in the epilogue, titled "Beyond Belief," I discuss forms of human-divine relationality in Uttarakhand by comparing the English-language term *belief* with the Indian-language word *manana* (lit., "to acknowledge"). I argue that manana involves entering into relation with deities; it implies practices of ritual reciprocity, of contact and exchange between deities and devotees. Manana is not an inward state, nor is it a one-way act; rather, it is an intersubjective, relational process. In this worldview, belief is something that is coconstructed—by both deity and devotee—through time, care, relating, and placemaking. Through describing the ways my interlocutors enacted manana, I show how religious practitioners in Uttarakhand have embodied and highly contextual ways of connecting to the supernatural beings who populate their world.

1

Making "Dev-bhumi," the Land of the Gods

Nagaraja's Places

One summer evening in 2010, I took a long bus ride to Danda Nagaraja temple, a growing pilgrimage site in Uttarakhand devoted to the worship of the god Nagaraja—literally, the "serpent king." In Uttarakhand, Nagaraja is revered as a form of the pan-Indian deity Krishna. As one of my interlocutors put it, "the 'land of the gods' [that is, Garhwal or Uttarakhand], has not been left untouched by the earthly activities [*lilas*] of Krishna, who is known here as Nagaraja."

Exhausted after weeks of traveling, I fell asleep and missed my stop. I woke to find the bus empty. We had stopped at a tea shop, and the bus driver told me I would have to wait until the morning for the next bus to Danda. Learning of my predicament, the owner of the tea shop, a caste-privileged Rajput, generously invited me to spend the night at his home nearby, where he lived with his mother, wife, and children.

Since I was on my way to Danda Nagaraja—a temple and pilgrimage center that is becoming increasingly popular with nonlocal tourists—I asked my hosts about it. The shop owner's mother, Mata ji, spoke in a dialect that was difficult for me to follow, but the other family members helped us communicate. She told me she was deeply devoted to the deity Nagaraja, who resided in the temple and was her family's "chosen deity" (*isht devata*). Yet, she seemed entirely uninterested in the temple. She had only been there once, decades ago, she said, even though she lived less than fifteen kilometers away from the famous site. Curious about her lack of interest, I asked why she had only visited once.

Mata ji said the temple had disappointed her because she had been unable to "see," that is, directly encounter (*darshan karana*), Nagaraja. Enclosed within the temple's central enclosure, which was usually locked, he was walled off from his worshipers, she reported. The only people who had unfettered access to him were Brahmin temple priests (*pujaris*): "They keep him [the god Nagaraja] all to themselves," she said. In our conversation, she repeatedly alluded to a feeling of being cut off from the god. In addition to the physical wall, the pujaris acted as a second, figurative wall separating the god from his devotees.

Mata ji contrasted her experience in Danda Nagaraja with *jagar* ceremonies in her home and village, where people could know and experience Nagaraja in a more intimate, immediate way (for more on jagar rituals, see chapter 4). Mata ji expressed the difference eloquently: "What use is a god you cannot see, one who does not speak or dance (*nach*)?" she asked.

Mata ji's poignant statement captures key disjunctures regarding how Nagaraja is worshiped and cared for in Uttarakhand, despite being one of the region's most revered deities. In large temple sites like Danda Nagaraja, worshipers encounter deities through the mediation of caste-privileged Brahmin priests, an experience they often describe, like Mata ji, as distal and removed. In jagar, they interact with gods as embodied presences via the mediation of caste-oppressed (Dalit) priests. These differences are also material: in jagar, Nagaraja is an embodied, flesh-and-blood *avatar* (incarnation),[1] while in temple settings, he appears as a silent, cloistered, and immobile *murti* (statue).

These differences have important stakes not only for how Nagaraja is worshiped and understood by his devotees but also for constructions of regional identity, state development and Hindutva projects, and histories of migration and conquest. In this chapter, I draw on fieldwork at two prestigious, regionally significant temples in Garhwal, specifically, Danda Nagaraja temple in Pauri District and Sem Mukhem temple in Tehri District. In Danda Nagaraja and Sem Mukhem temples, my interlocutors described Nagaraja as the "chosen deity" (*isht devata*) of Garhwal as a whole, not of a single family or village. In so doing, they identified him as a regional deity par excellence. They highlighted how worshiping him cuts across boundaries of class, caste, and geography. Moreover, because of Nagaraja's identification with the pan-Indian deity Krishna, he also braids together local religious cultures, including rituals of divine embodiment and oral narratives, with elite, Sanskrit-language textual traditions and temple worship. In Danda Nagaraja and Sem Mukhem temples, I tracked the emergence of region as a significant form and scale of placemaking. In these temples, Nagaraja and Garhwal—deity and region, respectively—serve as twin, mutually constitutive entities. I explore the narrative, historiographical, and infrastructural labor that enable this twinning.

Throughout this chapter, I ask: How is the region of Garhwal made into a *sthan* of the god Nagaraja, and what is the significance of this form of placemaking? To answer this question, we might first unpack the term *region*, or what some of my Pahari interlocutors referred to as *kshetra*.[2]

In her study of how pilgrimage practices in the Indian state of Maharashtra help forge a sense of region through the movement of human bodies across space, Anne Feldhaus discusses two distinct ways *region* is generally understood. In the first sense, region is a "large place," distinguished in scale from a "home," or domestic residence. In a second sense, region is a network of places that has special relevance for the people who inhabit it.[3] However, as Feldhaus observes, "Different regions often overlap in the same area, and different ... overlapping regions become salient in different contexts, even sometimes for the same person."[4] A "region," thus, has multiple geographical, historical, and administrative connotations and is not an unchanging, monolithic, or purely objective feature in the world.

In this chapter, I focus on how Garhwal-as-region is made by the movements of pilgrims and the god Nagaraja. To do this, I draw on narrative songs (*gathas*) performed during jagar rituals that describe the deity's movements: how he arrived in Garhwal; his fractious encounter with Gangu Ramola, a local ruler; and the establishment of the temples of Sem Mukhem and Danda Nagaraja. These narratives trace "sacred geographies" made up of connected places that, taken together, constitute a "region"—a place (*sthan*) that Nagaraja desires and comes to inhabit.[5] At the same time that these are stories of Nagaraja's belonging, they are also allegories about political and religious control of Uttarakhand more generally.

"Hindu-izing" Uttarakhand

In 1990, then president of the Hindu nationalist political party, the Bharatiya Janata Party (BJP), L. K. Advani, began a *rath yatra* (lit., "pilgrimage on a chariot"), visiting sites where Hindu temples had been supposedly destroyed by Muslim "invaders" during the medieval period and replaced with mosques. Advani's pilgrimage, which became part of the Rama-janama-bhumi (lit., "birthplace of Ram") movement, argued that the destruction of Hindu temples was emblematic of the violence that India's Hindu majority had suffered at the hands of Mughal and other Muslim rulers. Slogans such as, "lathi goli khaenge, par mandir vahin banayenge" (We'll take bullets and beatings, but we will build a temple there) and "Marenge, mar jayenge, mandir vahin banayenge" (We'll kill, we'll die, but we'll build a temple there) became the pilgrimage's rallying cries culminating in the violent destruction of the Babri Masjid in 1992. The Rama-janama-bhumi movement coalesced multiple, fractured "Hindu" communities through themes such as historical hurt and political wrongdoing.[6] While scholars have done important and critical work on "reclaiming" Hindu sites and power, in this chapter, I foreground how specific places, the *sthans* of deities, are the grounds on which these highly contested, politicized, and sometimes violent processes of reclamation occur.

Since then, Uttarakhand has increasingly become central to efforts by Hindu nationalist and cultural organizations to establish "Hindu" places across India.

Prime Minister Modi (also of the BJP) has made frequent and highly publicized visits to Uttarakhand's temples. The notion of Uttarakhand as *dev-bhumi* ("sacred landscape" or "land of the gods") has also been repeatedly employed to bolster the popularity and legitimacy of the Hindu nationalist BJP government, which came to power in a resounding victory in Uttarakhand's state elections in 2017. In 2017, on a visit to Kedarnath, Uttarakhand's most well-known pilgrimage destination, Modi declared, "Through the work we are doing in Kedarnath, we want to show how an ideal *tirth kshetra* [pilgrimage site] should be."[7] On another visit to Kedarnath in November 2021, he promised that "more pilgrims will visit Uttarakhand in the next decade than in the past century and the rapid development in the state will reverse the outward migration of young people," who leave Uttarakhand in large numbers in search of better employment opportunities in other parts of India.[8] For many commentators, a serving prime minister's visit to a Hindu religious site and commitment to develop it demonstrates yet another erosion of India's secular and constitutional values since the BJP came to power.[9]

The BJP's presence and political dominance in Uttarakhand centers on efforts to draw Uttarakhand and its majority Hindu population into the fold of Hindutva (lit., "essence of Hinduism"), an ideology that supports creating an ethnic Hindu *rashtra* (state) out of a constitutionally secular India. Those committed to India's secular and liberal ideals argue that Hindutva is authoritarian, casteist, and violent toward Muslims and other religious minorities. Indeed, as in other parts of India, anti-Muslim violence and racism, including calls to remove all Muslims from the region, have grown troublingly loud.[10] Those who promote Hindutva policies argue that they are merely promoting economic development and correcting the historical disenfranchisement experienced by Hindus at the hands of colonial powers and successive secular governments. In this imaginary, Uttarakhand, as a holy land for Hindus, plays large.

Under Hindutva, rhetorics of neoliberal development are intertwined with the Hindu-ization of the landscape, which includes temple building and the political mobilization of pilgrimage sites and practices as part of religious tourism.[11] However, as I show in this chapter, efforts to reclaim holy places in Uttarakhand through religious tourism and economic development and fold them into Hindutva are not without friction, as they occur in highly fraught and unstable local and regional contexts. We will see how resistances to Hindutva narratives and projects of placemaking also emerge from within communities that consider themselves Hindu. The god Nagaraja is a key site on which these battles are playing out.

Technologies of Development

The region of Garhwal hosts a vibrant and growing religious tourism sector, one that serves as a marker of regional identity for both outsiders and locals.[12] Every spring, usually in the months of April and May, millions from across India make a pilgrimage to what is known as the *Chhota Char Dham* (lit., "small four abodes/seats"). The *Chhota Char Dham* circuit consists of the temple sites of Yamunotri, Gangotri, Kedarnath, and Badrinath. This circuit enriches the state economy by providing employment to large numbers of Pahari workers and businesses.

During my fieldwork, there were wide-ranging efforts for Sem Mukhem and/or Danda Nagaraja to be included in the wider pilgrimage circuit and for it to be transformed from a four- to a five-temple route.[13] Indeed, many of Nagaraja's devotees spoke of Danda Nagaraja and Sem Mukhem, major Nagaraja temples, as the "fifth abode(s)" (*panchava dham*) of Garhwal.[14] I experienced these efforts to elevate the status of Danda Nagaraja temple from a local to a regionally significant temple firsthand when I visited it—after my short bus stop mishap—in 2010 and subsequently. During my visits, I interacted with many central actors in the temple economy, including Brahmin temple priests and temple patrons.

One wealthy patron I met, Mr. Pant, had been instrumental in the temple's transformation into an important pilgrimage destination. A native Garhwali, he had migrated out of the state and made a fortune in Haryana, where he owned several factories. When he turned sixty, he retired, entrusting the day-to-day operations of his factories to his children. He then moved back to Garhwal and began directing all his time, energy, and financial resources to "developing" Danda Nagaraja, as he put it, using the English-language word. Mr. Pant successfully lobbied district- and state-level government officials to complete the construction of a paved road to the temple, which put Danda on the map, quite literally.

He explained that while the inhabitants of Garhwal had known about the "greatness" of Danda Nagaraja for thousands of years, only now were people outside the area becoming aware. However, he added, "there is still a long way to go; we need to 'spread awareness' [*prachar*] about this place all over the country, so that even more people can come and reap its benefits." I came to learn that spreading awareness—prachar—includes not just developing the temple's infrastructure but also producing secular, scientific, historical, and religious narratives about Nagaraja and his temple. In other words, prachar is about mobilizing economic, state, and scientific capital to transform how Danda Nagaraja temple—and Nagaraja himself—are known and experienced.[15]

Other actors were also deeply invested in the temple's "development," including temple priests (*pujaris*), influential patrons, and local elites from the three villages that own the land on which the temple resides.[16] Like Mr. Pant, the temple priests also affirmed that although the temple was about 150 years old, Nagaraja had been "here" for thousands of years. Infrastructural changes accelerated dramatically in the mid-2000s after Uttarakhand achieved statehood. Until that point, Mr. Pant said, "Garhwal was just a backwater of Uttar Pradesh. State officials did not pay attention to what was needed in far-flung places like Danda. But now the state capital is close by [in Dehradun city] and all-important government officials know us, and we know them, so they are responsive to our needs, providing the 'facilities' [Eng.] to 'develop' [Eng.]." One of those necessary facilities was building a paved road from Pauri city to Danda Nagaraja (an approximately thirty-kilometer stretch). The road's completion boosted the inflow of pilgrims and capital to the temple. Local politicians and businessmen who facilitated this also capitalized on their association with the temple, regularly sponsoring large *pujas* and public recitations of the Bhagavata Purana, which were covered in all the local newspapers.

Nonresident Garhwalis constituted an important, fast-growing base of support for the temple economy, and because they were relatively prosperous, the pujaris and temple committee went to great lengths to cater to them. For instance, the pujaris decided that the annual temple fair should take place in April to coincide with schoolchildren's summer holidays, which made it easier for expatriate, middle-class Garhwali families to travel to the temple and attend the festival. In turn, these devotees infused capital into the temple economy. In fact, a signboard that displayed donor names showed that most were nonresident Garhwalis. The pujaris described how the temple complex had expanded since the mid-1990s, as guesthouses, restaurants, and other facilities had mushroomed around it. On my first visit to Danda in 2010, the temple authorities were also in the process of establishing a residential college for the study of Sanskrit language and literature, which had been assured accreditation by the state government.

Proponents of Danda Nagaraja temple to be a "fifth abode" offered several different arguments for the temple's significance. According to Mr. Pant, worshiping Nagaraja in Danda enabled devotees to "realize" or attain all their spiritual and material desires. For this reason, Danda was a *siddha pith* (lit., a "place of realization") that provided many "'practical' [Eng.] benefits for pilgrims," he said. "Whenever I sponsor a *katha* [recitation of the Bhagavata Purana], perform a puja, or simply sit under a tree to reflect upon God [*bhagavan*], I feel great peace," he said.

Mr. Pant had invited high-level government officials to visit Danda and experience the "practical" benefits of this place for themselves. He described how these influential visitors had become convinced of the untapped potential of this temple as a major pilgrimage destination (*tirth sthan*) and had only then agreed to build the road from Pauri city.

Mr. Pant also offered another reason for the temple's significance. According to him, the god Krishna—or Nagaraja—divides his time equally between Sem Mukhem temple in Tehri district and Danda Nagaraja in Pauri district. He told me the following story about how the god Krishna arrived in Garhwal: "After completing his *lilas* [earthly activities], Krishna decided to travel northward to Uttarakhand. But he knew that Uttarakhand was the 'land of the gods,' so he thought, 'How can I walk on this land, touching this hallowed ground with my feet?' So, he turned himself into a *nag* [serpent] and slithered on the ground to reach this place [Pauri Garhwal]. Since then, he spends six months of the year in Danda Nagaraja and six months in Sem Mukhem."

I was surprised that Mr. Pant's version of this story excluded many of the key characters and events known to Garhwalis about how Krishna came to reside in Garhwal. Although I knew my interlocutor was aware of these narratives (which I will discuss later in this chapter as well as in chapter 2), which are performed during jagar rituals, through this telling, he demonstrated a difference in how Nagaraja is known in Danda versus how the god is encountered in jagar. As the mother of the teashop owner whom I had met on the way to Danda had also indicated, these were two distinct forms of the god. Mr. Pant continued:

> Initially, when Krishna began to reside on this mountain [Danda Nagaraja] in the form of a serpent, people in the vicinity were unaware of his presence. However, every morning, a cow from Rin [a nearby village] would go to a particular spot on the mountain, deposit its milk, and return to the village. It did this on its own, spontaneously. When the owners of the cow would try to milk it, they would find, to their astonishment, that it had no milk left

to give. The villagers became curious about why the cow was not providing milk. So, one morning, he [a cowherd] followed the cow to the mountain and found that it was depositing its milk in a tiny depression in the ground on a *murti* [physical image] of a serpent, which was drinking the milk. Since the cowherd's discovery, the place where the murti was discovered is regarded as a *siddha pith* [lit., a "place of realization," that is, where one's prayers and wishes (*manauti*) are realized].

According to this story, Danda Nagaraja temple was constructed where the serpent's murti was discovered.[17] I was told that the murti was still present, housed in the temple's central enclosure. While I was in Danda, however, the central enclosure of the temple was not open to visitors. When I questioned Mr. Pant about this, he told me that murti was "very powerful" and, therefore, only revealed to devotees during special temple festivals, such as Krishna's birth. Although he had highlighted the temple's mytho-historical importance, he simultaneously downplayed the murti's contemporary relevance: "Nagaraja is present in every part of this temple. All you have to do is close your eyes, silence your mind, and you will feel his presence.... In the evenings, just sit quietly under a tree, and you will experience deep peace. Your thoughts and feelings will not wander; your awareness will become single-pointed [*ekagrat*], and you will stop worrying about everything that distracts you from god," he said.

In effect, Mr. Pant said that temple visitors didn't *need* to encounter Nagaraja as a murti—a material, localized presence—because the god's presence pervaded the temple. As he said this, I was struck by the contrast between encountering Nagaraja as an embodied presence in jagar rituals and his dispersed and depersonalized identity in Danda. I also noted Mr. Pant's internalized, yogic epistemology of "deep peace" and "single-pointed awareness." Mr. Pant described how he had invited scientists to "measure the spiritual 'vibrations' [Eng.] in Danda Nagaraja." Their measurements had "confirmed what we knew all along, that this place has tremendous power; it is truly a great siddha pith." According to Mr. Pant, the divine "vibrations" allowed temple visitors to achieve a profound release (*mukti*) in Danda, as opposed to the "minor benefits" one derived from consulting an oracle or sponsoring a jagar ritual. Mr. Pant's use of the scientific method to affirm the spiritual potency of Danda exemplifies the modernist vision that temple developers had for Danda. The pujaris used the authority of modern, Western science to bolster their claims about the religious efficacy of visiting Danda.

The temple's history, its significance, and the transformations underway at Danda Nagaraja were, however, contested. In some cases, those contestations came from within the temple economy itself, while in others, they came from outside.[18]

Fractious Identities

When I first arrived in Danda, the temple priests were eager to speak with me. At the temple complex, I followed pujaris in their day-to-day activities and chatted with them in the evenings after visitors had left. Developing a relationship with the pujaris was not an easy task, however. Once, after I had explained that my father was Sikh and my mother was Hindu, one of the pujaris became irritated. He asked me questions implying that I was lying about not being Muslim, and made condescending remarks about intercaste and interfaith marriages. While I was used to people asking probing questions about my name and family background, the pujaris' outspoken censure was disconcerting. Though I tried to develop a positive working relationship with the pujaris in Danda, we never fully recovered after this unpleasant interaction.

Efforts to develop and popularize Danda both positively and negatively impacted my research. On the one hand, pujaris and members of the temple committee were keen to speak with me because they believed my research could help inform an audience in and beyond Uttarakhand about Danda Nagaraja. On the other hand, they also expressed anxieties about what I would produce. These attitudes were unlike what I had experienced with jagar priests, who didn't seem concerned about the final product of my research. The pujaris encouraged—or warned—me to stay close to their "official" narrative about Danda Nagaraja, which they published both online and in printed pamphlets available at the temple. As a cautionary tale, one of the pujaris told me about a Garhwali writer who had interviewed him a few years earlier. The writer had published his work in Hindi with a local Garhwali press without seeking the temple committee's approval, so the pujaris had the text removed from every bookstore in Garhwal, he said boastfully. The temple authorities had stored the books on the temple premises. The pujari said that he was looking forward to the writer's return to Danda Nagaraja in the future, at which point the temple authorities would set fire to the texts in the temple courtyard in front of the writer.

Whether this story was apocryphal or not, it expressed the stakes of the "awareness-raising" programs around Danda and temple placemaking in contemporary India more broadly. Fortunately for both the pujaris and myself, I ended up working much more extensively with Dalit priests in settings beyond Brahmin-controlled temple sites. My commitment to doing so was partly shaped by the disdain caste-privileged Brahmin priests expressed toward Dalit ritual specialists. (Of course, their efforts backfired. Brahmin priests' near-universal derision of these practices made me *more* committed to exploring and understanding their literary, social, and political richness.) For example, one of the senior pujaris at Danda told me I shouldn't "waste my time" with jagar priests. They informed me I was making a "serious mistake" in learning about jagar. I should instead spend my time and energy working in Danda Nagaraja and other "pure" (*pavitra*) places of worship, they suggested. They pointed out that "since jagaris are illiterate, they do not have access to authoritative (*shastrik*) knowledge," which pujaris claim to possess. One pujari I met said all I needed to know about Nagaraja could be "found in the Gita-Bhagavat"—a shorthand for the broader Sanskrit-language textual tradition related to the god Krishna. "Go sit under that tree, and read this," the pujari told me, handing me a Hindi-language translation of the Bhagavadgita. I was offended by his dismissal of the jagar priests whom I had come to respect and trust. Nevertheless, to appease my hosts, I spent the next few days sitting under a tree in the temple courtyard reading the Gita.

Furthermore, they said, worshiping a god such as Nagaraja through divine embodiment in jagar rituals was less meaningful and efficacious than temple practices like puja, singing *bhajans* (devotional songs), and attending multiday Bhagavata Purana and Ramayana recitations. Pujaris' disparaging comments toward jagar echoed British colonial descriptions of these same practices, which were characterized as black magic (*jadu-ṭona*), ghost worship (*bhut nach*), animal sacrifice (*bali*), and "superstition" (*andha-vishvas*). Like colonial commentators, such as E. T. Atkinson (1973 [1882]) and E. S. Oakley (1905), pujaris similarly distinguished between so-called civilized (Brahminical) and primitive (Dalit) religions. For instance, referring to popular religion in Garhwal, Atkinson writes that, even though Garhwalis are nominally regarded as Hindus, "their social habits and religious beliefs are often repugnant to those who strictly observe the orthodox ceremonial usages of Hinduism."[19] Perhaps *repugnance* is too strong a word to describe the pujaris' attitude toward jagar, but the hierarchy between Brahminical and non-Brahminical forms of priestly power and authority is notable. As Richard Gombrich observes, one of the characteristics of the post-Vedic orthodox Hindu tradition, or what Gombrich calls "Brahmanism," is that it "denied all value to possession states." Possession, or what I refer to as divine embodiment, is screened out of Brahminical religion, which inculcates control. States of possession, in contrast, imply "losing one's self-awareness and self-control."[20] In other words, the authority of Brahminical religion is shored up by excluding certain practices, including divine embodiment, as non-Hindu.

However, in the temple courtyard, I was reminded of the fact that, despite their strong opinions, the pujaris did not own Nagaraja or his worship. Rather, many of the pilgrims I met at Danda also related to Nagaraja not solely as a temple deity but also as an embodied actor in jagar rituals. Many making the pilgrimage to Danda were fulfilling vows they had made during jagar ceremonies and divination and healing rituals. Further, when they saw me carrying around the Gita, I learned that only a minority of temple visitors whom I met had "read" the Gita or Bhagavata Purana, and even fewer had encountered these texts in Sanskrit. Finally, temple visitors did not see the pujaris in the same authoritative light that they saw themselves. They described pujaris' functions as performing a set of tasks—doing *arati*, chanting mantras, accepting and returning offerings, tying the sacred thread, and so on. Visitors to the temple had fleeting interactions with the temple Nagaraja and pujaris.

Even though pujaris distinguished between *their* Nagaraja and the embodied, "danced" Nagaraja of jagar priests and participants, for most lay devotees of Nagaraja, this was an abstract and artificial problem. For them, jagar was not antagonistic to temple worship; it was simply another way of knowing and interacting with Nagaraja. Even for urban, middle-class devotees who no longer sponsored or attended jagars, such rituals were an important part of their family traditions, and they did not dismiss or denounce them.

Land of the Gods: Origin Myths

On my visits to Uttarakhand after 2014, I began hearing alternate versions of the story of Krishna's arrival in Garhwal. In pujaris' version of the story, there was no mention of Krishna coming into conflict with a king named Gangu Ramola, nor was there any mention of Krishna asking this king for a place, or *sthan*, to inhabit—episodes that were central in the narratives about Nagaraja that I had recorded in jagar settings. Rather, the story of the god's arrival from the plains was contextualized within the history of Muslim conquest by both "upper" and "lower" caste Paharis. These (re)tellings occurred alongside the rise of the BJP in the constituencies of Tehri, Pauri, Almora, and Haridwar since 2004 but particularly since 2014, when the Nainital constituency (a stronghold of the Indian National Congress party) was abolished. Despite the rise in unemployment in the region due to the COVID-19 pandemic, most recently, in the 2022 state assembly elections, the BJP once again won a historic landslide victory, winning forty-seven out of seventy seats.[21] During election speeches, both Congress and BJP leaders evoked the notion of Uttarakhand as a sacred landscape, heralding themselves as the true stewards of "*dev-bhumi.*"[22]

One senior pujari narrated Nagaraja's arrival in Garhwal by saying that *all* the deities who inhabited Uttarakhand—"all 330 million of them"—had come to Uttarakhand from the plains of north India. Their arrival was related to specific historical events beginning in the tenth century onward, when north India came under the control of the first of several foreign rulers, beginning with the Ghurid dynasty. "Delhi used to be the seat of the gods before the Muslims got control of it," he said.[23] "When Muslims got control of Delhi, the gods fled to Uttarakhand.... Isn't this why you have come all the way here, to find your old gods?" he asked, winking at me. He knew I was from Delhi. Nagaraja was one of the first deities "to leave the 'plains' [Eng.] and arrive in Uttarakhand," he said. When I asked him to elaborate, he continued:

> When the Muslims arrived in Delhi, they asked the gods for a small place [*jagah*] to inhabit. The Muslims then began sacrificing chickens in this place in the way of halal [a religiously sanctioned form of animal sacrifice within Islam]. Before the arrival of Muslims, people did not sacrifice animals there. But after their arrival, blood began to be spilt everywhere, so the gods began moving away. The Muslims then demanded more land, on which they began sacrificing goats, so the gods moved away even further. Then, Muslims began reciting the Qur'an into the ears of cows [that is, prior to sacrificing them], and this, the gods could no longer bear, so they fled to Uttarakhand.... Before the arrival of Muslim conquerors, the gods were everywhere [in north India], but eventually, they had to leave even Gokul and Mathura [places significant in the mythology of Krishna]. This is why Uttarakhand is called the "land of the gods," because all the gods reside here now.

Both the jagar and pujari narratives of Krishna's arrival in Garhwal began with a request or demand for place. However, while the jagar narrative began with Krishna asking a local Garhwali ruler, Gangu Ramola, for a place to inhabit, in the pujari's narrative, a religious Other—"the Muslims"—demanded place and, in so doing, violently displaced Hindu gods.

In this story, as in many others, placemaking was not a socially or politically neutral or benign process. Rather, it was laced with violence. The Islamophobic tenor of the story—a mainstay of Hindutva projects—suggested that Hindu gods were repelled by "Muslim" practices, such as religiously sanctioned forms of animal sacrifice. This denunciation of animal sacrifice was, thus, also a way of critiquing non-Brahminical Hindu practices in Garhwal and folded together critiques of Muslims *and* Dalits, excluding them from rightfully belonging to the "land of the gods."

In addition to Brahmins, many Rajputs and Dalits from across Garhwal also narrated this story of how Uttarakhand had attained the title "land of the gods" to me. Rather than just an "upper-caste" Hindu narrative about fleeing "impurity," I found that the narrative existed across caste lines while retaining racist notions of Muslims both as ritually impure and as demanding. For example, a Dalit jagari described this story:

> The great battle between the Pandavas and Kauravas had turned the soil red in Kurukshetra. Here, during [Goddess] Kali's incarnation as Draupadi, the gods Hit, Binsar, Kshetrapal, and Ghandiyal were born from birds' eggs. Ghandiyal was the most senior of the gods. After growing up, he moved to Divar-patti, in Chandni Chowk [in Old Delhi]. Every morning, he used to bathe in the Yamuna River until the Muslims arrived and chased him away. He then traveled to Uttarakhand, and all the other gods followed him there. Why did Ghandiyal leave [Delhi]? Because the Muslims asked him for half a foot of land, and he gave it to them, but they kept asking for more. On this land, they started doing halal sacrifices of chickens, goats, fish, buffaloes, and even cows. With each sacrifice, Ghandiyal moved further away from them until he arrived here [Uttarakhand].

Thus, even though Dalit communities also practiced animal sacrifice, the jagari I spoke to said that their form of sacrificing animals was different from what Muslim communities did: "We also do halal," he said, "but we do it the *right* way, whereas Muslims do it incorrectly [*ulta*].... We must do animal sacrifices [*bali*] because the earth here demands it: unless it consumes the blood [of a sacrificial animal], its thirst is not quenched. That is its nature.... When we perform jagar, we ask the deity whether he wants a bali, and he tells us if he does or not." The jagari described how animal sacrifice practices were changing and "even dying out"—perhaps another effect of Brahminical Hinduism's growing influence in the region.[24]

However, my fears about the growing anti-Muslim racism in Uttarakhand becoming *dev-bhumi* and the rising influence of the BJP were assuaged somewhat by a conversation I had with two friends, Meena Joshi and her husband. I lived with Meena and their family while conducting fieldwork in Pauri Garhwal in 2011. Meena was a classically trained musician and came from an illustrious family of musicians and artists. Her husband was also a trained musician, but after getting married, he worked as a truck driver. Because Meena was a Brahmin and her husband a Rajput, the couple faced stiff opposition from their families when they married.

One day, while discussing the story of the gods' flight from the plains, we also began talking about Hindu-Muslim relations in Uttarakhand. At one point, Meena said, "Pahari culture is very different from the rest of India. Hindus and Muslims here have a long tradition of living together in peace." Her husband added: "This story you told us... is not about disliking Muslims. Not at all."

Meena continued, "When the gods left the plains and came to Uttarakhand, their devotees followed them. The devotees came from everywhere, Rajasthan,

Gujarat, Maharashtra.... I am a Pandit [Brahmin], and my husband is a Thakur [Rajput]. He has traveled all over India, but wherever he goes, they treat him like he is less than other Rajputs, just because he is from Uttarakhand. 'You are a *khashya* Rajput,'[25] they say. 'You are not a real Rajput.' Even I am not a real Brahmin to them!" Even though Meena was a Brahmin herself, she felt that "Brahmins from the plains" looked down upon Pahari Brahmins like her because many were nonvegetarian, consumed alcohol, and participated in religious ceremonies involving animal sacrifice, divine embodiment, and other practices deemed "impure" and unorthodox by Hindu communities in the plains. The same was true of Rajputs from the plains, she argued.

In a similar vein, Gerald Berreman observes that many Pahari Rajputs deny their khashya ancestry "on grounds that they are of plains origin. They say that the term refers to degraded people who are not really Rajputs, and they claim higher status for themselves."[26] Echoing William Sax and Berreman, Allen Fanger adds that Pahari Rajputs have been "undergoing Sanskritization-like efforts over the past several decades.... There is evidence that the Rajputs of Kumaon and Garhwal did not always wear the sacred thread and that Brahmanical ceremonial performance and values were not as important."[27] In contrast to these "lies," as she put it, Meena and her husband claimed that an overwhelming majority of Rajputs and Brahmins who called Uttarakhand home did not possess any khashya ancestry, as they had migrated to Uttarakhand from the plains. This included Meena and her husband's families, which were originally from Gujarat and Rajasthan, she said.

Meena and her husband were interpreting the story of the gods' flight from the plains in relation to the controversy around Pahari Hindus' khashya ancestry rather than through the lens of Hindu majoritarian discrimination against Muslims. They told me repeatedly that they had nothing against Muslims. Instead, they said, the story was popular among Paharis because it contained a kernel of historical truth: after the gods left the plains, their devotees followed them and settled in Uttarakhand. Therefore, this story also made a claim to purity: Pahari Hindus were not khashya interlopers or pretenders but rather "true" and "authentic" Brahmins and Rajputs.

A Renunciant in Sem Mukhem

Along with Danda Nagaraja, Sem Mukhem temple in Tehri District was one of the other primary dwelling places of the god in Garhwal. Sem Mukhem, which regularly appears in Nagaraja's jagar narratives, was said to have been the seat of the legendary kingdom of Ramoligarh, ruled by a king named Gangu Ramola. Narratives about Sem Mukhem tell of how Krishna came into conflict with Gangu after arriving in Garhwal. These narratives contain important lessons about affliction and healing (chapter 2) as well as how the worship of Nagaraja in Sem Mukhem becomes entangled with questions of regional identity and belonging, specifically histories of migration and conquest by "outsiders" who are thought to have transformed the religious terrain of Sem Mukhem.

As I did during my time at Danda Nagaraja temple, in Sem Mukhem, too, I interacted with pujaris, devotees, local villagers, and other key actors in the temple economy while living there for some weeks in 2010 and 2011. One of the people I spent time with was a renunciant (*sannyasi*) named Giridhar ji, who managed a small rest house on the road to Sem Mukhem and other important religious sites in Tehri. Giridhar ji, a local from Tehri, had been married and living a "householder's existence" but then decided to renounce worldly life and join a Hindu monastic order. Even though he still lived near his family, he had almost no contact with them. "They know to leave me alone, as I am no longer one of them. Our paths diverged long ago," he said. After becoming a renunciant, he devoted himself to setting up the rest house, which was built on a plot of land he acquired from a family acquaintance, and performed devoted service (*seva*) for pilgrims and other renunciants who knocked on his door.

I too lived in Giridhar ji's rest house and, over time, got to know him well. He was energetic, humorous, inquisitive, and someone who enjoyed intellectual debates. In the evenings after I would return from my fieldwork, Giridhar ji and I would eat together and discuss religion, history, and politics. Giridhar ji's own life story and the stories he told about Nagaraja helped me understand how Nagaraja and notions of regional belonging were bound together in Sem Mukhem.

Giridhar ji was also a passionate student of the Advaita Vedanta philosophical tradition and understood Nagaraja and other Pahari deities as manifestations of the Vedantic Absolute, Brahman. "Brahman has many names and forms," he said. "Some know Brahman as Nagaraja or Krishna, while others know him as Shiva, Sita-Ram, Devi-Mayya, or Hanuman. Ultimately, these are just names.... When we study the ancient texts, we learn that seeing these forms as separate from one another and from ourselves is a deluded view." Giridhar ji felt inspired and energized living in the vicinity of Sem Mukhem temple, which he identified as a place where "realized beings" congregated to meditate upon Brahman and achieve release from the cycle of birth and death.[28]

Over a few evenings, after his evening prayers, Giridhar ji narrated to me the story of Krishna's arrival in Garhwal, which I summarize below:

During Krishna's childhood, a fearsome serpent known as Kaliya Nag lived in the Yamuna River. Kaliya had polluted the river with his poison, due to which Nanda Baba's [Krishna's maternal uncle] cows fell sick and died.

One day, Krishna was playing with his friends, and his ball fell into the river, so he jumped in to retrieve it.

In the river, Krishna came upon Kaliya Nag and his wife. Kaliya was asleep, but his wife saw the beautiful boy and said, "Son, you have to leave, for if my husband sees you here, he won't spare you."

"But I have come here to awaken [*jagrit karana*] him," said Krishna. On hearing Krishna's voice, the serpent awoke and, as his wife had feared, attacked the boy. Because of the Nag's poison, Krishna's skin became blue, after which he came to be known as the "blue god."

When the Nag saw that Krishna was unaffected by the poison, he realized that the boy was a divine being.

Krishna climbed atop the serpent's hood and brought Kaliya to the surface with him. He emerged, dancing [*nachana*] on the serpent's hood, which amazed the villagers. The villagers, who had been worried about Krishna, rejoiced that he had returned.

Krishna told Kaliya that the villagers and their livestock on the banks of the Yamuna were suffering because of the deadly poison he released. "You must go away from here," he told the Nag. The Nag replied that if he did, the villagers "will attack and kill me." Krishna responded that, while dancing, he had left his footprint on Kaliya's hood, so now Kaliya was in his protection, and nothing would happen to him.

"*But where should I go? You must give me a place* [sthan]," he said to Krishna.

"Go north to the region of Garhwal and settle there," Krishna told the serpent.

"I will do what you ask of me, but I have one request: that you come to Garhwal and be with me."

"Okay. I will come to you. But I have many things to do, for which I have been born into this world. When my work is done, I will follow you to Garhwal," Krishna assured the Nag.

So, Kaliya Nag came to the land of the gods [*dev bhumi*], and Krishna performed the play [*lila*] for which he had taken human form. After the Kauravas and Pandavas fought each other, Krishna established his capital in Dvaraka. However, he found that his kin had grown feckless in their ways, so Krishna thought to himself, "After I leave this earth, these people will become completely lawless." So, Krishna drowned the city and took on the guise of an old Brahmin priest [pandit]; in his new guise, he followed in the footsteps of his devotee, Kaliya, north to Garhwal.

In the mountains, he encountered Gangu Ramola, a powerful ruler [*jagirdar*] who controlled Upper, Middle, and Lower Ramoligarh [a legendary kingdom in Garhwal]. On meeting Gangu, Krishna said: "I am an old Brahmin; I have nothing. Give me a place where I may live in peace."

Gangu answered: "I don't even have enough place to house my troops. I can't give you a place; you must go elsewhere."

Krishna, in disguise, replied: "Whatever you need done, I will do it. I won't do any harm—what could I possibly do to you? You are a great ruler, and I am just a poor Brahmin. Moreover, as a king, if you don't provide for the people, who will?"

But Gangu did not pay any heed to the pandit. So, as the pandit left, he made a vow that bad times would befall Gangu and his kingdom. In time, affliction attached itself to the kingdom in the form of drought and disease, destroying everything.

After narrating this, Giridhar ji said: "I don't know whether it's true or not, but people here say that the boulders you see dotting the hillsides in the distance"—he pointed to dozens of large, unusually shaped boulders—"were the cows, buffaloes, and goats that belonged to the inhabitants of Ramoligarh. Because of *nagadosh* [serpent affliction], animals turned to stone and all the crops died. People lost everything." He continued with the story:

> Because Gangu Ramola refused to give the pandit [Krishna in disguise] a place, the pandit went away. From Sem Mukhem temple, he went to Danda Nagaraja. Unlike Gangu, the people of Pauri [where Danda Nagaraja is located] gave the pandit a place. So, the pandit began living there happily. But over here, people were in serious trouble.
>
> In the olden days—in fact, even today—deities diagnose the causes of people's difficulties and solve them, much like medical doctors. . . . In the story, as told by my family's *gurus* [jagar priests], the inhabitants of Gangu Ramola's kingdom consulted the gods. They found that all the terrible things that were happening were because of the pandit's curse. The people collectively lamented the fact that they had not given him a place. One of these people, a wise person, went to meet with Gangu Ramola and said: "Since that pandit came here, we have been suffering greatly. Could it be that the pandit is behind all of this?"
>
> Gangu Ramola realized the truth and told his soldiers to find the pandit, capture him, and bring him to the palace. Gangu's soldiers traveled all over

Garhwal. Finally, they reached Danda Nagaraja. When they reached Danda, where the pandit was living comfortably, they told him he was being summoned by Gangu Ramola.

"The king who didn't give me a place when I asked him for it? Why should I come now? Forget it," replied the pandit. With help from the locals, the soldiers captured the pandit and brought him back.

On reaching Sem Mukhem, the pandit asked Gangu: "Why have you brought me here? What do you want?"

"We have been experiencing terrible things since you were last here: our animals have turned to stone, our crops have died, and there is no rainfall, so we can't grow any food."

The pandit replied: "I am no magician! What am I supposed to do? Why did you drag me here?"

But the people of Ramoligarh were unconvinced; they pleaded with him to do something. So, the pandit asked Gangu Ramola to bring him his astrological birth chart.

"If there is anything wrong, I'll be able to see it in your birth chart," the pandit said. "Your stars [lit., "houses"] are inauspiciously aligned. Perform a religious ceremony in the way I instruct you and all will be well again."

Gangu said: "No, you do the ceremony. You are the pandit, so you must perform it."

Everyone begged the pandit to do the puja, so he agreed. As a result of his efforts, the drought ended, and it began to rain; farm animals came back to life, and the people had food to eat. Gangu was happy, so he said to the pandit, "I made a big mistake when I refused you before; you are indeed great, so I will give you a place."

Gangu started constructing a dwelling place for the pandit. However, Gangu was still somewhat suspicious of the pandit, so he had the dwelling built far away from the village, on a mountaintop. When the soldiers began constructing the dwelling place, they came upon a large stone [*shila*] considered sacred by the people who lived in the area. This shila was called Sem Nagaraja—there was no *murti* [statue] there at the time, only a shila. The soldiers, who were ignorant, tried to break the stone to make space for the pandit's dwelling.

"Why are you destroying this sacred shila?" the pandit asked the soldiers.

"Pandit, you might be short of space [*jagah*], so we are trying to make space for you."

"There is more than enough space for me; no need to break the stone. I will use it as my pillow—and recline on it like Vishnu reclines on Shesh Nag."

In this way, the temple of Sem Mukhem was built around the shila, which became the central enclosure. Then, the soldiers began constructing the walls and the roof, but the pandit stopped them. "What need do I have for an enclosure when I can sleep under the sky?" So, in front of the shila, some leaves were strewn about to make a bed, and this became the pandit's *sthan*.

The pandit then performed many miracles. When the inhabitants of Ramoligarh saw these miracles, they thought, "He is truly a great god in disguise; he must be Krishna," so they started worshiping him with offerings of curd and butter. They came to his place every day, but he was usually in the high meadows by himself. They complained when they finally saw him: "We come to your place to see you [*darshan lena*], but you are never there, so how do we make offerings to you?"

The pandit replied, "Why do I have to be there for you to make offerings? Since that stone shila is my pillow, pour your curd and butter over it, and it will be as if I consumed it." After that, the people came to the pandit's place every morning to make their offerings to the shila.

When news reached the people of Pauri Garhwal [where Danda Nagaraja temple is located] that the pandit was Krishna in disguise, they felt ashamed for sending him away. They sent a group from Pauri to Tehri to bring the god back. The group reached the god and told him, "Gangu's work with you is done, so why don't you come back with us to Pauri, your original home? We have decorated your place and made it really nice for you."

The god replied, "When I was your guest, you grabbed me, beat me, and sent me away with Gangu Ramola's soldiers. So why should I come with you now?"

"You're right, but then we won't leave here either; we will stay here with you in Sem Mukhem, for we swore to the people of Pauri that we would not return without you."

Krishna forgave the people of Pauri and said, "I can do one thing for you: I will not come back with you to Danda Nagaraja, but I promise that whoever comes from Pauri to see me in Sem Mukhem will receive whatever they desire. I will fulfill all their wishes."

This story identifies Garhwal and Sem Mukhem as dwelling places, or *sthans*, of the god Nagaraja. The story also foregrounds longstanding tensions between two of Garhwal's administrative districts, Pauri and Tehri. While elements of Giridhar ji's story were familiar to me from Nagaraja's jagar performances that I had witnessed in villages across Garhwal—such as Krishna asking Gangu Ramola for a place, the affliction he unleashed on the people of Ramoligarh, and the building of Sem Mukhem temple—other aspects were entirely new. For instance, I had not known that Krishna had been forced to leave Danda Nagaraja.

Giridhar ji said that this "historical" episode explained why the inner shrine of Danda Nagaraja temple "remains closed" to this day. "Because Krishna did not return to Danda Nagaraja after he was sent away, the temple remains empty—he [the god] no longer resides there. Devotees still go to make vows and ask the god to grant their wishes, but they do not receive *darshan* ["see" or encounter the deity] there. To receive darshan, they must come here to Sem Mukhem," Giridhar ji said. As he said this, I remembered my interaction with the mother of the tea shop owner, Mata ji, whom I mentioned at the beginning of this chapter. During our conversation, she complained that the inner sanctum had been locked during her visit to Danda Nagaraja temple. She had felt cut off from the god. Giridhar ji's words affirmed what she had intuited: that the Nagaraja she knew and loved was not present in the temple.

Pilgrims to Sem Mukhem not only encountered Nagaraja in the form of the ancient stone, or shila, but also as a living serpent. Giridhar ji said devotees regularly glimpsed the god in "serpent form" in the mountains and forested areas surrounding the temple, especially in the vicinity of mountain springs, which connect the underground "serpent realm" to the world of humans. Once, after I encountered a large, venomous snake while walking in a secluded area near the temple, I was told that the snake's presence was a blessing, as Nagaraja had revealed (*darshan dena*) himself to me. Giridhar ji told me that "the area around the temple is a land of serpents—they are everywhere, so no one would dare plow this land. If anyone tries to farm here, snakes will emerge from every crevice, every direction, and drive people out." Killing or harming a snake, even inadvertently, would incur nagadosh, the dreaded serpent affliction (see chapter 2).

Because of the presence of these serpents, the area around the temple had been revered for millennia, even prior to the arrival of Krishna. Giridhar ji said, "The snakes who inhabit this area protect it from human encroachment, just like the rulers of Tehri protected their territory from foreign invaders." After the god's arrival and the building of Sem Mukhem temple, the rulers of Tehri Garhwal followed in Gangu Ramola's footsteps by serving as the temple's most devout patrons. They appointed the families of temple priests, known as the Sem Ravals, who still officiated in Sem Mukhem, Giridhar ji said. The mustard oil used in the temple lamps could only be pressed by the queens of the ruler of Tehri. When there were disagreements between priestly families, it was the ruler of Tehri (the *naresh*) who settled disputes. For the inhabitants of Tehri Garhwal, local sovereignty was bound up with the worship of Nagaraja in Sem Mukhem temple.

Mytho-Histories of Interregional Conflict

As we have seen, there are contrasting ways Garhwalis conceive of regional identity in relation to Nagaraja and his temples. Another important site for such identity production is the Hindi- and English-language scholarship of Garhwali historians and folklorists who have compiled, translated, and analyzed oral traditions, including jagar narratives, from across the region.[29] However, people like Giridhar ji expressed skepticism toward some of these histories. For example, I asked Giridhar ji why the pandit (Krishna) had told the soldiers not to break the shila, or stone. Giridhar ji smiled. "I am glad you asked about this," he said. "The pandit asked the soldiers not to break it because the shila was the real [asli] Nagaraja! It [the shila] was known as Sem Nagaraja even before the arrival of Krishna. It is because of this shila that Krishna became known as Nagaraja in the first place, so how could he have allowed it to be destroyed?" The inhabitants of the area had worshiped the shila for thousands of years prior to Krishna's arrival.

However, according to Giridhar ji, "The people of this area have forgotten their past.... Nobody knows who the people living near Sem Mukhem were—some say they were serpent worshipers, others say they were Buddhists. Some say they were worshipers of Shiva.... Others say they were Nagas [an ethnic group], while still others call them khashyas. At least, that is what I have read in history books, even though I don't trust everything I read," he said wryly.

When I asked why he didn't trust historians, Giridhar ji replied that their theories were often erroneous. The figure of Gangu Ramola was often depicted in historical accounts as a cruel and foolish person, but he was neither, claimed Giridhar ji. "Gangu Ramola was a powerful and ethical king who was deeply respected by the people here." Contemporary historians "don't know the first thing about his life.... They can't even tell you what his religion was! Was he also a serpent worshiper? Was he a Buddhist? No one really knows," Giridhar ji said. He described how several Garhwali historians who had written about Sem Mukhem had visited the temple and stayed in his rest house. During their visits, they had discussed their theories with Giridhar ji. "People around here, like the gurus who perform jagar in my village, say that the pandit in disguise was actually Krishna. Krishna, after the Mahabharata war, walked to Garhwal on his own two feet. But educated people [vidvan log] don't believe this.... Do *you* believe it?" he asked me.

I responded that I had heard that Krishna had come to Garhwal in the guise of a poor wandering mendicant (sannyasi) and not an orthodox Brahmin priest (pandit).

Giridhar ji was not impressed. "Whether he came as a sannyasi or a pandit, what difference does it make? If he was god himself, he could have taken any form he wanted, no?"

I nodded in agreement.

"But the scholars about whom I am speaking don't believe in god. They believe this story represents a big misunderstanding."

"How so?" I asked.

Giridhar ji responded: "They say the story was originally about a 'ruler of Dvaraka' [located in the state of Gujarat] who came to Garhwal a long time ago. When we say *dvaraka-pati*,[30] we immediately think of Krishna, but scholars say this is a mistake.... Scholars believe that the 'ruler of Dvaraka' who came to Garhwal was not Krishna at all, but some other king.... This ruler was called *dvaraka-pati* only because he was a great devotee of Krishna and not because he was the god himself."

According to scholars of the region, the true identity of the "ruler of Dvaraka" who came into conflict with Gangu Ramola was forgotten and filled in by the figure of Krishna. History was transmuted into myth. Giridhar ji added that some scholars imagined that "this king's city was destroyed by Muslim rulers" in the medieval period, which caused him to flee. The arrival of a pandit, a Hindu king, or Krishna himself—depending on which version of the story you find most compelling—also introduced orthodox Hinduism (*sanatan dharma*, in Giridhar ji's words) to Garhwal. Giridhar ji said that scholars believed that the pandit/Hindu king brought the Vedas, Upanishads, and *shastras* (authoritative Hindu texts) to Uttarakhand.

I was curious about how Giridhar ji explained the survival of traditional beliefs and practices, such as jagar, in this context. Using the example of the shila, the stone pillow again, Giridhar ji explained: "The pandit did not allow the shila of Sem Nagaraja to be destroyed, so the traditions of the people living in the area were preserved. This is why people still perform jagar, which only happens in Uttarakhand. The ancient deities continue to live among us ... but, at the same time, inhabitants of the region follow Hinduism." In other words, orthodox Hinduism did not entirely displace or erase traditional Garhwali religious forms; rather, they were assimilated. I wondered how "peaceful" this process was; as a technology of settler colonialism, assimilation can accompany violence and genocide.

I asked Giridhar ji about Gangu's refusal to give the pandit a place and the resulting destruction of Gangu's kingdom. To me, this part of the story signaled war and bloodshed. However, Giridhar ji rejected this version of events, which, he argued, rested on an image of Gangu Ramola as a selfish and cruel ruler. Instead, Giridhar ji said that Gangu had been a hospitable king to the migrants from the plains. "In the end, we know that Gangu Ramola gave the pandit a place because they were not really enemies," he said. "They understood that the only path forward was to live together in peace." As a result, the shila remained in place, and the pandit/Hindu king from the plains/Krishna was also given a new home.

To learn more about how these histories and mythologies mixed or remained distinct, I traveled to Dehradun, the capital of Uttarakhand, where I acquired a number of Hindi-language texts about Krishna in Garhwal, including one by a Garhwali historian named Shiv Prasad Naithani (1934–2021) that extended but also refuted many aspects of what Giridhar ji and I discussed. Despite being a prolific historian, much of Naithani's work remains untranslated into English and has not been seriously engaged with by English-speaking scholars of the region.

In his book, *Uttarakhand Gathoan ke Rahasya*,[31] which I translate as "The hidden meanings of Uttarakhand's oral epics," Naithani attempts to understand how Nagaraja came to be identified with Krishna and how he came to be the "chosen deity" of Garhwal. Rather than foreground tensions between the plains and mountains, as some of the other narratives I have discussed, Naithani argues that the oral epic describing how Krishna came to reside in Garhwal represents a communal memory of a centuries-old *interregional* conflict between Garhwal and Kumaon, the two halves of the modern state of Uttarakhand.[32] In my personal communications with local intellectuals, some characterized the interregional conflict as a conflict between Brahminical Hinduism and non-Aryan "tribal" traditions. According to Naithani, the narrative describes a history of competition and conflict between the rulers of Kumaon, represented by the god Krishna, and the rulers of Garhwal, represented by Gangu Ramola. Naithani argues that trade links between north India and Tibet (*bhot desh*) in the early medieval period made Garhwal's ruling elites wealthy and powerful.[33] The established rulers of Kumaon, the Katyuris (800–1200 CE), perceived the rise of Garhwal as a direct threat to their power and prestige. The Katyuris attacked and subsequently vanquished their Garhwali competitors—that is, Krishna vanquished Gangu Ramola.

According to Naithani, the Katyuri king of Kumaon, also called Kurmanchal, was known as Dvaraka-*pati*—literally, the lord or ruler of Dvaraka—an epithet for Krishna,[34] as I mentioned previously. The Katyuris were devotees of Krishna, which is why, in the oral epic narrative, the Katyuris are conflated with Krishna. The second reason is that the capital of the Katyuri kingdom was named Dvarahat,[35] which sounds similar to Krishna's home of Dvaraka, as an homage to the god. Over time, the historical ruler of Kumaon (Kurmanchal) and the god Krishna fused in people's minds.[36] According to Naithani, this explains how the collective memory of a specific historical conflict came to acquire a mythic, religious dimension.

Naithani claims that the Katyuris (i.e., Krishna) presented the ruling elites of Garhwal (i.e., Gangu Ramola) with an ultimatum: to submit peacefully or be invaded. The Katyuri's demand for control over land and resources corresponds to Krishna's demand for a sthan. As we know, Gangu Ramola rejected this ultimatum. As a result, the Katyuris invaded and overpowered Garhwal, which was represented figuratively as nagadosh, or "serpent affliction." The Garhwali rulers eventually submitted to the Katyuri king, originally referred to as Dvaraka-pati and later simply as Krishna. The temple in Sem Mukhem was originally dedicated to a deity known as Nagaraja, that is, the "serpent king". After conquering Garhwal, the victors built a temple for Krishna in Sem Mukhem, which established the Katyuris' political dominance over the region. These events "transformed the political culture and religious outlook of Garhwal" and resulted in the god becoming the "chosen deity" (isht-devata) of Garhwal.[37] In other words, not only was the interregional conflict between Kumaon and Garhwal about the control of trade, territory, and natural resources, but it also possessed a sectarian component. The Katyuri rulers were devotees of Krishna and, as such, had close links with the priestly families that controlled Badrinath, which is part of the prestigious "four abode" pilgrimage circuit and the most well-known Vishnu temple in Uttarakhand. While the Katyuris were Vaishnavas, the rulers of Garhwal were not—although there is little scholarly agreement about their religious affiliations.

Temples like Danda Nagaraja and Sem Mukhem were considered the products of a fusion between a localized, Indigenous Garhwali deity, Nagaraja, and the pan-Indian deity, Krishna. Even as these sites were transformed into a place for Krishna, older associations with serpent worship continued to live on, particularly in Sem Mukhem.

Conclusion: Myth and Memory

The aim of this chapter is not to ascertain the definitive truth about the "Brahmin/Hindu-ization" of Garhwal but, rather, to foreground how these historical processes continue to have meaning in the present context of regional transformations underway in contemporary Uttarakhand. My role as an anthropologist is not to discern whether the historical narratives I heard were objectively true or not but to understand why they are thought to be true. In these narratives, myth and history are blurred to radically different political effects: on the one hand, to assert an "authentic" and orthodox Brahminical Hindu identity by people considered marginal or "inauthentic" because of practices such as divine embodiment and, on the other hand, by those who seek to purge Pahari Hinduism of practices like jagar, which they view as deviations from scriptural, orthodox praxis. In other words, both those who support and decry divine embodiment use these narratives to further their arguments about the purity and authenticity of their practices.

Krishna and Gangu Ramola's encounter becomes an allegory about an encounter between different religious formations in Giridhar ji's account or interregional conflict between Kumaon and Garhwal in Naithani's account. In Giridhar ji's narrative, the pandit (Krishna) represents the "Sanskritization" of Garhwal's preexisting traditions and/or their absorption into the fold of a Vishnu-oriented (Vaishnava) religious framework,[38] whereas Gangu Ramola represents "unorthodox" Hindus or non-Hindus—either worshipers of Shiva, Buddhists, or members of so-called non-Aryan, tribal communities that followed an "animistic" religion that involved serpent worship. Giridhar ji compared the role of the Brahmin pandit in the story to the "great teacher" Shankara, who is said to have spread the religious and philosophical traditions of Brahminical Hinduism across India. Meanwhile, Naithani's interpretation is that the narrative describes a history of competition and conflict between the rulers of Kumaon, represented in the story by the god Krishna, and the rulers of Garhwal, represented by Gangu Ramola.

Giridhar ji was adamant that the story was *not* an allegory for the large-scale migration of caste Hindus to Garhwal after the so-called Muslim conquest of north India in the medieval period. According to these arguments, Hindu kings, who lost territories that eventually came under the sway of the Delhi Sultanate (1206–1526), migrated to places such as Garhwal to regroup and launch counteroffensives. In exile, migrant communities from the plains intermarried with the original, non-Aryan inhabitants of Garhwal, leading to the "*sanatan*-ization" or "Hindu-ization" of the region. According to Giridhar ji, if Brahmins and Rajputs had migrated to Garhwal in large numbers and changed the sociocultural landscape and ethnic makeup of the region in the process, they must have done so several hundred years prior to the thirteenth century and the founding of the Delhi Sultanate; perhaps there might have been multiple waves of such Rajput and Brahmin migration to Garhwal. Ultimately, for Giridhar ji, the story of Krishna's arrival was not about the military conquest and cultural subjugation of the original inhabitants of the region but about the gradual blending together of different communities and traditions over a long period of time. That is, the narrative of Krishna's arrival did not describe a singular event but, rather, a process of cultural transformation.

In contrast, Naithani's narratives did not foreground tensions between the mountains and the plains but instead focused on processes of mixing between two different Pahari regional cultures and communities. In his account, Krishna's arrival in Garhwal becomes emblematic of the successful military and cultural conquest of Kumaon over Garhwal, the two halves of the modern state of Uttarakhand.

Reflecting on these multiple, crisscrossing, sometimes dizzying accounts of the making of Uttarakhand as dev bhumi and, particularly, as a place where Krishna/Nagaraja resides, I am aware of the power of narrative. I wonder how my various interlocutors knew what they knew and what broader ideological agenda these stories serve. In the next chapter, we will see how people working in jagar settings understood the narrative of Krishna's arrival in Garhwal in relation to experiences of affliction and healing—accounts that were very different from those presented in this chapter. As I moved from Nagaraja's temple sites to jagar, the terrain of knowledge shifted beneath my feet. It revealed the instability of the processes of narrative and temple building, which often went hand in hand. Krishna/Nagaraja was everywhere in the region, but he was not the same wherever he went. As he moved between his many abodes, his multiplicity became a site of conflict. And the narratives told about him often seemed like ways of pinning him down.

2

Affliction and Healing

Prelude: The Dream

I told myself that I was interested in Nagaraja—who is known by some as a regional form of the deity Krishna—because his stories represented a deep and substantive engagement between pan-Indian, Sanskritic traditions and regional, vernacular, and oral narratives. But a dream and many conversations that unfolded afterward changed this. I learned that my connection with Nagaraja was beyond my rational or explicit control. Deities search for worshipers and, sometimes, researchers, too. It is not accidental who chooses whom. Neither is it necessarily conscious or rational. But deities and devotees somehow find each other. These encounters are not always pleasant, nor are they always consensual, though sometimes they are both.

I was living in an old house in a village in Garhwal.[1] The house had been unused for many years since the death of its sole inhabitant, an eccentric artist and intellectual. The house seemed frozen in time and home to material and nonmaterial remains of the past.

On one of my first few days there, exhausted from my travels, I decided to take an afternoon nap. I fell into a deep sleep. I dreamed I was walking down a narrow path away from the old house. I heard some people talking in the distance on top of a small hill. I tried to see who was speaking, but the bright afternoon sun blocked my view. All I could see was that someone was waving for me to join them. I climbed the hill, and as I got closer, I saw three religious mendicants (*sadhus*) with ash-smeared bodies. As I approached them, I realized that their skin was not ash-smeared but, rather, a deep blue color.

The sadhus were beautiful but also menacing. I suddenly realized that they weren't sadhus at all but forms of the god Krishna. I became afraid, but I kept walking toward them. I felt as if I were interrupting, but I decided to greet them. However, instead of folding my hands, touching their feet, or saying a respectful *pranam* (salutations), I extended my hand to shake theirs. As soon as I did this, I realized how incongruous and inappropriate this Western gesture was in the setting. "Why would I try to shake their hands?!" I asked myself angrily. But since my hand was already outstretched, I couldn't withdraw it, so I just awkwardly kept it outstretched. They looked puzzled by my intrusion and this strange gesture.

Then, the "Krishna" closest to me reached out his hand to meet mine. I looked down and realized my hand was covered with a dark blue powder, like the powder with which people mark each other on Holi. As he held my hand, I noticed the blue powder rubbing off on me. The blue color started traveling up my arm and spreading over my body. I watched this happen, spellbound. I felt myself suffocating and lost consciousness.

When I awoke in the dream, it was a starry, moonless night. I was outside my body, which was suspended in the air and slowly revolving in place like a satellite. The three Krishnas were standing around me. They were examining my body closely and reached into my torso with their hands. I could see them, but I couldn't feel anything. They were looking for something. I became afraid again. Somehow, I understood that they weren't trying to hurt me but rather help me. One of them reached in and found something that resembled a dark, viscous tar in my body and pulled it out.

I woke up sweating profusely. I was back in the old house. Despite the disturbance that the dream had caused me, as I came to, I realized I felt light and buoyant. I was breathing easily for the first time since arriving in Garhwal two or three months prior to this dream. I felt as if my senses had sharpened somehow: I could clearly see, hear, and smell everything around me.

I stood up and walked to one of the room's windows. In the distance, I saw the bright yellow roof of a Nagaraja-Krishna shrine. How could I have missed seeing the temple before? I wondered.

It took me many months to work up the courage to tell this dream to Ram Lal, a *jagar* performer with whom I was working at the time. He laughed when I told him. "It's good that you started your research with such a dream because the story of Krishna and Gangu Ramola also begins with a dream," he said.

I took the dream and the sighting of the shrine as a sign. I felt Nagaraja was giving me permission to search for him.

> In modern Athens, the vehicles of mass transportation are called *metaphorai*. To go to work or come home, one takes a "metaphor"—a bus or a train. Stories could also take this noble name: every day, they traverse and organize places; they select and link them together; they make sentences and itineraries out of them. *They are spatial trajectories.* [Emphasis mine.][2]

"So, Mori Lal tells me you are interested in learning about Nagaraja," Ram Lal said. "What have you heard about him?" he asked me.

I met Ram Lal through a mutual acquaintance named Mori Lal (no relation), who was also a jagar performer.[3] Eager to show Ram that I had done my homework, I summarized the story of how Nagaraja (Krishna) arrived in Garhwal,[4] a story that centered on his encounters with a local king named Gangu Ramola. Even as an outsider, I heard these stories told many times. Sometimes, only parts of the story were narrated quickly, such as while putting a child to sleep, while at other times, such as in domestic jagar rituals, the story was densely elaborated, stretching out over many hours, with rich commentary and ritual fanfare. Most Garhwalis are so familiar with the story that they do not remember hearing it for the first time, as A. K. Ramanujan has said about the Mahabharata and Ramayana epics.[5] The story's imprint on the imaginations of people in Garhwal is similar to how stories like "Cinderella"—or perhaps more contemporaneously, the Disney and Pixar universe of stories—circulate in Euro-American settings; except here, multiple versions exist with different narrators emphasizing different events and encounters between Nagaraja and Gangu Ramola.

After summarizing the story to the best of my ability, Ram Lal said, "Yes, that's more or less correct." But his tone made it clear that I had missed something.

"There is more to the story," he said. "For example, you didn't mention that Nagaraja inflicted *nagadosh* upon Gangu because of his failure to grant him a place (*sthan*) to rest." I was struck by Ram's emphasis on *nagadosh*, which I translate as "serpent affliction."[6] While Nagaraja, the "king of serpents," is the deity who inflicts the specific kind of affliction that is nagadosh, Ram's question opened up a broader line of thinking around *dosh*—suffering, or more precisely, affliction itself—as an act of divine intervention.

This chapter explores the nature of divine affliction and the afflictive nature of deities in Uttarakhand by analyzing different scenes in the Nagaraja and Gangu Ramola story, which follows a trajectory from misrecognition and affliction to recognition and healing. My understanding of these events and their significance for theorizations and practices of affliction and healing draw from many conversations I had with ritual specialists, such as jagar priests (*jagaris*) and mediums (*pasvas*), and lay people in Garhwal.[7] When ordinary Paharis experience dosh, they seek out oracles and jagaris to heal them. For ritual practitioners charged with diagnosing and healing misfortune, illness, or suffering in their communities, the Nagaraja and Gangu Ramola story is key to understanding how a deity could be transformed from an afflictive to a benevolent presence. For the ritual practitioners with whom I worked, understanding the afflictive nature of deities helped explain their presence in the world, the forms they take, and how they act in relation to their human worshipers.

The term *dosh* describes a constellation of interlocking disturbances—psychophysical, social, and environmental—that can affect both humans and nonhumans alike. Dosh is one possible (but not the only) relation between humans and divinities in Uttarakhand, and it is a concern that animates people's everyday practices and thoughts, particularly when they experience difficulties, misfortunes, or illnesses in their lives that are not easily explained by other causes. I translate *dosh* through the English-language term *affliction* because both connote something more than physical devastation. As the philosopher Simone Weil describes, affliction leaves people "mutilated," valueless, and worthless. Affliction can involve the twinned and catastrophic impacts of physical pain *and* social humiliation or degradation. For Weil, affliction reveals the inherent fragility of human dignity that can be shattered anytime by the unforeseen contingencies of necessity and force that leave the "victim writhing on the ground like a half-crushed worm."[8] The story of Nagaraja and Gangu Ramola share many resonances with the kinds of affliction Weil describes, despite the radically different contexts. Among many other lessons that can be drawn from the Nagaraja and Gangu Ramola story, the narrative reveals how all humans, no matter how powerful, are vulnerable to the power of deities and how deities are also influenced by human behavior and action. Misrecognition alone can lead to devastation, while recognition can bring reward.

There are also other sources and origins of affliction. If a person crosses or harms a deity, a nonhuman associated with a deity (such as a snake), or a place where a deity resides, even unintentionally, an afflictive form of a deity can enter their body and become lodged in them. In Uttarakhand, dosh "attaches" to people in several ways. For example, people may fall victim to dosh due to prevailing astrological conditions at the time of birth. This form of dosh is diagnosed by oracles, as well as by astrologers known as *gantua*,[9] and it often comes to light before a couple is married when their astrological birth charts (*kundali*) are matched. Second, dosh may be connected to particular kinds of imbalances in the humors (*doshas*), which in Ayurveda consist of three elements: *vata*, *pitta*, and *kapha*. Affliction may also attach itself to a person as the result of negative actions committed in a previous life. These forms of dosh often commingle and combine. My interlocutors described affliction as a dynamic process rather than as an isolated event.

In Uttarakhand, affliction is understood as a harmful attachment. When gods "attach" themselves to humans, they often do so as afflictive presences. People in the region say that "affliction," or dosh, is hard to throw off. Dosh can come in many forms: illnesses that affect humans or livestock, misfortune, bad luck, or environmental degradation, such as soil infertility. Rather than a "symbol" of the deity's anger or displeasure, dosh is the angry deity who causes harm if their desires—which often center on demands for "place"—are denied. Dosh "clings" or "attaches" (*lagana*) itself to bodies, persons, and places and requires expert intervention to dislodge.[10]

As we will see, the Nagaraja-Gangu Ramola saga also reveals the centrality of a particular kind of spatial logic in practices of affliction and healing.[11] Just as affliction is understood as the deity "attaching" themself to a person against their will, healing or a harmonious human-divine relationship is often described as the ability or willingness of a devotee to "make place" for a deity. In particular, healing rituals are efforts to make place for afflictive, *un-placed* manifestations of divinity. When successful, ritual practitioners can transform dosh into a nonafflictive, creative, and desirable form of the deity. Understanding the dialectics and capacities of both affliction and healing within deities themselves is central to notions of well-being and flourishing in Uttarakhand. At the same time, in focusing on deities' capacities for affliction, the narratives that follow are certainly also cautionary tales, reminding humans to tread carefully.

Before diving into the series of encounters between Nagaraja and Gangu Ramola, it is first necessary to know something more about the nature of deities like Nagaraja.

The Hooked Thorn

Garhwalis acknowledge that all Pahari deities are beings "of power" (shakti); they are both destructive *and* creative. Healers and ritual specialists must learn to manage deities' destructive potential while harnessing their creative capacities. To illustrate, the jagari Ram Lal described an episode from the Mahabharata epic:

> Deities are like the Narayan Astra [*astra* is a powerful weapon]. You must bow [*nak mastak*] before them. Performing jagar, undertaking a pilgrimage to Sem Mukhem temple, [or] making sacrificial offerings are all ways of bowing down to deities. You must bow to them. If you try to manipulate or misuse them, they will destroy you....
>
> We see this in the story of Ashwatthaman [a warrior who sided with the Kauravas in the Mahabharata war], who employed the Narayan Astra and almost destroyed the world. Even the Pandavas had to bow down before this weapon, or else they would have died.
>
> Krishna told the Pandavas: "I know the secret [*rahasya*] of this weapon. Bow to it and give up your arms, and you will be saved." But Bhim [one of the Pandava brothers] did not listen, and the right side of his body started to rot.
>
> Krishna said, "Bhim-sen, I acknowledge your greatness and bravery, but this one time, please bow down." Bhim relented and bowed to the weapon, which then became ineffective. Duryodhana [the leader of the Kauravas] said to Ashwatthaman, "So what if this weapon failed once—try again!"
>
> Ashwatthaman refused: "If I use it again, it will destroy me. It will not be made peaceful [*shant*] again."
>
> Deities are the same way: you have to bow to them, and then they become peaceful. But if a person, for his own nefarious purposes, goes to a deity and says, "Don't become peaceful," that can backfire.... People use deities to harm and lay curses [*ghat lagana*] on others, but in the end, they end up destroying themselves.

Like the Narayan Astra, which has world-destroying potential, gods demand obedience. Even important humans—the key actors of the Mahabharata, the Pandavas and Kauravas—are forced to submit to their power. As Ram told me, while it is possible to harness or weaponize the power of deities (in the form of *hankar-jankar*, that is, "black magic"), those are dangerous and ultimately self-destructive practices.

This capacity to harm or inflict suffering is understood by jagar practitioners and ordinary Paharis alike as an effect of deities' inherently complex and contradictory nature. One of the first narratives I recorded about Pahari deities' propensity to both harm and heal was performed by Ram Lal during a jagar ritual dedicated to Nagaraja-Krishna. This story, which I summarize below, involved mythical winged beings called *garudas* and described the emergence and resolution of divine affliction, or dosh:[12]

In order to obtain the *paiya* tree that [Krishna's uncle] Kansa had demanded, Krishna had to travel to the serpent realm. On his way there, in a place called Dhaulagudiyar, he encountered 360 wing-less garudas. These garudas had been without food for twelve years. They were hungry, but because Krishna respectfully addressed them as "uncle" [*mamaji*], they refrained from devouring him, even after the god invited them to eat him if it would satisfy their hunger.

"Where are your wings?" Krishna asked the garudas. They replied that they had attacked a bird from Surudkot and eaten his grain, so the birds of Surudkot had cut their wings off as punishment.

Krishna decided to help the garudas get their wings back. On arriving in Surudkot, he told the birds there that because they had taken the garudas' wings, dosh had attached itself to them. "If you want to be cured," he told them, "you must return the garudas' wings."

One by one, the birds of Surudkot became sick with a terrible fever; they were close to dying. Krishna, then, took on the guise of a *pandit* [Brahmin priest], wearing saffron robes and carrying sacred texts. "In order to remove the dosh and be cured," he advised them, "make an initial offering of two garuda wings."

After they made this offering, four of the birds of Surudkot were cured. Seeing this, they began gathering the 720 wings that were still needed. However, they only managed to return 718 wings to the garudas.

One of the garudas who was blind was left wingless. And for each wing that was unaccounted for, two birds remained sick. Krishna stressed to the birds of Surudkot that the wings of the blind garuda had to be returned because this garuda, being both blind and unable to fly, was totally defenseless, which was a grave injustice.

In the end, the birds of Surudkot managed to find the remaining two wings, and the dosh that afflicted them was removed. The *pandit* then revealed himself as the god Krishna. Happy that their wings had been returned, the garudas asked Krishna how they could be of service to him, and Krishna, knowing that he would need them later on, told them they should appear whenever he called them.

When Ram and I discussed this story later, he said that its central message was that Nagaraja-Krishna could "sometimes be the disease [*bimari*] and sometimes the 'doctor' [Eng.].... He [the god] spreads the disease and also cures it [*ilaj karana*]." In other words, Pahari gods like Nagaraja were known and experienced as agents of both harm/destruction as well as healing.

During the performance of a particular kind of song known as the Brit Barma,[13] with which jagar rituals begin, jagaris recite phrases that invoke what Ram described as the "face" (*chahara*) and "identity" (*pahchan*) of the deity. Specific phrases in Nagaraja's Brit Barmas characterize the god as an unpredictable, mercurial being. One, for example, describes how, "with a smiling face, he [the god] strikes from behind" (*mukhdi hasli, picchli dhansli*), while another describes the god as "the hooked thorn of the jujube berry tree" (*ulta ber ka kanta*). Early one morning, as Ram and I left a village where he had just performed a late-night jagar for Nagaraja, Ram summarized the episode to which "mukhdi hasli, picchli dhansli" referred:

> There used to be a demon named Kaliyavan. He received a boon that he could not be killed by any ordinary means. So, in order to defeat him, Nagaraja devised a plan. Nagaraja proposed a marathon race: whoever tired first would lose. The race took place in Mathura, close to a cave where a sage named Mushkunda Maharaj, who was immersed in deep sleep, lived. While Nagaraja and Kaliyavan were running their race, Nagaraja led Kaliyavan into the cave and jumped over the sleeping sage's body. But Kaliyavan was unable to leap over Mushkunda, and the sage awoke with a start. The sage had been given the boon that whoever woke him up from sleep would immediately be killed by his angry gaze; this is exactly what happened.

Ram explained that when he had sung "mukhdi hasli picchli dhansli" in the Brit Barma he had just performed, audiences knew he was referring to Nagaraja as a trickster; they understood the phrase to mean that the god did not confront his enemies head-on but rather used guile and cunning. Deities like Nagaraja are known to be playful (*mukhdi hasli*), but there is also a darker, destructive edge to their play (*picchli dhansli*). The gods' ways were *ulta* (crooked), "the opposite of what they seem," Ram said, alluding to Nagaraja's use of cunning in relation to Kaliyavan.

Moreover, deities such as Nagaraja are also tricky because their methods were often morally ambiguous, and their aims were hard to decipher. Ram added:

> To those who are poisonous [*jaharile*], Nagaraja manifests as poison. This is why he is known as Nagaraja, not because the god is [literally] a snake but because his actions [*karma*] are like those of a snake.... Nagaraja's stories show us that Nagaraja is a "destroyer of demons and benefactor of devotees" [*asuron ka kal, bhakton ka dayal*]. When he gives to his devotees, he gives generously, but when he is angered by someone, he destroys them root and branch.

Ram also offered another way of describing Nagaraja's duplex character: "Nagaraja destroys his enemies, but he does so out of love [*pyar se*]," he said.

I was confused by the phrase "out of love," so Ram clarified that deities like Nagaraja destroyed adversaries such as Kaliyavan in order to save the sociomoral order (*dharma*) and alleviate the burden of sin (*pap*) that weighs the world down. While the deity's intentions were pure—they acted to serve humanity and the greater good—they nonetheless engaged in dubious acts to achieve their purposes. For example, in the Mahabharata, Nagaraja (Krishna) acted through other people. Ram said: "Krishna did not himself pick up arms; instead, he orchestrated circumstances in such a way as to achieve his aim [the restoration of dharma]." For Ram, this mode of indirect action, once again, underscored deities' penchant for wreaking destruction "out of love," that is, in pursuit of a greater, yet sometimes unspecified, good.

The duplicitous nature of deities is also often described through the metaphor of "the hooked thorn of the jujube berry tree" (*ulta ber ka kanta*). The *ber*, or jujube, tree is common in Uttarakhand, and its thorn frequently hooks itself into the flesh of humans and animals. Ram explained that the interesting thing about this thorn is that "when you try to pull the thorn out, it tears your flesh as it leaves the body, causing even more damage. But if you push it in deeper, it becomes easier to extract. . . . So, you have to be very careful in extracting such a thorn," he said. Ram Lal and the jagari Dhanvir ji, Ram's teacher, likened this capacity of deities to "attach" themselves to persons or places to the hooked thorn of the ber tree; deities, too, operated in this counterintuitive way. Like the hooked thorn, the presence and activity of deities in the world could also be painful, and they had to be removed carefully and strategically. As Ram explained, "Surrendering to it, bowing to it, becomes the only way to extract it; once you surrender, it releases you from its grip. . . . If you fight, [the deity] fights back," Ram said.

Jagaris also explained that the infliction of affliction and suffering was not necessarily, or not only, a negative event but was more ambivalent. According to Dhanvir ji, illnesses and misfortunes could be occasions for personal and relational transformation. For example, affliction could be Nagaraja's way of "erasing the pride of the prideful," Ram stated. "Even when [the god] hurts you, he does so for your own benefit," he said. However, in a less optimistic vein, Ram added that gods may also act selfishly even while they act as if they are benefiting others. From this perspective, not all experiences of illness and misfortune are random or accidental. They are not *always* intended to harm, but this does not mean that they are always necessarily beneficial either. Affliction occupies a morally ambiguous zone; it has to be contextualized in relation to the afflicted person's moral dispositions, their actions, and as a direct or indirect expression of divine agency.

In my conversations with Ram Lal, Dhanvir ji, and other ritual practitioners, I also learned that the deity's form (*rup*) is just as contradictory as his activity (*lila*) in the world. My interlocutors often said that, in Uttarakhand, one may encounter god anywhere, at any time, often in disguise. A jagari whom I met through Ram and Dhanvir ji commented that this was why Garhwal was called "the land of the gods" (*dev bhumi*). . . . One must remain alert to recognize a god or else "fall victim to his *lilas* [games]"—which are not without dangerous consequences. As John Stratton Hawley argues, god's lila involves reversal, deception, and even thievery, and one of the main functions of lila is to undermine everyday assumptions about the world.[14]

Let me now turn to significant episodes in the Nagaraja and Gangu Ramola story that are revelatory of the dimensions of affliction and healing that I have described. I want to emphasize that there were many different versions of this story; some flowed like tributaries or offshoots of a central narrative, while others became their own rivers, stand-alone stories in their own right. They were told to me by multiple storytellers whose different versions and interpretations I try to honor here, yet they all follow the same grain of affliction and wrongdoing to healing and resolution.

Kaliya Nag

The relationship between Nagaraja (Krishna) and Gangu Ramola spans lifetimes. According to some jagaris, the two first met when Krishna was an infant. One day, Krishna was playing on the banks of the Yamuna River with his friends. The golden ball they were playing with fell into the water, where the terrifying serpent being, Kaliya Nag, lived. Krishna jumped into the river to retrieve his ball and encountered Kaliya Nag and his consort, Padmavati. Padmavati begged Krishna to leave before Kaliya Nag awoke from his sleep, but Krishna ignored her warning.

On awakening, Kaliya Nag threatened Krishna, telling him he would be killed if he didn't leave immediately. Krishna warned Kaliya of his "arrogant" (*ghamandi*) attitude. Kaliya then coiled himself around Krishna, squeezing the life out of him. In response, Krishna enlarged himself, revealing his divine form. Kaliya Nag and Padmavati understood that this was no ordinary child. Kaliya begged Krishna for forgiveness and pledged his eternal devotion to him. Krishna then rose out of the water, dancing (*nachana*) on the hood of the awakened (*jagrit*) serpent to the amazement of all the inhabitants of Gokul. Krishna told Kaliya to leave the Yamuna and travel northward to Garhwal and the city of Ramoligarh, where he promised to make him a powerful ruler. Krishna also promised to join his devotee, Kaliya Nag, there one day. In one version of this story, Kaliya Nag is reborn as the cruel and arrogant king Gangu Ramola, who, in his new incarnation, forgets his commitment to Krishna. Many years later, after the end of the Mahabharata war, Krishna sees Ramoligarh in a dream and becomes deeply drawn to it, setting the stage for another encounter between them.

Other performers told a different version of the story. According to Chander Singh Rahi,[15] a famous jagar performer and Garhwali intellectual, Kaliya Nag was *not* reborn as Gangu Ramola. Rather, after leaving his abode in the Yamuna River, Kaliya met Gangu Ramola, the ruler of Ramoligarh, in Garhwal. Kaliya Nag asked Gangu for a place to inhabit, but Gangu attacked Kaliya with a sword, dismembering his body. Since harming a serpent is a grave offense, by killing Kaliya Nag, Gangu invited *nagadosh* upon himself and his kingdom. According to the jagar performer Dhanvir ji, Krishna felt compelled to avenge the death of his devotee, Kaliya Nag, after learning what transpired between Kaliya Nag and Gangu Ramola. In this version, Krishna's arrival in Garhwal had to do with him fulfilling his promise to his devotee, whom he had pledged to protect and care for in their first meeting in the Yamuna River and who had remained loyal to him.

Dhanvir ji and other jagar performers claimed that these details were well-known among older performers but were regularly omitted in contemporary performances. According to Dhanvir ji, younger jagar performers no longer learn and perform these narratives with the same rigor and attention to detail as before. While "newer" tellings of the story emphasize Krishna's dream of Ramoligarh and his desire to be reunited with Kaliya Nag (reincarnated as Gangu Ramola), the versions told by older jagar performers emphasize how Gangu had murdered Kaliya and thus had already fallen victim to nagadosh prior to even meeting Krishna. The events described by older performers like Dhanvir ji change the affective tenor of the story significantly, making Krishna's reason for going to Garhwal both more urgent and less pretty. Krishna was driven by anger, grief, guilt, and a desire to avenge a wrongful death. As I will describe later in the chapter, these details make explicit profound understandings about the nature of affliction, healing, and placemaking in the region.

The Jogi and the Arrogant King

In the following sections, I rely on the Garhwali poet and playwright Lalit Keshwan's telling of the Nagaraja and Gangu Ramola story. I draw on it here because of how Keshwan ji emphasized and explained the causes of dosh, or divine affliction, as related to Krishna's search for place. In 2010, I was introduced to Keshwan ji by the jagar performer Chander Singh Rahi and the Garhwali musician Uma Shankar Chandola. Rahi ji informed me that, even though Keshwan ji was not a jagari himself, "What Keshwan ji does not know about Nagaraja is not worth knowing.... What jagaris sing [about Nagaraja] these days is not even half the story.... Sadly, the songs of previous generations of jagaris are fast disappearing, but a few still keep those traditions alive." As Rahi ji had intimated, Keshwan ji proved to be extremely knowledgeable; I was particularly impressed by his erudition and evocative, layered telling of the Krishna and Gangu Ramola story. Much of Keshwan ji's story, which I summarize in the following pages, was narrated and discussed in the presence of Rahi ji and Chandola ji.

Keshwan ji's version did not include any mention of Kaliya Nag; it began with a Krishna who was exhausted after the Mahabharata war and eager to find a place to recuperate. Keshwan ji's story went as follows:

> In the city of Dvaraka, the god Krishna told the divine sage Narad about a dream he had had the previous night in which he had seen the most beautiful place on earth. Krishna said to Narad, "Please find this place for me." After searching far and wide, Narad found it in *dev bhumi* [lit., the "land of the gods"] Garhwal. On returning to Dvaraka, Narad informed Krishna that a prideful king named Gangu Ramola ruled over this land and that he had brought nothing but misery to its people.[16]
>
> "Nowhere in those villages is there a single temple to be seen," said Narad. "Gangu doesn't allow his people to honor their gods and goddesses; rather, he commands his subjects to worship him alone, proclaiming that he is the only one worthy of devotion in the world: 'If someone greater than me exists, let him be brought before me,' he says."
>
> Krishna prepared to go to Garhwal to further investigate. On his arrival, he saw a crowd of people gathered at the periphery of a village. Disguised as a *jogi* [wandering mendicant], he joined the throng of onlookers. In the midst of the crowd, a jagari sang:
> "Last night, Narayan [a form of Vishnu]
> came here in a dream.
> On the mountain of Sem [Mukhem]
> slept Narayan.
> Come to our Ramoli, O Narayan.
> Come and witness our drama, Narayan.
> Who shall we tell our sorrows to, Narayan?
> What injustices are occurring, Narayan!
> Gangu drinks the milk from our cows

and takes all the grain that we grow.
See our desperation and misfortune, O Narayan.
Our ancestors are crying out, Narayan.
Break Gangu's pride, Narayan.
Leave Dvaraka and come, Narayan."

As the song was being performed, Gangu arrived and dispersed the gathered crowd. "How dare you utter someone else's name," he said. "You must utter only my name; I alone am everything."

Later, Krishna, still in his jogi's disguise, went to Gangu's palace and spoke to the king: "Gangu Ramola, give me a place (*sthan*) where I may live in peace. I have fallen in love with this land and want to reside here. I am your true god, Nagaraja. I have left Dvaraka and come to your door as your guest; whatever I have, I offer to you, in return for your hospitality."

Paying no heed to the jogi's words, Gangu said: "I don't care who or what you are," he replied. "I won't give you even a handful of dirt, let alone a place to live, anywhere in this kingdom. If you were really a god, why would you come begging to me? I won't build you a temple, nor will I give you a scrap of land. Go back to where you came from."

In this version of the story, Krishna, in disguise, travels to Ramoligarh and asks Gangu for a place to live. In addition to dominant explanations in classical accounts of Krishna's entrance into the world and his activities within it—which are usually explained as the god's altruistic service in upholding the normative order (*dharma*), testing or helping his devotees, or his desire for autotelic play—here, Krishna is also driven by a desire for "place," or sthan. He dreamed of beautiful Ramoligarh and simply wanted it. Gangu, on the other hand, driven by excessive "pride," denies the god a place. This denial, in turn, leads to Krishna inflicting—or manifesting as—nagadosh (serpent affliction), which we will see in the next section.

This narrative brings together several important themes about the nature and desires of deities like Nagaraja as well as the sources of dosh, or affliction, including excessive pride or arrogance—that is, *ghamand*, *ahamkara*, or *garv*—which Gangu Ramola was exercising in spades. When I asked Maheshu Dhami, an elderly ritual medium (*pasva*) of Nagaraja, why Gangu was so vociferous in denying Krishna a place, he offered a compelling interpretation: "Gangu was like that; he saw Krishna as an 'untouchable.'" According to Maheshu ji, Gangu had brought dosh upon himself because he had *looked down upon* a stranger, a nobody, a wandering mendicant. Initially, I understood the story as positing a relatively straightforward connection between Gangu's arrogance and his denying Krishna a place—a denial that would invariably have severe consequences in the next part of the narrative, bringing much affliction and suffering. In other words, I imagined Gangu's arrogance as the root cause of affliction.

Yet jagar performers, mediums, and lay devotees insisted that dosh had multiple etiologies: it was dependent on many different causes and conditions. They impressed upon me that "arrogance" was both a cause *and* effect of dosh. For instance, when the jagari Dhanvir ji and I discussed the relationship between arrogance and affliction one afternoon, he invoked the Ramayana epic: "[King] Ravana had the whole city of Lanka made of gold," Dhanvir ji said. "No man has more than 5–10 kgs of gold, but Ravana had a whole city. So, Shiva burnt it down, even though he himself had built Lanka. When someone has so much arrogance [*ghamand*], God destroys [*chur karana*] it then and there."

"So, you are saying that ghamand causes dosh?" I asked.

"No, no, you have it wrong. Dosh causes ghamand!" Dhanvir ji replied, amused. "Look at Gangu's arrogance. He told Krishna that he would not even give him a handful of dirt, let alone the place that he desired."

According to Dhanvir ji, Gangu's arrogance was itself a manifestation of the dosh that was produced when he killed Kaliya Nag. In Gangu's case, "He acted in the way he did [toward Krishna] because he was already suffering from the dosh of killing Kaliya," Dhanvir ji claimed. In other words, in his experience, arrogance was merely the symptom of a deeper, underlying dosh; arrogance belied a more intractable, hidden fault or misdeed. Dhanvir ji went on to say that deities manifest as affliction in response to many kinds of provocations, including the arrogance from which Gangu suffered as well as his act of denying Nagaraja place.

Arrogance was thus both a cause and an effect of dosh. It was a cause of dosh in that it provoked Nagaraja-Krishna to act, as Shiva had acted against Ravana. But arrogance was also an effect of dosh; dosh had given rise to Gangu's arrogance and impelled him to act in short-sighted and self-destructive ways. The ritual medium Maheshu ji confirmed this, saying, "The dosh of the deity attaches itself [to a person] when that person thinks they are greater than others, when they have too much *ahamkara* [lit., "I-doing," or arrogance]; that is when they stop remembering god." For Maheshu ji and others, dosh arose out of a nonrelational, hollow individualism and mistaken sense of superiority toward others. When people "forgot about" or neglected their relationships with divinities, other human beings, and the natural world, dosh befell them. Maheshu ji had once said that if a person ends up harming a snake, that person is probably already suffering from other "troubles" (*pareshani*) or afflictions. Both Dhanvir ji and Maheshu ji suggested that arrogance and affliction were constitutive of each other.

Affliction

Keshwan ji's version of the story continues. The impasse between Gangu Ramola and Nagaraja grows into a full-blown conflict:

> Krishna warned, "Gangu, honor the guest who comes to your door. You are not in your senses; until I receive a sthan in Ramoligarh, I will keep coming to you." Then he disappeared into the forest. The jogi kept coming back, as he said he would, but Gangu continued to refuse him. Finally, Gangu decided to put an end to this harassment and followed the jogi into the forest.
>
> In the wilderness, a voice rang out from a mountaintop, "Hey Gangu, come up to the top of this peak."
>
> Gangu and his warriors began climbing the mountain but soon encountered a large serpent sunning itself on their path. Without thinking, Gangu lifted his sword and cut the serpent in two. On reaching the mountain top, he found no one there.
>
> On returning home, Gangu narrated what had happened to his wife, the queen Menavati. Yet, even before he could finish, he began complaining of a terrible headache. As she massaged his temples, Menavati told Gangu that he should not have killed the serpent. "That was no ordinary serpent," the wise Menavati said. "It was surely a divine serpent. As the descendant of Nagas yourself, you have committed a heinous crime."[17]
>
> Meanwhile, Gangu's pain increased. "Quick, fetch me some water to quench my thirst," he begged. "My mouth has become dry, and my head is going to explode; that serpent is still dancing before my eyes." Menavati handed Gangu a pitcher of water, but when he looked inside, he saw only blood.
>
> Gangu's suffering grew. He lay curled up in bed for days, feverishly tossing and turning. His entire body was covered in rashes and boils. Meanwhile, Gangu's messengers reported that all the water in the villages had dried up; cattle and livestock were dying for no apparent reason; the soil in the fields had become saline; and parasites had destroyed all the crops. The people had never experienced a catastrophe like this before.

This narrative describes the afflictive manifestation of a deity that clings to persons and places as disease and destruction. Angered by the repeated refusals to his request for sthan, Nagaraja manifests as dosh, an afflictive presence that ravages not just the arrogant king Gangu Ramola but all the human inhabitants of Ramoligarh, as well as animals, crops, and the natural environment. In this story, dosh is directly related to Krishna's denial of place: his affliction is literally an effect of his "un-placed-ness." In this form, the deity not only causes harm; they *become* disease. As Dhanvir ji put it: "Just as gods can have many manifestations [prakop], dosh also takes many forms." Dhanvir's use of the word prakop—an angry, fiery "outbreak" of divinity—seemed appropriate in this context. Nagadosh, or serpent affliction, was thus a destructive ontological manifestation of Nagaraja-Krishna relating to his unresolved desire for place. In Keshwan ji's version of the story, Gangu Ramola's refusal of the wandering mendicant pushes Gangu, his subjects, and the natural order to the brink of destruction.

Some jagar participants' interpretations of this story are shaped by their own experiences as ritual mediums and, in particular, focused on the use of their bodies as instruments of divine agency and expression. As Maheshu ji explained: "Because Gangu had so much arrogance, god had to enter his body." Much like the hooked thorn, Nagaraja lodged himself inside Gangu Ramola in order to produce transformation through affliction. Maheshu ji's claim that Nagaraja-Krishna had "entered" Gangu's body mirrored his own experiences as a ritual medium. Just as the deity entered Gangu, the deity also entered and inhabited Maheshu ji prior to and during jagar. For example, Maheshu ji described how he knew whether Nagaraja would be "danced" (nachana) by him because, days prior to a jagar, his skin would become covered in rashes and boils, and he would suffer from blinding headaches, much like Gangu Ramola in the story. He described these bodily afflictions as nagadosh, signs that portended that Nagaraja would make himself present in the ritual. In other words, nagadosh did not simply symbolize the god's impending appearance; rather, nagadosh *was* the god, albeit in a disguised, hot, "*ugra rup* [excessive form]," as Maheshu ji described it:

> When you examine the boils [phora-phunsi] that come from nagadosh, you see that they are slightly different from regular boils. These boils are white [varun] in color, like smallpox pustules; because they are white, one knows they are different from ordinary boils.... The rashes [dag] are different, too; they are like the scratch marks [kharoch] of a wild animal. They are deep scratches.... These things happen to ritual mediums [pasvas] before a jagar, or they happen to the medium's family members.

Maheshu ji explained that these abscesses were caused by the heat [garami] of the deity on the body. For him, being "possessed" by a deity was not an instantaneous irruption of divinity; rather, the god was already in/on the body of the medium days prior to the ritual in an incipient, partial, and afflictive form.

According to Maheshu ji, Nagaraja can be transformed from an afflictive into a healing presence during the course of the ritual if they are "given place" (*sthan dena*) in the body of the medium. The act of making place for the deity within the body of the medium "opened space" for the deity to be experienced in a desirable, creative form. As in the Gangu Ramola narrative in which Nagaraja forcibly takes hold of Gangu Ramola's body and of the region as a whole, jagar performers similarly described the human body as a place that a deity inhabits for the duration of the ritual. Thus, from a placemaking perspective, "deity possession" is understood as the localization of divine presence in relation to—that is, within, upon, and through—human bodies.

However, my interlocutors also pointed to important differences between bodies-as-places and other physical sites of presence, such as homes, villages, and temples. For one, bodies were regarded as important yet highly unstable sites of presence. As a ritual medium who regularly embodied the deity Bhairavnath told me, "By dancing [*nachana*] the god [Bhairvavnath], place is made for the god [in the body]. But bodies [*sharir*] . . . and the places where the lamps burn [the homes of worshipers where jagar rituals are performed] are also different." He went on to say that the body "as place" was a special site of presence because it was a "vehicle" (*vahan*) that carried the god to more stable or permanent places of dwelling, such as temples and the homes of worshipers.

The narrative of Nagaraja-Krishna's encounter with Gangu Ramola dwells on a specific form of affliction that is particular to Nagaraja, which is nagadosh or serpent-affliction. Significantly, Keshwan ji's story describes how Gangu killed a snake. In Garhwal and other parts of India, the act of killing or causing harm to a snake, either deliberately or unintentionally, is extremely inauspicious. In Garhwal, this is a particularly serious offense because Nagaraja's identity is closely tied to that of snakes; an act of violence against a snake is regarded as an act of violence against Nagaraja (on a narrative level, by juxtaposing Gangu denying the mendicant place with his killing of a snake, the story connects the two). This sequence of events and wrongdoings triggers a catastrophe for Gangu Ramola and his kingdom. In some versions of the story, Gangu is transformed into a beggar, wandering aimlessly, haunted, and afflicted with terrible hallucinations.

"This is what the deity's dosh does," the medium Maheshu ji said. "I have seen it myself." When I asked him to say more about the effects of nagadosh in the narrative of Nagaraja and Gangu Ramola, he explained: "The whole [human-ecological] balance breaks down." Maheshu ji argued that nagadosh is more than a narrative trope; it is something that people experienced in their daily lives. As he described:

> When a *nag* [snake] gets caught in a plow, people get nagadosh. A serpent never gets stuck in a plow just like that; there is always a reason. If it happens, *it means you are also suffering from other* pareshanis *[troubles] in life; that's when*

the snake gets caught in your plow. You must sacrifice your bull, your plow, whatever you are wearing at the time [when the snake gets caught in the plow], your jewelry, your animals, everything. Sometimes, you have to even give up the plot of land [that you are farming] for some years. You can't accept a single rupee for any of it. If you do, then there is no benefit [to your sacrifice]. If you don't do these things, you will continue to see it [the snake] in some other form or another [such as in dreams and hallucinations]....

Before the snake comes on the plow, you will see the snake on your path—it is a sign, and if you don't heed it, then it [the snake] will attach itself to your plow. Before such a thing happens, people see the snake here and there, and most people understand that they must perform worship for Nagaraja, do a jagar, go to his temple, make an offering of *rot-prasad* and *pithai* [various kinds of ritual offerings]....

You can be certain it is nagadosh when you milk a cow to find insects in the milk. If it is a very severe form of dosh, you will find there is blood in the flow of milk....

Different deities present with different kinds of dosh. Nagaraja's *prakop* [lit., "outbreak" or "manifestation"] often shows itself in cows and buffaloes, because he [Nagaraja] is a *dudha-dhari-nag* [lit., milk-bearing snake; i.e., he loves milk and curd and protects and cares for dairy cows].[18]

Despite these warning signs, people often don't not realize they are afflicted with nagadosh. Missing the signs of nagadosh was, after all, itself a mark of one's "sickly" status—an imbalance that desensitized a person to the significance of these occurrences. People in Garhwal draw on a range of methods to diagnose dosh. Many seek the help of an oracle to diagnose and treat dosh, and it is often only during the ritual ceremony that the origin of the dosh is revealed to them. As Maheshu ji put it, "The deity [consulted in the oracle's healing room or during the performance of jagar] will tell you, 'Hey, you have Bhairav's dosh or Narsingh's dosh or Nagaraja's dosh.'"

In other cases, dosh may be revealed in a person's dream. Maheshu ji explained:

If you are suffering from nagadosh, you might see a snake in your dream. You might see that the snake has been cut, that someone has cut it.... So then, you go to see an oracle, and the oracle will confirm it. He will say, "You have cut a snake, so now you are suffering from dosh." At that time, *you may not even know you have cut a snake*....

This is what happened to a person in my village who was suffering from nagadosh and had to go to Sem Mukhem [to heal his condition]. This was six months ago, in late October. After he returned from Sem Mukhem, he performed jagar for two nights in his home. I was there. During the jagar, he found out that he had had this dosh for many years; he must have killed a snake at some point and not been aware of it. His brother would regularly see snakes in his dreams [in his dream, he would see a snake drowning in a river close to their village], so he knew there was a problem in his family.

Maheshu ji and other ritual specialists informed me that accidentally cutting or injuring snakes was common, especially while people are engaged in agricultural activity, such as harvesting crops or plowing and tilling the land. People explained that because snakes are cold-blooded creatures, they come out of their dark and cold dwellings to warm themselves in the sun in the late mornings or afternoons—the same time when people are working outside. As humans clear forests and expand into previously uninhabited areas, they encroach more deeply into the territory of wild animals. Thus, in recent years, it has become increasingly common for people to come into contact with venomous snakes.[19] Moreover, the natural habitats of snakes and other wild animals, such as leopards, are increasingly threatened because of the expansion of towns and villages and the ever-growing number of infrastructural and industrial development projects across this ecologically fragile Himalayan region.

In my conversations with Maheshu ji and others, my interlocutors often pointed to the connection between notions of place, or sthan, and the importance of establishing spatial (and moral) boundaries between zones of human habitation and activity, on the one hand, and surrounding forest lands, on the other. In light of this connection, Nagaraja-Krishna and other deities' desire for place was related to the obligation of human beings to respect the integrity of the natural world and protect it from human exploitation. Similarly, implicit in the concept of dosh and nagadosh was the idea that "balance" (santulan) had to be maintained between the natural and social orders and that unchecked human encroachment into the wilderness was destructive to both. For instance, referring to depictions of nagadosh in the story of Nagaraja-Krishna's encounter with Gangu Ramola, Maheshu ji said that the "whole [human ecological] balance breaks down," by which he meant that human sickness and the material devastation experienced by the inhabitants of Ramoligarh arose when the always-tenuous equilibrium between the human society and nature was disrupted. In the story, after Gangu enters the forest in search of Nagaraja-Krishna, he kills the snake that he encounters on his way, which we know is a grave moral offense. Soon after this, Gangu loses his kingdom and becomes sick and destitute. In light of these events, according to my interlocutors, Gangu's act of submitting to Nagaraja-Krishna and "making place" for the deity was also about respecting the integrity of the natural world and protecting it from insatiable human encroachment.

Healing (and Still Some Affliction)

Returning to the narrative of Nagaraja and Gangu Ramola, as the latter is still in the throes of a crisis. His body is fevered and pox-ridden; he is on the brink of death. His kingdom suffers from an unrelenting famine. The rivers and fields have dried up. Humans and nonhumans alike suffer, seemingly without end. Keshwan ji's narrative continues:

> "The people say the jogi is their only hope, for he has special healing powers," a messenger reported to Gangu. "It is as if a deity is dancing [*nach*] on him."
>
> Gangu dismissed the messenger, but upon his queen's urging, he finally agreed to see the jogi [Nagaraja-Krishna in disguise]. When the jogi reached Menavati, she fell at his feet and begged him to save her husband. The jogi responded that he would do whatever he could. He instructed Menavati to prepare a seat for him, arrange a tray of "pearls" [*moti*; grains of uncooked rice that serve as ritual instruments in jagar and *bakkya* rituals], sprinkle some water from the Ganga River to purify the area, and seat Gangu in front of him. Like an oracle, the jogi moved the pearls around in the tray, tossed them in the air, and caught them again. He scrutinized the pearls to decipher their patterns and decide how to move forward.
>
> The jogi addressed Gangu Ramola: "Gangu, you have killed a serpent, so nagadosh [serpent affliction] has attached itself to your kingdom of Ramoli. You have insulted your *isht devata* [chosen deity] and that is why all the water in Ramoli has dried up, the cow pens are empty, the grain in the granaries has been reduced to hay, and the soil has become saline. Even your ancestors have become angry with you. Devotee, water has turned to blood in front of your eyes, food has become poison; you cannot eat, drink, walk, or sleep; your whole body is covered with rashes and boils. Isn't this so?"
>
> Gangu, who was sobbing, said that it was indeed true. The jogi instructed Menavati to place an offering to Nagaraja on the tray and express her innermost desire [*manauti*] to him. "Vow to Nagaraja that you will worship him till the end of your days," the jogi instructed Gangu, "and that you will make a temple for him in Sem Mukhem."
>
> After Gangu and Menavati did what was asked of them, nagadosh was removed from Ramoligarh, and everything went back to how it had been

before the jogi's arrival. Deeply grateful to the jogi for restoring his health, Gangu said: "Deity, you have saved me; please forgive me. I dedicate [*samarpit*] all places [*sthan*] unto you. You asked for one place, but I will give you seven," namely, Albala Sem, Talbala Sem, Asin Sem, Badasin Sem, Aruni-Varuni Sem, Loka-Bhuka Sem, Gupt Sem, and Sem Mukhem. The jogi then shed his disguise and revealed the truth of who he was [that is, Krishna]. Nine months later, at the age of eighty, Menavati gave birth to two sons, Siduva and Biduva.

The story reveals the importance of human-divine relationality in ensuring human flourishing and well-being. However, what this narrative powerfully shows is that healing is not the opposite of affliction; rather, the two are interwoven.

Gods do not only fulfill the desires of humans, but humans must also fulfill the desires of their gods. Gods rely on their worshipers to "make place" (*sthan banav*) for them; in turn, their devotees are rewarded and blessed with health, prosperity, and protection. Because dosh, including nagadosh, is an un-placed, or dis-placed, form of a deity, its cure entails making the deity peaceful (*shant*) through acts of placemaking. For Gangu, placemaking also entails shedding his arrogant nature and submitting to Nagaraja-Krishna. In the story, then, place is made for the god both literally and figuratively: Gangu constructs a temple for Krishna in Sem Mukhem, *and* he humbles himself before Nagaraja-Krishna, recognizing his true power and identity and becoming his devotee.

In short, the afflictions that had become "attached" (*lagana*) to Gangu—his killing of a snake, arrogance, and denial of Krishna—are alleviated through acts of literal and figurative placemaking. For example, in cases of nagadosh, oracles may tell afflicted persons to sacrifice or donate something valuable to the deity. Maheshu ji described how it was common for "devotees to be told to make two snakes, out of gold or silver, and offer them into the river, undertake a pilgrimage, sacrifice a goat, or some other thing" in order to pacify nagadosh. These devotional acts become a way to actualize the god's creative potential while curbing their destructive effects. Both Gangu Ramola *and* Nagaraja are transformed through placemaking. At the moment the god is offered sthan, he sheds his wandering mendicant disguise to be recognized as Krishna, revealing "the truth of who he was." In this way, he becomes more fully present to his devotees in a form that is beneficial rather than harmful to them. Acts of making place for the god—whether through divine embodiment, making a shrine at home, or contributing toward the building of a temple—are, thus, mechanisms of healing. Placemaking is a way of containing the god's "excessive" (*ugra*) and destructive qualities—that is, keeping the god "in place." Significantly, in Maheshu ji's understanding, placemaking not only "opened space" for the god to come into being in a nonafflictive mode, but it also kept the god "in place," that is, delimited.

It is important to note the different kinds of affliction that comingle in the story. What does this tell us about the nature of affliction and healing in Uttarakhand? First, we learn that affliction begets affliction in a process of escalation and intensification that can easily spiral out of control. No one is free of affliction because astrological, humoral, and karmic faults are the effects of living in this world, which I will refer to as Dosh One. As Murphy Halliburton observes, the idea of "cure" is sometimes not possible, nor is it the only, or most desirable, option.[20] Dosh One can be the product of environmental conditions, such as poor-quality food or water, karmic imprints, environmental degradation, the configuration of astrological houses at the time of birth, and thousands of other factors. While healing cannot resolve all these negative forces, people can mitigate the effects of these karmic, astrological, and humoral "faults" through practices of placemaking. In the Nagaraja and Gangu Ramola narrative, for example, Gangu is originally afflicted by the sin of killing a snake (or Kaliya Nag, in different versions) as well as his arrogance (Dosh One). The affliction that Nagaraja imposes upon him, which I call Dosh Two, is different from those other afflictions because it has the potential to counteract them. While Dosh Two—the devastation of his body and the region—is experienced as a negative state, it contains the possibilities for healing. This is why Ram Lal described even the harmful, destructive presence of a deity as a form of "grace" [kripa]. In other words, Dosh Two—the afflictive deity that can be transformed into a benevolent one through placemaking—can act as a prophylactic against the effects of underlying *doshas* (Dosh One). Dosh Two does not necessarily change those base conditions of suffering and affliction that are a part of human life and experience, but the treatment of Dosh Two, placemaking, can guard against various forms of disease and misfortune. In other words, while some afflictions cannot be "cured," they can be transformed into occasions for healing.[21]

Affliction and healing are understood as two aspects, or phases, of a single process.[22] Healing is never straightforward; it does not go smoothly from affliction to the removal of affliction. Rather, different forms of dosh act upon each other to generate the potential for healing. While Dosh Two can be understood as an afflictive manifestation of a deity, depending on how this manifestation, or "outbreak," is handled, it can lead to greater suffering, or the deity can be transformed into a source of healing. Finally, in transforming Dosh Two through placemaking, the potential for healing must be actualized by the sufferers themselves; after Nagaraja-Krishna arrives at Gangu Ramola's door, the onus to make place for the god rests with Gangu.

The nature of affliction—like Pahari divinities themselves—is thus inherently paradoxical. Affliction, though often harmful, painful, and even torturous, has the potential to bring humans and deities closer together. Rather than one being an antidote to the other, then, affliction and healing are closely related, sometimes uncomfortably so. At times, listening to Ram Lal and Dhanvir ji's analysis, I wondered if the intimacy of affliction and healing could be used to justify victim-blaming: that people were somehow responsible for their own suffering. This seemed uncomfortably close to neoliberal logics of social Darwinism to me. Further, at the time, someone close to me was battling a life-threatening illness, and the notion that their suffering was a mark of "grace" did not sit well with me.

"If someone gets sick or injures themselves, would you say this happened because they themselves were at fault [*doshit*], that they deserved it?" I asked Dhanvir ji.

"No, not at all," he replied. "You are seeing what happened to Gangu as a punishment, but I am saying that it was actually god's grace [*kripa*]." While I had understood Gangu Ramola's experience of nagadosh as a form of divine retribution, Dhanvir ji emphasized its salvific effect. Ram and Dhanvir ji underscored the fact that *affliction* and *healing* are often indistinguishable from each other. Just as Nagaraja came to Garhwal disguised as a wandering mendicant, healing came to Gangu disguised as affliction.

Healing may look like affliction, suggesting the instability and unpredictability of divine play. These details reveal a deeper ambivalence around how people relate to Pahari deities—as tricky or crooked beings, "like thorns of the *ber* tree."

3
Political Divinities in the Village Square

Dance of the Pandavas

In late 2010, I took a long bus journey across Garhwal. On the bus, I unexpectedly met Sharad ji, a retired government official whom I had met many months before. He was very friendly and remembered that I was researching Garhwali ritual performance traditions. I was on my way to a temple festival in Uttarkashi District at the time, but Sharad ji urged me to change my plans and accompany him to Dyongarh, his native village, where a *panno* was scheduled to take place in a few days. Panno, or *pandav nrtya*, "dance of the Pandavas,"¹ is a nine-day long performance of the Mahabharata epic, in which village deities are "danced" (*nachana*) or embodied.²

Following my ethnographic instincts, I agreed. After a few hours, Sharad ji and I disembarked at a bus stop near Dyongarh. Sharad ji told me he would join me in the village after a few days and handed me over to Karan Singh, one of his neighbors. Together, we hiked nearly ten kilometers—down winding, unpaved paths—that cut through dense forests, orchards, and fields until we finally arrived in Dyongarh. At the end of the long journey, Karan Singh, a fit, middle-aged man, hadn't broken a sweat, while I was completely exhausted despite being half his age.

On the long walk, Karan Singh told me about Dyongarh. Since no Brahmin families lived in the village, for important religious events such as panno, Brahmin priests (*pujaris*) from neighboring villages were brought in to officiate. Karan mentioned that while most of the inhabitants of Dyongarh belonged to the Thakur (Rajput) community, a small number of Dalit families—whom he referred to as "*Das-log*"—also lived in the village.³ In Uttarakhand, *D/das* (lit., "servant," sometimes used in the sense of "servant of god") is employed as a surname, a generic term for Dalit people, and denotes a class of musicians who perform during religious festivals and wedding parties. As such, the musicians who performed during the panno also belonged to the Dalit community and were called *das* or *auji*.

Auji is a term that denotes a specific caste or *jati* whose so-called "traditional" occupations include tailoring and music.[4] While not all the aujis I met in Dyongarh and surrounding villages worked as professional tailors or musicians, some worked as both. On our way to Dyongarh, Karan and I walked past a cremation ground that was used by Dalit families. Rajputs and Brahmins in the area used separate cremation grounds—which were maintained by Dalits—on the banks of a tributary of the Ganga River. "So death is not the great equalizer, after all," I said ironically. Surprisingly, Karan smiled at my dark humor. I came to learn that he identified as a follower of Gandhi and was critical of "untouchability" (*chua-chut*). Karan and I went on to discuss the myriad of ways Dalits were discriminated against in Uttarakhand, including how they were forbidden from accessing wells and other water sources that were controlled by caste-privileged communities. He informed me that access to clean water was one of the biggest challenges faced by people in the area. Dalits, in particular, struggled to collect water from the few sources that Brahmins and Rajputs did not control.

Over 70 percent of Uttarakhand's population relies on rain-fed terrace farming in this largely mountainous state.[5] While most Dalit families in and around Dyongarh do own land, their landholdings are classified as "marginal" plots, that is, measuring less than one hectare.[6] They can cultivate enough vegetables, lentils, rice, and other crops to feed their families, but they rarely have any surplus to sell in the local markets to supplement their incomes. The plots of land belonging to caste-privileged agriculturalists, on the other hand, are generally much larger, because of which Dalits are also reliant on livestock farming to sustain themselves.

As Karan explained, "One of the main difficulties for Harijans [the word Gandhi used to refer to Dalits] in these parts is that they have to walk far up the hillsides to cut leaves and grasses to feed their animals, thatch their roofs, collect firewood.... Grazing livestock is the most serious problem since all the [high-altitude] pastures belong to the upper castes. Due to this, Dalit families can only support a very small number of animals, hardly enough to get by." Since caste-privileged people prefer to live at higher altitudes—closer to the main village temples—this also enables them to control the most desirable pasturelands. This means that Dalits, who live at lower altitudes, struggle to feed their animals.

"This is the main reason why so many Harijan families live in poverty," he said. "But things are changing rapidly, as upper castes realize that it is in their best interests that everyone is uplifted, because then everyone prospers." At this point, we encountered an acquaintance of Karan's, who began walking with us. The conversation moved on to other topics. As such, I was unable to question Karan about why he thought "upper castes" were more invested in the so-called upliftment of Dalits than before. What did he mean when he said that things were "changing rapidly" for Dalits?

I ended up staying with Sharad ji's family in Dyongarh for the next few weeks. Pannos usually take place in November, the season of epic performances (*gatha lagana*), Sharad ji told me. While the days are still bright and warm when the sun is out, the nights are bitterly cold. The panno I was to attend had been organized by the village headperson—or rather, the husband of the woman who was officially the village headperson.[7] Village heads often serve an important function as ritual sponsors (*jajaman*) since they represent the village community. The panno is a public, communal event: it is funded by the community, attended by nearly all members of the village, and takes place in the village square. Because of my proximity to Sharad ji, the voices and insights of those in his socioeconomically privileged circle shaped my interpretation of the panno. However, as I had done in other villages, I also prioritized meeting with and learning from Dalit musicians themselves.

Dalit Life and Expertise in Dyongarh

Over the next few weeks in Dyongarh, I interacted with Dalit families in the area who worked as musicians, farmers, tradespersons, and private- and government-sector workers. Because my attention was focused on the panno, I ended up spending a lot of time around the thoughtful and talented Ishvar Das and his shy teenage son, Munnu, both of whom played the drums and sang for the duration of the panno. They sang and played percussion instruments called the *dhol* (a large double-headed, bass-heavy drum) and *damaun* (shallow kettledrum) for the duration of the nine-night performance. Despite being central to the ritual proceedings, Ishvar ji and Munnu ate and drank away from the performance, maintaining caste-based purity-pollution taboos.

During the afternoons, the aujis laundered, ironed, and mended the costumes of the Pandava brothers and other panno performers, and, in the evenings, they sang, played the drums, and invited the deities to descend upon their mediums. While they were extremely busy, the aujis sometimes had time in the mornings to talk while they were doing their household chores. However, to my frustration, I was rarely able to meet with the aujis without a Rajput villager present. One of Sharad ji's relatives or contacts insisted on accompanying me to Ishvar ji's home, saying, for instance, that they were concerned that I might get lost to and from his home, which was located on the outskirts of the village. Once we arrived at Ishvar ji's home, my Rajput companion would hover about, surveilling our interactions.

Sometimes, when I asked the aujis a question, our minder would answer for them. The aujis would silently nod along. Once or twice, when I managed to shake my tail, as it were, and spend time with the aujis alone, they offered me tea and biscuits, which we consumed as we talked (a small rebellion, breaking caste taboos). On most occasions, however, when our conversations were monitored, the aujis did not bring out any refreshments because they knew that Rajputs would not accept food and drink from Dalit persons.

While my Rajput companions were present, the aujis and I talked about their drumming practices and ritual expertise; discussing a "sensitive" topic like caste was out of the question. Such conversations would not only have irritated my Rajput hosts but also embarrassed, if not endangered, the aujis. Despite steering clear of topics like caste, the time I spent with the aujis raised eyebrows. Some Rajputs stopped inviting me into their homes even though I was an honored guest of one of the most influential families in the village.

"Upper-caste" surveillance was one impediment to discussing caste during my fieldwork but not the only one. Because I am not Dalit and caste has a profound impact on social interactions in rural Uttarakhand—as it does across South Asia and other parts of the world—I sometimes hesitated to bring it up for fear of reproducing its violence in the context of our interaction.[8] Instead, by focusing on Dalit musicians, performers, and healers and on forms of knowledge and expertise that had been honed by these communities, I wanted to disrupt the popular, bureaucratic, and scholarly understanding of Dalits as simply "voiceless victims of violence and injustice."[9] My interlocutors also conveyed to me that, while the reality of caste impacted their lives in important (and painful) ways, their lived experiences, self-understandings, histories, and practices could not be reduced to an externally defined position in the social hierarchy. Over time, as a sense of trust and understanding developed between us, my Dalit interlocutors began initiating conversations about caste themselves. It became no longer a question of the fieldworker eliciting information but rather receiving what his Dalit interlocutors chose to offer.

One morning, I visited Ishvar ji and found him and Munnu servicing the large *dhol* that he played throughout the panno. I asked them if there was something wrong with the drum, but Ishvar ji laughed and said that old dhols such as his were delicate (*nazuk*) beings. He told me that he had inherited this dhol from his father, who had also worked as a musician. After his own death, Ishvar ji said, Munnu would inherit the instrument. Even though Ishvar ji possessed a newer, costlier dhol, which he would play during weddings and other nonreligious events, he preferred playing his father's old dhol during religious rituals such as panno. Ishvar ji and Munnu showed me some of their other drums, which included a *nagara*, another kind of kettledrum, and *daur*, or *damru*, a small double-headed drum that is usually played indoors during *jagar* ceremonies (healing rituals involving drumming, the performance of sung narrative, and divine embodiment). When the pair performed jagars, Munnu accompanied his father on the *thali* (lit., "plate"), a cymbal-like percussion instrument. Ishvar ji added that he did not possess a *hurka* (a drum that resembles a *daur* and is also employed during jagar rituals), but some members of his extended family played this instrument as well as the increasingly rare *mashakbaja* (bagpipes).

Ishvar ji told me that while he was sometimes invited to perform jagar not only in the homes of Dalits but also caste-privileged people, this was rare because he was from a family of aujis and not jagaris (jagar priests), terms that represent two distinct classes of Dalit ritual specialists.[10] While there exist many overlaps between the ritual expertise of both performers, I was told that aujis generally perform during public rituals in outdoor settings, such as communal events called *mannad* and *bhandara*, pilgrimage processions, temple festivals, weddings, Ram-*lila* celebrations and, of course, panno. Since aujis play outdoors, they know the larger and louder dhol, which is usually accompanied by the *damaun* or *nagara*. Since jagaris, on the other hand, hold small-scale, private rituals in domestic settings and usually perform indoors (see chapter 4), their instruments are smaller drums such as the *daur* and *hurka*, both of which are regularly paired with the *thali*.

Across Uttarakhand, the popular perception exists that jagaris enjoy a higher status as ritual performers than aujis. This disparity may be related to the fact that jagaris are invited to enter the homes of caste-privileged Hindus on a more regular basis than aujis. Some jagaris are also initiated into the use of powerful magical incantations that have the capacity to heal as well as harm. Ishvar ji, however, disagreed with this distinction: "It depends on the person," he said. "Some jagaris deserve all the respect they are given. But many do not. It is the same way with aujis. . . . Some aujis are well-versed in the all the narrative-songs of the gods, from beginning to end. When they play their drums, the gods always come." Ishvar ji complained that some people who called themselves jagaris did not deserve this title. "They are *burtiyas*," he said dismissively. A burtiya is a ritual performer who may have some knowledge of drumming but is not an expert singer-storyteller. On the other hand, Ishvar ji said he personally knew of many aujis who were not only accomplished drummers but also skilled narrative performers.

Ishvar ji claimed that, according to a text called the *Dhol Sagar*—literally, "Ocean of Drumming"—the sacred knowledge of drumming was passed down from Mahadev (Shiva) and Mahadevi (Parvati) to the aujis of Uttarakhand.[11] Ishvar ji said that knowledge (*gyan*) of this text had been "given" to him by his father, who, in turn, had received it from his ancestors in an unbroken chain that went back many generations. Many ritual musicians with whom I worked mentioned the *Dhol Sagar*, but I never encountered this text in written form, so I asked if he had a physical copy in his possession. He said that written copies of this text exist, but it is most often transmitted orally from teacher to student. Ishvar ji described the *Dhol Sagar* as a compendium of different rhythmic patterns called *bol*—literally, "speech"—that drummers memorize, recite, and perform on their drums; bol refers to both the vocalization of these rhythmic patterns by drummers as well as to the vibratory, rhythmically-articulated "speech" of the drums themselves. Ishvar ji said that knowledge of these bol enabled aujis to "call" the deities to "manifest" or "appear" in/on the bodies of their devotees, such as during the performance of panno, to which I now turn.

Performing Panno

This panno was performed to honor Goddess Bhagavati, whose temple, was in direct view of the performance. For nine nights, actors performed episodes from the Mahabharata epic, a long and bloody conflict among five brothers, the Pandavas, and their cousins, the Kauravas. On the first night, Draupadi, the wife of the Pandavas, was "danced" (*nachana*) by a woman from the village. On the second night, the five Pandavas were introduced, and they remained in the *maidan* (the village square or large, open public ground where the village congregates) for the remaining nights, orbiting the central ritual fire (*dhuni*) with prop bows, arrows, and maces in their hands. Whereas Draupadi's embodiment was understood as "possession," the men who *represented* the Pandavas were not "possessed"; they were not ritual mediums who *became* the Pandavas. The Pandavas were represented by five tall and handsome men who wore their power and privilege as rich Rajput landowners with practiced ease. Every night, they wore white turbans and tunics that had been washed and ironed earlier that day by the aujis.

As the musicians narrated episodes and introduced central characters of the Mahabharata, sometimes they muted their drumming. Following brief periods of verbal narration, there were bursts of drumming and dance during which the voices of the musicians could barely be heard at the edges of the maidan. The musicians sang of the Pandavas' legendary exploits and travails, and, some nights, the headman and the actor representing Arjuna joined the musicians in the narration. Along with the singing and drumming, divine embodiment featured prominently in the panno. In addition to characters from the Mahabharata making an appearance, important local gods like Ghandiyal, Kuleshvar, Dhara Devi, Bhagavati Devi, Unishor, and Nagaraja were also "danced." Some audience members also entered into *nach* spontaneously, that is, various deities "came over" them unexpectedly during the panno.

Each night, the performance followed almost the same sequence of events. After the villagers returned from working in the fields, they ate dinner with their families and then congregated in the maidan. The aujis built a ritual fire and tuned their instruments outside the temple (as Dalits, they were not allowed to enter the temple). At the commencement of each evening's performance, a few men belonging to caste-privileged communities—the Rajput men representing the Pandavas and the visiting Brahmin priest—sat in the Bhagavati Devi temple and performed a private evening worship. Within the temple, in a smaller enclosure that was shielded by a curtain, a receptacle containing a small quantity of soil had been sown with wheat on the first day of panno. This wheat, I was told, would grow miraculously by several inches during the nine-day panno—a miracle of the goddess who resided in the temple.[12] When the aujis began drumming, the night's performance began.

Before the first night of the panno, the headman welcomed guests into the village square, told people where to sit, and ensured that the performance began and ended on time. In a booming voice, he also introduced the epic characters and sometimes summarized episodes to explain what was happening in the performance.

The headman introduced me to people in the village whom I interviewed about panno and the religious practices—such as drumming, storytelling, and divine embodiment—that constitute it. One of the villagers I became close to during this time was a man in his late twenties who appears in my fieldnotes as Barabar (which literally means "equal," but is used to mean something like "cool" in English). I nicknamed him Barabar because of his fondness for the colloquial Hindi-Urdu specific to Mumbai, which he used in amusing ways. Dyongarh was Barabar's ancestral village, but he lived and worked in Mumbai in a "hotel" (restaurant). He had come home for the Divali holidays to spend time with his family and had lots of free time to show me around. Many people commented on our friendship. However, they saw Barabar as a "troublemaker" and worried, half-jokingly, that he would lead me astray.

Before the performance began, Barabar commented that I was learning a lot about local deities during my time in his village. Gods and goddesses, Barabar said, were like "politicians" (*neta*), and we both laughed.[13] He referred to the panno not as a "dance" of divine embodiment, like other villagers did—but as an expression of *netagiri*, a Hindi-language word that translates to the English-language term "politicking." In using the term *netagiri*, I was struck by how Barabar evoked negative connotations of deities as self-interested and sometimes untrustworthy political actors. Barabar's statement intrigued me. What did it mean to liken a deity to a politician?

Like the English-language term *politicking*, the Hindi word *netagiri* implies engaging in political activity and persuasion for self-interested goals. Like human politicians, deities can appear as skillful rhetoricians and ambiguously powerful players in everyday life. Also like politicians, village deities are responsible for upholding the normative order and its attendant hierarchies, but they can also operate "above the law" or subvert normative principles when it is necessary and/or convenient for them. Additionally, like human politicians, political divinities sometimes ally themselves with marginalized communities while at other times with elites. It all depends on what is beneficial to them. In other words, such alliances are often provisional, temporary, and tactical.

Whereas in other chapters, I focus on how "place" is made for Pahari deities at the level of the body, home, temple, and region, in this chapter, I show how deities are encountered as "political divinities" in village settings.[14] Pahari gods and goddesses are not always encountered as political divinities; they tend to appear in this way when they become active in the public sphere, particularly during important religious festivals like panno, which are attended by whole villages or sometimes groups of villages. Further, while people often liken "political divinities" to human politicians, there are also key differences between them. For instance, political divinities appear to their worshipers immediately and in person when they are "called," whereas human politicians are less accessible, rarely traveling to and interacting with ordinary citizens in remote villages of Uttarakhand. More importantly, unlike human politicians, the power and authority of a political divinity are associated with ensuring the orderly and integrated functioning of the human-social, natural, *and* divine realms. That is, not only are political divinities tasked with maintaining the fertility of agricultural lands and the health of livestock, but they must also protect their worshipers from nonhuman agents of disease and misfortune, such as ghosts and ghouls (*bhut-pret*).

In panno, deities are invoked by an entire village community rather than by a single individual or family. In return for safeguarding the collective well-being and material interests of the community, they make significant demands not just on individual families but also on whole villages. During such festivals, the maidan becomes a key site of divine presence and human-divine interaction. In addition to hosting public religious events, shared, public village grounds are also used for village council (*panchayat*) and village association (*gram sabha*) meetings. As such, the maidan is not only geographically central but also crucial to village politics. Adjoining Goddess Bhagavati's temple,[15] one of most important religious structures in Dyongarh, the maidan is seen by village inhabitants as a seat of sacred *and* secular power, where citizens in rural Uttarakhand relate to and understand their government, which includes divinities.

These spaces also offer opportunities for deities to interact with their "constituents" or worshipers, garner their support, resolve disputes, and exert influence on village life. Through divine embodiment, prominent village gods and goddesses involve themselves in local decision-making processes and intervene in matters of collective importance. In addition, during these ritual performances, deities may also advocate for their own interests—which are not always aligned with their constituents' needs. As a result, unlike other ritual performances, which follow a more or less predictable form, divine embodiment in collective settings is a more fluid, situational, and pragmatic activity with tangible, far-reaching, and surprising outcomes.

This understanding of divine embodiment in relation to village politics in Uttarakhand resonates with Hildegard Diemberger's work on female diviners and oracles in Tibet.[16] Diemberger argues that "spirit possession" plays a critical role in local politics in Tibet. She writes that "during difference among the leadership, when critical decisions had to be made, female diviners are reported to have determined the outcome. *This was, however, a limited and contextual power*" [italics mine].[17] Similarly, in Uttarakhand, although deities influence political institutions and civil society by involving themselves in local decision-making processes, their powers are also "limited and contextual." They cannot act unilaterally to "magically" will into being a certain desirable situation. Rather, they need to persuade audiences to think and act in accordance with their desires. Divine embodiment emerges as an important tactic of persuasion in this context.

Despite being a public, collective ritual, divine embodiment in the context of panno can be exclusionary. Through their participation in these rituals, political divinities' politicking may involve demarcating and buttressing social boundaries. In the ethnographic examples I offer, divine embodiment in public spaces does—and does not—empower people of lower social rank. In the second half of the chapter, I describe how a political divinity instigated a village crisis during the panno by demanding an expensive tax or tribute, which led to a contentious public exchange. In the end, the village crisis was resolved through acts of politicking by both human and divine actors, demonstrating how public rituals of divine embodiment are sites of negotiation between competing interests and entangled with concerns about local governance.

Ambiguous Inclusions

During the panno, I noticed that those who engaged in *nach* from caste-privileged communities often embraced the aujis, touching the foreheads of the performers to their own or gently caressing their faces with their hands. This intimate physical contact was striking because of the aujis' status as so-called untouchables and the careful maintenance of purity-pollution taboos in other contexts. But in the maidan during the performance, the otherwise strictly enforced boundaries between caste-privileged and Dalit villagers became somewhat porous.[18] Such moments of inclusivity and ritual communitas have been described extensively in the anthropological literature on divine embodiment. In fact, the capacity of divine embodiment to empower and elevate people of lower social rank is one of its defining features, something that was also on display in the maidan in Dyongarh.

My caste-privileged interlocutors explained this intercaste physical contact by stating that, during the performance of panno, the aujis serve as key intermediaries between deities and their worshipers and are, therefore, no longer considered "untouchable" (*achhut*). Instead, during the performance, that is, within a circumscribed ritual frame, their identity as powerful and respected "servants of the gods" comes to the fore. The word *servant* is a literal translation of the word *das*—the surname of the performers in Dyongarh but also a term widely employed for professional performers who specialize in drumming, storytelling, orchestrating nach, and mediating human-divine contact in public settings, as I mentioned previously. In other words, during the panno, as deities "come over" their mediums, the aujis are also transformed. Whereas in everyday life, physical contact between caste-privileged and Dalit persons is actively discouraged, in the maidan, it is not only permissible but desired by the Rajput mediums of the gods.

Why did the caste-privileged ritual mediums—or rather, the embodied gods—seek out such contact? In addition to demonstrating the deities' abiding love for their "servants," what else does the breaking of social taboos in this context accomplish? My interlocutors in Dyongarh stressed divine agency, which is something that has often been overlooked in scholarly discussions about divine embodiment.[19] Some villagers in Dyongarh argued that the gods who were embodied in the maidan did not differentiate between "high" and "low"—that is, between Rajputs and Dalits—because the deities "were above such concerns." When I asked what this phrase meant, one of my Rajput interlocutors told me that deities, unlike human beings, did not care about the caste (*jati*) of a person. My interlocutor went on to say that only deities possessed the power or capacity to withstand contact with so-called untouchables, who are stigmatized as inherently and dangerously "impure" or "polluting." According to this view, a Rajput person embracing a Dalit indexes the presence of a god in/on the body of the former because most caste-privileged persons shy away from such dangerous contact with "impurity." From this perspective, ritually mediated contact with Dalits does not challenge or transform caste hierarchies but actually reinscribes them.

What intercaste contact in the maidan did do was affirm the powerful—and magnanimous—nature of the embodied deity, brought into relief against the "low" social status of the aujis. Because the intimate physical contact was performed by a *deity* acting via a caste-privileged person—and *not* by the Rajput villagers or aujis themselves—for some of my interlocutors, this gesture represented the deities' willingness to "lower themselves" to the level of the Dalit musicians. For this reason, even though physical contact between Rajput and Dalit persons, from a sociological perspective (rather than an indigenous or theological one), can be interpreted as "boundary-breaking," it is also not necessarily subversive in the sense of challenging normative social hierarchies. Rather, these gestures of physical intimacy are a kind of ritually circumscribed social transgression that is not only licensed by deities but also, in effect, performed by them (via their human mediums). As such, this gesture can be read as a self-serving one on the part of a deity: it confirms the deity's privilege and freedom, indicating that they can bend social rules and violate caste taboos if and when they desire. In this sense, deities follow classical Indian theories of kingship and governance by granting special dispensations to the "lowliest" among their constituents, their "servants" (*das*), thereby tempering their enforcement of social order and hierarchy (*danda*) with occasional acts of compassion (*kripa/daya*).[20] However, like kings and modern politicians, the largesse of deities often demands something dear in return.

Ambiguous Exclusions

Divine embodiment in the maidan was both a (limited) site of inclusion and boundary-breaking with respect to caste, *and* it was also about exclusions and negotiations of community membership. One night during panno, unidentified deities "came over" two women in the audience. One of the women, who happened to be my friend Barabar's mother, danced rhythmically and gracefully. The other swayed and lurched around the maidan in a highly erratic manner. She veered toward the aujis, grabbed and pulled on their drums, then raced dangerously close to the ritual fire burning in the center, making the audience collectively gasp with fear. The village headman folded his hands and bowed reverently in front of Barabar's mother, but he confronted the second woman, holding and shaking her. Scolding her in front of the entire village, he told her to stop doing "drama," using the English word. "This is no place for *harami nach*" [lit., "forbidden dancing"], he bellowed. The underlying meaning of the headman's statement was that the woman's nach was illegitimate and inauthentic.[21] She seemed visibly embarrassed by this public admonishment but did not stop dancing right away. People around me surmised that she was trying to save face even though she had been "found out." A few women in the audience laughed quietly under their shawls and sari ends.

What made people think the woman was feigning divine embodiment?[22] I asked Barabar how he and the headman had been able to gauge whether her nach was authentic or not, and he replied that they knew because she was no longer a member of their village. Even though she had been born in Dyongarh, upon getting married, she had moved to her husband's place of residence, a small neighboring town. As per the patrilocal norms followed in the area—i.e., after marriage, a woman "leaves the village of her birth (her *mait*) . . . and moves to the home of her husband (her *sauryas*)"[23]—she was now a resident and citizen of her husband's father's birthplace. In so doing, "She is no longer a part of her natal family and should not, for example, observe birth and death pollution for them, but only for her husband's family and lineage."[24] Because the woman was married, she was now an "outsider" (in relation to Dyongarh, her *mait*) and therefore unable to participate fully—and authentically—in the ritual. Rather than the maidan functioning as an open and egalitarian space, it is also shot through with gendered exclusions that reinforce patriarchal and patrilineal norms.

My interlocutors also had other ways of gauging the veracity of divine embodiment that had to do with experience and "somatic modes of attention."[25] Barabar told me that he had confronted this woman before, and she had intimated that she was under the influence of "some powerful deity." But then, when the headman accosted her, she quickly relented, having no choice but to give up her "drama" [Eng.], he said. My companion continued: "Did you notice how [the woman who was accused of feigning nach] suddenly became all calm [*shant*] after the headman confronted her? That would not have happened if some divine power had truly overcome her."

This event demonstrated how divine embodiment in the maidan is a highly regulated practice; it is not available to anyone and everyone. Only particular people—in this case, "legitimate" members of the village community—have the right to embody village deities. By excluding or delegitimizing certain bodies and subjects from nach, the village community and its boundaries are shored up. In the words of J. Z. Smith, divine embodiment in the maidan serves as a "*focusing lens*, marking and revealing" significant aspects of village belonging.[26]

Crisis in the Maidan

During the panno I attended, I observed how Pahari deities operate as "political divinities" by intervening directly in village governance. In this section, I describe how the deity Nagaraja, the "serpent king," instigated a village crisis in Dyongarh by demanding an expensive tax or tribute. During the panno that occurred the year before I visited Dyongarh, I was told that Nagaraja had demanded that the villagers provide him with a drum made of silver (*chandi ka dhol*). Since this is an expensive tribute, the god promised he would ease their burden by providing half the capital needed for the silver drum and that the villagers would be responsible for the other half. Not wanting to displease the god, the villagers agreed to collect their share of the funds; each family in the village had contributed 750 rupees toward the purchase of the silver—*chandi ka chanda* (lit., "donations for silver"), as one of Barabar's friends alliteratively put it.[27] So far, so good.

But on the fifth night of the panno I attended, this deal took a disturbing turn. On this night, the Mahabharata episode known as the "slaying of the rhinoceros" was to be performed. I was excited because I had never seen this episode, though I had been told about it numerous times.[28] The rhinoceros in the story was represented by a pumpkin, which was to be smashed by Arjuna, one of the Pandava brothers, at the climax. Yet, before the performance began, while people were still streaming into the maidan, the village headman made an announcement. While he and a few of the village elders had been inside the goddess temple, he said, the god Nagaraja had spoken to them. The headman informed the audience that the god had decided *not* to provide half the funds needed for the silver drum. In other words, the villagers were responsible for the entire sum. Each family would have to give an *additional* 750 rupees for the drum.

This announcement led to an uproar. The audience members talked angrily among themselves, trying to absorb the news. The headman continued: "As you know, not making the drum is not an option, for this is what the god wants, and we must comply with his wishes, as hard as it may seem. Also, we need to collect the money in the next few days. We need to buy the silver as soon as possible; time is running out." The urgency in the headman's statement reflected the collective understanding that misfortune and illness would befall the village if they did not comply with the god's demands. One of the well-off villagers with whom I was sitting suggested that the villagers pool their money as soon as possible to ward off the punishment or affliction (*dosh*) that would surely befall the village if the deity's wish was refused (see chapter 2).

Yet, not everyone agreed with the headman's urgency. Someone in the audience protested: "How are we going to come up with such a large sum so quickly? This is our hard-earned money; we barely have enough left over from paying our debts from last season and feeding our families; now you want us to raise even more money for this silver drum, for which we have *already* contributed?" I was sitting with Barabar and a group of young men who started heckling the headman loudly. One of them pointed out that if one of the villagers had broken their promise and backed out of a deal, they would be punished for their actions. The headman, visibly irritated, turned away from the hecklers.

The deity's demand precipitated a crisis not just for individual families who had to shoulder an extra financial burden but for the village as a whole. The conversation shifted from the extra funds required to questions about where the silver drum would be housed once it was bought. The person who served as the designated medium of the Goddess Bhagavati argued that the silver drum should not be housed in Nagaraja's temple in Dyongarh but rather in a larger temple that was shared by the *patti*, a group of approximately twenty villages. However, this suggestion was contested. One of the prominent landowners in the village replied: "There is no way our village is going to provide all this money for the silver so that people from other villages can enjoy the fruits. The drum, once it is made, will remain in our village, in our own temple." The person seated beside me whispered that the deity's "big temple" already had ten silver drums, so it hardly needed another.

As I came to understand, the deity's demand for the drum was not merely a whimsical or selfish desire; it also affected the prestige of the village. In discussing where the drum should be housed, the village's standing in relation to neighboring villages was at stake. The greater a village's financial contribution to the larger shared temple, the more it could assert itself in intervillage disputes over water rights, the distribution of shared grazing lands, road-building and maintenance, and so on. Donating the drum to the larger regional temple would make the village more visible vis-à-vis other villages. In this sense, it could be argued that the demand for a silver drum also benefitted the deity's constituents symbolically and materially.

However, not everyone in the village agreed, especially the poorer families who could ill-afford a second donation of 750 rupees without any immediate benefit or guarantee of support. In the midst of the heated back and forth in the maidan, the headman suggested—in an uncharacteristically conciliatory manner—that poorer families in the village be exempted from the collection (*phant*). At this, many in the crowd, especially the economically better-off villagers, became furious: "Then why should anyone pay? If others don't pay, why should we be forced to cover their share?" The younger men in the audience became especially rowdy.

The argument about the silver drum soon transformed into an argument about the villagers' everyday concerns and difficulties. Some people began complaining about sanitation and hygiene issues in the village and how certain persons left trash outside their doors and on public paths with little regard for others. They argued about peoples' lack of "community spirit" and enthusiasm for public works like temple renovations and building projects. People mentioned that the village school was in dire need of supplies, such as desks, chairs, and writing materials. They protested the exorbitant price of everyday necessities in the shops, saying that the village council needed to do more to make predatory traders and shopkeepers lower their rates. Of utmost concern was the lack of progress in constructing the main road leading to the village—which had been funded but was still not ready even though the village council had assured everyone years ago that it was close to completion. "This is why our costs are so high," some villagers exclaimed, "because you [the village council members and powerful elders] are not applying adequate pressure on the district officials to finish the road!"

Sensing that he was losing control of the congregation, the headman brought the public airing of grievances to an abrupt end: "Tomorrow morning there will be a meeting [*baithak*] of the whole village. Everyone must come, no matter what other work they may have; attendance is not optional. But any family that does not bring their share of the collection money will be severely penalized," he announced to the crowd. The headman's remarks left no room for further argument, even though the villagers continued to chatter among themselves.

I thought the matter was laid to rest and hoped that I would see the "slaying of the rhinoceros" before the night's end. However, things took an even more unexpected turn.

Failed Negotiations, Successful Politicking

The public airing of grievances did not conclude the crisis. That same night, after the panno resumed, Nagaraja made his appeal directly to his "constituents." Around midnight, the god's medium emerged from the temple and sat down at the edge of the performance ground. His body started to tremble and jerk, his jaw clenched and unclenched, and he started to sweat and mutter incoherently, all signs that the deity was "coming over" (*ana*) his medium. Suddenly, the medium, hissing angrily, turned to the headman and gestured that he approach. The headman, with hands folded and head bowed, walked over to the embodied god.

"Don't you recognize me?" the god asked the headman, slurring his words as the audience strained to decipher his meaning. "Who am I?" he asked. Then, referring to various deities, including Draupadi, who had made appearances alongside the Pandavas in the performance ground, he stated: "No one who has danced before will dance tonight; now only ghosts and ghouls [*bhut-pret*] will dance!" Later, when I asked Sharad ji about this exchange, I was told that the god was indicating that the deities in the maidan would be replaced by less benign or benevolent beings.

On hearing this announcement, members of the audience were clearly disturbed. The musicians kept on playing, and the medium who had made the ominous pronouncement about the imminent arrival of ghosts and ghouls continued to endure his bodily spasms, his gaze distant and unfocused. Another medium, of a local deity named Unishor, who had danced for a short time the previous evening, arrived and sat down beside Nagaraja's medium.[29] A white muslin cloth was draped around Unishor's shoulders and bare, wiry torso; his hair was open, reaching down to his waist. The medium was from an economically deprived, predominantly Dalit village in the area. When this person had arrived from his village earlier that evening, he had prostrated himself at the bottom of the temple steps and touched the feet of the village elders to seek their blessings, but because he was Dalit, he had not entered the temple. As the musicians picked up the tempo, Unishor's medium got up to dance, mesmerizing the audience with his display of speed, agility, and power. He moved as if propelled by some external force, as if something outside his body was hurling and spinning him around. In comparison, the movements of the medium who embodied Nagaraja were rhythmic and stable, almost monotonous.

Together, these beings raced to the edge of the performance ground only to be drawn back to the central fire like moths to a flame. While they danced in front of the spellbound audience, the (male) medium of Goddess Bhagavati stormed out of the temple and also began dancing.[30] The goddess skipped and hopped across the maidan, waving her arms by her side as if imitating a bird in flight. She seemed suspended in air as clouds of dust arose around her feet. Suddenly, the goddess stopped dancing. She rushed to the ritual fire located at the center of the maidan and picked up a heavy, burning log. Brandishing the log above her, she charged the audience. There was a loud commotion in the crowd. A group of children seated in the front backed away in fear as the enraged goddess approached. Older audience members jumped in front of the children, forming a protective barrier around them. The goddess stopped in her tracks, and the headman and some village elders rushed to meet her. She was yelling, but her words were not fully legible to my companions and me. The elders tried to wrest the burning log from her, but they were careful not to touch the goddess, as this would have angered her even more. The Brahmin priest ran to join them—the first time I had seen him leave the temple area. He sprinkled an auspicious ritual substance—a liquid mixture called *panchamrit* (lit., "five nectars")—on the goddess, which had its desired effect of calming her. However, she was still trembling violently, and it was clear to everyone that she was extremely upset. The elders asked her what the matter was as they doused her with panchamrit and encouraged her to sip from a pitcher of water.

The embodied goddess continued to scream and resist for some time. She finally became more composed and coherent. She exclaimed: "The shoes! The shoes! Why are there shoes in my temple?" The priest begged her to forgive them, and everyone scrambled to pick up the audience members' shoes and sandals that had been strewn at the edges of the maidan outside the goddess temple. People grabbed their offending footwear—which they had taken off when they sat down to watch the evening's performance—and hurled it away from the temple. Seeing this, the goddess became calmer and allowed herself to be led away from the audience toward the center of the maidan.

Meanwhile, the other two mediums continued dancing as before. Instead of stopping or even slowing down, Nagaraja's medium started to speed up. His movements became angry and chaotic; like the goddess before him, he too started veering toward the audience every time he circled the fire. The audience, especially the women and young children, still reeling from the onslaughts of the enraged goddess, retreated. Everyone was on their feet, on high alert, unsure what to do. To rein in and slow down the beings spiraling out of control, the aujis relaxed the tempo of their drumming, but to no avail; the dancing beings seemed to pay no heed to the musicians or village elders.

The villagers with whom I was sitting interpreted this threatening display as a warning or punishment for contesting Nagaraja's demand for a silver drum. After consulting with the village elders and the Brahmin priest on the temple steps, the village headman was advised by his confidantes to "cool" the god's ritual medium down and make him peaceful (*shant*). After several moments of awkwardly following the medium around the performance ground to try to catch hold of him, the headman finally succeeded. The medium was reseated at the edge of the performance ground. The headman tried engaging him in conversation, but there was no response, so the Brahmin priest was beckoned. The priest applied a sacred vermilion powder to the medium's forehead, sprinkled panchamrit on him, and whispered incantations into his ear, which seemed to awaken and alert the medium.

The deity, or what/whoever he had become, started to speak, but even those in his immediate vicinity, namely the headman and the priest, had to lean in to hear his words. By contrast, the headman spoke loudly to make clear to the audience that he was interceding on their behalf. He asked the deity to give the village more time to collect the money needed for the silver drum. Or, he said, the deity might reconsider fulfilling his pledge to provide half the needed capital. He explained that it was very difficult for the villagers to come up with the additional funds "since there is a *ghata* [a deficit of funds] in the village." The headman spoke to the god with folded hands, looking down. On hearing the headman's request, the god flew into a rage, saying that he didn't care about "any deficit." "Stop talking nonsense! I don't want to hear excuses," he exclaimed, lunging forward to strike the headman, who dodged the blow nimbly. "What deficit? What deficit [*kaisa ghata*]?" he shouted repeatedly.

"Forgive me, lord," the headman replied while his interlocutor vacuously parroted the headman's speech. Staring off into the distance, he was clearly in no mood to negotiate with the headman or the village.

The divinities' displays of anger put an end to the villagers' protests. It seemed inevitable that the villagers would have to collect additional funds for the drum; refusing the deity's demand seemed impossible now. The mood of the audience changed from indignation and irritation to quiet resignation. The only thing left to do was seek the deity's blessings now that he seemed more calm and stable. The headman was the first to approach the deity, who reached into a tray that had been placed beside him, grabbed a handful of rice and vermilion powder, and smeared it roughly across the headman's forehead. This gesture signaled the end of the evening's events. The audience lined up behind the headman. Not sure how long he would be present in this form, they did not want to miss their chance to be blessed.

At eight the next morning, I returned to the maidan to find the village meeting in progress. Like a bus conductor, the headman held a ticket book in his hands. He sat behind a rickety office desk that had been placed at the center of the maidan, close to the smoldering embers of the fire from the previous night. In front of his desk, a snaking line had formed, with one male member from each family in the village (including the poorer families), each carrying the additional 750 rupees needed for the drum. The headman collected the money and provided receipts to the villagers. Methodically, one by one, he checked off people's names in his ledger in an act of divine bureaucracy.

Conclusion: Divine Embodiment as Rhetoric

After the dust had settled, there was much talk about what had happened. While many mistrusted the village authorities, no one openly questioned the deities' desires or agency. In other words, what had happened was not just a power grab between differently positioned human beings. Deities were known to make exorbitant claims on their worshipers in exchange for protecting and providing for the village. However, I couldn't help but wonder if I had witnessed an elaborate ruse on the part of village elites who had used Nagaraja's demand for a silver drum to extract additional revenues from the village. Indeed, villagers were highly suspicious about the collection of money. They suspected that village authorities and the deity were colluding against the interests of the majority. Some told me that since the powerful landholding villagers would invariably be entrusted with buying the silver and paying the merchants and artisans to make the drum, they would likely "eat" some of the money themselves. Villagers had resisted what they saw as an unjust tax by the deity and had also challenged the village authorities and their management of public affairs. Public opinion suggested that by not providing his share of the needed funds as he had promised, the deity had acted improperly or unethically.

Yet, despite this, what had convinced the villagers to put aside their protests was the deity's presence. When the deity appeared directly before the audience, people did not overtly challenge him. Rather, the deity's angry appearance interrupting the panno quelled the debate. That is to say, witnessing the deity state his demands directly, in the flesh, had a much more persuasive effect than hearing about them secondhand. The embodied presence of the deity—as a social actor that was acted upon in the here and now of the maidan—was instrumental in subduing dissent and manufacturing the collective consent of the village. The deity had verbally reminded the village of his power—"Who am I?" he repeatedly and threateningly asked the villagers. In saying, "Now only ghosts and ghouls will dance," the deity—or some other supernatural entity who replaced him—also threatened to put a stop to the villagers' beloved panno and overrun the maidan with dangerous forces. Through these threats and tactics of persuasion, all of which involved divine embodiment, the deity convinced the reluctant villagers to meet his demands.

In public settings like the maidan in Dyongarh, through divine embodiment, deities interact with their "constituents," garner their support, and exert influence on village life. At the same time, this crisis also reveals how the position of a deity, like that of an elected politician, is not unimpeachable. Deities can be questioned, even reprimanded, for not meeting their obligations to their worshipers.

The public nature of the debate arising from the deity's demand for a silver drum also demonstrates how, as a local "political divinity," a deity is answerable to the village community. In doubling the tribute required for the silver drum, the deity was taking a risk; if a political divinity is seen to be abusing their authority, they can fall out of favor with some members of the community. Just as a deity depends on their constituents for their fame and fortune, constituents depend on them for health, security, and prosperity; their relationship is imperiled when one or the other party fails to meet its obligations. The precarity of this relationship was laid bare in the debate that took place; the villagers pushed back against the deity's demands while also being wary of the consequences of disobeying the deity.

The public, collective setting where the divine embodiment occurred also *allowed villagers to air their everyday grievances.* While these kinds of debates do not always occur during panno, the appearance of the deity as a political divinity in the maidan made space for discussions of social importance to occur. This airing of grievances was the most candid public exchange among people of different socioeconomic standings that I witnessed during fieldwork. As political divinities, the embodied gods played an important role in creating an atmosphere conducive to such a frank, heated exchange. From rich landowners to poor day laborers, Rajputs and Dalits, men and women, old people and young, everyone shared their concerns about the socioeconomic welfare of the village.

The airing of grievances in the maidan resulted in greater accountability from village authorities. In the village meeting that occurred the following day, village authorities were forced to answer for the delays in the road-building project. The headman promised that he and his delegation would once again visit the district magistrate's office to ensure the road would be ready in time for the next harvest. For final arbitration on matters relating to rising costs and the acquisition of building materials, a village council (*panchayat*) meeting was scheduled for the following week. Therefore, the debate that had spontaneously erupted during the panno was not only a space of critique but also a space where a new agenda for the village was collectively forged.

Understanding deities as "political divinities" helps us see how people in Uttarakhand construct a particular ontological and ethical worldview toward authority and governance. In this worldview, local authority does not exist in a purely secular realm; rather, when it comes to collective decision making and debate, village institutions work hand-in-hand with deities and other supernatural beings. At the same time, public rituals of divine embodiment also shed light on the kind of power that political divinities and politicians alike can wield. It was precisely because the deity's power and authority superseded that of the village elites that allowed the less privileged villagers to openly challenge the latter and vent their frustrations. As my interlocutors described, everyone in the village was equally answerable to the deity—no matter their class or caste. In this sense, the direct and immediate experience of a political divinity through divine embodiment had an empowering effect on ordinary villagers, though, of course, this was temporary and tempered by the additional tax that was levied on them.

Prior to the fiery and threatening display in the performance ground, villagers had resisted what they saw as an unjust tax by the deity, and, in the process, village authorities and their management of public affairs were also challenged. Yet the "dance" of the deity in the maidan had a powerful impact on the villagers.

In Uttarakhand, divine embodiment is not only a private or subjective experience; it is deeply enmeshed in the social and political fabric of everyday life. The immediacy of divine embodiment enables nonhumans to meaningfully engage with the human-social world and its shifting realities. As embodied presences, deities are seen as firmly rooted in *this* world and not some otherworldly, transcendent realm removed from the everyday concerns of ordinary people. Through divine embodiment, deities make their presence felt and wishes known in real time; they then subsequently convince (or coerce) worshipers to think and act in ways that are desirable to them. The voices and agency of deities shape and are shaped by local political and social concerns. While Pahari deities uphold the normative order and its attendant hierarchies, they can also subvert normative principles when it is necessary and/or convenient for them. As my interlocutors described, much like human politicians, deities will only make alliances to the extent they benefit them personally. And, much like human politicians, political divinities are also at the mercy of their "constituents." They risk losing their "seat" and falling out of favor if they don't deliver on their promises.

View of the Himalayas

Harvest season; author with interlocutors

A jagar priest

A woman is comforted by family members during an intense healing ritual

An embodied deity addresses his worshipers during a jagar ritual

An embodied deity dances

An embodied deity and his worshipers during a public ritual

Divine embodiment during a jagar ritual

An exorcism on a ghost-afflicted woman

A jagar priest drums outside a temple

A jagar priest drums during a jagar

Jhakar Saim temple

A deity is carried by his worshipers

A deity dances during a public ritual

4

Undoing Love

Ghost Affliction and Patrilocal Marriage

Bhut and Chhal

In previous chapters, I discussed how place (*sthan*) is made for deities; in this chapter, I focus on how ritual "placemaking" is performed for deities *and* their worshipers. I am particularly interested in rituals designed to integrate married women into their affinal homes and families.

At the time of marriage, Hindu brides in Uttarakhand leave their natal homes to reside permanently in their affinal homes with their husbands and in-laws.[1] For a new bride, adhering to the patrilocal norms followed in the region makes the transition from natal home (*mait/maike*) to affinal home (*saras/sasural*) an emotionally difficult process. As a bride makes the physical journey to her husband's home—often through heavily forested, unpopulated areas, some of my interlocutors described how "fear might pierce her heart, and a *bhut* [ghost] may enter her." New brides are particularly vulnerable to bodily attacks and possession by malevolent supernatural agents known as *chhal*, a subcategory of bhut, the spirits of men and women who died untimely and/or violent deaths and now wander restlessly in the wilderness beyond the boundaries of human settlement. In the Kumaon region of Uttarakhand, from which the ethnography of this chapter is drawn, chhal almost exclusively attack young women. However, many of my Kumaoni interlocutors also used the words *bhut* and *chhal* interchangeably.

I was told that young brides were vulnerable to chhal, or "ghosts," on their way to their marital home because these beings were "attracted to the clinking sound of the glass bangles" that brides wear at the time of marriage. Ghosts can also enter and inhabit the bodies of young women and girls before they are married.

These ghosts might remain inactive or dormant within their female hosts until after marriage when they begin to cause "trouble" (*pareshani*) in the home of their in-laws. Young women "caught" by ghosts may exhibit a variety of psychological and physical symptoms, including bouts of depression, rage, mental disorientation, debilitating headaches, and body aches. I refer to women's "possession" by these malevolent supernatural agents as "ghost affliction." I was told that many ghost-afflicted women lost their ability to speak, perform their domestic duties, and/or bear children. Sometimes, they lashed out inappropriately at their in-laws or refused to leave their beds for days on end. Not only women but also their infant children may fall sick or even die because of ghost affliction.

To ascertain and address the cause of her maladies, the afflicted woman's in-laws consult their family deities in domestic *jagar* rituals. If the ritual shows that the woman is suffering from ghost affliction, embodied deities persuade and compel the ghost to release its hold on the woman in addition to prescribing other ritual remedies. In Uttarakhand, as in Tamil Nadu and other parts of South Asia, "The untimely dead tend to 'catch' young married women who consequently suffer from psychic and reproductive disorders. These spirits must, therefore, be 'made to run away.'"[2] In Kumaon, bhut and chhal are exorcised from their hosts through the performance of jagar.

One meaning of the Indian-language word *chhal* is "deception" or "deceit." By entering, inhabiting, and impersonating young women, chhal appear as something they are not.[3] During the affliction, their hosts, too, become Other to themselves. A second meaning of *chhal* is also a bhut, or ghost—a dissatisfied spirit of a person who has died an untimely or violent death. A jagari once told me that "bhut become caught between the world of the living [*nar lok*] and the world of the dead [*mrityu lok*] because of their desire for human love." He suggested that, at the time of marriage, a young woman becomes an easy object for a ghost to "attack" or latch onto because of her social, emotional, and physical liminality. Moreover, as a past participle form of the Sanskritic verbal root *bhu*, literally, "to be," the word *bhut* also denotes "the past."[4] *Bhut kal*, for instance, is a grammatical term for the English language "past tense." Bhut can thus be thought of as melancholic remnants of the past that refuse to abate or give way, negatively affecting people and places in the present. Jagar exorcisms performed for bhut- or chhal-afflicted brides are designed not only to dis-possess the bride from the ghost but also to dis-possess her from her affective attachment to her past life and natal home to facilitate the bride's absorption into her marital family—that is, to "make place" for her in the home of her in-laws.

As I describe in the second half of this chapter, these meanings of *chhal* and *bhut* overlap but also diverge from how many Kumaoni women who experienced jagar exorcisms described ghost affliction. According to the women I spoke with, ghost affliction is about more than an existential affinity between ghosts and brides. Their narratives emphasize how ghost affliction shapes and is shaped by a wide range of relational and material hardships that women endure in the context of patrilocal marriage in north India. They experience these jagar rituals of exorcism, of divorcing themselves from their pasts, with ambivalence.[5]

This chapter draws substantially from my experiences and observations over four months while staying with a family in Bani whose daughter-in-law (*bahu*) was being treated for ghost affliction. However, throughout my years of fieldwork in this region, I observed gendered differences in how people understood and explained the propensity of ghosts to afflict brides. While men generally told me that ghost "attacks" were rare occurrences and none of the women in their family had suffered from it, women told radically different accounts of how ghost affliction was common and that each of them had experienced it. They interpreted and contextualized ghost affliction as a structural rather than individual problem, revealing how women conceive of patrilocal kinship as a potentially harmful or afflictive process.

In this chapter, I describe how jagar exorcisms seek to separate or "single out" the married woman from the ghost that afflicts her. This is simultaneously a process of extricating the woman from her natal kin and "making place" for her in her marital home. According to the dominant patriarchal perspective, a married woman's "past self" must give way for a new social reality to come into being. My interactions with formerly ghost-afflicted women reveal how women and ghosts alike are disciplined by family elders and deities through conventions of patrilocal marriage that frame the diagnosis and treatment of ghost affliction. In my analysis, I privilege women's embodied and first-hand understandings and lived experiences of ghost affliction and its relationship to marriage and patrilocality. While I show that jagar exorcism rituals are designed, in part, to complete a woman's transition to her marital home, the narratives of the women I spoke with reveal the incompleteness and ambivalence of this process and the lingering presence of Others who continue to coexist with them even after their so-called assimilation into their affinal homes.

Ghost Affliction

In some anthropological studies interpreting afflictive possession among women,[6] possession by spirits or ghosts is seen as a symbolic medium for subverting dominant social and political orders, particularly by marginalized groups such as women and lower-caste people.[7] In contrast, Isabelle Clark-Decès (previously Nabokov) sheds light on the hegemonic aspects of possession rituals in South Asia. In her penetrating ethnography, *Religion Against the Self*, Clark-Decès argues that in the possession rituals she observed involving married women in Tamil Nadu who were possessed by demonic agents known as *pey*, the female individual was psychologically fragmented and "split apart" in order to account both for her personal experience and reproduce her normative role within the dominant culture of oppression.[8] Clark-Decès reveals how rituals designed to dis-possess women of demons that have caught them pressure "women and their spirits into articulating a sense of self that is entirely alien to them."[9] Furthermore, she writes, "These exorcisms enforced a reality that was not debatable and could neither be challenged nor contested."[10] Thus, rather than making room for social critique, these exorcism rituals coerce afflicted women into conforming to patriarchal expectations.

In exorcism rituals for ghost-afflicted women in Uttarakhand, I observed dynamics like those described by Clark-Decès. However, whereas in Tamil Nadu, Clark-Decès argues that "the source of a woman's alienation was *locked in her head*, in her antisocial and life-threatening fantasies of extramarital sexuality,"[11] in Uttarakhand, ghost affliction and its treatment were less about controlling women's sexuality and more about ways to resolve the social and physical dislocation, disruption, and insecurity inherent in practices of patrilocal marriage. It was not that concerns about women's sexuality were absent, but they were folded into the many difficulties women must undergo in and after marriage. Drawing on feminist anthropological scholarship on kinship and affliction in South Asia, I argue that chhal affliction in Uttarakhand arises in response to "the *failure* of family, kinship, and marital relations."[12]

At the same time, this chapter does not reduce ghost affliction to a symbolic representation of (more real) psychological and/or social conflicts. Rather, I see chhal affliction as part of a sequence of cascading psychic, social, and material hardships that women are subjected to after marriage. For instance, as a new bride enters her marital home, she may be viewed as an object of suspicion and considered dangerous, "having the capacity to corrupt a man's loyalty to his parents and brothers."[13] These anxieties, in turn, make a bride vulnerable to accusations of chhal attack and affliction. However, as the women I spoke with described, the ghost also crystallized a number of other fears women brought with them to their affinal homes: fears about how they would be treated by their husbands and in-laws; rearing children and providing their in-laws with male heirs; learning to live without the support and care of their natal kin; becoming fluent in new forms of labor, including various agricultural tasks that they may have been shielded from in their natal homes; balancing domestic responsibilities with academic and professional pursuits outside the home; and so on.

Ghost affliction and its treatment thus shed light on kinship "as a precarious social process,"[14] wherein the precariousness of relations "coalesce in women's distresses,"[15] which can include spirit attacks and afflictive possession.[16] Knowing and treating affliction becomes a way for individuals and communities to grapple with what Sarah Pinto terms the "gendered fallout of kinship."[17] As Pinto writes, "The work of kinship, like the work of medicine"—and I would add, the work of some ritual, including jagar—"may happen at points of breakdown, the places where vulnerabilities in and to relations, in and to kinship, accumulate."[18] In their narratives of illness and rehabilitation, my female interlocutors described ghost affliction as a site of such accumulation and breakdown. Ghost affliction was coterminous with narratives of the physical, emotional, and relational disruptions produced by patrilocal marriage. In reporting on these interactions, I honor the slippage that occurred between the ritual exorcism and women's everyday lives to reveal how patrilocal marriage affects and is affected by chhal affliction.

For women in patrilocal and patrilineal kin arrangements, the loss of kin and security "is not only an ordeal of the interior emotions; it also produces new creatures in the world"[19]—ghosts with "horrifying agency."[20] Loss and hardship become attached to ghosts just as ghosts become attached to married women. Such ghosts are not any less "real" because they are known in relation to social and emotional disruptions of various kinds; rather, as this book shows, nonhuman beings in Uttarakhand intervene in matters of personal and collective importance in tangible and far-reaching ways. Interpreting "possession" "as a psychological event" or "as a social or sociopolitical event that trades in power relations" does not preclude viewing it "as a 'real' incursion of spirits and deities."[21] Thus, rituals such as jagar are sites of fluid, pragmatic, and situational negotiation between humans and between human and nonhuman actors.[22]

Accretions and Erosions

If ghost affliction is related to a bride's continued or excessive attachment to her past (bhut), jagar exorcism rituals are designed to "cut" a bride off from the ghost, from her natal home and kin, as she is emplaced within her affinal family. In the performance of jagar, the "cut" is framed as a way of healing chhal affliction and caring for the suffering daughter-in-law—in a way, normalizing the violence that women often described during the ritual.

One summer, while I was visiting the home of an old friend in Kumaon, I was invited by Deepak Bisht and Nitin Bisht, cousin brothers in their thirties, to attend a series of jagar ceremonies in their village, Bani.²³ I was told that the jagars were to be performed to treat Nitin's sister-in-law (his younger brother's wife), the newest daughter-in-law, who had been experiencing various "obstructions" (*vighan-badha*) and "troubles" (*mushkilein*). Nitin's father was the head of the large extended family and chief sponsor (*jajaman*) of the ceremonies.

The marriage had happened eighteen months earlier. Kiran, the bride and new daughter-in-law, had entered her marital home from a village on the other side of the valley from Bani. Soon after her arrival, Kiran started displaying symptoms of ghost affliction. She had been experiencing migraines, body aches, and bouts of physical weakness and mental disorientation, leaving her bedridden for days. In particular, I was told that she complained of a "great weight on her body" that made it impossible for her to move. In addition, she was unable to "straighten her legs," which were bent, stiff, and painful. Given the seriousness of her symptoms, a jagar was performed, and the family gods were consulted. After the initial diagnosis of ghost affliction by the deities, a series of rituals were performed over the course of several months, culminating in a final exorcism that included a goat sacrifice in a forested area outside the village.²⁴ (During my time in Bani, I participated in the last two jagars in the ritual sequence but did not attend the final sacrificial ritual in the forest.) While these rituals were ongoing, Kiran had become pregnant and given birth to a son who was a few months old by the time the ghost was fully exorcized.

Three generations of Deepak and Nitin's family lived together in their ancestral home, which had been recently expanded to accommodate their growing family. Deepak and Nitin's fathers were two of six brothers. The eldest had died some years ago, and one of them did not live in Bani; the four remaining brothers continued to inhabit the ancestral home with their wives, sons, and daughters-in-law. All of their daughters were married and resided in their affinal homes, and all but the youngest brother's sons were married with children. They were a large, industrious, caste-privileged Thakur (Rajput) family that owned fruit orchards and agricultural plots.²⁵ Deepak and Nitin told me—with some pride—that, unlike many other landholding families in the area, none of their cousins had sold off their share of ancestral lands or out-migrated.²⁶ Processes of development in Uttarakhand have been uneven, benefiting families with significant social capital and connections. On a recent visit to Bani, I learned that Deepak had "entered politics [*rajaniti*]" and that his wife had become an elected member of their village council (*panchayat*), constituting an influential and prestigious role for her and the family.

Deepak and his male kin relied on multiple sources of employment, including participating in the burgeoning tourist, construction, and real estate industries. In addition to managing his family's fields and orchards, Deepak and his younger brother also worked for the local water department and helped outsiders purchase, develop, and maintain property in the area. Over the last few decades, there has been a growing demand for land in Kumaon. Many urban north Indians with disposable incomes are seeking to build holiday homes and take advantage of Uttarakhand's temperate summer climate. Not everyone in Kumaon is happy with the growing influx of outsiders from Delhi and other parts of India. Deepak's father was one of many who had shared their ambivalence about this with me.

One afternoon, Deepak's father told me how one of his neighbors had sold his agricultural lands to a hotel developer in the early 2000s. The neighbor's family had burned through the money they received from the sale of the property and were soon left with nothing. Because of this, the neighbor had to go back to the person to whom he had sold his land and beg him for a job. "He [the neighbor] now works as a servant [*naukar*] on the property he once owned.... This is a common story," Deepak's father said. His words reflect the social and economic pressures experienced by locals due to the increasing numbers of non-Pahari residents in Uttarakhand since the 1990s, the time when India's economy was opened up to the world or "liberalized." Other families are forced to send young men for educational opportunities or seasonal migration. With every generation, normative practices of patrilineal inheritance fragment ancestral landholdings to the point where family units are no longer able to sustain themselves solely through agricultural production. In addition, within Uttarakhand, since tourism, including religious tourism, has become one of the fastest growing spheres of employment in this ruggedly scenic part of India, many young men spend the summer season serving the industry as restaurant and hotel workers, taxi drivers, and other service employees far from home.

When the men leave, sometimes for long periods of time, their wives and parents are left to manage the agricultural work at home, with most of the burden falling on the women. Yet, as both men and women pointed out to me, more women than ever before are finishing school and going to college, supplementing family incomes from agriculture with higher-paying, white-collar jobs. Of course, as in other patriarchal contexts, these additional incomes do not lessen any of women's household responsibilities, even though men are sometimes anxious that women might start rejecting traditional forms of labor, marriage, and kinship. Moreover, more general anxieties about "cultural erosion" were expressed in public conversations about divorce. For instance, in one of our conversations, Deepak's mother and her female companions from the village said that they did not personally know any family that had been through a divorce. In the same breath, however, the women lamented the fact that divorce was on the rise all over the region—not just in urban areas but also in rural ones.

A pervasive patriarchal fear in joint families—as has been well documented by studies of kinship in South Asia—is that daughters-in-law, desirous of greater social and economic independence, will break the "intergenerational family contract"—namely, that modernization, urbanization, migration, demographic transition, new lifestyle aspirations, and the spread of Western values will erode filial obligations and collective familial interests in favor of individual interests.[27] The fear is that "modern" women might persuade their husbands to break from their families, turn brother against brother, sell their land, and move away to towns and cities. In such apocryphal narratives of family breakdown, metonymically linked to broader socioeconomic changes, women are portrayed as loci of danger and instigators of familial strife. These anxieties also undergird and indirectly inform narratives and rituals of ghost affliction.

Accelerated social and economic transformations in the region mean increased disturbances and disruptions to kin relations and networks. The practice of jagar is flourishing not in spite of but because of rapid socioeconomic transformation in Uttarakhand. For example, when I asked Deepak's mother and other female elders why they had to perform so many jagars for Kiran, they said that they were required to perform jagar regularly "to protect [*surakshit rakhana*] their family traditions.... Of course, there is a monetary cost [*kharcha*] to all of this, and in the past, when we were young, people did not have the resources to perform jagar so often. But now that people have the 'facility' [Eng.], how can they not care for their traditions?" Rather than a narrative of modernization, in which traditional jagar practices would be imagined to be dying out, the women emphasized the increasingly urgent need to "protect their family traditions." Jagars and the deities invoked in them were experienced not only as protective barriers against the encroachment of chhal and other negative supernatural influences but also against the social effects of modernization, urbanization, and changing gender norms.

Family Matters

Each of the jagar ceremonies I attended took place at night after the family finished dinner and lasted for about two hours. A middle-aged Dalit jagari named Satyaram ji led the ceremonies, which involved the performance of narrative song, drumming, and divine embodiment. Satyaram ji sang and played a large *dhol*, a bass-heavy percussion instrument, while a younger man accompanied him on a smaller kettledrum.

Although I heard several rumors about the ghost troubling Deepak's family, the family itself was reluctant to discuss them with me. I was told that any mention of the ghost in everyday life—that is, outside its proper ritual setting—ran the risk of strengthening its hold on its victim. However, some of Deepak's Rajput neighbors told me about cases of ghost affliction that had occurred in their own families but were now resolved. For instance, one village elder told me about a woman who died while collecting firewood in a nearby forest. She slipped and landed on the sticks she was carrying, which penetrated her chest and killed her instantly. Her "restless and unhappy spirit" then entered my interlocutor's niece when she was still a young, unmarried girl. Another night, over drinks, I was told by one of Dinesh's neighbors about a schoolgirl who had been killed several years ago by a nonlocal Muslim laborer who had come to Kumaon to repair a road in the vicinity of the murdered girl's school. After her death, many girls in the school "fell sick," he told me.

In both accounts, ghost affliction was understood as a relational rather than an individually bound phenomenon. Writing about a similar case of "mass hysteria" that afflicted schoolgirls in Nepal, Aidan Seale-Feldman argues that a Nepali understanding of ghost affliction foregrounds "the way in which affliction may be decentered from the individual and shared and transferred between bodies."[28] I was also acutely aware of the Islamophobic tenor of the second narrative, the way ghost affliction was articulating with political intolerance and Othering.[29] These narratives have been gaining force in a climate of growing anti-Muslim sentiment in Uttarakhand and other parts of India in recent decades.

However, there was another way chhal affliction was about intimacy, relations, and relatedness. Deepak's family priest, the jagari Satyaram ji, told me that "the bhut troubling the family" originated from "a forested area in the direction [bhag] of the daughter-in-law's natal village." In saying this, Satyaram ji indicated that the ghost was somehow related to Kiran's natal home but not to Deepak's family.[30] He did not have the expertise to know the exact relationship, he said; that was only something a jagari connected to Kiran's natal family could do. According to him, his job was to "send the bhut back to where it came from." If Kiran's condition did not improve after the jagars performed for her in her marital home, she would be sent back to live with her natal family temporarily. Her natal family would have to consult with their family deities to decide how to move forward with her treatment. However, according to Satyaram ji, sending Kiran back to her natal home was a last resort: it would be seen as a failure on the part of her marital family and deities. Satyaram ji assured me this would not happen. None of the women he had treated over the years had failed to get better, he reported with pride, although he knew of a handful of women who had failed to be cured of ghost affliction in their marital homes. In one case where a woman had failed to be cured, it had turned out that she was not afflicted by a ghost at all, but rather, by the *dosh*, or "fault," of the deity Bhairav (see chapter 2).

In other cases, bhut emanated from women's marital homes and villages. Satyaram ji told me about a woman in a nearby village who had committed suicide soon after marriage as a result of excessive and recurring demands for dowry from her in-laws. The spirit of this woman had become "attached" (*lagana*) to another woman in the village. These two women were not related as kin, but they were connected by virtue of their social place as in-marrying brides. Satyaram ji suggested that the afflictive spirit of the woman who had died wanted the village to acknowledge and remedy the injustices she had endured as a young bride. To this end, she had chosen another bride as her host and vehicle to communicate with the wider community. Eventually, after the cause of their misfortunes was diagnosed, the village community pacified the angry spirit by constructing a shrine for her. Every year, during important religious festivals, the spirit was remembered and worshiped by the family who caused her to take her own life, Satyaram ji said.

The afflicting spirits could be gendered male or female. Dangerous supernatural entities that are gendered male can also become attracted to women of marriageable age.[31] When I asked Satyaram ji about the gender of the being afflicting Kiran, he told me it was female, as determined by Golu Devata and conveyed to the Bisht family in a previous jagar. However, because the bhut was from elsewhere and not connected to the Bisht family, its identity remained unknown. He reminded me that his job was simply to "send the bhut back" to its place of origin, which was in "the direction [*bhag*] of" Kiran's natal village. He also told me that Kiran's natal family would play no role in Kiran's exorcism—they would not be consulted or asked to participate in any of the rituals. He said this was because Kiran was now a member of the Bisht family and, as such, her welfare was their responsibility. Separating Kiran's natal and marital homes—and her past and present self/s—was a central theme in the rituals I attended, complicating the idea of "home" in the lives of married women.

In the jagars I attended at Deepak's home, the "chosen deity" (*isht devata*) of the family, Golu Devata, was embodied by a younger brother of the family patriarch and sponsor (*jajaman*) of the ritual. Golu Devata—also known as Goljyu, Gvarral, and Goril—is one of the most beloved Kumaoni deities. He is frequently referred to as a *nyaya devata* (lit., "god of justice") because he is known to protect his devotees from oppression and exploitation.[32] In local histories (*itihas*), he is also identified as a historical figure, the ruler of the erstwhile kingdom of Champavat. His temples, such as Chitai, are imagined as courts (*darbar*) where devotees can petition the god to assist them in their personal and collective difficulties by writing their prayers on pieces of paper. In jagar, however, devotees petition the god directly as an embodied actor in the here and now. In addition to Golu Devata, the god Ganganth,[33] another well-known Pahari deity, was also "danced" (*nachana*)—that is, made present in/on the body of his designated medium during the jagars I attended in Deepak's family home.

Immediately before the jagars began, oil lamps were lit and placed in a hollow niche in the wall in the front room. These lamps invited the family deities to enter the ritual space and inhabit their mediums. A gentle glow and dense clouds of fragrant incense filled the room as Golu Devata and Gangnath danced to Satyaram ji and his accompanist's drumming. The sound of the drums ricocheted off the mud-plastered walls of the room; at times, the music was loud and busy, but there were also periods of little or no drumming when the focus was on verbal exchanges between the family members and deities. The most vocal participants in the ceremonies were Golu Devata and Nitin's father, the chief sponsor of the ritual.

As a guest of the family, I was invited to sit beside Nitin's father and the other elders. The jagaris and other ritual participants sat on opposite sides of the room, facing each other; the mediums of the family deities were seated directly in front of the jagaris. As the jagaris began drumming, the mediums knelt on the floor and started trembling and swaying to the music. After some time, they jumped to their feet and began "dancing" in expanding and contracting circles. At times, they danced while kneeling on the floor, and the wooden floor bounced with the weight and energy of their movements. During moments of relative quiet, when Satyaram ji softened or stopped his drumming, he would take this opportunity to smoke the *bidi* (cigarette) that he had stowed away above his ear. Between ponderous puffs of smoke that spiraled into the clouds of incense, he refereed the back and forth between the human and nonhuman actors present.

In the first jagar I attended in Deepak's home, the initial volley of drumming lasted about fifteen to twenty minutes. Then the deities "came over" their mediums, and Golu Devata spoke. His speech had a sing-song, melodic quality; it was punctuated by a hiccoughing, stammering break between lines, which added a staccato effect to his otherwise lilting words. It was strangely pleasant and hypnotic to listen to but, at times, also difficult to follow. To introduce himself to the ritual participants—not that he needed this introduction—he began by speaking/singing about his birth and early life. I was surprised to hear the medium—or rather, the god—sing his own story. In most of the other jagar rituals I attended, jagar narratives were sung by professional storytellers, jagaris. When I later asked Satyaram ji why the god had sung the story and not him, Satyaram ji laughed and said, "Who better to sing the story than the god himself? After all, he was there!" He added that sometimes embodied deities sang if they were moved to do so, such as if they were meeting their devotees after a very long time. Furthermore, while not every god would sing jagar, Golu Devata was the "king of Champavat" and, as such, was able to do things other gods could not. Satyaram ji also confided in me that not every medium of Golu Devata was able to sing the god's story as well as Deepak's uncle, Dayal Singh ji, who embodied the god. "Dayal ji lives a very pure life. He doesn't eat meat, drink [liquor], or do anything like that. So, the god has given him many gifts," Satyaram ji said, expressing his admiration for him.

"The earth is my mother. The sky is my father...." In a soaring voice, Golu Devata began to sing, first invoking his ancestors: "I was born in Supi.[34] My maternal uncle is Saim Devata.[35] ... Let my voice reach you, O Uncle. My power and devotion come from you, O Uncle."

Addressing his uncle, Golu Devata told the story of his early life. While most participants had heard some version of this story narrated many times before, there was always the possibility of tellings bringing forth new details and incidents that were unknown to members of the audience. Deepak, for example, was unfamiliar with the story about Golu Devata as a child when he was in Saim Devata's courtyard, which happened to be Jhakar Saim temple (see chapter 6). Golu Devata spoke of a cedar tree and a white oak tree that provided shade to the courtyard. He said the former secreted milk, while the latter emitted water. One day, prior to bathing in a river outside the temple, a menstruating woman hung her clothes on the cedar tree. This ritual "impurity" caused the tree to stop secreting milk, fall on the woman, and crush her to death. When the tree fell, one side of Saim Devata's body was also affected—in Deepak's words, "It started to rot"—rendering the god immobile.

I wondered what this gendered narrative about affliction meant to the participants of the jagar and how it articulated with ghost affliction, if at all. The story seemed to be about the destructive potential of female power (shakti) and the need to contain it. It promoted suspicion toward women's bodies and identified them as the source of affliction and harm. I thought about ghost affliction and the significance of a new daughter-in-law submitting to the authority of the elders and deities of her marital home.

After singing about his early life, Golu Devata addressed the family: "May you continue receiving happiness and not sorrow. You have invited me into your home and offered me a token of your devotion [lit., "two flowers"], so may you be blessed, and may sadness and misfortune be kept at bay."

The god offered to help the family resolve their predicament in return for their continued relationality and hospitality. Golu then turned and pointed to the ghost-afflicted daughter-in-law, Kiran, saying whatever the ghost wanted, he would provide. "I will take it to its real destination, where it belongs. That is my responsibility. After I do this, the girl will face no more difficulties; she will be fine."

The god then advised the family on how to get rid of the ghost. Picking up a few grains of uncooked rice from a metal platter by his side, on which lay various ritual objects and substances, he said that by counting the grains of rice, they would come to know if their ritual efforts would bear fruit or not. According to this practice, if the family was handed an even number of grains, it would serve as an auspicious sign; the daughter-in-law would be cured without difficulty. However, if an odd number came up, it was a bad omen. The god placed the rice grains in the hands of a male family member and, without looking at them, said, "The grains of rice have increased [*badh gaye*]," meaning that the family had received an odd number of rice grains. Golu informed the family that this had happened because, in the previous jagar, the family had been told to perform the next ritual within three months, but the family had exceeded this prescribed time. The deity scolded the family, stating that their tardiness had contributed to Kiran's deterioration. In this instance, like others we have seen in this book, deities were not only diagnosing affliction and misfortune, but individual and kin well-being was also directly connected to the family's adhering to the deity's demands, a sign of their devotion to him.

In a loud voice, the ritual sponsor, or jajaman, affirmed the truth of the god's words and expressed his dissatisfaction about the family's current situation: "The first three months since the previous jagar, she was totally fine, nothing happened, but as soon as three months went by, her health went bad again. *Parmeshvar malik*," he cried out, addressing Golu Devata as the family's protector and guide, "What is the matter with her?! Tell me what I should do, what materials are needed, and I will do the *puja* [ritual worship] immediately.... Just don't let her health get any worse." He repeated this a few times before Golu responded.

Acknowledging the patriarch's plea, Golu continued: "Well then, why didn't you do the necessary investigations after three months had elapsed, like I told you to?"

The jajaman replied vaguely, "We had our reasons.... Time went by. It's true that we didn't complete the rituals in time. But now, I'm ready and happy to do the final ritual tomorrow if you wish." Rather than refer to a literal "tomorrow," the jajaman was conveying his acknowledgment of the urgency of completing this ritual process.

Seeing that the jajaman was eager to get on with the exorcism, the god gave the family instructions for the final ritual: "The puja will be done in the direction of the daughter-in-law's natal home; from the forest, you will be able to see Kafal [Kiran's village]. Remember, when you do the puja in the forest, you should be able to see her natal home clearly. Do not forget! Do the puja above the stream that leads to her natal home." The god told the family that the puja required the sacrifice of a single goat. Hearing the god mention a goat to be sacrificed, the jajaman asked if the animal needed to be of a specific color. Black, white, or brown, or would a multicolored one do? The god seemed uninterested in this point and somewhat annoyed at the interruption; he ignored the jajaman and continued with his instructions. The family also had to construct a shrine to honor the ghost. "The ghost will consume the goat's blood, and the meat will be cooked and eaten by those performing the puja," Deepak informed me later. The family members and neighbors who performed the sacrifice and cooked and consumed its meat were forbidden from setting foot inside the home of the sponsor for at least three days.

During these discussions, the jajaman interrupted once again about the appropriate color of the goat, a question that struck me for its specificity. Golu finally answered that a multicolored goat would be fine. The tone became somber again as Golu added: "Before you do this ritual, send the girl to visit her natal home. Because afterward, it is not advisable for her to go there for three months. So, send her now! Or we can do the final ritual now, and she will have to remain at home for the next three months." These directives—both the location of the ritual and the restrictions on Kiran's movement—affirmed the importance of the bride's natal home and her relationship to it in addressing ghost affliction. By keeping the daughter-in-law in her marital home, the ritual enacted a separation between her natal home and past life, on the one hand, and her new life as a daughter-in-law, on the other. However, this separation was not without difficulty.

As the conversation turned to scheduling the final ritual, the family discussed whether it was better to perform it before or after the upcoming harvest festival called Harela, which was two weeks away. The jajaman said it was best not to wait: "Let's perform the puja now; it's better than her [Kiran] falling sick constantly. Yes, let's do it now! We don't need any more time," he told the god. Still hiccoughing, stuttering, and trembling as he spoke, the god said: "Okay, but in case you can't find an appropriate sacrificial animal or if you face any other issues related to money or time, I can stop her [Kiran's] symptoms—at least for a few days."

I was struck by the easy back and forth between the family and Golu Devata compared to other ritual contexts I observed. Even though he had posited a significant list of demands, the deity was surprisingly accommodating to the family. The god then described some of the items the family needed to collect for the final ritual: "A black cloth, glass bangles, lentils, rice, cloves, betel leaf.... All of this is to be placed in a box and left at the shrine after you complete the puja."

The jajaman, practical and detail-oriented as ever, responded: "You have mentioned a great many things, lord. In case I forget something, would you write down a list [*parchi*] of things that are needed? I don't want that there be any more obstacles in the performance of this puja."

The request that the god write up a list struck me as amusing. Would he whip out a pen and paper at that moment while stuttering, trembling, and in the throes of *nach*?

As I looked around, I saw that a family member was studiously taking notes while the deity spoke, to make sure none of the ritual items were missed.

The jajaman then addressed the ghost who was inhabiting Kiran. His tone was somber and his words tentative:

> Don't worry about anything. I will provide whatever you desire; I will take you to your place [*than*], wherever that may be, but please don't trouble this blameless girl anymore. She has done nothing to you.... I will make an offering that will quench your thirst. If you are hungry, I will feed you. If you are thirsty, I will offer you drink. If you get lost, I will help you find your place again. I guarantee you, I will carry you on my own head and situate you in your place. When you lose your sense of direction, I will help you regain it.

While the jajaman communicated his message to the ghost, Kiran, looking down at the floor, was silent. Technically speaking, the jajaman was addressing the ghost and not Kiran, but I couldn't help wondering how Kiran understood and experienced this moment. Was she only overhearing these words addressed to someone else, or did she also feel implicated? Was the jajaman also telling *her* that when she was lost and disoriented, he would make place for her?

Now, Golu Devata addressed the ghost. At first, his voice was calm and reasonable: "You became hungry and thirsty, and you brought your desires with you. But it is time for you to leave her [Kiran] alone. Come, I will sate your desires; I will take you back to your place."

Suddenly, his affect shifted, and he became loud and threatening. "I try to convince those who can be convinced, but if they don't listen, I am forced to use force; I use my tongs. You should show me your power, and I will show you mine.

I eat hot, and you eat cold!" His mention of "eating hot" was related to deities' fondness for swallowing pieces of burning coal and licking various metal instruments, such as tongs and tridents, that had been heated in the ritual fire.

In the midst of this address, verging on scolding, Kiran's five-month old son was handed to her. Seated in her lap, he started to cry. Above the wails of the crying child, the god continued haranguing the ghost, "Just because we have addressed you kindly, don't think you're a big deal."

At this point, the rhythm of the drumming changed, becoming louder and more intricate. This signaled to the participants that they should approach the god to receive his blessings prior to his departure. Family members approached the god one by one. Folding their hands, they bowed, picked up a few marigold flowers from a metal tray, and gently placed the flowers on the god's head. As their hands moved from the tray to the god's head, they moved across the god's body gracefully, touching his knees, elbows, shoulders, and head. But despite the conclusive gestures, the ritual was not yet concluded. As the deity was blessing the ritual participants, Kiran left the room. We soon heard that she had become confused, dizzy, and then had fainted. "She is unwell again," the sponsor announced to the family. Concern and fear were palpable.

Unmasking an Imposter

"Everyone is worried about her," the sponsor turned to tell the god, who was still present in the room. The god asked that the daughter-in-law be brought to him. Meanwhile, he reassured the sponsor, saying, "Whatever is happening to her will not last, so be strong." I heard family members whisper to each other, "She is ill again; the bhut will not leave her so easily." One of them said: "The god is with us. Let him look at her. He'll know what to do."

While family members discussed Kiran's situation in hushed tones, the jagari Satyaram ji continued drumming. Even though I had heard it all evening, it now sounded louder and more intense. I felt the sound penetrate my body, making it hard to breathe. I was suddenly claustrophobic and felt like bolting out of the room. I was confused about what was happening. I wondered if my symptoms were the result of my sitting too close to the throbbing drums, breathing in copious amounts of incense, or the heat of so many bodies in such close proximity. Or had my body tensed up once I realized that Kiran had fallen sick? I knew that Kiran's fainting was serious, and I did not want to draw attention to myself by either running out of the room or fainting. I tried distracting myself by listening to the sound of the smaller kettledrum instead of Satyaram ji's dhol, which sounded more soothing. Like rain. Or was it actually raining outside? I wondered. As I struggled to hold myself together, Kiran was carried into the room by two older female relatives. Her eyes were closed; she looked weak and tired. She was seated cross-legged in front of the god.

"We need to clear this final hurdle; everyone is very worried," the jajaman said to the deity.

Kneeling in front of her, the god loomed over Kiran while swaying rhythmically to the music. He addressed the ghost: "I have folded my hands and bowed before you, beseeching you to kindly leave the girl. But you do not listen. . . . Do you want to see my power [shakti] or my devotion [bhakti]? Even after all this, do you still need to see it?!"

The ghost/Kiran let out a loud, piercing wail. Deepak later explained that this was the first time the ghost, which had been covertly inhabiting Kiran all along, had publicly revealed itself. Responding to the ghost's emergence, the god lunged toward the ghost/Kiran and seemed to grab them by the hair and spin their body across the floor. The ghost/Kiran lay writhing on the ground. Without making contact with Kiran's body, the god punched and slapped the air around the ghost/Kiran, who then raised themselves off the floor and began kneeling and swaying like the god. The ghost/Kiran moved across the floor on their knees to escape the god's onslaught. At one point, the god placed his hands on the ghost/Kiran's head and neck. The god's touch made them fall back to the ground, where they curled up and trembled in a fetal position. The ghost/Kiran lay shaking on the floor for some time.

Later, Deepak asked me about this moment: "Did you feel the god's power?" Though I nodded yes, this sequence of events was shocking to witness. My physical unease transformed into an emotional unease. I could not believe that the god had attacked Kiran, even if she were not herself but a ghost. The exorcism and its gendering looked—and felt—violent. I glanced at Kiran's husband, who was looking on impassively. The physical altercation did not seem to surprise him, even if it was being waged upon and through his wife's body.

The god addressed the ghost/Kiran, who was still trembling: "Now, take my tongs. First, you take them; then, I will." Deepak later explained that for the bhut to have grabbed hold of the god's metal tongs would have indicated that they were ready to submit to the authority of the god. However, before the ghost/Kiran could respond, the jajaman yelled out: "I was willing to give her [the ghost] whatever she desired, and yet she did not listen to me." Addressing the ghost directly, he said: "If there is something that is not on the list [of ritual items for the final exorcism] but should be, just tell me! There are so many people here asking about your welfare—do you like it? Is this what you want? Everything we are doing is for you. Does all of this make you feel good? You are suffering, but does that mean we are happy?" The jajaman clearly understood the ghost as a being who was suffering and in need of care. The ghost may have been suffering from a specific injury, but the jajaman also recognized the ghost as inherently a creature of suffering: the product of an untimely and violent death, trapped in a limbo between this world and the next, driven by unfulfilled desires.

The affective tenor of the jajaman's outburst oscillated between empathy and censure, like much of the ritual itself. Throughout the jajaman's monologue, the ghost/Kiran continued shaking. Once again, I felt uncomfortable by who was being interpellated: Was it the ghost or Kiran? When the jajaman, Kiran's father-in-law, scolded and blamed the bhut for all the trouble it was causing, to what extent was Kiran "herself" being blamed? Was he shaming her for becoming a victim of ghost affliction and worrying the family? During the ritual, Kiran's dangerous Otherness was articulated through the presence of the chhal/bhut. Kiran was fashioned through the ritual as both self and Other, daughter-in-law and ghost—a state I refer to as existential doubling. This moment revealed the epistemic murk that can occur when the bodies and agency of humans and nonhumans merge. It was precisely this existential doubling that the exorcism sought to resolve by separating out and locating each of them in their rightful place: Kiran in her marital home and the ghost in a place in the forest overlooking Kiran's natal home.

After the jajaman's address, the ghost/Kiran began crying. They slowly got up from the floor. "Why are you crying so much?" the jajaman asked. "Is there something else you want? Tell us, what is it? Tell us who you are and where you are from. All this crying and screaming doesn't help anyone! What is your problem? Why are you troubling her [Kiran]?" Again, the jajaman's tone became conciliatory.

Golu Devata/Dayal Singh ji also spoke to the ghost: "I've folded my hands [to you]; I've done everything I can. But now you must vow to leave this blameless girl." He told the ghost to lay its hands on the sacred metal plate (*thali*) he held before them.

Speaking to other ritual participants, the deity said: "When she touches the plate, the ghost should say, 'I won't cause any more trouble.' Then the ghost will not return. If she does return, I will turn her to ash."

Deepak later told me that destroying the bhut in this way was seen as a last resort "because the deity did not want to incur the sin [*pap*] of violence."

The god then made the ghost/Kiran place their hands on the plate and vow to leave the family. Without saying anything, the ghost/Kiran touched the thali, silently assenting. As they did, the jajaman added: "So far, I have only summoned one deity, but if you choose not to listen, I will call many more, and then you'll be forced to obey!"

While smoking, Satyaram ji also chimed in, speaking-singing like the deity: "As much power as a deity has, the *guru* [or jagari, that is, Satyaram ji himself] who makes the deities dance possesses double of that. So be careful! When I drop my sticks [used to play the dhol] into the fire, they don't burn!"

Golu Devata then threatened that he was a fair and just being, but if anyone—even a member of his own family—acted or spoke falsely, the deity "would cut them down with only a handful of rice." Then, as abruptly as before, his tone and affect once again softened: "I will take you from here," he sang to the ghost, "like a new bride, wearing gold ornaments, bracelets, with the middle parting of your hair filled with red powder.[36] ... Just like a beautiful bride, I will take you to your rightful place," the deity sang. Once again, the ghost and Kiran—a young married woman whose own "middle parting was filled with red powder [*sindur*]"—were conflated.

As the deity sang to the ghost, I became aware of some commotion at the front of the house. The door opened and two young men who were leading a goat with a rope around its neck entered. The jajaman yelled to the ritual participants gathered by the doorway to move aside. This was to be the sacrificial goat—a "multicolored" one—as per the previous exchange between jajaman and deity. As the goat was led into the ritual space, it began bleating loudly in an almost-human voice; it was clearly agitated.

The men who had led the goat inside loosened its leash so that it could move about. Every now and then, it stopped and nudged someone with its bony head and short horns. In response, some of the participants folded their hands in a gesture of respect while the jagaris lightly splashed the goat with water from a nearby river that they had collected in small steel cups. The deity, who stood and loomed above the other ritual participants, also repeated this gesture. After the goat had been splashed a few times, its whole body twitched and shook like a wet dog vigorously drying itself. When I later discussed this part of the ritual with some family members, they told me that splashing the goat was a gesture of respect and a way of "inviting" the goat to assent to its role of being sacrificed. Without this assent, the ritual could not proceed. The vigorous shaking of the goat's body was a sign that the goat had understood and accepted its fate. (Of course, in addition to constituting a "gesture of respect," the splashing of water could have also helped precipitate the twitching and shaking.) The goat's sacrifice was thus construed as the "self-sacrifice" of an important, respected, and beloved member of the household.

The ritual moved to the next phase, which was to "transfer" the ghost from Kiran to the goat.[37] Literally, the ghost had to be "swept" (*jharana*) out of Kiran's body and put in/on the goat. Golu Devata approached Kiran, made her stand up, took off the reddish bandana she was wearing around her head, and tied it around the neck of the goat. Kiran's long, dark hair fell over her back and shoulders in untidy streaks. The deity positioned himself behind Kiran and started combing, separating, and disentangling each strand of her hair with his fingers. He performed the following actions deliberately and repeatedly. In a series of fluid motions, he waved some invisible substance or entity—the ghost that was being released from Kiran's hair, I was later told—on/into the goat that was standing beside her. Kiran was then asked to take off her bangles, necklaces, and jewelry and place them on a cloth in front of her. Along with her other clothes and objects, this pile was to be taken to the forest and buried there after the goat sacrifice. The goat and Kiran's belongings were to be offered to the ghost as a "substitute" for Kiran.[38]

It was now time to send the goat away to be sacrificed in the forest, the jajaman said, directing the two men who had brought the goat in. He also instructed them to shut all the doors and windows of the house so the ghost would be unable to return. A few relatives and neighbors participating in the sacrificial ritual were to "do a puja, sacrifice the goat, consume some of it, and take the rest home with them." Some of my male interlocutors described the sacrifice as "just a 'party' [Eng.]; you won't miss much." Those who participated in the sacrifice were forbidden from reentering the Bisht family home for at least three days, so even though a "party" in the forest sounded intriguing to me, I was disappointed that I couldn't attend because I was living with the family. By shuttering the doors and windows of the house and banning participants in the sacrificial ritual from reentering the home, a physical separation was created between the goat, which now carried the ghost, and the family.

As the goat was led away, the jajaman addressed one of the male relatives who had brought the goat: "Don't come back here for three days! It doesn't matter how urgently you need me; just don't come!" One of the women elders in the room jokingly responded: "What do you mean for three days?! Knowing him, he won't be back for another three months," by which she meant that this relative was too self-involved to care about the family anyway. Everyone in the room laughed as the relative sheepishly led the goat away. Some of the women left the room and returned after a few minutes with trays of chai, signaling a closure to the evening's ritual.

The jagar exorcism brought the chhal/bhut who had been inhabiting Kiran out of hiding. Yet, the ghost's surfacing did not erase Kiran. The ritual entailed a doubling in which both daughter-in-law and ghost were simultaneously addressed. For example, the sponsor's admonishment—"There are so many people here asking about your welfare—do you like it? . . . Everything we are doing is for your benefit. . . . You are suffering, but are we happy?"—were directed both toward Kiran and the ghost.

The sponsor's demands and censuring of the ghost/Kiran articulated simmering "commonsensical" critiques of daughters-in-law[39] as potentially disruptive and untrustworthy figures in their affinal households.[40] As Kalpana Ram argues, in the eyes of her in-laws, the daughter-in-law embodies ambiguity and danger, "having the capacity to corrupt a man's loyalty to his parents and brothers."[41] Kiran's interpellation into ritual interactions between the god, the ghost, and her marital family reveals the gendered violence and trauma—both physical and nonphysical—that can be woven into exorcism rituals for ghost-afflicted women.[42] Specifically, in jagar exorcisms, the "cure" for ghost affliction consists of "singling out" the daughter-in-law to effect a break between her and her ghost-double and absorb her into her new familial context. In addition to the ghost losing power and agency and being subjected to violence during the ritual, the daughter-in-law must also leave behind her premarried life and connections to her natal home. In fact, the "cure" for ghost affliction requires that she be forbidden from returning to her natal home for a stipulated period of time.

The ritual was an intense witnessing experience. My inner state often felt out of step with the emotions of my male companions, at least what they outwardly displayed. I was both disturbed and intrigued by their stoicism, which made me curious about how Kiran and the other women had experienced this ritual and other cases of ghost affliction. I wanted to know how the "cut" between past and present, natal and affinal home, was experienced by women who have themselves been afflicted by chhal/bhut. I had little idea that this investigation would challenge many of the "truths" I had been told by male members of the Bisht clan.

Everyday Afflictions

The men in Kiran's marital home described ghost affliction to me as exceptional. But women themselves who had been through it described it as one of many "gendered vulnerabilities" they underwent in their everyday lives as an effect of patrilocality.[43] Women theorized afflictions, including ghost affliction, not as exceptional but rather as coextensive with the gendered struggles and difficulties of everyday life after marriage.

After Kiran's exorcism ritual, I asked to speak with her directly to learn more about her experiences and interpretations. However, nothing came of my request. Since I was grateful for how welcoming and open the Bisht family had been, I didn't press the matter further. I was keenly aware of how my positionality as a male outsider limited my access to women in the family. Much later, I also learned that the family feared that talking about the ghost might cause it to reappear. To learn more about what women themselves thought about ghost affliction, yet without upsetting the gendered choreography of the household, I decided to join them in their agricultural labor. My time in the village coincided with the harvest season. All the women of the household were busy loading and storing cauliflower. As elsewhere in rural India, where close to 75 percent of full-time agricultural workers are women, here, too, women carried the burden—quite literally—and all of it was unpaid. Every day, they carried heavy loads in sacks up a hill to their storage site next to the main road. By lunchtime, they had made ten to fifteen trips up and down this hill. It was backbreaking work.[44] Initially, when I started spending time with them, one of the men of the household accompanied me. If I asked the women a question, he would answer for them. But after a few days, they stopped accompanying me, and the women and I began to speak more freely. They were amused to see me out of breath, drenched in sweat, and struggling to keep up with them.

Over the course of several days, the women I spoke with included Deepak's wife, Malini, Nitin's wife, Kanchan, and a middle-aged woman named Sona ji, who was also married into the Bisht family. Initially, I asked them about the etiology, symptoms, and treatment of ghost affliction. Unlike what I had been told by men in the family, they told me ghost affliction was a ubiquitous phenomenon. Women used everyday idioms to describe ghost affliction—words and phrases such as *tabiyat kharab hona* (ill-health) and *pareshani* (trouble).

While men in the family had described ghost affliction to me as a rare occurrence, all three women I interviewed had experienced ghost affliction soon after marriage. They described their symptoms as consisting of fever, headaches, dizziness, spontaneous "dancing" during jagar rituals, as well as an inability to work or get out of bed in the morning. Like the men, they linked the presence of chhal/bhut to untimely or unfortunate deaths. Sona ji described chhal/bhut as the spirits of people who had died suddenly. She explained that if someone "drowned in a river, fell off a cliff, or was murdered, that person's sprit would begin to wander about in that area." This spirit would then "catch" or become "attached to" a young woman passing through the area.

In her account, Sona ji also identified the time of marriage and the multiple dislocations—emotional, psychological, physical, and geographic—experienced by brides as the moment when women became especially vulnerable to attack by chhal. Sona ji explained that the chhal had most likely "caught" Kiran when she had journeyed from her natal village, Kafal, to her marital home in

Bani. "This is why the puja [the goat sacrifice] has to done in the forest facing her *maike* [natal home]. That's where the ghost caught her, so that's where it must return." Sona ji articulated the important linkage between ghost affliction, patrilocal marriage, and Kiran's literal and figurative journey from natal to marital home, which the rituals had also made explicit.

However, whereas the exorcism ritual had foregrounded the agency of the ghost, women related ghost affliction to the everyday hardships they experienced after marriage. In other words, they did not limit the suffering and dislocation captured by ghost affliction to the moment of marriage or to the journey between natal and affinal home; rather, it extended into a daughter-in-law's future. All three women, who were differently placed generationally, described ghost affliction within a broader economy of gendered hardship and suffering that they faced. Everyday stresses in their lives affected and were affected by ghost affliction. Despite having different experiences of marriage and belonging to different generations, all three women understood the difficulties of patrilocal kinship for women. In their accounts, affliction was not only physiological but also social, psychological, and physical. Similar to Veena Das's theorization of "ordinary" afflictions, women understood their gendered vulnerabilities as afflictions that "are assimilated within the normal and yet not fully absorbed by it."[45] For example, women connected ghost affliction to their physical, mental, social, and material well-being, including their ability to work in the fields, take care of farm animals, bear children, particularly male heirs, take care of their husbands and in-laws, and their many other domestic responsibilities. In these ways, conversations about ghost affliction were simultaneously conversations about marriage itself.

All three women described marriage not as a singular event but as a series of difficulties and adjustments. The first difficulty was selecting a suitable groom and the bride's lack of agency. Sona ji said she was only seventeen years old when she got married. "When choosing a partner, the girl and boy have some say, but the final decision rests with the parents. Of course, parents don't want anything bad for their children," Sona ji said. "But then, who can see the future? It is fate. Some women are unlucky, and things go badly for them." Sona ji indicated that despite her parents' best intentions, a woman could find herself in a bad marriage with a difficult husband or in-laws. She mentioned that she knew of several women who had been verbally and physically abused by their in-laws. She added:

> In the past, girls didn't go to college, so they got married early. They had to get used to their new responsibilities from a very young age. Back then, if a girl didn't get along with her in-laws, she was finished—she would go mad, screaming and crying and fighting with them. Her life was finished! There

was nothing she could do; she had to put up with it or kill herself. But today, it's different. If they [new daughters-in-law] don't like it, they can leave, get a divorce. But then, they [the divorcees who remarry] will have to hear about it [suffer repercussions] in their new homes.

I was surprised to hear Sona ji describe divorce as something that happened frequently since I had not met any divorcees during my fieldwork. However, she insisted that divorce was "very common," although she noted that their family had been spared. "We've had some problems, like everyone else, but we bear it. Everyone has to bear a little hardship, right?" I nodded my head, but the younger daughters-in-law were silent. In Sona ji's remarks, divorce marked an erosion of Pahari cultural identity; it was a troubling sign of the sweeping socioeconomic changes and globalization that had affected Uttarakhand but were imagined as having come from "elsewhere."

The marriage event itself was also traumatizing and difficult. Even if a bride's natal home was in close physical proximity to her marital home, the symbolic weight of the journey from "daughter" to "daughter-in-law" was profound. Physically traveling to her in-laws' place—often through uninhabited, forested areas, outside not only the figurative but also physical confines of her natal home—tested the bride's "strength" and made her vulnerable to preying ghosts. In other words, the symbolic and physical journey of marriage linked to women's susceptibility to negative, external supernatural forces.

"Before marriage, girls are usually okay, but then, after marriage, chhal come after them. And then her [the bride's] in-laws must take care of it," Kanchan explained. In addition to connecting ghost affliction and marriage, in saying this, Kanchan was also citing how brides were dependent on their in-laws for healing them. For instance, when I asked what part a bride's natal family played in curing ghost affliction, the women told me they had no role at all, as their daughter had already been "given over" to her in-laws. In this way, jagar healing rituals effected a transfer of responsibility for the welfare of the bride from her natal family to her in-laws, as Satyaram ji also suggested. They marked the social fact that the bride's in-laws, not her natal family, were now responsible for her well-being, and the bride was subject to their actions. These rituals, though done in the name of making women well, also brought out a disconcerting truth about where women now belonged. Despite the fact that a bride was "given over" to her in-laws at the time of marriage, the women I spoke with acknowledged the incompleteness of this process in the form of lingering affective and moral ties between a bride and her natal kin, often bolstered through the physical proximity of her natal village, which might bring up memories, longing, and desires for her past.

A jagar ceremony was required to enact the final "cut" between the bride and her natal kin while ritually binding the bride to her husband and his family. Similarly, both marriage and jagar transitioned brides from their natal to marital homes, entailing a figurative erasure of the former. The culmination of the jagar, the goat sacrifice, can be read as a way of acknowledging and honoring a bride's natal home while separating her from it or wresting her from the negative pull of her past life.

Despite its associations with a single, paradigmatic event—marriage—women narratively wove stories of ghost affliction with accounts of everyday, gendered vulnerabilities. While we were discussing ghost affliction, Sona ji steered the conversation toward other more mundane matters, specifically, the labor involved in agricultural work and women's everyday lives more generally. Whereas men described ghost affliction as a result of women's "hearts [*dil*] being weak [*kamzor*]," women offered a different explanation of vulnerability. When I asked why men didn't get attacked by chhal, Kanchan explained: "Because men go everywhere; they have the right [*adhikar*] to go anywhere, even to the cremation grounds [when someone dies]. But women aren't allowed to go to such places." Kanchan suggested that because men came into contact with negative external forces on a more regular basis as a result of their gendered privilege, they developed a spiritual resistance or immunity to those forces. "Their hearts become strong [*majbut*]," she claimed, whereas women's more restricted lives made them susceptible to chhal attack and affliction. In this way, the women pointed to patriarchal control over their bodies and movements as a reason for their susceptibility to chhal attack.

Chhal attack was something women had to learn to endure, much like they had to endure "all the household responsibilities" after marriage, as Sona ji put it. I asked whether she had household responsibilities before she was married. But Sona ji said no:

> In our *maike* [natal home], our mothers and fathers take care of everything. After marriage, not only do we have to manage all the housework, but we also have to leave behind our brothers and sisters, mothers and fathers, and move away. So when I first came to my in-laws, I was very unhappy—I used to cry all the time [she laughs]. I used to go into the forest to cut grass, drowning in thoughts about my mother and father, worrying about them. And then I would just sit somewhere and cry. It was very hard—women here have a hard life.

For Sona ji, marriage marked an abrupt cut from her previous life, which was characterized as full of love and care. Her new life as a daughter-in-law, by contrast, was characterized by a sense of profound loneliness, worry, and melancholy—she was "drowning" in thoughts of her past and her natal kin, as she put it. At the same time, in this state of unease, she was required to build new habits, get to know her in-laws, and learn to handle new responsibilities. The other daughters-in-law of the household were her only succor during this time.

Malini also pitched in: "It was very tough for me after marriage, too—everything breaks down after marriage.... Even things you cannot do, you have to get used to them, you have to learn. Everything changes. It takes years to get used to a new place." I was drawn to Malini's phrase, "everything breaks down after marriage." It signified the ways marriage and its aftermath are experienced by women not just as the "making" of new relations but also the unmaking of prior relations and lives.[46]

In Uttarakhand, the making and unmaking of marital relations also took place in a divine register. In addition to learning about their new family, married women also had to acquaint themselves with new family deities. As Malini explained: "For example, here we do puja for Golu and Haru-Harit [two well-known deities in the region]. But, in my natal home, it was Saim Devata and Mayya-Devi [two other deities]; now I don't perform ritual worship for them [the latter]." The women explained to me that, after marriage, daughters-in-law had to learn how to worship new family deities properly; for some, it took a long time to develop their own personal relationships with them. Even if a daughter-in-law was already acquainted with the gods worshiped in the home of her in-laws, the way each family related to a deity varied according to the personalities and proclivities of family mediums. Beyond this, relating to unfamiliar deities was not a one-way relationship; the family deities also had to get to know the new daughter-in-law.

Thus, the jagar exorcism also held an important purpose of making relations, making place, for the daughter-in-law. As my female interlocutors commented, the fact that a married woman's natal family had no role in the treatment of ghost affliction expressed that, after marriage, she was wholly in the care of her in-laws and a member of her affinal home. As such, jagar allowed the bride and her affinal family, as a social unit, to interact with each other and express care in a ritually formalized way. As some of my male interlocutors, such as Deepak and Nitin, suggested, a daughter-in-law's period of affliction and healing, which often spanned many months as it did in Kiran's case, represented a kind of probationary learning period for her. During this time, there was some leeway in terms of expected domestic chores. As my male interlocutors suggested, the woman's oversights could be forgiven more easily by her in-laws because, as someone who was possessed by ghost, she was not truly or fully herself.

Being Singled Out

Women's accounts of ghost affliction and the ritual itself suggest that the moment of marriage does not complete the transition from a woman's natal to affinal home. Women described the jagar exorcism, which chastises and violently displaces or separates the chhal/bhut from the bride, with ambivalence. This ritual was another equally important mark of this transition, of separating women from their past selves.

When I asked Sona ji about her own experience of ghost affliction, she dismissed the episode, visibly embarrassed: "It was a light episode," she said. "It just happened. Soon after I got married, I must have gone into the forest, and then not known an 'attack' [Eng.] had happened. After that, my mind must have become weird [*ajib*]," she replied. By this, she meant that she had been attacked by a ghost and had become mentally or emotionally unwell without knowing it. I was struck by the general, dissociated quality of her account, as if it had happened to someone else.

"But it happened to me in a very light [*halka*] way," she repeated. "I didn't start dancing [*nachana*] or anything like that."[47] But as Sona ji continued, the seriousness of her affliction came to light: "But a goat still had to be sent [sacrificed] for me," she said. "The jagar had to be done because soon after marriage, I lost two of my children because of chhal." Her first child was only a few weeks old when they died, and the second had been eighteen months. Sona ji's voice lowered to a whisper. I felt the pain of Sona ji's revelation, and we sat in silence to honor the moment. The other women also became quiet. After a while, they got up to continue working, but Sona ji sat in silence. I stayed with her.

After a few minutes, Sona ji continued: "After the jagar was done, everything became okay. I had more children after that, and they're all fine." Saying this, her face brightened; she once again seemed like her cheerful, talkative self. Shifting the focus away from herself, she said, "The same thing happened with Malti *didi* [a female relative who had been with us the previous day]; she, too, lost her child." Then, pointing to Malini, who was just out of earshot, she whispered: "It happened to her as well. Yes, pujas have been performed for each of us."[48] . . . Although the worst happened to Chetan's wife [Kiran], all of us have faced this trouble."[49]

I remembered the uneasy feeling I had had during the exorcism, and I asked Sona ji about the process of going through it. She described it as "strange": "Everyone is looking at you; watching you closely," she said. But, she insisted that her experiences were not "as bad" as Kiran's. She described how Kiran's behavior had been a source of great shame and embarrassment to herself because she had been "dancing" with her hair open in front of everyone. "In the mountains, we cover our heads as a sign of respect toward our elders. But, the other day [during the jagar I attended], you saw how she was, with her hair open—didn't you see her? Well, after that happens, the woman who dances feels ashamed," Sona ji explained. For women, these feelings of embarrassment and shame (*sharam*) were associated with publicly displaying symptoms of ghost affliction, such as "dancing" with head uncovered and hair opened in front of their in-laws and elders. These symptoms were more stigmatizing than others—such as fainting, suffering from fever, being unable to get out of bed, and so on—as they also signaled a breakdown in gender norms. In their affinal homes, it is customary for young women to behave modestly, so to lose control in this way was remembered as a mortifying experience for the women who had experienced it.

Despite the fact that their attachments to their pasts and their natal homes were "worked upon" through jagar, all three women expressed a sense of loss, painful disconnection, and longing for the love and comfort of their natal homes. Malini's natal home was about a half-day journey away by road, and she was only able to go there once every three months for two or three days at a time. Malini's in-laws allowed their *bahus* (daughters-in-law) some time away from domestic responsibilities for special occasions, such as attending a village festival or the wedding of a close family member, but these were limited occasions. Moreover, the women not only needed their in-laws' permission to visit their natal homes but were also dependent on their husbands to drive them and pick them up. Sona ji described how things were when she got married: "When I first came to my in-laws, I wanted to go back to my parents all the time, but there was no road back then. And no phone. Back then, we didn't have cell phones like everyone does today, so it was much harder [to stay connected to your natal home after marriage]. Many other, less privileged women in the village were not allowed to leave at all because they had responsibilities of taking care of children and animals—duties that could not be offloaded to anyone else."

Conclusion: Jagged Narratives

Unlike the dominant narratives of jagar I heard in Bani—narrated by men—in which ghost affliction was described as an uncommon and aberrant event, women themselves viewed it as a structural, gendered, and everyday reality. Whereas men described ghost affliction as a question of individual failure and rehabilitation, my female interlocutors highlighted issues such as patriarchal control over women's bodies. Women consistently pointed to how the day-to-day challenges they faced made them vulnerable to multiple forms of affliction; they were ill-prepared to deal with the negative supernatural forces that lay in wait for them in unknown and new habitats and the transitions that took them there, which were full of hardship, vulnerability, and danger. My interlocutors also talked about how their lives in their natal homes did not prepare them for the social and material difficulties they confronted in their marital homes, such as being viewed with suspicion by their in-laws and enacting new, unfamiliar forms of reproductive labor. They spoke of feeling like strangers in their new homes and shedding tears as they remembered their parents and siblings from whom they had been cut off. These experiences of social dislocation, precarity, and Otherness were also closely bound up with accounts of ghost affliction, and questions about the latter would often elicit responses about the former. Thus, in women's narratives, rather than being an isolated, rare, and purely supernatural condition, ghost affliction was part of a broader ecology of hardship and suffering—from leaving behind their natal homes to learning to navigate a new terrain of kinship after marriage to bearing children, toiling in the fields, and learning new forms of labor.

Unlike widely circulating narratives about the waywardness, forwardness, and danger of daughters-in-law whose liminal presence can cause ruptures in the mythical "unified" joint family,[50] women who had experienced ghost affliction described their presence in their new homes as marked by social dislocation and Otherness—of being haunted, as it were, by memories and attachments to their former life in their natal home. An important and recurring theme in each of the women's accounts of marriage was that they felt a dissonance between the comfort and care of a woman's natal home and the material hardships associated with life in the home of their in-laws. This dissonance inherent in patrilocal marriage rendered the bride both inside and outside, self and other, in relation to her affinal home. That is, in the immediate postmarriage period, she was simultaneously an integral member of her husband's family and a stranger to her in-laws. Significantly, a new bride's experience of social Otherness within a new familial context parallels the phenomenon of ghost affliction, wherein an ambiguous and dangerous supernatural interloper inhabits the bride's body, producing a state of "existential doubling." In nested frames of Otherness, the ghost, the bride's shadowy double, exists as a stranger within her as she becomes a stranger within her new home.

The driving force behind the ritual intervention in ghost affliction is to "make place" for a married woman within her new, affinal home; it is designed to adjust the woman to her new living conditions by "cutting" her off from her natal home and past life and enacting new connections with family members and deities. For example, during one of the jagar rituals I attended, the deity Golu

Devata had mandated that the afflicted daughter-in-law, Kiran, not be allowed to visit her natal home for at least three months following the final ritual. Thus, enforcing a period of complete separation between Kiran and her natal home became an important factor in the timing of the final ritual. In "singling out" Kiran, that is, effecting a separation between the ghost and Kiran, the exorcism ritual was designed to incorporate Kiran into her new social role and familial context. Because the word *chhal* is used interchangeably with *bhut*—a word that means "ghost" but also the "past"—the ritual treatment married women undergo in the home of their in-laws is understood to dis-possess them of the supernatural agents that afflict them as well as the affective ties that bind them to their "past life" and kin membership in their natal households. In this way, chhal/bhut exorcism is a socially and ontologically transformative rite of passage that extends and completes the marriage ritual—to make an in-marrying woman a full and loyal member of her new household.

But while jagar rituals are designed to cut a married woman off from the ghost that afflicts her and from her natal home and past, women's own narratives run counter to this logic of "singling out" through cutting. In my fieldwork, ghost affliction emerged as a shared experience that bonded women of different ages who had all undergone the privations of patrilocal marriage. The stigma of ghost affliction was not borne individually and, in the minds of women, was not divorced from the social and material realities of patrilocality and the labor involved in the dissolutions and articulations of kinship. In women's narratives of affliction, broadly conceived, other connections among women (that exceeded kinship) also surfaced, as did mutually constitutive connections between ghost affliction and gendered experiences of patrilocal marriage. Rather than appearing as an individualized disorder with supra-mundane etiology, ghost affliction was reinterpreted as a quotidian, historically constituted, and collectively endured phenomenon. While jagar rituals are aimed at "singling out" married women, the narratives of women themselves reveal how ghosts of the past continue to live beside them, reappearing every time a new bride appears on the horizon.

5

Out of Place

Lives of Oracles and Priests

Outcast(e)

What does it mean to feel "out of place," and what does it mean to find your place, to be found? This chapter is about the often tumultuous lives of storytellers, musicians, oracles, and healers whose lives are shot through with the contradictions of caste-based violence, deprivation, the struggles of migration, and experiences of loss and suffering, including homelessness, unemployment, familial conflict, cycles of substance dependence, and bouts of "madness." My interlocutors described these experiences as different ways of being *out of place*: of feeling marginalized, lost, sick, or unmoored. They described being called to serve the gods as priests and ritual practitioners after these periods of intense turbulence as finding their way home.

This chapter tracks how ritual experts in Uttarakhand, particularly *jagaris* (ritual experts who preside over and mediate rituals of divine embodiment) and *bakkyas* (oracles) find their way "home,"[1] both literally and figuratively.[2] It is about how they learn to listen to gods and how gods call them home, endowing their lives with purpose and meaning. Their stories emphasize not just human agency but also how human and divine connections can be harnessed to experience fulfillment and healing for both gods and religious practitioners. At the same time, they also show how being *in* place is never settled; particularly for those who occupy positions on the margins, place must be constantly made and remade.[3]

One of the most pressing contradictions that jagaris and bakkyas encounter in their everyday lives is between their relatively prestigious roles as priests and healers—that is, as figures of religious authority—and their identities as members of caste-oppressed communities. The jagaris and bakkyas with whom I have worked since 2010 belong to communities that are legally designated as Scheduled Caste (SC)[4] in the Indian Constitution.[5] Members of these communities continue to endure forms of violence and oppression across India. While some of my interlocutors self-identified using the acronym SC, others also employed the term *harijan*, a term popularized by Gandhi to mean "person of god," as well as *Dalit*, which literally means "crushed down" or "oppressed."

As a socioeconomically and caste-privileged Indian man born to a Sikh father and Hindu, Brahmin mother working with jagaris and bakkyas, I had to navigate a complex terrain of fieldwork relations. My positionality both opened up and foreclosed connections. For one, I benefited from structures of inequality that harmed my Dalit interlocutors. Early in my fieldwork, several caste-privileged people told me that Dalits were known for lying, stealing, and cheating; "You can't trust them," I was told, as they dissuaded me from living and working with ritual practitioners who belonged to Dalit communities. In fact, all through my fieldwork, my work and time with my Dalit interlocutors was constantly, though discreetly, surveilled by caste-privileged people (see chapter 3) who claimed they needed to be wary and watchful of Dalits because of their allegedly well-known criminal proclivities.[6] While my own socioeconomic privilege was never threatened, by working, traveling, and living with Dalit practitioners for extended periods of time, I damaged my relationships with some caste-privileged Rajput and Brahmin persons. Some cut off contact with me, while others stopped inviting me into their homes, preferring to meet with me in more neutral, public settings, such as restaurants and tea stalls, where caste taboos were not as strictly observed. At the same time, this estrangement with caste-privileged community members helped me establish trust and intimacy with my Dalit interlocutors, making it easier to talk candidly about caste-based violence.

For example, one of my interlocutors, a jagari named Champal Mistri, discussed how his community was perceived by "upper-caste" (*uch jati*) people one evening while we were eating dinner in his home. We had just returned from a *jagar* in a neighboring village that Champal had presided over.[7] As Champal and I ravenously consumed the mountain of *dal bhat* (lentils and rice) on our plates, he described the casual but persistent casteism that he and his family were subjected to in their everyday lives: "They [upper-caste people] think we are all gangsters [*daku*]," he said, and we both laughed. Even though he was being serious, the word *daku* (from the Hindi word *dakait*, which is where the

English word *dacoit* comes from) conjured iconic images from Hindi films from the 1970s and 1980s. Further, Champal was conjuring a long history of legal discrimination against caste-oppressed people in which, under colonial laws such as the Criminal Tribes Act (1871), entire communities, castes, or "tribes" were criminalized.[8] I looked carefully at Champal, an earnest, scholarly man in his mid-forties, with a week-old stubble, who was dressed in a road-worn cotton kurta. It was absurd to imagine him as a gangster, which is partly why we had both laughed at his statement.

Champal explained that much of the "crime" that was attributed to caste-oppressed communities was a direct result of the fact that they were socially and economically marginalized. "Yes, they [the youth] sometimes do wrong things, but that's because they don't have anything. . . . I admit, we [Dalits] have a bad reputation," Champal said. He went on to say that when Dalits engage in theft or other forms of petty crime, it is widely reported in the media. However, when Thakurs (Rajputs) and Brahmins engaged in the same behaviors, "no one speaks about it publicly, let alone writes about it. . . . Is it like this where you live, in America?" Champal asked me. "It's not very different," I replied, describing how slavery had shaped contemporary American society and the ways Black people and people of color are criminalized and incarcerated in disproportionately high numbers.

Champal's point about the everyday discrimination meted out to his family and community is also reinforced by recent local and national political events. Since 2014, when the right-wing Bharatiya Janata Party (BJP) government under Prime Minister Modi came to power for the first time, the social and political climate across north India, including in Uttarakhand, has changed significantly. While the more secular-leaning Indian Congress Party narrowly won state assembly elections in Uttarakhand in 2012 (by one seat), by 2017, the tide had significantly turned toward the Hindu nationalist BJP, which won a landslide victory in the state.

During my visits to Uttarakhand in recent years, my Dalit interlocutors talked at length about the rising tide of upper-caste violence and Dalit responses to these trends. For instance, they cited a case in which a Dalit man was lynched by an upper-caste mob for allegedly "entering a flour mill in their village and rendering it impure."[9] Some jagaris recounted atrocities committed against their relatives and neighbors who were beaten up and even killed for eating and drinking in the vicinity of upper-caste people or entering a Hindu temple. In 2016, Dalit activists in Dehradun District filed legal petitions and organized demonstrations to demand that Dalits be allowed to enter and worship in local temples against the wishes of Brahmins, who have traditionally forbidden this practice.[10] In 2018, the Uttarakhand High Court ruled that Brahmin priests must allow Dalits to enter and perform ritual worship in "all religious places and temples."[11] My interlocutors, however, had little faith in the enforceability of this legal order given the deep-rooted and pervasive nature of caste oppression. They argued that the rising tide of upper-caste, Hindu nationalist violence had contradictory effects: on the one hand, Dalit groups are now more organized than ever, and there is greater solidarity and less infighting among different Dalit caste communities, or *jatis*; while on the other hand, the fact that the violence against these communities is often either explicitly or implicitly sanctioned by the state has a chilling effect on political dissent.

Like other members of Dalit communities, bakkyas, jagaris, aujis (see chapter 3), and other Dalit religious specialists face grinding discrimination. However, they also happen to be figures of religious authority and expertise; they mediate between local deities and worshipers, including those who are of "higher" caste than them, such as Brahmins and Rajputs. For instance, as specialists, the professional role of jagaris is analogous to that of Brahmin priests who, in temples and other ritual spaces, also mediate contact between deities and their worshipers. In this role, jagaris also garner a great deal of respect; they are needed and lauded for their ritual and textual expertise. Not only do jagaris "call" (*bulana*) deities to enter and inhabit human mediums and interact with their worshipers, but they are also skilled ritual musicians, healers, and storytellers who can influence the behavior of deities in powerful ways.

Because of jagaris' ability to "call" or "invite" local deities to enter and inhabit the bodies of mediums and interact with their worshipers, people from caste-privileged communities are sometimes wary of the power that jagaris wield. As one of my Brahmin interlocutors told me, "jagaris' association with powerful gods and goddesses makes people afraid. They fear that a jagari will misuse their power and put a curse [*ghat lagana*] on them." In employing the phrase *ghat lagana*, my interlocutor was alluding to the fact that certain religious specialists, such as oracles and jagaris, are said to command supernatural beings to harm their adversaries.[12] Aside from such innuendo—which was more commonly directed toward oracles than jagaris—jagaris are understood to perform a range of crucial religious functions and, as such, are treated more respectfully than other Dalits.

When I asked Champal why jagaris are treated with more respect by upper-caste people than their other caste fellows, Champal put it differently. Rather than emphasize the power of jagaris and oracles to harm, he emphasized how jagaris *healed* deity-human relationships (although, of course, the power to harm and heal are interconnected). For Pahari people, Champal said, relationships between humans and divinities are as integral as relationships between members of a family, neighbors, and friends. And much like human bonds, "relationships with divinities also experience their ups and downs," Champal said. That is, such human-divine relationships are not only deep-rooted and deeply felt, but they are also dynamic and unpredictable; they change and sometimes even break down. The consequences of such relational disruptions, sometimes referred to as *dosh* (lit., "fault"), can be dire: humans and animals can become ill or suffer, or there can be environmental and ecological devastation, such as famine or crop failure (see chapter 2).

In Champal's description, when the tenuous balance between the social, natural, and supernatural orders is disturbed, it sets off a chain reaction that leads to greater destruction and suffering for all. According to Champal, "Upper-caste people know of these dangers as well as anybody else," so to protect themselves and their communities, Thakurs and Brahmins are forced to enlist the services of skilled jagaris, even if they happen to be Dalit. In other words, jagaris are indispensable to the process of maintaining social and cosmological order. However, I was also told that, since the early 2000s, the number of Thakur and Brahmin ritual specialists who play the drums, perform deities' narrative songs, and mediate between deities and worshipers has been increasing. Whereas professional jagaris traditionally belong to Dalit communities, caste-privileged people are now starting to do this religious work for themselves. My interlocutors explained this shift as related to increasing caste discrimination in Uttarakhand. As one said: "They [caste-privileged communities] are training their own people to perform jagar, so they don't have to call [Dalit] jagaris into their homes."

We had finished eating. Champal's wife cleared our plates, and Champal stretched his legs and lit a bidi. Though I thought our conversation might move on to other topics, Champal returned to the question of caste and criminality. "Valmiki [the legendary poet-sage who composed the Sanskrit-language Ramayana] was a *daku*, too, you know," Champal informed me. I told him I was surprised to hear this. Champal continued:

He [Valmiki] was an outcaste and an unlettered country bumpkin [*anpadh-gavar*]; people looked down upon him. One day, he accosted some people traveling down the road, pulled out his knife, and took their belongings. While this was happening, a saintly person [*sant*] came their way—Valmiki wanted to rob him, too. On learning what Valmiki wanted, the sant said, "I will let you take my belongings, but I have one condition. Go home and ask your wife and children if the kind of merit [karma] you are accumulating in order to feed and clothe your family is also shared by them or whether it is yours alone."

Valmiki tied the sant up and went home and asked his family: "Are these sins [*pap*] mine alone, or do they also belong to you?" His family laughed at him when he asked this question. "This is your karma alone," his wife said, "just like mine is to feed and take care of the children. It is my responsibility to take care of the children and, unlike you, I don't have a choice in the matter. But if the day comes when I must steal from someone or do whatever else needs to be done, it will be me who does it [takes responsibility for it]."

On hearing these words, Valmiki went back to the sant, who asked him, "So, now do you understand?" After that day, Valmiki renounced his life as a daku. The sant said, "Now that you have left this work, repeat Rama's [the divine hero of the Ramayana epic] name." But Valmiki was illiterate, so instead of saying "Rama, Rama, Rama," he uttered, "*mara, mara, mara*" [lit., "I am dying"]. He was perishing because of his bad karma! On saying this [acknowledging his wrongdoings], his [vocalization of the] letter "a" became elongated, and "*mara, mara, mara*" became "Rama, Rama, Rama." From that point onward, he started composing the Ramayana.

On one level, Champal's story is about the importance of renouncing worldly ties. It argues that a person's karma—the de/merit that accrues from their actions—is theirs alone and that the sins and attachments of worldly life are a hindrance on the path to salvation. Following the correct path, that is, renouncing the world and devoting oneself to god, can result in radical self-transformation and the creation of beauty, as Valmiki is traditionally known as the *adikavi*, the "first poet".[13]

In the context of our conversation about caste and criminality, however, this story also reveals the tension between how jagar performers see themselves and how they are seen by a casteist society. The subtext of Champal's story is that Valmiki and the figure of the jagari are similar because they sing the legends of the gods into existence; Valmiki was the "first poet" who brought the story of Rama to the world, while jagaris sing of the earthly exploits of local deities in jagar rituals, so both are known for their transformative use of poetic language and music. Moreover, like the rehabilitated daku in Champal's story, Champal also saw himself as someone who had succeeded in renouncing harmful worldly attachments. However, an important point of difference between Valmiki and the figure of the jagari is that, while the former's prior identity as a daku had been all but erased, the latter continues to be stigmatized as a socially inferior Other.

Jagaris have to constantly straddle these complexities in their everyday lives. Many only experienced a sense of social value and importance after they became professional jagaris and bakkyas. They described the earlier periods of their lives as fraught with multiple challenges that come with being caste-oppressed Pahari men. While not all jagaris and bakkyas are men, and I spent time interviewing and working with women ritual specialists as well,[14] here, I focus on how Dalit men *found place* in relation to longstanding patterns of out-migration for adult Pahari men due to a lack of local employment opportunities.[15] As studies of out-migration from Uttarakhand show, migratory pressures are highly dependent on factors such as household size and per capita land holdings. For historically marginalized SC/ST communities, who are more likely to be employed in casual work and own small plots of land, the pressures to migrate out of the state are higher.

Jagaris and oracles thus navigate a challenging social landscape and find (some) respite from those challenges through their work as religious specialists. Their place in the world—their social and professional identity—is largely dependent on the gods for whom they perform rituals. Identity and belonging are also narrated through an idiom of homecoming: after being lost and adrift in the world, religious specialists are "called home" to serve the gods.

Ujval: Migration and Marginalization

Despite the fact that Ujval Das understood his work as a jagar performer as hereditary—"It is in our blood," he said—his journey to this path was fraught. Like most jagaris with whom I worked, Ujval Das described his vocation as a patrilineal inheritance. Many jagari lineages went back at least three or four generations and were mediated by jagaris' fathers and paternal uncles. (Some of the women oracles I met had learned from their husbands). Even though Ujval's father had been a jagari, Ujval lived through a period of great confusion and anguish in his twenties before being "called by the gods" to perform jagar.

Ujval Das's life story is emblematic of the many psychological, social, and material difficulties that affect Pahari men and Dalit Pahari men, in particular. When he and his brother were young boys, their mother died. His father remarried soon after, and subsequently, two more children were added to the household. While life continued more or less smoothly for everyone else (or appeared to), Ujval resented his stepmother. Because of his antipathy toward her, Ujval started "going down the wrong path," as he put it. He stopped attending school when he was in the fifth grade and started spending time with other troubled boys in the surrounding area. While his other siblings went to school, helped with household chores, and found ways to supplement their family's income, Ujval spent his days drinking homemade liquor, getting into fights, and engaging in petty crime, he said.

Before "going down the wrong path," Ujval described how, as the eldest son of a jagari, he had been taught to play percussion instruments known as *dhol* and *nagara* and provide vocal accompaniment when his father was invited to perform jagar. However, as Ujval's relationship with his family soured, he began neglecting his apprenticeship as a jagari as well as his other familial responsibilities. His parents began to see him as a burden (*bojh*): he was not working or contributing to the material well-being of the family, but instead, wasting his time "running around with local hooligans." When he was sixteen, Ujval was effectively thrown out of the house and told by his father to "move to the [North Indian] plains" to find employment. Though his family was at one level trying to protect Ujval from the recurring cycles of drinking, crime, and trouble with village authorities, Ujval felt that his family had abandoned and exiled him.

Though Ujval was blamed for his expulsion from the village, the districts of Almora and Pauri Garhwal, the latter being where Ujval was from, have the highest rates of long-term outstate migration and "recorded an absolute decline in population in 2011 over 2001."[16] Based on data collected from ten sample villages in Pauri District in Garhwal, a report by the National Institute of Rural Development (NIRD) in India found that "migrants have comparatively better educational attainments as compared to their non-migrant counterparts."[17] Yet, demographic statistics about out-migration are not designed to capture the tumultuous nature of these experiences for young men, particularly those who are Dalit and already disadvantaged, like Ujval. The fact that Ujval dropped out of school at an early age made it more difficult for him to find employment in the neighboring state of Uttar Pradesh. The NIRD report also notes how migrants from SC communities struggle to take advantage of new opportunities because of higher rates of poverty, lack of access to educational opportunities, qualifications, and, as Ujval also observed, fewer "family connections" or networks of economic support for Dalit migrants to rely on outside of Uttarakhand (a fact that is also confirmed by other large-scale surveys of out-migrants). Ujval added that while upward mobility was possible for a small fraction of Dalit migrants, for most, their lives became harder, and their economic situations worsened after leaving Uttarakhand.

Ujval ended up in Moradabad, an industrial city in Uttar Pradesh, where his relatives found him a job working for a plumber. However, Ujval came to work drunk one day and was fired on the spot. Within a few months of moving to Moradabad, he was unemployed, unhoused, and depressed. He was too ashamed to tell his father what had happened or ask for financial help. He lost all contact with his family and "felt like his life was over," even though he was still a teenager. When I asked him why he couldn't find another job in Moradabad, he blamed it on the lack of a caste-based support network: "When rich pandit [Brahmin] and Thakur people go to the plains, they are able to find lots of work, but I didn't have any family connections." Ujval was implying that upper-caste migrants to the plains already had a greater measure of social capital and financial security than Dalits such as him, which made it easier for them to make a life outside of Uttarakhand. Describing this time in his life, Ujval added, "I was troubled for a long time. Sometimes I couldn't sleep, sometimes I couldn't eat; sometimes this, sometimes that. Someone was always unwell in my family.... I was lost. I couldn't support myself where I was, but I couldn't go back either."

In addition to drinking heavily, Ujval also started using other substances, including opioids. "During this time, I wanted to die, and came close to dying many times," he told me. Ujval also started "hearing voices" and "seeing things that were not really there.... I would see people who had been dead for many years walking around in front of me.... I saw my own mother one day, and I knew I was going mad." Ujval tried to quell these waking visions by drinking and drugging himself into a stupor, but the visions followed him: "I started hearing voices in my sleep. I was seeing things, but they were not like dreams." One night, Ujval realized he could not continue like this anymore. He said: "I cried for what I had done, I cried for my family, I cried for my mother. I wanted to die, but then Goril [Ujval's family deity] came to me. He said, 'You are like this because you have abandoned me—you have abandoned your *gaddi* [a jagari or oracle's "seat"].' After Goril, one by one, a procession [*julus*] of gods and goddesses came to me—Mother Bhagavati, Bhairavnath, Narsingh, Mahasu.[18] ... They all came."

This was a turning point in Ujval's life. Ujval realized that he was being called to perform jagar by his lineage deity, Goril (also known as Goljyu or Golu Devata [see chapter 4]). "Goril *devata* helped me find my path," Ujval said. He realized that the voices and visions he was experiencing were trying to help, not harm, him: "I was being called back home to serve the deities, as my forefathers served them.... So, I decided to go back to Pauri, even though I thought that my family would reject me. But they welcomed me back; the gods had spoken to them, too. They knew what was happening [to me], so they were happy when I came home." Although Ujval did not know it at the time, the deities had also spoken to Ujval's father and told him that they had chosen Ujval to be their priest—that is, they had called him to begin his work as a jagari. During the time Ujval was away, his father had developed health problems and become very frail. He was no longer able to handle the rigors of the road as a performing jagari.

When Ujval returned to his native village, he began accompanying and helping his father, a process that enabled him to learn and grow as a jagari in his own right. Over time, Ujval's relationship with his father healed. Ujval gained his father's clients' trust, and his father slowly retired as a ritual performer. By the time I met Ujval, he had been working as a jagari for almost twenty years. As a jagari who had inherited his craft, Ujval had not only inherited the "marks" (*linga*) of his priestly lineage—which included material instruments of ritual significance, such as the *chaurgai*, *chhattar*, and *nad*—from his father but also a network of clients. Ujval had also been initiated into the use of certain mantras (incantations) that have the power to heal and harm. (These initiation rituals sometimes take place on cremation grounds.) Priests of Ujval's lineage had served particular families in the surrounding area for generations; being connected to these families also meant being in relation with their deities and the designated mediums who embodied them.[19] Ujval visited and performed jagar for his clients regularly in conjunction with cyclical Hindu festivals or during times of crisis and difficulty. As he explained, "Sometimes I am asked to put on a jagar if someone in the home has fallen sick or if something bad is happening, like someone experiencing a string of bad luck."

In addition to performing jagar, Ujval supported his family by working as a tailor. Although working as a jagari did not bring Ujval and his family enough financial support to sustain them—as he said, he was not "hired and paid" to do this work but was "invited" to perform jagar and offered a few hundred rupees (in purchasing power parity, between $50–$100 USD) as *guru dakshina*, an offering to one's guru—it was clear that being a jagari was meaningful for him on other registers, as spiritual, emotional, and social labor, particularly in the aftermath of what he had suffered earlier in his life. I asked Ujval if the upheavals in his life had made it easier for him to empathize with the sufferings of those for whom he performed jagar. "I don't know if that's the case," he replied, "but my troubles [*kashta*] certainly brought me closer to God [*bhagavan*]."

As a jagari, it was Ujval's responsibility to facilitate interactions between many different deities and their worshipers, a role that is only possible if he maintains equanimous relations with them too. As Ujval put it: "Once I began to trust in God, I was able to find my path." In order to mediate between different deities and human communities, Ujval offered a monistic conception of divinity that recognized and respected differences between individualized deity forms or manifestations: "Goril showed me that all the deities are branches of a single tree," Ujval said. I came to understand that as Ujval's relationship with Goril deepened, he came to see how distinct, localized, and immanent forms of divinity participated in a greater whole. As a result, rather than speak of specific divinities by name, Ujval used the more generic words *bhagavan* and *ishvar*—which evoke an abstract, nonspecific, and singular conception of divinity—to describe the deities with whom he worked. Although Ujval was well versed in the histories and practices of specific local deities who inhabit Uttarakhand, by employing nonspecific terms such as *bhagavan* and *ishvar*, he demonstrated an important professional ethic: as a jagari, he was obligated to serve many different deities regardless of his own personal or familial loyalties.

Since being called to serve as a jagari, Ujval's life situation improved significantly. "It is because of God's grace [*kripa*] that everything is okay now—there is no trouble in my life," Ujval said. However, it had been a long and painful journey to get to this place.

Jaipal: Permeable Boundaries

I met Jaipal, a bakkya (oracle), during the wedding reception of a mutual acquaintance who lived in Uttarkashi District in Garhwal. I was immediately struck by his tall, imposing frame and air of authority. He wore a beard and had long, waist-length black hair, which he tied and kept hidden under a baseball cap when he was not meeting with clients. He was around sixty years old and had a youthful air about him. In his healing room, where the deities inhabited and spoke through him, he unfurled his hair and used it to great dramatic effect.

Jaipal was a local celebrity who was well-known for his healing powers. Prior to meeting him, I had heard a lot about him. For instance, I was told that women who were struggling to conceive often visited him because he was particularly skilled at healing afflictions related to reproduction and fertility. One trusted friend informed me, "Some years ago, a Muslim woman who had been married for over twenty years came to see Baba ji [a term of respect] all the way from Kolkata because she was unable to have children. She had visited many holy men and many doctors over the years, but no one was able to help her. But soon after meeting Baba ji, she became pregnant with a child." Jaipal's powers were reinforced by the long distance she had traveled to reach him (all the way from West Bengal) and the fact that she was not even Hindu. Still, she had been healed.

On meeting Jaipal, I told him what people had said about his healing powers. He nodded but clarified that the focus should not be on *his* agency: "All I want to do is help people. *Not me*, actually, but Baba ji [the deity Bhairavnath, who "spoke" through Jaipal] wants to help people," he said. Rather than take credit for the "miracles" (*chamatkar*) for which he was known, Jaipal attributed agency to the deity who spoke and acted through him, namely, the god Bhairavnath.[20] Bakkyas like Jaipal are identified with their deities most closely during the performance of oracular healing when their bodies are inhabited by them. However, even after the ritual has been formally completed, the residual effects of embodiment linger in the bodies and persons of bakkyas. A degree of ontic indeterminacy thus envelops all oracles: they are themselves, but because of their vocations, they are also someone/something else. In Uttarkashi, for example, people expressed this contiguity by using the honorific *Baba* or *Baba ji* to refer not only to the deity Bhairavnath but also to Jaipal himself. For instance, one day, as Jaipal was walking down the road, a person standing beside me pointed to him and said, "The deity is coming toward us." I amused myself imagining what it would be like for Jaipal, a god in the world, to do mundane things like buy groceries or drink tea at a roadside stall.

Although Jaipal had built a powerful reputation, like other healers whose life histories I heard, his, too, was rife with struggle. "It's good when you can support your family, but it was not always like this," Jaipal told me one day. Jaipal had lived in the city of Patiala in Punjab for many years. He had returned to his village in Garhwal less than a decade prior to our meeting. Although he was in perfect health now, Jaipal had been gravely ill while he had been away. "I came back to Garhwal because I had to save my life," he said.

In Patiala, Jaipal worked in an electronics appliance shop, and he sent money that he earned to his wife and child who remained in Garhwal. He returned to Garhwal only once or twice a year for a few days at a time. Unlike Ujval, who had struggled to find work outside Uttarakhand, Jaipal had fared significantly better. While his separation from his family had been difficult, he grew accustomed to his modest but comfortable life in Patiala: "I had very little money, but I never went a day without food or shelter," he told me, a fact that he now understood to be the god Bhairavnath's blessing. "He has always taken care of me, even when I didn't know that he was doing so," Jaipal said.

One day, Jaipal was driving his motorcycle on a busy road in central Patiala when a drunk driver plowed into him with his car. Jaipal's vehicle was crushed, as was one of his legs. At the hospital, the doctors told him that his back and left leg had broken in multiple places and needed to be operated on. "I was taken to the hospital on Sangrur Road, but when the doctors tried to fix my leg, it started to swell up. It became so large that the doctors couldn't operate. The doctors said, 'We can't handle this. You'll have to go to another hospital.'"

Jaipal knew then that he was in a hopeless state since the government hospital he had been taken to was one of the best in Patiala. He was then sent to a private hospital for treatment but was told he would have to wait for two or three months to receive treatment, which was also significantly more expensive than the government hospital. During this time, Jaipal was stuck at home, nursing his mangled leg and back with no one to help him and no way of supporting himself and his family. The only person who was able to offer him solace during this trying period was his wife, who was in Garhwal. They spoke to each other on the phone every day.

During one of their phone conversations, Jaipal's wife told him that she had started visiting an oracle who embodied the deity Bhairavnath. "My wife told me that Bhairav Baba had spoken to her and said, 'For now, I [the deity] have only broken his [Jaipal's] back; let's see what more I do; this is just the beginning . . . He doesn't act in accordance with what I command.'" Bhairavnath, via his oracle, had given Jaipal's wife some grains of uncooked rice that were infused with the deity's healing powers. She was told to send the rice to Jaipal and ask him to consume five to ten grains a day. Bhairavnath advised Jaipal's wife that Jaipal should "eat these pearls [rice grains] every day, and then, if he [Jaipal] feels some benefit, he should come home. He should leave his job in Patiala and sit down in my [Bhairavnath's] *mandir* [temple/healing room]." Meanwhile, Jaipal's condition only worsened:

> My [injured] leg and back got worse, and then there was unbearable pain along the whole left side of my body. The doctors couldn't do anything about it; no one could help me. All they said was, "Go to some other hospital, do this test, do that test." How could I go anywhere in my condition?!
>
> One of the doctors examining me said that my leg would have to be amputated in order to save my life. I was even willing to do that. . . .
>
> Meanwhile, I kept eating Baba ji's [Bhairavnath's] *prasad* [lit., "divine grace"; in this case, the sanctified grains of rice that Jaipal had been given]. Every day, I ate a little bit, even though I was sure I would die there [in Patiala], far away from home.
>
> As I lay in bed waiting to die, I started to hear Baba ji's voice within me. He told me that no one could cut my leg; they could not even cut my hair!
>
> My hair started growing very long. My hair used to be long before Baba ji said this, but not like it is today. Before Baba came to me, I had baby locks [*jata*]; people in Punjab even thought I was a *sardar* [a turbaned Sikh]. In '86 [during a period of violent civil unrest in Punjab], there were police checkpoints everywhere, but the police never stopped me—even though I looked like a brigand! [Jaipal meant that even the police were intimidated by him.]

Jaipal attributed his recovery to Bhairavnath's intervention and the grains of rice that the deity had prepared for him. He told me that these grains had been infused with the healing powers of the deity, so by consuming them, Jaipal was incorporating the deity's power—and, by extension, the deity himself—into his own body. Subsequently, the deity started communicating with Jaipal directly, forbidding the doctors to amputate his leg.[21] As the deity's presence entered his body, Jaipal's leg began to heal. Eventually, Jaipal recovered the ability to walk.

Although Jaipal could have gone back to working in the shop in Patiala, he could not forget Baba's advice that he should leave Patiala and make a new life for himself in Baba ji's mandir. Jaipal said, "Baba ji told me, 'If you want to die there [in Patiala], then die, but if you want to live, then come to my mandir. My *bhaktas* [devotees] and *sants* [saints] never experience any lack.' So, I did. I left everything and found Baba ji's *gaddi* [seat]." At the wedding reception where I met Jaipal, as he and I washed down morsels of goat carpaccio with homemade rice wine, he told me:

> "It is by Baba ji's grace that I am able to feed my family.... I am the father of one child. If I do not lead anyone astray but only help the people who come to me, the benefits of my meritorious actions will be enjoyed by my child. For this reason, I have never hurt or manipulated anyone.... Whatever people give me in return is enough.... Even when I am not on my *gaddi* [seat], people still leave money in my *thal* [metal tray]. Saints and devotees never experience any lack, that I know."

Jaipal returned to Garhwal and began his new life as the deity's oracle.[22] After the illness that almost killed him, Jaipal's relationship with the deity deepened.

Although Jaipal has a charismatic personality, being in his presence and in the presence of other oracles was often an unsettling experience. In his company, I became aware of the slipperiness of divine presence, of how deities *and* humans co-occupy the bodies of bakkyas and other ritual mediums, their presence(s) often leaking into each other. I was both fascinated and terrified when the permeability of oracular bodies became clear. One afternoon, as we sat in the courtyard of his house and talked, Jaipal told me: "People from all over come to me seeking help, *while some come to test me.*" He looked at me pointedly as he said this, as if I had doubted him in some way. I assumed I had said or done something to offend him, so I apologized, but he ignored me: "When people like that [people who want to "test" Jaipal and/or his deity] come to me, I start to feel hungry. So, I heat my tongs in the fire and eat them [lick the red-hot tongs]. The more I eat, the fuller my stomach becomes.... I then start to think, if I hit my head with these tongs, then my head will feel better, too. When I do this, sometimes the tongs bend, but I don't feel a thing."

After saying this, he began garbling his words. Yet, he continued to hold my gaze as if he were making perfect sense. I didn't know what to do or what to make of his behavior—and this not-knowing combined with the deity's power—made me nervous. On probing the sense of unease this produced in me, I was forced to confront my own deep-rooted compulsion to demarcate the boundaries of individual personhood. While I had become accustomed to the idea of permeable and dividual personhood in ritualized enactments of divine embodiment, I was surprised at how anxious it made me when it made itself present in the everyday world.

Thankfully, it seemed that, over time, Jaipal/Bhairavnath also got used to *my* presence, my "tests," as he put it. As our relationship deepened, too, his shifts in personality became less frequent and disruptive, enabling us to have long, illuminating conversations about his work.

Ram: The Performer

In the final jagari life history, I describe Ram Lal, with whom I worked closely over many months. In Garhwal, I accompanied him as he performed his duties as a jagar priest, and he visited and stayed with my family in New Delhi. In our travels together, Ram introduced me to his teacher and other jagaris, oracles, and mediums. Like Jaipal, but even more so, Ram Lal's life was reshaped by a disability. Like Ujval, he used intoxicants to cope with trauma, and, also like Ujval, his life and journey were marked by his caste status. Like Jaipal, he blurred the lines between being a storyteller as ritual and everyday practice.

Ram Lal could not remember a time when he had sight. As he told me the first time we met, when he was in his thirties, "God may have taken something from me, but he has given me many other things in return. . . . For me, since I was a child, I've had the habit that whatever I hear, I 'note down' [Eng.]," he said. I asked him what he meant by "note down," and he responded that he committed everything to memory because he could not read or write. In one incident that stayed with me that happened early in our relationship, I learned how Ram's phenomenal memory served him. One day, we met a person who offered to introduce us to an oracle. Ram and I were on our way somewhere else, so I asked this person for his phone number and wrote it down on a piece of paper. Two weeks later, I realized that I had lost the number. I complained to Ram when, without pausing, he promptly recited the ten-digit number—a number he had heard only once, many days prior. While the example of the phone number might seem trivial, it explained how Ram was able to retain and reproduce the long and complex narrative songs (gathas) of multiple local deities with ease. Not only was he able to perform a large number of gathas, but he could also perform other variants of the "same" narrative that he had learned, or "noted down," from other jagaris. In comparison, I felt painfully slow and unable to retain the simplest things without writing them down and going over them with him dozens of times.

Indeed, Ram possessed an encyclopedic knowledge of Pahari performance traditions, and his expertise had made him a widely respected jagar performer at a young age. Ram had not been born into a family of jagaris. His father was a carpenter, he told me. Yet Ram said he had been born with a love for performing jagar:

> I have been interested in jagar since I was very young. When I was a child, my parents would sponsor jagars themselves. I have been playing *daur-thali* [percussion instruments used by jagar performers] since I was two and a half.... This is an old thing for me. Today, I think, so what if I have an instrument of ten or fifteen thousand [rupees]? I must keep my *daur-thali*; it represents the very beginning of my art [*kala*]....
>
> My guru is Dhanvir ji.... I learned everything I know from him. He used to come to our place to perform jagar, and I used to sit down beside him. Back then, I couldn't play the *daur-thali* because I was too young; I couldn't match his melody with my undeveloped [*totali*] voice, so I would just listen to him and carefully "note" [Eng.] everything he did. And today, even though I am asked to perform in *daur-thali* "programs" [Eng.] all over Garhwal, I can't say I'm a "success" [Eng.] because a guru [teacher] is a guru, right?

Although Ram had started out as a jagari without many of the advantages of hereditary performers, he established a strong reputation for himself and cultivated a wide network of clients. His fellow jagaris and clients spoke highly of his knowledge and skill, and over time, I came to understand why. He not only performed jagars in his own village and neighboring areas but also in more distant places, which was unusual for most jagaris, who tended not to be as ambulatory as Ram.

Ram was from a small, mixed-caste village consisting of a few dozen households in a high-altitude area of western Garhwal. Ram's village was located close to an important regional temple. Since the late nineties, the growing popularity of this pilgrimage destination has provided an economic boost to villages in its vicinity. The flowering of this temple's economy was contemporaneous with Uttarakhand's achievement of statehood, which happened shortly after the (neo)liberalization of the Indian economy in the 1990s. In Ram's village, caste-privileged families owned the largest share of agricultural lands and were socioeconomically significantly better off than their Dalit counterparts. Dalits in Ram's village provided agricultural labor to wealthy landowners in their own village as well as in neighboring areas; they also worked in low-wage professions, including as tailors, carpenters, bricklayers, and barbers. Because demand for seasonal agricultural labor waxed and waned throughout the year, there were periods when work was scarce, and people were forced to live off meager savings or borrow money from local moneylenders. In addition to engaging in agricultural work, some in Ram's village also worked in restaurants, shops, and other businesses that catered to temple visitors. However, the economic effects of the burgeoning temple economy were highly stratified; while the changing landscape had helped more socially and economically privileged Brahmins and Rajputs, few benefits "trickled down" to Dalits.

As I got to know Ram, I realized that even though Ram and Ujval had arrived at their vocations in different ways, there exist remarkable parallels in their stories of struggle. For instance, echoing what Ujval said about his own youth, Ram also lamented how he had been a burden to his family in his early years. Because of his visual impairment, he required more care and attention than his other siblings. While his siblings went to the village school, there was no school for blind children close to his village, so, for the most part, he was deprived of formal schooling.

When he was still a young boy, he started visiting the jagari Dhanvir ji, who lived in a neighboring village. Describing himself as highly driven even then, Ram sought out Dhanvir ji to learn music. Ram learned quickly. At home, he would practice the songs he learned from his teacher using whatever musical instruments he could make or find—such as "a steel plate and spoon as percussion instruments"—he told me, laughing. Immediately recognizing the boy's extraordinary talent as a singer and musician, Dhanvir ji began asking Ram to assist him in his work.

Even though his parents worked hard, his family was very poor, he said, so they were anxious for their children to contribute to the household. His parents did not take Ram's interest in music and performing jagar seriously. "They thought I was wasting my time learning about drumming and such things because 'How can a blind person travel to faraway places to do jagar?' they said." Instead, his parents and relatives told him to pursue other work, such as helping in a relative's roadside shop, since Ram was skilled in basic arithmetic and accounts despite not being formally educated. He tried this for a while as a teenager but soon tired of it and left his job. Like Ujval, Ram's relationship with his family began souring in his teenage years, and after a heated argument with an older relative, Ram left home. By leaving home, Ram wanted to show his family that he could take care of himself: "I wanted to show them that I could go anywhere I wanted, so I could work as a jagari, too," Ram said.

After breaking with his family and leaving home, Ram traveled to Haridwar and Rishikesh, two busy towns famous for being destinations of religious tourism in the Himalayan foothills. Living in these places was "like living in a different world," he said, even though he was still in Uttarakhand. But while the first few months away from his native village were enjoyable, because Ram was unemployed, things soon became difficult. He struggled to find shelter and lived where he could "on the pavement or in the courtyards of various holy persons' [sadhu-sant] complexes."

Despite the challenges he faced, Ram's pride kept him from going back home even though he was poor and unhoused. Ram's descriptions of life in Haridwar and Rishikesh shared many similarities with Ujval's account of being lost and destitute in Moradabad. For instance, during this time, Ram confessed that he engaged in various kinds of "intoxication" (*nasha*), as he referred to it. I was surprised to hear this, as I had never seen Ram drink alcohol, smoke marijuana, or even a bidi or cigarette in all our time together—whereas Ujval was still quite fond of drinking and smoking. For Ram, substance use was a way of coping with the stresses of being on his own; after the novelty of being away from home had worn off, the hard realities of being unemployed, poor, and unhoused set in.

It was difficult to get a precise hold of what Ram's life was like during this time. He rarely talked about this period, and when I asked him about it directly, he changed the subject or talked about it in the most general terms. "It was difficult but also illuminating," he said vaguely. In certain rare moments, however, when he offered more details, his tone and affect suggested that this period was charged with a sense of shame. Even though we were not that far apart in age, our relationship was like teacher and student; he was my friend but also my guide. In light of this hierarchy, it was uncomfortable for him to talk about what he had experienced. Because of his reticence, I stopped asking him about these experiences. They only came up obliquely, such as when we talked about our romantic histories or during liminal moments like when we were trying to fall asleep under the stars after a late-night ritual.

The picture that emerged from Ram's recollections of being adrift in Rishikesh and Haridwar was that his emotional and physical state began to deteriorate rapidly during this period. So, in search of solace and healing, Ram started undertaking arduous "pilgrimages" (*jat*) to "places of realization" (*siddha pith*) across Uttarakhand. As he put it, "In each of these places, I began to feel the highest god [*parameshvar*] more and more strongly. I discovered that he is the root [*mul*] of all the deities, who are different forms [*rup*] of his being. He is everywhere . . . in every living being, even though we cannot see him. People call him *parmeshvar*, Brahman, Mahadev, but these are just names; ultimately, he has no name [*nam*] and no form [*rup*]." Realizing this "truth" (*sachhai*), Ram began to perceive divinity in every "river, tree, and stone." He added: "When I discovered this, my relationship with the gods changed. . . . They became friendly with me." During this time, he said, he found the sense of fulfillment and security he was seeking "because no living or nonliving thing can harm you if you are under the protection of the highest god; everything is this world moves because of him."

As Ram's suffering gave way to a sense of clarity and calm, he decided to return to his village, where his family welcomed him back and arranged for him to be married. Ram also resumed his apprenticeship under Dhanvir ji, not only accompanying his teacher when he performed jagar but also performing jagar on his own. Because of his musicianship and abilities as a storyteller, Ram quickly developed a large client base. His rise was meteoric, for "within two years of returning [home], I was asked to perform at a radio station in Haridwar in a proper studio," he told me with pride. Achievements such as these cemented his reputation as a skilled performer and marked the culmination of his journey from being Dhanvir ji's apprentice to being a respected jagari in his own right.

Ram was an extraordinary ritual performer with a clear and resonant singing voice and remarkable skill as a drummer. He could sustain ritual action and audience attention in ways I had not seen before. On one occasion, Ram described the ritual efficacy of drumming in the following way: "The sound of the drum causes trembling [kampan] in the body [sharir]." By "trembling," Ram was referring to how deities become present in/on the body of a human medium during ritual performances involving divine embodiment. When a deity descends upon their medium, the medium begins to display signs of "possession," which include trembling/shivering (kampan), swaying, or disordered speech.

A moment later, Ram clarified: "The drum actually causes trembling in the heart [hriday]." I was curious what he meant by "heart," assuming that Ram was not describing the heart merely as a physiological organ of the body. He answered: "All the goddesses [devi] reside in the hriday." Ram added that "goddesses" were our "life force" (pran), that is, the subtle energy that pervades and animates our entire psychophysical being, including our breath, senses, emotions, intellect, and physical body. In other words, Ram understood the heart as the powerful, energetic (that is, physiological, emotional, *and* spiritual) center of a person's being.[23] In contrast to the body (sharir), which evokes fixed or congealed matter, hriday suggests a sense of fluidity, depth, and spaciousness; it refers to an open, "lively interior," to borrow Yohanan Grinshpon's phrase.[24] Ram continued describing how the rhythms of the jagari's drum—its vibratory "speech" (bol), as he put it—communicated with the deepest, most expansive and vibrant aspect of our being. The drums brought the hidden depths where "the goddesses reside" to the surface, thereby opening and enlivening the body. According to this description, the medium's "trembling" marked a moment of permeability when not only deity and human but also surface and depth came together.

However, Ram repeatedly stressed that the ritual power of drumming could not be reduced to a mechanical or predictable process: "The drums cannot force the deities to dance; we can only invite [nyaute] them." As such, the rhythms (chal) of the drum not only communicated with the "heart" of the medium but also with the deity. So, while the expertise of the drummer mattered, the desire and agency of the deity to appear mattered more, and it exceeded human control. As some ritual performers with whom I worked were fond of saying: "The deities are like the wind (hava); they come and go as they please." This was precisely why ritual specialists like Ram were needed—because making deities present through ritual drumming and other means was a deliberate, effortful, and collaborative process. Ram said that if drummer and deity enjoyed "good relations" (sambandh), they were able to "understand" one another.

While Ram had previously used the word *bol*, or "speech," to refer to the drum's rhythms, here he employed the term *chal*, which connotes a "way of moving."[25] I noticed that Ram was using the word *chal* to refer to two distinct yet related concepts: one, the physical "movements" of dancing deities, and second, the rhythms of the drum, that is, the temporal ordering or patterned "movement" of individualized drum strokes. With respect to chal's first meaning, Ram said jagaris could recognize an embodied deity merely by their chal, that is, how they moved, walked, and the rhythm of their footfall, before they spoke or identified themselves. Even though he could not see the deities, he could identify them through their distinctive dance. With respect to chal's second meaning, Ram said there were different rhythm patterns to welcome or invite the deities into the ritual and others to send them away; some rhythms energized or sped up the deities' "dance" (*nach*), while others slowed or calmed their movements. If, for some reason, the drummer wanted to change how the deity was "dancing"—maybe the deity was becoming too "hot" and needed to be "cooled" down—the drummer could do this by varying their own rhythmic chal. "Gurus and deities are always communicating with each other. If the deities want to dance a certain way, we [gurus] cater to them. This is why they follow us," he said, suggesting a symbiotic relationship. Manipulating this mysterious articulation was key to a drummer's expertise. Ram's remarks made clear that jagaris' rhythmically mediated attunement to the desires, moods, and behaviors of embodied deities was a form of ritual artistry or skill that needed to be nurtured over decades.

This delicate collaboration between deity and drummer also had the potential to "break down," as Ram put it. Sometimes, for example, during rituals of divine embodiment, deities might descend not only upon designated mediums and random audience members but also drummers. While I never witnessed this happen to Ram, I did see it occur with another drummer who regularly accompanied him. This second jagari played on a metallic, cymbal-like percussion instrument called the *thali* (lit., "plate"), while Ram played the *daur*, a double-headed drum. Whenever a deity unexpectedly "came over" the second jagari, he would stop drumming, his eyes would roll back, and he would start shaking and exclaiming, "Command me (*adesh*)," indicating that he was under the influence of a deity. Ram saw these incidents as moments of ritual failure, as jagar priests must always "remain composed," he said, to effectively mediate relations between deities and ritual participants. When a jagari lost awareness and control of himself, he could not continue drumming, and the ritual had to stop. Because this was an undesirable kind of "possession," Ram referred to it using the English-language word *attack*. "As you know," he said, "when a person dies, death enters the person through their eyes. Similarly, when a god 'attacks' [Eng.] a jagari, he does so though their eyes." Ram asserted that eyes served as portals or gateways (*dvar*) for deities and other nonhumans to enter and exit the human-social world.

Ram, the Seeker, and Some Ethnographic Truths and Fictions

That Ram's success as a jagari came despite his disability caused some ripples and ambivalence in his community. In other words, as a person of so-called low-caste standing with the additional "burden" of his disability, his success as a jagari was *out of place*: it was unexpected and perhaps even improper. One of Ram's Dalit neighbors told me that many people were jealous of his success: "It's not only upper-caste people who feel this way. Members of our own community get angry with him." Ram's strong personality only made these feelings more fraught. I learned that many in Ram's community described him as argumentative, stubborn, and difficult. Ram had told me that when he was younger, people tried to push him around. "Because I am blind, they think I am weak," he explained. I imagined how Ram must have taught himself to stand up for himself in a way that others read as argumentative.

My friendship with Ram grew. He quickly became a confidante and teacher, answering my never-ending questions with patience and care. Ram had questions for me, too; he was curious about my life in New Delhi and the United States, so I invited him to stay with me in my apartment in Delhi. Unlike other people I had met from Uttarakhand, who had generally negative things to say about big cities like Delhi—overwhelming with noise, pollution, and traffic—in

Delhi, too, Ram was fiercely independent. He enjoyed exploring the city using the new metro system. Ram said he wanted an "unlimited" metro pass of his own; in addition to its obvious utility, it carried a special romance for him. The freedom and power of limitless travel that the pass represented for him was exciting. He described the metro pass as a "passport" that could allow him to travel anywhere, including outside the country. Pass in hand, Ram adeptly navigated the chaotic cityscape with ease. In some ways, I felt we had exchanged roles: now he was the relentlessly curious ethnographer, asking me questions and "noting down" everything we experienced.

In Delhi, Ram was *like* an ethnographer, but after we returned to Garhwal, he became one. Since Ram was often present during my interviews, he became familiar with my style and approach. Every now and then, Ram would chime in with questions of his own, drawing my attention to things I had overlooked. Before I knew it, we had become cointerviewers. If we were talking to someone and they said something interesting, Ram would turn to me and say, "Take out your recorder, this is important." As I took out my recorder, Ram would take over the questioning. Because Ram was asking questions from a position of knowledge and expertise, whereas I was interviewing people from a place of relative ignorance, Ram asked our interviewees questions that would never have occurred to me. His questions opened lines of intellectual inquiry that were of immeasurable benefit to me, so I was happy to let him take the lead.

In describing our research endeavor, I would tell interviewees that "we are doing research [*shodh*] about Uttarakhand's culture and history [*sanskriti aur itihas*]," or "we are doing research about local gods and goddesses and their worship in jagar." However, when Ram answered this question, he departed from my usual response by substituting the Indian-language term *shodh* for the English-language word *discovery*. So, Ram would say something like, "We are doing 'discovery' [Eng.] about Uttarakhand's gods and goddesses." I thought his use of the word *discovery* was an elegant slippage. it *Discovery* seemed like a better word than my formal and arcane *shodh*.

However, over time, Ram's interview style began departing more and more from mine. When he took charge, he often failed or forgot to ask for verbal consent before turning on the voice recorder, and instead, began interviewing people in the tone and affect of a Hindi-language television news reporter, holding my voice recorder in front of the interviewee like a reporter's microphone. Some recoiled from the sudden shift in affect while others warmed to it, flattered to be taken seriously. I didn't know what to make of this, but I let it go on because Ram seemed to enjoy the process and his newfound role in my project.

One day, Ram's introductory statement, "We are doing 'discovery' [Eng.] and interested in local deities," glided into him introducing us as reporters from "the Discovery Channel." All our interlocutors were familiar with the TV channel, which has been present in India since the 1990s, airing science and nature documentaries in multiple Indian languages. The fact that I often carried a small video camera with me did capture my desire to one day make a documentary film about the ritual practices we were exploring. If Ram was particularly interested or inspired by something someone had said, he would tell me to turn on the video camera. I had limited memory storage, so I had to either record over prior recordings or pretend that the camera was on. Ram would then hold my audio recorder directly in front of the interviewee, turn to the camera, and say, in the bright affect of a TV journalist: "Greetings, ladies and gentlemen, I am Ram Lal, and with me is 'cameraman' [Eng.] Amitabh Singh."

I now also had a stage name: Aftab was now Amitabh, a name that was easier for people in Uttarakhand to recognize and pronounce and was instantly stripped of its Persian/Urdu origins to be more Hindi/Hinduized for our "audience." I was also now Ram's "cameraman," rather than his cointerviewer. I felt a flood of emotions. I was in awe of Ram and did not want to intervene or interrupt his flow. I rationalized his flights of fancy as harmless. He is a natural storyteller, after all, and that's not something you can turn on and off, I reminded myself. As a jagari, Ram brought the storyworlds of the deities to life, so why should his everyday reality be less imaginative, poetic, or performative? Another part of me also found it amusing to be demoted from ethnographer to cameraman. Ram's gesture of flipping the usual power hierarchy between "researcher" and "research assistant" tickled me, given critiques of anthropology's coloniality.[26] At the same time, I was growing a little concerned. Even though Ram was asking excellent questions that elicited illuminating responses, he would paraphrase and elaborate on our interviewees' responses for the benefit of the camera. Often, Ram's gloss was more interesting than what our interviewees had offered, but at the same time, I was uncomfortable with the fact that our interviews were becoming a one-person show. As Ram seemed to grow more confident in this mode, I decided to intervene. Whenever we met with someone I wanted to speak with in a more focused and intimate way, I told Ram I would conduct the interview. Ram, I was relieved to learn, was happy to take a backseat when asked.

But performances have a life of their own. One day, Ram and I were planning to attend what we thought was a religious ceremony at a nearby temple. However, on arriving at the temple, we realized that the event was actually a large political rally organized by a right-wing Hindu nationalist group. The chief guest at the event was a well-known local politician who had been invited to speak, and hundreds of people had gathered to see him. As dignitaries made speeches and garlanded each other, and devotional songs blared over loudspeakers, Ram decided it would be a good idea to interview people at the event. With his trusted cameraperson at his side, Ram started interviewing members of the audience, asking penetrating questions about Hindutva—that is, the political ideology of contemporary Hindu nationalists—and how Hindutva related to local Hindu beliefs and practices.

Ram then decided to interview the political dignitaries themselves, who were seated in and around the makeshift dais that had been erected for the event. Ram pushed through the crowd to gain access to the chief guest. As Ram and I approached the dais, a couple of burly, tough-looking men in crisp white kurtas stopped us in our tracks.

"Let us through! We'd like to speak with the chief guest," Ram Lal told the men, who I assumed were part of the politician's security detail. The men did not relent, so Ram protested: "Why are you stopping us? We are from the Discovery Channel and have a few questions for him. I am Ram Lal, and this is my cameraman, Amitabh Singh."

The men didn't know how to respond, so they let us move ahead. But before we reached the politician, a more senior and even more menacing-looking member of the politician's contingent intercepted us. He was also dressed pristinely in white, like the men before him and the politician himself, but in every other way, he looked like a goon.

"Who are you?" he asked Ram. His tone was intimidating. Threatening.

Ram repeated his Discovery Channel spiel. The goon was unimpressed. A small group of other fierce-looking members of the politician's contingent surrounded us. One of them shouted out: "If you're from Discovery Channel, where are your papers [credentials]? Show us your papers!"

Instead of de-escalating, Ram escalated the situation: "How dare you question us like this!" Ram retorted, visibly angry. "But fine, why not. We'll show them to you." Then, turning to me, Ram said, "Show them our papers."

My heart sank. I didn't know what to do—I didn't have any press credentials or any affiliation with the Discovery Channel. Not knowing what to do, I rummaged around in my backpack, pretending to look for the papers. The only official identification I had was my Indian passport, so I pulled it out and showed it to our interrogators.

"What's this?" asked the head goon. I apologized and said that I had left our "papers" behind in our guest house. I made a half-hearted statement about going back to get them.

"Come on, let's go," I said to Ram under my breath, but he continued arguing with the politician's security detail. Things were getting more heated by the minute. "Who do you think you are, treating people like this? We are simply doing our work. We're not here to cause trouble," Ram yelled as more people gathered around us.

I was afraid for myself and for Ram, who was creating a commotion in the courtyard of a temple surrounded by upper-caste people and Hindu nationalists in a climate in which egregious forms of violence against Dalit people had been committed. One of the security men brushed Ram aside, grabbed my backpack, and started rifling through my things. The head security guard took my video camera from me and looked at it suspiciously. "What have you recorded? Show me."

I knew Ram and I had to get away, so I held him by the arm and pulled him away, gesturing to the guards that I would be right back. Before they could stop us, Ram and I started weaving through the crowd, trying to find our way back to the main road. "Hey, come back!" the goons yelled, and I could hear them call in reinforcements to chase us down. Somehow, Ram and I managed to get through the crowd and make it to the road; we continued running until we were out of breath.

After making our escape, Ram and I didn't exchange words for some time. Finally, Ram broke the silence and said, "Those guys were assholes. We should have told them off for their behavior!" In response, I did something I regretted. It was not so much what I said but how I said it: for the first time in our relationship, I raised my voice and vented the anger and irritation I was feeling. I demanded to know why it was necessary to talk about the Discovery Channel in the first place: "All of this was totally unnecessary. There was no need to interview that politician—none of this has anything to do with our work. This was a totally pointless and foolish exercise.... Why were you trying to pick a fight with those goons when they could have done anything to us?" I said, my voice raised.

As I was saying this, I was surprised by how worked up I was. Looking back at this moment, I think I was ashamed of how we had run from the scene. Or rather, how *I* had run. Ram had been willing to fight and stand up for himself while I had acted like a coward. Instead of dealing with my shame, I lashed out at him. Ram was taken aback by my harsh rebuke, as I had always been respectful toward him. My outburst had called into question the very foundation of our relationship—the sacred relationship between teacher and student. I felt terrible. I could sense how hurt and betrayed he felt. I tried to apologize, but Ram's face was impassive. We walked in silence, and I hoped that we could get over this so things could go back to how they had been. Over the next few days, we resumed our work but didn't talk about what had happened at the rally. Ram stopped taking the lead in interviews even though I encouraged him a few times. My outburst seemed to have fractured the delicate rapport we had established.

A week or two later, while Ram and I were traveling by bus, a fellow passenger who was clearly inebriated started talking to me, asking me what I was doing in Uttarakhand. Ram answered that we were doing "discovery" about jagar and local deities. The drunk passenger snorted, muttered something rude under his breath, and turned away. After a few minutes, he turned to me again, saying loudly, so that others on the bus could hear: "Why don't you look into something useful instead, why all this superstitious stuff? Do you know the names of the plants and trees you see?" he asked pointing outside our window. "Do you know about the different crops that grow on this land? Do you know how much effort and time it takes to grow these things? If not, then what do you know?! If we [farmers] didn't grow this food, the whole country would starve!"

People were turning their heads to look at us. I felt embarrassed but also acknowledged that his points were valid. I didn't know as much as I would like about agricultural practices in the region. I tried to calm him down: "Yes, you are right, there is a lot to learn. I would like to know these things."

He cut me off. "How can you learn anything if all you do is run around from one temple to the next? How can anyone learn anything about the world like that?"

Ram interjected, trying to defend me: "It's alright, forgive us, please leave us alone. What do you want from us? We're just trying to do our job."

"What do you mean you're just doing your job?!" the person responded. "I could drink your job up in a cup of mild tea [that is, your job has no value/substance]!"

Ram and the other passenger exchanged heated words for some time until the passenger's stop arrived and he stumbled off the bus. I was relieved that the unpleasantness was finally over. I didn't know how Ram felt about it until the next day when, during another conversation, Ram brought up the incident: "If somebody were insulting a politician or someone important, everyone on the bus would have said something. If somebody were insulting a Thakur or a pandit [Brahmin], everyone would have shouted him down. But because we speak the truth [*sachai*], no one came to our defense."

I realized that Ram was referring not just to our interaction with the belligerent drunk on the bus but also to our run-in with the politician's goons. Even though he did not name me directly, I felt implicated. After all, I had also criticized him for saying that we were working for the Discovery Channel, and my censure of him mapped uncomfortably onto centuries of caste-based oppression and silencing, of me, a higher-caste person chastising a lower-caste person like Ram.

Ram continued, his voice quivering with emotion:

> Because, as jagaris, we speak the truth, no one can harm us. But when someone searches for truth, some barrier 'automatically' [Eng.] presents itself, without fail. I have many relatives, but none of them ever ask us, "What kind of 'discovery' [Eng.] are you doing? What benefit will come of your work?" No one asks this. Instead, everyone questions the value of the work. They ask: "What does 'discovery' even mean?" People remember God when something bad happens, and then they call us [jagaris], but at other times they forget.... They [upper-caste people] often say things like, "I will drink your job in a cup of mild tea," but they can't do anything to us because we speak the truth.

I knew Ram well enough to know that he only rarely aired grievances about casteism and what it meant to be a jagari (and even more rarely, what it meant to have a disability). It was striking to me that he distinguished between the everyday violence of caste-based oppression and insults that he had to survive and a deeper commitment to what he described as a search for "truth" or "speaking the truth." This distinction also made me reflect anew on how Ram had dramatized our research endeavor as a television show. For Ram, "speaking truth" (*sachai bolana*) and "adhering to the truth" (*satya nibhana*) had broader significance. They were not merely questions of speech and reality in a narrow sense; they suggested a way of seeing and relating to the world that was attuned to the hidden supernatural forces that govern people's lives.

Realizing and acting upon these forces set religious specialists such as Ram apart from ordinary people. As someone who spoke and adhered to truth, a sense of righteousness empowered Ram; it made him fearless, enabling him to assert himself not only as a jagari in the ritual sphere but also in his everyday life, giving him a sense of flexibility and malleability. He could assert a small (mis)truth about us being part of the "Discovery Channel" because there was an underlying, deeper truth in which he believed: that we were in search of the gods.

6

Playing in the Rain

Scenes from a Himalayan Pilgrimage

> For the place-maker's main objective is to speak the past into being, to summon it with words and give it dramatic form, to *produce* experience by forging ancestral worlds in which others can participate and readily lose themselves. To this engrossing end . . . the place-maker often speaks as a witness on the scene, describing ancestral events "as they are occurring" and creating in the process a vivid sense that what happened long ago—right here, on this very spot—could be happening *now*.
> —Keith Basso, *Wisdom Sits in Places: Landscape and Language Among the Western Apache*

> On pilgrimage to the same site . . . different persons and groups judge each other keenly, often adversely, because there is heightened awareness of deviations in practices and ideologies.
> —Bonnie Wheeler, "Models of Pilgrimage: From Communitas to Confluence"

The Inner Lives of Gods

Every year, during the monsoon season, deities from across the region of Kumaon, Uttarakhand, travel back to their natal home, a temple site called Jhakar Saim. The god who resides in this temple, Saim Devata, is identified as the maternal uncle of many of the region's deities, including Golu Devata (whom we encountered in chapter 4). Deities are said to have spent their happy childhood years playing together in their uncle's courtyard.

Once a year, Saim Devata's divine nephews—the key actors in this pilgrimage—are led back to Jhakar Saim by their worshipers and by *jagar* priests, or gurus, who play the drums, sing, and dance with deities in this journey of celebration and renewal. While some devotees accompany the gods to and from Jhakar Saim, others eagerly await their return to their home villages. The deities travel back to Jhakar Saim to show respect to their uncle and relive their joyful childhoods. Renewed and energized, divinities then transfer their newfound vitality to their devotees. Bonnie Wheeler writes: "While pilgrimage is a journey to and through a sacred space, it is usually also a journey *back* or *away* from that space. Pilgrims who recuperate from raw contact with the sacred and return home inevitably carry some new quality—moral, spiritual, or even material—as part of the pilgrimage memory."[1]

Because the pilgrimage is a ritual of renewal, it is fitting that it occurs during the rainy season, a time of not only dissolution but also rebirth. After the hot and dry summer months, the monsoon rains bring new life to the Himalayas. Heavy, dark clouds roll through towns and villages; they enter and exit one's home without warning or invitation. The monsoons are also a time of violent catharsis, with the increasing occurrence of landslides and flash floods exacerbated by extractive development projects. Mountainsides crumble, rivers overflow their banks, and roads, bridges, and other built structures are swept away. It rains for days on end as the hard exteriorities of the world liquefy.

In Jhakar Saim temple, an ancient tree connects *patal lok*, the subterranean realm of disorder and vitality, to *nar lok*, the familiar, terrestrial world of duality and differentiation, name and form. "The gods are like the many fruits of a single tree," I was told by one interlocutor, as "they began their lives in Jhakar Saim, but then go on to settle [*basana*] in other places, to work in their chosen professions [*karobar*]." My interlocutor meant that once Saim Devata's nephews grew up and left their childhood home, they fanned out across Kumaon, taking responsibility for the sustenance, health, and protection of the region's worshipers through different occupational roles. Yet, even deities need some "vacation time" and the chance to reconnect with one another. Once a year, they are given a much-needed respite from their adult responsibilities—an opportunity for joyful play [*khel*]: "When the deities travel back to their uncle's courtyard [*angan*], they remember their happy childhoods and begin to dance [*nach*]," my interlocutor added. Through "dance," deities express joy at returning to see their maternal uncle as well as sadness about the ultimate irretrievability of their happy, carefree pasts.

During the rainy season, one late July, I accompanied a party of pilgrims from the village of Bani to Jhakar Saim. I had been living in Bani, a village in Almora District, for a few months with the family of my friend and close interlocutor Deepak Bisht (see chapter 4). During this process, I met several gurus, mediums, and devotees who taught me about this pilgrimage. I was told by residents that, until the mid-1990s, it used to take many days to complete the pilgrimage journey from Bani to Jhakar Saim. Today, however, because of extractive developmental efforts, including building new roads and bridges, Jhakar Saim was more easily accessible to pilgrims who were able to complete the pilgrimage in a day.

The pilgrimage culminated around a ritual fire (*dhuni*) in Jhakar Saim's temple courtyard. Four gurus from Bani played their drums, sang, and led human and divine pilgrims from Bani to the temple. In the temple courtyard, embodied deities danced around the ritual fire and blessed their worshipers. The deities blessed some young women who had accompanied them from Bani by lobbing pieces of fruit into their *dupattas* and sari ends, which they held open like baskets. In the Jhakar Saim temple courtyard, each group of deities and devotees had a certain amount of time around the fire while the next group watched and waited their turn. On one occasion, I saw a deity from another village being dragged away from the fire by his minders. The deity did not want to stop dancing and make way for the next contingent of deities; his gurus chased him around the fire to catch him and compel him to leave, but he resisted their efforts. They finally caught up with him, and I watched as the anguished deity was led away from the fire.

When I asked one of my companions what we were witnessing, he said that the deity, Harjyu, was unhappy because he did not want to leave the temple and go back to his hard life managing the everyday affairs of his worshipers. "Deities, too, need a break from time to time," he said. Watching this somewhat comical but also poignant scene unfold, I was struck by the disjuncture between the dominant image of Harjyu—as a fearsome, commanding figure—and his image now—like a small child being dragged from the playground.

Soon after Harjyu was dragged away, it started raining heavily. Everyone in the temple courtyard scrambled to take cover. I found shelter under the awning of a nearby guest house beside a smelly diesel generator that was roaring because the rainstorm had caused a power outage. From my vantage point, I could see the deserted temple courtyard clearly. When I looked toward the firepit, I saw that Harjyu's medium—a middle-aged man of around sixty with chiseled features and a slender yet powerful physique—had returned. He was alone by the smoldering fire, seated on his haunches and gazing into the distance with a forlorn expression. As he sat there, the medium cradled his head in his arms and started shivering in a way that suggested the presence of a deity in/on his body. But as I looked more closely through the sheets of falling rain, I realized that he was not only trembling but also sobbing, wiping tears from his eyes.

The deity sat there without anyone attending to him or even aware of his presence. After some time, however, a person from his village party came looking for him. He approached the deity warily, standing beside him but not uttering a word. This time, the person did not try to drag Harjyu from the fire. Instead, he lit two cigarettes, handing one to the deity and taking the other for himself. The deity sat trembling, crying, and smoking in the empty courtyard. Even though I had no idea why he was crying, I felt a desire to console him. Yet, I knew approaching a deity without a guru present could be dangerous, as embodied deities can often act in volatile and unpredictable ways.

When the rain stopped, pilgrims started streaming back into the courtyard, and my view of the firepit was blocked. When I did see it again, Harjyu and his companion were gone.

Afterward, reflecting on this scene in the deserted temple courtyard, I was left with a sense of bewilderment. Harjyu's behavior felt like a performance but, without the usual ceremonial fanfare, audience, or throngs of human worshipers and onlookers, what did this performance signify? Who was it for, and what was it supposed to achieve? What did it mean for me to be watching the deity during this intensely private moment? And finally, why was he crying? The moment revealed to me the inadequacy of scholarly terms like *performance*, *ritual*, and *possession*, which do not capture the complex, subtle, and often unexpected textures of divine presence in the world. Such terms fail to convey the humanity, the simple everydayness, of the scene I witnessed: a deity sitting alone, smoking, and crying in the rain.

Mixing and Flowing

Mina ji, the aunt of one of my close friends in Bani, said that the pilgrimage to Jhakar Saim was a time of "mixing" or "mingling" (*mishran*).[2] The word *mishran* has connotations of sweetness and gentility; it captures how human and divine modes of existence come poignantly together during rituals like pilgrimages. *Mishran* also highlights other integrative aspects of the Jhakar Saim pilgrimage, which weave together disparate people, places, and practices in a historically meaningful and moving expression of regional belonging. Mina ji described the pilgrimage as providing people from across Kumaon an occasion to meet and celebrate together. Deities also had a chance to meet and mingle during the pilgrimage, I was told. At certain times during the pilgrimage, separate and distinct human embodiments of a single deity—such as Harjyu-s, Gangnath-s, and Golu Devata-s from different villages—came face to face. The effect was like being in a hall of mirrors; I repeatedly witnessed possessed mediums of the "same" deity encounter each other in fleeing moments of (self-) recognition.

The pilgrimage was also important for devotees to mingle. For instance, Mina ji was excited that her recently married daughter, who now resided in a distant town, would be returning to her natal village, Bani, to perform the pilgrimage. Jhakar Sem was also personally meaningful to Mina ji in another way. She had first met her own husband during the pilgrimage many years ago. "The festive atmosphere [*mahaul*] of the trip allows boys and girls to spend time with each other," she explained. "Those who attend college meet and talk there [at school], but those who don't have to make the best of such occasions [that is, public festivals]," Mina ji said with a mischievous laugh. She explained that the carnivalesque atmosphere of the pilgrimage allowed for interactions between members of the opposite sex to be looser and less restrictive than in everyday life. Also, jagar priests from different parts of Kumaon could perform together in spontaneous acts of *jugalbandi*, or musical dialogue. These dialogues often had a competitive edge to them, as some gurus, through virtuosic displays of musicianship, succeeded in luring their colleagues' deities away from them.

The pilgrimage also brought together different kinds of religious sites, both those that were highly localized and those of transregional importance. Pilgrims' (and deities') movements through these spaces established a continuity between them; by virtue of being on the pilgrimage route, each was considered important in its own right. For my interlocutors in Bani, performing ritual worship in a humble goddess shrine in their village was as integral to the pilgrimage as visiting Golu Devata's grand and ancient temple in Chitai, for instance.

In bringing these different orders of place into meaningful relation, the pilgrimage gave rise to its own profoundly felt, historically deep, geographically circumscribed, and religiously significant sense of region, or *kshetra*.[3] The Indian-language word *kshetra* has many meanings. For example, Kumaon and Garhwal are generally identified as the two large kshetras that constitute the state of Uttarakhand. In addition to possessing historical and cultural significance for Pahari people, these designations have important political and bureaucratic ramifications for the modern state of Uttarakhand. The seven districts of Garhwal and six of Kumaon constitute two separate administrative and revenue divisions of the state,[4] possessing their own governmental organizations.[5] However, the sense of region or kshetra that emerges from the pilgrimage—constituted by a set of "connected places" within approximately a hundred kilometers of each other[6]—does not conform to any fixed, official, or bureaucratic conception of "region." Furthermore, the experience of kshetra that the pilgrimage to Jhakar Saim generates bears no relation to popular administrative and cultural understandings of Kumaon and Garhwal as administratively, linguistically, culturally, and historically distinct. It is, therefore, important to disentangle the idea of kshetra as a lived and highly localized experience of place from modern political notions of districts and states. The kshetra produced by the bodily movements of non/human pilgrims trace the geographical contours of a mythologically/historically significant—but not cartographically represented—"region."

During the journey to Jhakar Saim, pilgrims' movements within/between sites of religious significance also revealed the dynamic and emergent properties of "place" itself. The pilgrimage shows that "the character of a place," such as a village, temple, or region, "is not somehow a product only of what goes on within it but results too from the juxtaposition and intermixing there of flows, relations, connections from 'beyond.'"[7] The places that pilgrims move within/between during the pilgrimage to Jhakar Saim are not only "open to the outside,"[8] but they are also "internally multiple."[9] "Reconceptualizing place in this way," Doreen Massey writes, "puts on the agenda a different set of political questions. There can be no assumption of pre-given coherence, or of community or collective identity. Rather *the throwntogetherness of place demands negotiation.*"[10]

Similarly, Karen Pechilis sees pilgrimage as a "form of negotiation between the unfamiliar and familiar, between journey and non-journey."[11] Echoing Pechilis, Bonnie Wheeler writes that "pilgrimage is a ritual activity marked simultaneously by *communitas* and by competition. Pilgrimage is not a monolithic institution; it shifts meanings as often as it shifts ritual centers."[12] Studies of pilgrimage should thus account for both the articulations and fissures that characterize pilgrimage.

Building on the work of Massey, Pechilis, and Wheeler, this chapter foregrounds the negotiations and tensions inherent in pilgrimage as a practice of "placemaking." It shows that, aside from knitting together disparate sites of religious practice, the cross-cutting movements of embodied deities, devotees, and gurus in pilgrimage can also have highly destabilizing and disruptive effects. On the one hand, the pilgrimage to Jhakar Saim wove together modest village shrines and large, well-known temples, such as Golu Devata's temple, to produce an integrative experience of regional belonging. On the other hand, the pilgrimage also aggravated underlying, often irreconcilable, tensions within Pahari Hinduism, specifically between distinct forms of religious power and practice, such as between Brahmin and non-Brahmin priesthoods and their respective spheres of authority. During the pilgrimage, gurus from Dalit communities led their deities from villages across Kumaon to temple sites that were managed by Brahmin priests, or *pujaris*.[13] These encounters were often tense, if not outright hostile. The presence of jagar priests in prestigious, Brahmin-controlled temple sites brought into relief continuities and antagonisms between two hierarchically differentiated—yet equally important—forms of priestly authority in Uttarakhand. Moreover, in these temple sites, deities were not only offered Brahmin-mediated worship, or *puja*, as temple images and icons but were also encountered as embodied actors through divine embodiment, or *nach*, that is, "possession." Tensions between Brahminical and non-Brahminical priestly authority were spatialized in the distinction between the interior of the temple, on the one hand, and the outer courtyard, on the other, which were actively maintained throughout the pilgrimage. For instance, the inner chambers (*garbha-griha*) of Brahmin-controlled temples were reserved solely for *puja*, while gurus played their drums and embodied deities danced in the temple courtyard.

Thus, "mixing" (*mishran*) in the pilgrimage to Jhakar Saim also includes social boundaries being produced or reinforced. Mixing does not mean that everything dissolves; rather, substances may also remain distinct from one another. Liquid and sediment both may form. This chapter shows how regional Hinduisms, including Pahari religion, are not homogeneous, unified wholes but rather constituted by entrenched, often irresolvable, tensions and conflicts.

Going Home: Gendered Mixing

The Jhakar Saim pilgrimage both enacted and subverted dominant gendered relations. The pilgrimage, though performed by deities gendered male, enacted a quintessential female experience: that of married women returning to their natal homes for a reprieve from their marital homes.[14] The pilgrimage was thus a deeply affective experience for both deities and female devotees, allowing for public expressions of vulnerability and loss that were absent in other ritual contexts.

The morning of my first Jhakar Saim pilgrimage, I woke up at dawn in Bani to meet my fellow pilgrims in what they had described as a "place of the goddess" (*devi ka sthan*). On arriving there, I found that it was just like any other traditional, two-story house in the area, with beautifully carved wooden shutters, thick, solid stone walls, and a buffalo pen on the ground floor. I was told this was an important religious site in the village because it belonged to a multigenerational family of ritual mediums who embodied multiple local goddesses. "Goddesses of our village love this place," my friend Deepak told me as we approached the house.

Outside the house, a large crowd had already gathered by the time we arrived. In the center of the yard, a ritual fire was lit. Every now and then, the jagar priests and mediums who had congregated in the upper level of the house would peek outside their window like nervous actors from behind a stage curtain. As we waited in the yard, a few tardy gurus and mediums, dressed in colorful dhotis, tunics, vests, and turbans, darted upstairs to join their fellow gurus and mediums. While the ritual performers inside the house were all men, about three-quarters of the people gathered outside were women. The women huddled around the ritual fire while men in the yard, standing a little further away from the house, smoked bidis and chatted among themselves.

As the ritual fire roared to life, the crisp morning breeze carried smoke toward us, stinging our eyes. The billowing smoke merged with the dense morning mist, through which the oblique rays of the rising sun were diffracted. As the sun rose, the gurus within the house started playing their drums. The fire crackled, and the gurus' drumming grew louder and more intense. Even though the ritual mediums were hidden from view, their intermittent shouts and yells as the deities "came over" them could be heard clearly in the yard. The deities began "dancing"; we could not see them yet, but we could hear their rhythmic footfalls on the wooden floor of the old house, which added a muffled, bass-heavy counterpoint to the click-clacking drums of the gurus.

The gurus exited the house, followed by the village deities, who made their way to the ritual fire to dance and meet with their devotees. As the deities circumambulated the fire, female devotees approached them with folded hands. The women touched the deities' feet, embraced them, and hung heavy garlands of marigold flowers and crisp twenty- and fifty-rupee notes around their necks. The women showered their deities with flower petals and handed them brightly wrapped packages of fruits and other edible offerings to sustain them on the long journey to Jhakar Saim. The deities embraced the women, accepted their offerings, and placed them on a large metal platter next to the fire.

Some of the women—especially the older women in attendance—channeled divine presence and "danced" alongside the deities. Prateek, a friend of mine, found his aunt becoming animated and veering too close to the ritual fire, alarming her family. Prateek was afraid she might collapse, so he tried to lead her away from the deities, but she continued dancing. The men accompanying the deities on their journey to Jhakar Saim bowed to the "dancing" women, touched their feet, and asked for their blessings. Hoping that the deities' departure would calm the women, Prateek walked over to the gurus and told them that it was time to lead the deities away from the place of the goddess and begin their journey to Jhakar Saim.

Prateek told me that seeing off the deities was especially important for the older women of the village because only a few of them would be able to accompany the deities to Jhakar Saim. The journey was a long and taxing one, and some were not physically able to undertake it, I was told (even though their energetic dancing indicated otherwise). In reality, many of the older women had responsibilities in the household, such as taking care of children and animals, which limited their ability to travel outside the village. Moreover, only a few representatives of each family—usually younger men and women—undertook the journey on behalf of their kin. (Families who had lost a member in the past year did not participate in the pilgrimage.) Women elders who were not making the journey had a chance to see off their beloved deities, wish them a safe and happy journey, and implore them to return home quickly. "They are like mothers sending off their daughters-in-law [*bahu*] with sadness," Prateek said. In turn, the deities were tender and affectionate toward the women, gracefully accepting their gifts and assuring them that they would soon return. Prateek added that if village women are like mothers-in-law to the deities, "Gurus are like their [deities'] husbands. . . . Just as a husband drops his wife off to her natal home and then returns to pick her up after a few days, gurus . . . take the deities to their natal home [that is, Jhakar Saim] and subsequently bring them back to the home of their in-laws [that is, to villages such as Bani]."

The journey to Jhakar Saim began but also ended in a "place of the goddess," namely, the goddess Nanda Devi's ancient temple in the town of Almora. The fact that the journey ended in a Nanda Devi temple was both practically and symbolically significant. During the pilgrimage, various caravans of the village tended to become separated. Meeting in Nanda Devi's temple provided everyone with an opportunity to reconvene and settle accounts with one another, as numerous expenses had been incurred over the course of the pilgrimage, such as bus and taxi fare, food and snacks, temple offerings, and so on. As William Sax has observed, the famous Nanda Devi pilgrimage also replicates the goddess's journey from her marital home to her natal home.[15] From Shiva's high abode in the Himalayas, she journeys to her natal home/s, that is, villages in the foothills. Nanda Devi, like other married women, returns to her natal home periodically, where she is welcomed warmly and with great fanfare. After her brief visit, she once again returns to her marital life with Shiva.

The deities' pilgrimage to Jhakar Saim mirrored and ritualized married women's emotionally charged experiences of moving between their marital and natal homes. As Shanti ji, a middle-aged woman from Bani, put it, the deities' journey to Jhakar Saim—the abode of the deities' *maternal* uncle, she reminded me—was a visit to their natal home. For this reason, she said, married women felt especially connected to this pilgrimage and looked forward to it every year. Yet, unlike the pilgrimage of the goddess Nanda Devi, the deities with whom I traveled between Jhakar Saim and Bani were all male. The dissonance between the deities' "male-ness" and the enactment of a quintessentially female-gendered experience—that of returning to one's natal home within the norms of patrilocality—led to a rearrangement or queering of gendered relations and subjectivities both among deities themselves and between male and female devotees. For example, deities who were otherwise known to be commanding, even terrifying, presences demonstrated their gentleness and vulnerability.

The deities' reenactment of married women's journeys from their marital to natal homes also revealed the deep emotional weight of the experience. Most women who marry outside their villages and towns do not get a chance to visit with their natal kin frequently; when they do, it is often for only a few days. Similarly, local deities also get to visit Jhakar Saim infrequently—specifically, once a year during the monsoon season. For married women, returning to their parents' home is a joyous time, while leaving again can be painful. For deities, too, the pilgrimage is a time of celebration as well as deep sadness and loss: on leaving Jhakar Saim, deities are often inconsolable. They cry, bargain, resist, and lament their departure from Jhakar Saim—as we saw with the deity Harjyu, who refused to leave the ritual fire.

Telling me how deities sometimes cried when they left Jhakar Saim, Shanti ji said that the deities' sadness reminded her of what she felt as a young, newly married woman when she had to return to her marital home after a too-short, infrequent visit to her natal family. For female devotees, seeing their formidable deities reduced to tears was a profoundly moving sight. It was particularly affecting because they were reminded of their own losses as married women.

Marking Boundaries

Yet, through the pilgrimage, it became clear that "mixing" had its limits. Much like a solution of mud and water, not everything is liquified. Some sediment remained. In terms of which sacred spaces were included or excluded from the pilgrimage, for instance, it became clear that mixing was not an indiscriminate and totalizing process. Rather, pilgrims selectively enacted distinctions between different religious sites in the performance of pilgrimage.

After leaving the place of the goddess, deities, devotees, and gurus climbed a hill to reach a sprawling complex of open-air shrines and other ritual spaces in Bani. First, they gathered around the ritual fire (*dhuni*) of Guru Gorakhnath, a legendary saint, yogi, and leader of one of the largest religious orders in northern India, the Naths. Approaching the roaring fire, devotees were careful not to step on the large flat stones on which ritual mediums would sit as they awaited their deities' arrival during late-night rituals of divine embodiment. "These stones draw the deities toward their mediums," one of my companions explained. As such, these sacred objects were not to be stepped on. On the day of the pilgrimage to Jhakar Saim, however, there was no need to sit and wait for the deities to descend as they were already in attendance. Instead, while the gurus played their drums, embodied deities paid respect to Guru Gorkhanath by circling his dhuni.

Every now and then, as the deities circled Guru Gorakhnath's dhuni, the musicians would stop drumming to allow the deities to address those who had gathered through forms of spoken and sung "speech." The deities told priests and devotees that they were anxious to reach Jhakar Saim. "Please lead us there, O Das," the deities sang, addressing their priests, or gurus, as "servants." (While the word *Das* is sometimes employed in a derogatory fashion to refer to caste-oppressed people in Uttarakhand, in this context, it was used respectfully.) With great exuberance, the deities sang: "With your drums, show us the way, O Das! We want to see our family again!" The gurus punctuated the deities' words with short, concentrated bursts of drumming. During this back and forth, one of my companions explained to me that the deities were acknowledging the power of the gurus' drums, which "open the deities' path [*rasta*] and take them to where they need to go." According to my interlocutor, who was himself an accomplished drummer and musician, without the gurus' drums, the deities "would be unable to see where they were going." My companion pointed out that even though the path of the deities overlapped with the paved and unpaved roads that the pilgrims traversed, the deities were not following the road but, rather, their gurus. "The deities follow their gurus' drums wherever they take them," he said.

Following these exchanges at Guru Gorakhnath's dhuni, the deities began to circumambulate other structures in the area in a clockwise direction. From the dhuni, the deities moved to a goddess shrine that housed two- and three-dimensional images of various goddesses, such as Bhagavati Devi. Following their deities, devotees folded their hands and bowed their heads before the goddesses. Everyone then walked to an ancient pavilion dedicated to the worship of Saim Devata, whose primary abode was in Jhakar Saim, where they were traveling, but who also inhabited other shrines and ritual sites across the region. This pavilion, with its stone pillars and dark, hidden recesses, was the oldest structure in the complex; it was where gurus, mediums, and other participants conducted public, late-night rituals of divine embodiment in Bani. The ancient structure looked like it had been carved out of the hillside; the ashy mounds of previous ritual fires were still visible. At the end of the day, after returning from Jhakar Saim, the deities congregated outside Saim Devata's pavilion while the villagers celebrated their return.

The villagers circumambulated the structures in the complex three times. Yet, some structures in the complex were intentionally excluded from their circumambulations. The structures that the deities—and, by extension, the villagers—excluded were a Shiva temple, a Krishna-Vasudev temple, and an ornately built space for the public, ritualized recitation of sacred texts, such as the Valmiki Ramayana and Bhagavata Purana, by Brahmin priests. Many of the excluded structures were newly constructed or renovated—in the familiar style of modern Hindu shrines in Uttarakhand and much of north India—and made of plaster and cement. The excluded spaces were all maintained by Brahmin priests, who were not in attendance. The Shiva and Krishna-Vasudev shrines were padlocked. I asked my interlocutors why certain shrines were included in the deities' circumambulations while others were not, but they only said, "This is how it had always been." Unsatisfied with this response, I asked whether it was because some sites were maintained by Brahmin priests while others were not or whether some were dedicated to pan-Indian deities while others were dedicated to local and regional ones, but again, I did not receive a definitive answer.

The Enclosure and the Courtyard

In the next leg of the journey, as the pilgrims made their way to their first temple stop, tensions between distinct modalities of expertise, divine presence, and authority—what I express here as tensions between the "enclosure" and the "courtyard" of the Golu Devata temple in Chitai—became clear.

After their circumambulations, the village party descended to the main road, where they embarked on their journey to Jhakar Saim. Several jeeps, vans, and buses had been hired by the villagers for this occasion. Prior to the advent of roads and motor vehicles in the area, the journey to and from Jhakar Saim used to take several days, but now the pilgrimage could be completed in a single day. However, some still choose to make the pilgrimage on foot for various reasons, such as to fulfill a vow made to a deity or express gratitude for finding a job, doing well on a school exam, giving birth to a child, and so on. The pilgrims—including the ritual mediums who were not really showing outward signs of being under the influence of a deity because the gurus had stopped drumming—bade farewell to the villagers who would not be accompanying them on their journey.

The journey to Jhakar Saim had an unrushed, meandering quality to it. The pilgrims made several stops, including at Golu Devata's famous temple in Chitai, the meadows and springs surrounding Jhakar Saim, the temple courtyard in Jhakar Saim, the ancient temple complex of Jageshwar, and Nanda Devi's temple in Almora, among other places. They also made unplanned stops. For example, temple committees and community organizations sponsored numerous roadside kitchens to feed pilgrims as an act of religious service (*seva*). As we drove by, the organizers of these roadside kitchens flagged down passing vehicles and invited pilgrims to stop and accept their hospitality. Energetically vying for the attention of passing pilgrims, representatives of these kitchens engaged in acts of competitive giving as they tried to outdo their "rivals" in terms of eager *seva*, generosity, and hospitality. At one point in the morning, the driver of our jeep was won over by one of these groups. Next to tall loudspeakers playing devotional music, we ate heartily: fresh rotis, dal, raita, spicy vegetables, and sweet rice pudding, followed by multiple cups of hot, cardamom-infused tea. Later in the day, after these sites had fulfilled their function of feeding hungry pilgrims, their kitchen tents and seating areas were dismantled and carried away. They left no trace, I marveled, on the way back to Bani.

Golu Devata's temple in Chitai is one of the god's most famous temples in the region. Like Sem Mukhem and Danda Nagaraja, Chitai is a regionally important site (see chapter 1). It hosts visitors from both rural areas and urban centers in Kumaon and elsewhere in India. During the summer months, Kumaon is overrun by Pahari expatriates and affluent tourists from across India, particularly from the sweltering plains, who are fond of vacationing in "hill stations" such as Nainital, Bhimtal, and Mukteshwar. These tourists flock to Chitai in air-conditioned buses and cars; Golu Devata's temple is a popular cultural attraction for them. Meanwhile, in the same hot season, many Pahari expatriates return to their ancestral towns and villages in the area. For them, visiting with their families includes seeing and being seen by Golu Devata in his temple in Chitai and/or via jagar.

According to his devotees, centuries ago, Golu Devata used to rule over the kingdom of Champavat in Kumaon. Today, he inhabits Chitai as an impartial arbiter of justice (*nyaya*) who aids the downtrodden and fulfills their prayers.[16] Some of my interlocutors in Bani described the temple to me as the god's *darbar*, his royal court, where he could be petitioned for assistance in a range of other/worldly matters, such as finding employment or having children. Visitors to the temple write their wishes (*manauti*) on small slips of paper that are affixed to the temple walls. When their wishes are granted—which is very common, I was told—those who have benefitted from the god's generosity offer large, heavy, metal bells, which can be seen all over the temple complex, including hanging off the branches of trees. Periodically, when the temple cannot contain any more offerings, the bells are taken down and sold to metal traders in the area.

On arriving in Chitai, our party of pilgrims entered the temple gates and congregated in an open space that was in view of—but also a considerable distance from—the central enclosure of the temple, which was the primary attraction for other temple visitors. While other visitors queued up for long periods of time in front of the central enclosure of the temple to receive *darshan*—that is, to see and be seen by the deity who resided within—the party from Bani bypassed this space. In so doing, they also bypassed the Brahmin priests who managed the temple and mediated contact and exchange between the resident deity and the throngs of temple visitors. Instead of obtaining darshan at the central enclosure, the pilgrims from Bani occupied a corner of the complex where the gurus immediately started playing their drums, and the deities commenced "dancing." The pilgrims formed a circle around their gurus and deities and clapped their hands and sang "Jai Golu," "Jai Harjyu," and so on, naming the deities in attendance. As we were in Golu Devata's temple, he was the first among the deities to speak. Dressed in a white kurta and bright red waistcoat, he sang to his gurus and worshipers:

> The king of Champavat [the deity refers to himself in the third person]
> Joyfully welcomes his subjects [to his temple/court].
> We [deities, gurus, and worshipers] rejoice together,
> As we travel back home [to Jhakar Saim].
> Show us the way, O Das [jagar priest],
> Show us the way home.

While claiming dominion over his temple in Chitai and the ancient kingdom of Champavat, the god asked his "servants," that is, his gurus, to lead him and his human and divine companions "back home," that is, to Jhakar Saim.

I noticed that while the other temple visitors could see and hear the pilgrims, they mostly tried to ignore the boisterous party from Bani. Some standing in line to gain access to the central enclosure of the temple—with hands folded and eyes closed in quiet, serene prayer—were clearly confused and disturbed by the loud drumming, singing, and dancing. Others glared into their smartphones or shot irritated glances in our direction. Responding to their unwelcome looks, one of my companions from Bani commented on the irony of the situation:

"They [temple-goers] come all the way here to see Golu Devata, but they don't want to see him when he is standing in front of them," he whispered to me.

My interlocutor's words revealed how two distinct models of worship were being brought into (tense) relation in Chitai. On the one hand, Brahmin priests mediated contact between Golu Devata and his worshipers in and around the central enclosure of the temple. On the other hand, in the temple courtyard, gurus, that is, Dalit priests, facilitated interactions between Golu Devata and his worshipers through divine embodiment. While Golu Devata appeared in the central enclosure as a silent *murti* (temple image), in the courtyard, he was seen and heard as a human avatar (incarnation). While some temple visitors communicated with the god via the written word, that is, by inscribing their wishes on slips of paper that were hung on temple walls, others interacted with the god through speech, song, and dance.

To enable these distinct modalities of presence, practice, and authority to coexist within a single space, interactions between religious actors needed to be carefully choreographed. The Dalit gurus and Brahmin priests did not interfere with each other's work. In fact, they did not speak, nor did they acknowledge each other's presence. Despite some whispered words and a few curious, perplexed, and angry looks, the different groups of visitors carved out their own spheres of activity and influence within the temple complex.

However, this tenuous choreography of proximity and distance—which was enabled by the Dalit priests who confined themselves to the periphery of the temple—also had the potential to break down, leading to chaos and confrontation, which I will describe in the latter half of this chapter. When ritual protocols periodically break down in this way, tensions between distinct ontologies of religious practice, which are always simmering below the surface, erupt into view.

Meadow, Spring, Tree

After Chitai and a few brief stops along the way, the villagers from Bani congregated in an open meadow a couple of kilometers away from Jhakar Saim. During the journey, we endured several thunderstorms that had descended upon us from seemingly nowhere, stalling all movement and activity. During the monsoon season, rain clouds vanished as quickly as they arrived; these shifts seemed even more extreme when traveling by road in the Himalayan mountains. Each valley felt like its own self-contained weather system. After battling the elements, we were almost at Jhakar Saim, where the weather was sunny and bright. After arriving in jeeps and buses, pilgrims sat down in a large circle in a meadow. Like before, the gurus started playing the drums, and the deities got up to "dance," expressing their delight at being so close to their beloved uncle's abode. They embraced each other and blessed their worshipers, some of whom began dancing alongside their deities.

From the meadow, the pilgrims walked to a natural spring near Jhakar Saim temple, where they bathed alongside pilgrims from other parts of Kumaon. The spring was known to have special healing properties, and many of the pilgrims had brought bottles and canisters to take the water home with them as *prasad*, a material manifestation of divinity.[17] Over the centuries, the stone steps leading to the ancient spring and the pool that had formed around it had become worn and smooth. There were a few small manmade structures around the spring, but for the most part, it still existed in its natural state, amid boulders and trees, open to everyone.

Vinod, a friend from Bani, told me that the spring connected the underground realm of chaos and vitality to the world of human activity and form. He added that, in jagar songs, Jhakar Saim was identified as the deities' place of origin because "all the deities [in Kumaon] have emanated [*ubharana*] from it [the spring]." The spring had "never stopped flowing," he said. It was a source of "divine power," so deities returned to it periodically to restore and rejuvenate themselves.

Bathing in the spring was thought to be especially beneficial for women who wanted to become pregnant. For this reason, many new brides from Bani had undertaken the pilgrimage to Jhakar Saim. Clad in colorful saris, they were the first to descend into the pool surrounding the spring. Initially, I thought it was merely the cold water that was making them tremble and shout, but my companions told me that it was due to the presence of deities in/on their bodies. The deities blessed some of the women by "coming over" them, Vinod said. Deities also came over some of the men who descended into the pool. Onlookers urged the deities to play: "*Khelo! Khelo!*" they chanted, clapping their hands. Like children, the deities in the water splashed each other; like long-lost friends, they embraced each other. In the pool, some of the deified women began embracing men who were not their relatives. The men became visibly uncomfortable and retreated from the contact. The women's family members, who had been watching them closely, immediately jumped into the water to stand between their female kin and the men.[18] But not all physical contact was policed. In some cases, deities caressed each other's faces and touched their foreheads together. My companions mentioned that the deities who were greeting each other so lovingly were doing so because they had not seen each other in a long time. "Some of them live very far from each other and only get a chance to meet during the pilgrimage," Vinod explained.

In the midst of this delightful scene, dark clouds appeared. One moment, it was bright and sunny, and the next, it was raining again. Sunlight mixed with the falling rain to produce mini rainbows that danced around us like butterflies. Instead of dampening the fun, the rain added to the intensity of the carnivalesque mood.

Watching the deities play, I wanted to join them in the water. However, I regretfully refrained. I had been unprepared for this part of the pilgrimage and had not brought a change of clothes or towel with me to dry off in the rapidly cooling evening. Later, when my friends learned that I had not bathed in the pool, they expressed their disappointment. Prateek said that, as a result of not going into the water, my *darshan*—that is, my encounter with divinity—had been left incomplete. My interlocutors advised me to come back to the spring and complete my darshan another year, which I promised to do. For my interlocutors, bathing in the spring was a form of darshan. Related to Indian-language terms for "seeing" and "sight," darshan has been characterized in Western scholarship as seeing and being seen by a divinity, such as in the form of a temple statue.[19] But in the ritual sensorium of the pilgrimage to Jhakar Saim, darshan also implied playing in the rain and water with the deity. In this multisensory, joyful encounter with divinity, devotees joyfully "mixed" with divine presence.[20]

After bathing in the spring, the pilgrims made their way to the temple complex of Jhakar Saim. Similar to what had occurred in Chitai, most of the pilgrims from Bani bypassed the temple's central enclosure, which housed garlanded icons of divinities that were marked with a sacred red powder (*pithai*), sandalwood, turmeric, and other ritual substances. Many temple visitors were lined up outside this enclosure, waiting to catch a glimpse of the deities inside. The pilgrims from Bani again ignored the enclosure, instead choosing to congregate around a large ritual fire that was burning in the temple courtyard.

However, unlike my companions, I queued up outside the enclosure. I had never been to the temple before, and I was pulled by the force of habit; lining up to see the deity was more familiar to me than the forms of divine presence that my companions were showing me.

While I was standing there, one of my companions saw me from across the courtyard. He ran up to me and asked why I was waiting there. "Come on, you can have your darshan some other time. The *murti* is always there; come to the *dhuni* [ritual fire] instead," he insisted, pulling me away. Leaving the queue, I was struck by the pilgrims' differing attitudes toward darshan in the spring versus in the central enclosure. While they were dismayed that I had missed my encounter with divinity in the spring, seeing the god in the temple enclosure was not a priority.

I joined my fellow pilgrims at the dhuni. Since I had been unable to visit the enclosure, I asked them more about it. One replied that the central enclosure had been built around the trunk and roots of a tall deodar (*diyad*) tree that, once upon a time, used to secrete milk. The milk used to collect in a pool where the central enclosure now stood. Saim Devata—the visiting deities' maternal uncle, often described in jagar narrative songs as an immobile and mute being—lived within this tree (or rather, the tree externalized the deity's deep, mysterious innerness). Like the spring, the tree connected the dark, power-filled netherworld to the world of humans. Yet, while both spring and tree connected separate ontological domains in a similar way, the pilgrims had markedly different attitudes toward them, dismissing one while valorizing the other.

I attribute this difference to the fact that, while pilgrims acknowledged divine presence in the central enclosure of Jhakar Saim temple, their approach to pilgrimage prioritized divine embodiment over Brahminically-mediated temple worship and the religious authority of Dalit priests over that of Brahmin priests. The pilgrimage articulated different contexts of practice—such as divine embodiment and temple worship—while also maintaining distinctions between them. In this sense, not everything was articulable—not everything could be "mixed" or brought together. Implicit, long-simmering tensions, historical antagonisms, and solidarities between gurus and temple priests and between local and nonlocal religious practitioners also shaped the pilgrimage experience, as we will see in the next scene.

Fire: The Confrontation

The visiting deities "danced" around the ritual fire in the Jhakar Saim temple courtyard. Tended to by a Brahmin temple priest, the fire burned in a square, ashy pit, which was shielded from the rain by a *mandap*, or canopy. Four short, sturdy walls separated the firepit from the gathered deities, gurus, and worshipers. As the gurus played their drums, deities circumambulated the fire and blessed their devotees. Throughout the day, various parties of pilgrims arrived and departed the mandap. While one party occupied the mandap, the next waited and watched. Village parties had sole control of the mandap for approximately thirty minutes at a stretch. Periodically, the deities dancing around the fire would be joined by others waiting in the wings, and for around ten minutes, there would be some overlap between the two groups. Gurus of the new party would start drumming alongside the outgoing gurus, giving deities from one village the opportunity to interact with their counterparts from other villages.

As they danced around the ritual fire, the deities identified themselves through spoken and sung speech and greeted and embraced each other. The incoming gurus matched the rhythms of the outgoing gurus, playing softly at first but then becoming louder and more assertive with time. Finally, the new drummers drowned out the outgoing group as new deities replaced the old. The outgoing gurus then led their deities and devotees away from the fire to circumambulate the temple complex before departing.

Before the party from Bani could have its turn at the dhuni, it started raining heavily again. Everyone in the temple courtyard scrambled to find cover. To escape the rain, a few of my companions and I found refuge under an awning in the verandah of a guest house (*dharamashala*) on the temple premises, located a few dozen meters away from the dhuni. At the time, the guesthouse was fully occupied by a contingent of saffron-clad renunciants (sannyasi) who had traveled to Jhakar Saim from an ashram in the city of Haridwar in the foothills of the Himalayas. The renunciants were in Jhakar Saim to participate in an *akhand Ramayana* performance: a multiday, "unbroken" or continuous recitation of the Sanskrit-language Ramayana epic attributed to the legendary poet-sage Valmiki. At any given time, a handful of sannyasis could be seen milling around the temple complex, performing chores, sweeping their rooms, drying their saffron robes on a clothesline in the verandah of the guesthouse, drinking tea, or doing other everyday activities.

The sannyasis kept their distance from the dhuni and the pilgrims. At one point during the day, as a couple of sannyasis walked past the dhuni, they grimaced and plugged their ears with their fingers, disturbed and irritated by the loudness of the gurus' drums. However, most of the sannyasis spent their days in a corner of the temple complex attending to the ritual recitation and far away from the dhuni. Those who needed a break spent their time indoors in their rooms in the dharamshala, with windows and doors tightly shut to keep out the commotion in the temple courtyard.

After it started raining, I found myself in the sannyasis' verandah. I attempted to engage some of them in conversation. They told me they had been sent to Jhakar Saim by a "great soul [mahatma] from Haridwar." The mahatma was affiliated with a well-known religious order (*akhara*) based in Haridwar.[21] On hearing its name, I immediately recognized the order from local news reports: in recent years, a number of prominent members of this akhara, who were associated with far-right Hindu nationalist groups, had made threatening and hateful comments about religious minorities, specifically Muslims.[22] One of the sannyasis told me that the mahatma had a "special relationship" (*khas sambandh*) with the temple priests in Jhakar Saim. Because of their relationship, members of his order had a standing invitation to visit and stay in Jhakar Saim for as long as they desired. He said that the "quiet atmosphere" of this remote mountainous region was particularly conducive to the performance of akhand Ramayana, which required great "concentration and effort" (*dhyan aur parishram*). As he said this, I sensed he was criticizing the pilgrims for spoiling the "quiet atmosphere" of this place with their noisy rituals. He also seemed to be drawing a negative contrast between the virtues of "concentration and effort," which he associated with the sannyasis' practices, versus their absence in the pilgrims' dancing and drumming rituals.

When our party arrived at the *mandap*, there were already a few parties of pilgrims waiting for their turn around the ritual fire. We waited and watched as other deities danced around the fire. I barely noticed the temple priests who were standing in a corner, keeping a watchful eye on the unfolding events.

Before it was "officially" our turn, some deities from our party decided to join the deities who were already dancing. The four gurus from Bani were led by a wizened elder who was a masterful drummer and possessed a soft singing voice. When he saw that some of his deities had decided to enter the fray, he started drumming, matching the rhythms of the gurus who were already playing. However, his voice could not compete with the loud and robust voices of the younger gurus before him. He was unable to break through, which delayed our turn around the fire. With an air of irritation—and perhaps jealousy—he looked on as the deities from his party, one by one, began following the gurus of the other group. Even though he was unable to win back "his" deities and gain control of the mandap, he did not give up. He decidedly took charge of the mandap by physically pushing the other gurus away.

The deities from Bani took up more space around the fire as their arcs around the mandap grew wider and more energetic. The energy of the previous group of deities could no longer match the newer, fresher deities who were finally able to take over the ritual space. At the fire, it seemed the deities could no longer contain their joy at being back in their uncle's courtyard. They embraced each other and blessed their devotees from Bani, who had gathered in a tight circle around them. Every now and then, pausing in front of their devotees, deities embraced them or placed their hands on their heads. The deities handed their devotees fruit and flowers to bless them.

Many young, newlywed women from Bani stood at the edge of the mandap, in the innermost ring of onlookers, waiting to be blessed. They took off their colorful *dupattas* (scarves) and held them open in front of them like baskets. As the deities passed them, they lobbed apples, pears, and flowers into the women's scarves. I was told these blessings would help the young women give birth to healthy children and ensure the prosperity and safety of their families. I watched as one young woman wearing a red sari, glass bangles, and *sindur* (a sacred red powder) in the parting of her hair—which indicated that she was a newlywed—waited patiently. I knew her from Bani as a relative of Golu Devata's red waistcoat-wearing medium. Golu Devata saw her from the other side of the mandap and, on his next circumambulation around the fire, made his way toward her. As he moved toward her, he hopped over the short barrier that separated him from the fire, scooped up a small handful of ash from the firepit, and then immediately jumped out of the firepit. His movements were swift and smooth, and as such, I barely noticed them. After hopping out of the firepit, he completed his arc around the fire, approached the waiting woman, and marked her forehead with the ash he had obtained from the firepit.

As soon as Golu Devata marked the young woman's forehead with ash, one of the temple priests ran toward the deity and grabbed him by the arm. The deity recoiled, pulled away from the priest's grasp, and continued circling the fire. "Hey, what are you doing?!" the temple priest exclaimed as he chased the deity. He caught up with him and, this time, held him by the shoulders. The deity cried out as if he had been physically injured by the contact. His piercing cry startled the pilgrims. The deity started clenching his jaw and trembling and shaking uncontrollably, and some villagers from Bani loudly protested the roughhousing of their deity.

The mandap erupted in chaos: the villagers closed in around Golu Devata to protect him from further assault, while temple priests (*pujaris*) from different parts of the temple ran toward the priest who had confronted the deity. One of the pujaris had run over to a group of sannyasis to inform them of what was happening. Numerous sannyasis came running to the site of the confrontation to support the pujaris; before we knew it, more than twenty had surrounded the pilgrims.

All of this happened quickly, in a matter of seconds. Initially, people were confused, but as word spread among the pilgrims that their beloved Golu Devata had been harmed by a temple priest, confusion gave way to anger. The villagers were furious: "How can you lay your hands [*hath lagana*] on our deities like this?" they asked, astonished that a priest had disrespected and physically threatened one of their deities.

Despite pushback from the pilgrims, the temple priests, held their ground. They were outnumbered, but, at the same time, they were adamant that the pilgrims were in the wrong. While the villagers looked on in shock, the gurus continued playing, and the other gods continued dancing. However, the deities' dance was different now: their movements seemed jerky and agitated, whereas earlier, they had been smooth and graceful. After having been grabbed by the shoulders, Golu Devata had managed to break free, spin away from the pujari, and resume his circumambulations. Realizing he was incapable of stopping the deity on his own, the pujari turned to the gurus for help. He rushed toward the gurus and commanded them to stop drumming: "Stop it, stop it!" he shouted. "Stop everything!" However, by this time, the pilgrims had also formed a circle around their gurus to shield them from the pujaris' ire and allow them to keep playing.

One of the villagers from Bani, a well-built young man, confronted the pujaris angrily: "What happened? What are you doing?" he asked.

"How could he [Golu Devata] have entered the firepit like that?! What gives him the right to do such a thing?" the pujaris responded indignantly.

During this heated exchange, on one of his rounds around the fire, Golu Devata came to a stop in front of the pujari who had grabbed him and simply stared at him. For a few moments, neither the deity nor the pujari backed down until another pilgrim from Bani pushed through the crowd and inserted himself between Golu Devata and the pujari, breaking the tension between them. He folded his hands, bowed, and requested the pujari to back away as the deity resumed his dancing.

Although this gesture defused the situation to some extent, it was not entirely resolved. A few sannyasis tried to make their way through the crowd and reach the pujaris and deities at the center of the melee. Knowing the sannyasis were there to help the pujaris, the pilgrims held them back and kept them from advancing. Unable to move forward, the sannyasis stationed themselves on raised platforms of various kinds around the temple courtyard—such as on walls, roofs, balconies, and at the tops of flights of stairs leading down into the temple courtyard. From these elevated positions, they literally loomed over the pilgrims and could see the action at the dhuni and communicate with the pujaris who were at the center. Some of the sannyasis threatened the pilgrims: "Leave them [pujaris] alone, or we won't leave you!"

Seeing the sannyasis arrayed around them, the gurus tried to de-escalate the situation by backing away from the dhuni. They resumed playing their drums so that the deities—and, in turn, the villagers—would follow them. The gurus circled the fire; after two or three rounds, their circumambulations started becoming wider, more expansive. The deities and villagers followed, albeit reluctantly at first. Gradually, the party from Bani started circumambulating the entire temple, not just the dhuni. As we followed the sounds of the gurus' drums around the temple, I asked one of my companions from Bani what we were doing, and he whispered to me that the deities were bidding farewell to their uncle by circling the temple five times. The long, circuitous circumambulations also served another purpose: taking the time to slowly circle the temple allowed the villagers to regain their composure and leave the temple in a dignified manner. The villagers' retreat from the temple immediately after their confrontation with the pujaris and sannyasis would have been experienced as an ignominious retreat.

The villagers did their circumambulations, but their heads were lowered. They were fuming, still angry about how their deities had been treated, but had resigned themselves to leaving quietly. I was glad that cooler heads had prevailed and that we had managed to avoid a serious confrontation. Yet, feelings of hostility between the pujaris and sannyasis, on the one hand, and the pilgrims and gurus, on the other, were still palpable. While the pilgrims walked with their heads down, the sannyasis glared at them from their perches around the complex, seemingly challenging them to do or say something provocative.

As we circled the temple, a few of the sannyasis walked over to the large diesel generator located near the guesthouse and turned it on. The deafening noise of the generator drowned out the gurus' drums—a final act of disrespect toward the pilgrims before they departed. For one middle-aged woman who had been walking in front of me and grumbling under her breath about the insolence of the pujaris and sannyasis, this act was the final straw. She looked up in defiance at a sannyasi in front of her who happened to be making a call on his cell phone.

"Who are you calling?!" the woman shouted at the sannyasi, trying to be heard above the din of the generator. "You can call whomever you want, but they won't be able to save you.... Don't force our deities to show you their power!"

The sannyasi looked down at her—he seemed puzzled by her outburst—while the villagers around her tried to calm her down. They held her by her arm and asked her to keep walking. Her outburst had been contained, but she had made it clear that she was not afraid of the sannyasis. As the pilgrims kept her moving, she continued to vent her frustrations, her voice at full volume barely audible above the generator:

"How can these people from outside [*bahar ke log*] touch our deities?! What do they know of this place [*Jhakar Saim*]? Our ancestors have been coming here for thousands of years. Do they think they can just buy [*kharidana*] up everything here and kick us out?"

Her compatriots nodded in agreement but were eager to leave the temple premises as quickly as possible before things escalated once again.

The journey back to Bani was tense and somber, but there was also a desire not to dwell on the incident. On our way back, I asked the wife of a friend, Chatra, about the woman's outburst. She said that she sympathized with her and that she was justified in feeling hurt and frustrated. Chatra said, "Our deities represent the village, so when they are insulted, our whole community [*samaj*] is insulted." She added that the women in our party had the deepest reverence [*shraddha*] for the deities, and they were hurt by what had happened at the dhuni. Chatra reminded me of how village women had embraced and blessed the deities prior to their departure from Bani, giving them food and other offerings to sustain them on their long journey. The journey to Jhakar Saim, she said, was particularly poignant and meaningful for women because women were reminded of their sorrow at leaving their natal homes after marriage and how happy they feel when they have a chance to return.

"Like our deities, we miss the happy years in our natal homes [*maike*], with no responsibilities, no difficulties," she said. Chatra commented that Lakupati, the woman who yelled at the sannyasi, was an otherwise mild-mannered, quiet woman who would not have acted the way she had if she had not been deeply affected by the pujaris' and sannyasis' insulting behavior toward the village deities.

"And then, how would you feel if you were thrown out of your own natal home like that?" she asked rhetorically. "It's not a good feeling."

Conclusion: Cohabitation and Conflict

After the altercation at the ritual fire in the temple courtyard, I discussed the incident with some of the gurus from Bani who had led the pilgrimage to Jhakar Saim. One of the gurus told me that if the conflict had escalated, the gurus would have been held responsible by the police and other relevant authorities, as they were leading the party of pilgrims. The volatility of the moment demanded that the gurus act, which they did by trying to lead the pilgrims away from the fire and the standoff with the pujaris. This was not an easy task. The villagers, especially the younger men, had become very agitated and were preparing for a physical altercation with the pujaris. It was the intimidating presence of the sannyasis surrounding the pilgrims that seemed to sober some of the young men from Bani, yet others continued to admonish the pujaris.

Commenting on the deities' reaction to being manhandled by the pujaris, one of the gurus asked rhetorically: "Our deities eat fire; how can you touch them and not get burned?" He proceeded to explain the gravity of the pujaris' actions to me anecdotally, describing a jagar he had officiated in the past. He said that one of the men of the sponsoring family had arrived at the ritual drunk, and this had greatly offended the family deity, Gangnath. The deity confronted the man, who retaliated by physically pushing the deity "because the man was clearly not in his senses." Infuriated, the embodied deity placed his hands on the man's head, and the man fell unconscious. Because of this insult, the deity told the family that he would never again return to their home. The deity then left his medium and vanished.

The family tried to revive the man who had collapsed, but they did not succeed. The man remained unconscious for many days. The guru informed the family that the only one who could help the man was the deity who had promised never to return. The family was advised to sacrifice a buffalo at a nearby Gangnath temple and beg him to return so he could revive their family member. After the sacrifice, the deity finally consented, and the man—who had been unconscious for over two weeks—was brought to him. During the jagar that was performed to revive the man, Gangnath "blew air all over the man's body, and he came back to life." The point of the guru's story was that local deities, such as Gangnath and Golu Devata, possessed power over life and death, and so for human beings, even temple priests, to manhandle such deities was unthinkable. My interlocutor suggested that if Golu Devata's devotees had not intervened at the dhuni in Jhakar Saim, the deity could have severely harmed the offending pujaris.

In subsequent conversations with people involved in the incident, including two temple pujaris, I learned that the altercation was, in large part, about the perceived transgression of religious boundaries in Jhakar Saim. In particular, the pujaris felt that their own religious authority had been challenged by Golu Devata's actions at the dhuni. The pujaris were situated in various places across the temple complex, and one of them tended to the ritual fire in the courtyard. The pujari sat on the short concrete barrier that surrounded the firepit. From early in the morning till late at night, temple pujaris took turns sitting in this spot; one of them was always at hand to mark the foreheads of temple visitors with sacred ash from the dhuni, among other functions that he performed. With hands folded, in a gesture of respect, visitors would approach the pujari and place some money on his metal platter, which contained small mounds of red powder, uncooked rice, flowers, incense, and other ceremonial objects and substances. The pujari received their offerings, marked their foreheads with ash, and tied a red thread around their wrists. He would also hand them small paper sachets containing the sacred ash for visitors to carry home with them. During the pilgrimage, I barely noticed this pujari because very few pilgrims approached him, and the gurus and deities at the dhuni did not interact with him at all. It was only after the altercation that I realized the importance of the pujari as the caretaker of the dhuni.

By jumping into the firepit and collecting and applying sacred ash to his devotee's forehead, the god had violated the delicate ritual choreography that mediated relations between deities, gurus, and temple priests. Golu Devata had transgressed a boundary between two separate domains of priestly power and authority. The "inside" of the temple—that is, the inner sanctum as well as the space within the boundary walls of the firepit—was controlled by the temple priests. In contrast, the "outside," that is, the temple courtyard and the space outside the walls of the firepit, was reserved for the embodied deities and their gurus and devotees. By collecting some ash from the firepit and applying it to his devotee's forehead, Golu Devata had appropriated the ritual function set aside for the temple priest seated on the boundary wall. The temple priests who protested the deity's transgressions did so to remind the party from Bani about their status as "outsiders" and guests in the temple, even though they claimed a form of ancestral ownership over it via their deities. Thus, by undercutting the authority of the temple priests, Golu Devata precipitated a crisis of ownership, belonging, and pride, which ultimately led to the pilgrims from Bani being sent away from the dhuni.

The events brought into relief two competing views of ownership and belonging in relation to Jhakar Saim. According to the pilgrims from Bani, the dhuni—but also the temple as a whole—belonged to their village deities, who related to Jhakar Saim as their natal home and place of origin. Yet, it was clear that the pilgrims related more to some parts of the temple than others. For example, the inner sanctum, where many of the temple priests were stationed, was not regarded as an essential site of darshan for the pilgrims. Instead, the deities, gurus, and pilgrims from Bani collected around the dhuni in the courtyard of the temple, which constituted the focal point of ritual activity for them. While the pilgrims claimed ownership of the temple for their deities, for the temple priests, the pilgrims were simply guests. The pujaris saw themselves as the primary custodians of the temple, and, as such, their authority not only superseded the gurus' but also their deities'. The deities were allowed to dance around the firepit but not permitted to cross the barrier and enter it.

The dhuni was thus constituted as a site of ritual power on multiple levels: while it shone with the fiery energy, or *shakti*, of the dancing deities and pulsating drums that propelled them forward, it was also a site where the priestly authority, or *adhikar*, of Dalit gurus was brought into tense relation with that of Brahmin priests. For the most part, these two forms of priestly authority managed to coexist at the dhuni without overt conflict, though this was not exactly harmonious but more the product of mutual avoidance and noninterference. The gurus and their deities, on the one hand, and the temple priests, on the other, shared space at the dhuni, but mostly, they left each other alone.

However, when the temple priests confronted Golu Devata and his followers, I realized that tensions between these distinct modes of religious authority and practice had been there all along. My interlocutors from Bani told me that tensions between Dalit gurus and Brahmin priests were a familiar feature of Pahari religion. "Some of these temple priests really resent our gurus," one of my friends from Bani claimed, because the deities only "follow" their gurus.

Postscript: Non-Pahari "Outsiders"

After leaving Jhakar Saim temple, as I discussed Lakupati's outburst with Chatra, Deepak joined our conversation. I asked both of them, "But what did Lakupati mean when she said the sannyasis cannot just 'buy [*kharidana*] up everything and kick us out' of Jhakar Saim?" Deepak laughed at my question.

"Who knows? She probably thinks the sannyasis are just like other people from the 'plains' [Eng.] who are buying up land and property in our area."

Deepak said that he, personally, did not have anything against people from the plains who were choosing to migrate to and buy property in the mountains. In fact, he was involved in the growing real estate market and had brokered a few lucrative land deals in recent years.

On the other hand, some of my interlocutors *were* deeply concerned about these demographic changes (see chapter 4). For instance, Deepak's father told me at another time that some of his neighbors had sold off their ancestral lands and now worked as wage laborers in the construction business and other service industries, and these locals were "treated very poorly." There, locals had been reduced to "servants" (*naukar*) and second-class citizens in their own lands, he complained.

During this conversation with Deepak's father, generational divides about the future of Bani and Uttarakhand, more broadly, became clear. Deepak's father pointed out that many younger people in the area—like his son Deepak—were quite happy with this influx of "plains-people," who they believed would enrich the local economy and provide the younger generation with much-needed jobs. "Young people don't want to work in agriculture anymore; they want to live easy lives with the amenities and comforts of people in big cities," he claimed. Tourists and pilgrims who traveled to Uttarakhand from all over India provided a significant source of income to people in the flourishing service industry in the state, such as restaurant and hotel workers, taxi drivers, tour guides, and so on.

For example, in subsequent visits to Jhakar Saim, I befriended some local shopkeepers who sold religious souvenirs and materials for temple worship—such as garlands, sweets, fruits, etc.—to temple visitors. These shopkeepers and merchants reiterated that out-of-state visitors had helped enrich the local economy; they also said that the number of such visitors had been increasing steadily, about which they were happy. One of the shopkeepers said that, in the past, such visitors used to stop in Jhakar Saim on their way to other, more famous, nationally known pilgrimage centers, such as Badrinath. "Today, however, Jhakar Saim has become their final destination ... because people are looking for quiet and secluded places to stay, so they like to spend long periods of time here," he said.

Shopkeepers and merchants around Jhakar Saim credited the rise in the number of visitors to ongoing developmental efforts by the state. These projects included the construction of new roads and bridges, which had increased accessibility in this mountainous and forested terrain. They also mentioned that the temple guesthouse had been renovated and expanded in recent years to house the growing influx of visitors, especially overnight and long-term guests, such as the sannyasis from Haridwar. These conversations reminded me of analogous developments in Danda Nagaraja and Sem Mukhem that I described in chapter 1, especially with regard to capital investment and a sustained focus by temple authorities on economic development (*vikas*) and growth.

On the other hand, it is important to note that such economic development has come with severe costs to the environment. Much of the Himalayan state of Uttarakhand is located in a zone of acute ecological fragility and, every year, residents have seen an increase in the frequency of landslides, flash floods, and other deadly environmental disasters in the state.

After accompanying the pilgrims from Bani to Jhakar Saim, I returned to the temple a few more times. On these visits, I had a chance to speak with some of the sannyasis who had seen and participated in the altercation at the dhuni. While I had a sense of why the pujaris had acted in the way they did, I was still unsure of why the sannyasis had chosen to jump into the fray with such gusto. Was it simply because they were guests of the pujaris and felt obliged to help them, or were there also other factors at play?

The sannyasis told me they had come to Jhakar Saim in search of a tranquil environment to perform the *akhand* Ramayana and immerse themselves in "prayer [*puja-path*] and contemplation [*samadhi*]." Instead, they had been confronted with throngs of "noisy" local pilgrims and their dancing deities. Some of the sannyasis told me that initially, they had been intrigued and amused by the colorfulness of what they saw: the drumming, dancing, and singing in an unfamiliar language. But the novelty of this experience had worn off by the time the party from Bani arrived at the temple. By then, the sannyasis were eager to return to a quieter, less boisterous sense of place. When I witnessed them walk by the temple courtyard where Dalit gurus were playing their drums, some of the sannyasis covered their ears and grimaced, expressing *ghrina*, which Joel Lee characterizes as an "emotion-concept similar to disgust."[23] Just as a person's "odor" may mark them as "low-caste" in the north Indian contexts studied by Lee,[24] in Jhakar Saim, the pilgrims' ritual sensorium also marked them as "outsiders" in relation to this "peaceful," Brahmin-controlled temple site.

The sannyasis' frustration had been building for many days, so when the altercation between the villagers and pujaris broke out, the sannyasis were quick to jump in and teach the rowdy villagers a lesson. The sannyasis noted that they had been as tolerant as possible toward the Pahari pilgrims and their practices, but when they heard that the pilgrims were "attacking" their hosts, the temple priests, they ran to their defense. As one of the sannyasis put it, "We love peace [*shanti*] above all else, so when peace is threatened, we are there to protect it at all costs, even if it means taking up arms.... This is the nature of the vow we keep as sannyasis."

During our conversations, the sannyasis asked me about my work, and I told them I was learning about the worship of local Pahari deities, jagar, and other rituals involving divine embodiment, such as the pilgrimage to Jhakar Saim. When I said this, one of the sannyasis asked me, with some derision, why I was so interested in the "delusions" (*bhram*) of "unlettered" (*anpadh*) villagers. Another, in a more conciliatory mode, conceded that the Absolute, Brahman, took many forms, including as local Pahari divinities, but then also asserted that local practices, especially divine embodiment and animal sacrifice, were associated with inferior and partial (*adhuri*) forms of knowledge and devotion. "It is easy for people to become caught in the nets of illusion, so it is our [the sannyasis'] work to cut through these nets, which is why we wear such clothes [saffron robes] and forsake worldly concerns." For the sannyasis I spoke with—none of whom were from Uttarakhand—the worship of local Pahari deities through divine embodiment ran counter to the textual traditions (*shastra*) that they upheld. For the sannyasis, the local practices I was interested in were seen to perpetuate illusory, nonrational modes of knowledge and practice.[25]

Some of the sannyasis participating in the akhand Ramayana recitation lamented that Sanskrit-language traditions—including Valmiki's Ramayana—were being ignored and forgotten by local Pahari people. When I asked them why they thought this, as everyone I had met in Uttarakhand, especially the jagar priests, respected and celebrated these classical Hindu traditions, they said, "Look at what is happening here in this temple [Jhakar Saim]: we [the sannyasis] have been chanting the Ramayana for many days and nights, but no one has joined us in this important endeavor.... They [the pilgrims] sing and dance around their fires, instead of asking, 'Why are we born into this world, what is the nature of reality, what is the nature of Self?'" I had encountered such dismissiveness toward local Pahari practices many times before in my interactions with temple priests in Sem Mukhem, Danda Nagaraja, and other places. For instance, as I described in chapter 1, temple priests often described caste-oppressed jagar priests as "unlettered" (*anpadh*) and therefore lacking in access to legitimate and authoritative sources of religious knowledge and training.

This pilgrimage to the temple of Jhakar Saim culminated in an altercation, revealing how such places and practices of placemaking can be deeply fraught and affectively charged. In the altercation and the unresolved social dynamics and inequalities it revealed, the (always incomplete) process of "mixing" became clear. In the pilgrimage to Jhakar Saim, mixing occurred between different religious sites and the actors who manage, frequent, and inhabit them, as well as between different modalities of divine presence in the world. For instance, during the pilgrimage, "adult" divinities displayed attributes that were viewed by their worshipers as "child-like"; as they remembered and relived their happy childhoods on the way to their beloved uncle's abode, deities became playful and exuberant. Through the pilgrimage, deities sexed male reenacted a quintessential female experience—that of returning to her natal home. And finally, in terms of the places that the pilgrimage touched, we saw how mixing occurred provisionally. The temple of Jhakar Saim was itself divided spatially between the temple's central enclosure and the courtyard, as movements of differently positioned ritual actors of "high" and "low" caste were carefully controlled.

Epilogue

Beyond Belief

On one of our trips, the *jagari* Ram Lal and I were invited to a wedding reception in Tehri Garhwal. I was always happy to go to such parties with Ram because it gave us a chance to let our hair down, have a few drinks, and chat with people in a looser, more informal way. At the party, I was introduced to a Dalit woman who said she had seen me at a *jagar* ritual a few weeks earlier. She asked what I had been doing at the jagar, and I briefly described my research to her. After listening, she asked me if I "believed" (*manana*) in the gods and goddesses I had encountered during my fieldwork.[1]

Before I could respond, she added: "An educated person such as yourself couldn't possibly believe [*manana*] in such things, right?"

Her description of me as an "educated" person—a mark of social and economic differentiation—and as a patronizing outsider who might look down upon local Pahari practices triggered a defensive reaction in me. Though I am an upper-class, urban, non-Dalit, and non-Pahari person, I did not want to be mistaken for a stereotypical outsider. So, I responded that, of course, I believed in them. I said that the world was infinitely more mysterious than "educated" people such as myself knew. And though I was educated, I did not see myself as an arbiter of truth and reality. Moreover, I said that I trusted what my interlocutors had told me over the years.

Yet, the question of whether or not I "believed" in divine embodiment and the reality of local deities haunted me throughout my fieldwork. Though I feigned certainty in this encounter, in truth, my answer is constantly evolving. After hearing me out, she offered the following insight: "The gods and goddesses are only real [*asli*] for those who believe [*manana*] in them."

I nodded along, indicating that I understood what she meant. But later, I became less sure. Did she mean that the existence and agency of Pahari deities was a matter of subjective perception? Was she questioning the existential reality of deities? Was she pointing to the existence of multiple ontologies? Or was I misunderstanding her completely?

Over the next few days, I went over my field notes and located other instances when people had said similar things to me. In one recorded exchange with a jagar priest named Champal Mistri, he used almost the same exact phrase as she did while also asserting the objective reality (*hakikat*) of deities. According to him, deities were as real as "mountains, rocks, and trees." He added, "One may or may not know about the existence of a particular mountain or river; one may have never visited this place, but this doesn't mean it isn't there."

The jagari Ram Lal helped me further decode these concepts. Through our conversations, I learned that "belief'—a deeply-held feeling about whether something is true—was not an appropriate translation for the word *manana*. Rather, the verb *manana* differs from—and exceeds—the English-language term *belief* in significant ways. According to the anthropologist of religion Roy Rappaport, *belief* is primarily an inward, private state tied to intrasubjective states and processes through which persons come to identify (with) what is true and real.[2]

Rappaport's definition of *belief* does not exhaust the semantic range of this word in popular parlance, which comes closer to the meaning of *manana*. For example, Jack Eller notes that, in vernacular English:

> "Belief" is a word with three quite distinct senses. First, it can be used . . . to claim that a proposition is true, such as "God exists." . . . Second, it can be used in the sense of "confidence" or "trust," as in "I believe my wife will pick me up from the airport"; here, the existence of my wife and the airport are not the issue. Third, it can be used in the sense of "commitment" or "value," as in "I believe in democracy," in which one is not disputing the existence of democracy but the goodness of it. These senses can be conjoined or disjoined in any particular language or religion, and their interrelation can change over time.[3]

The Indian-language word *manana* possesses a similarly broad range of meanings, including the three connotations of *belief* outlined by Eller. However, in Eller's first understanding of *belief*, *manana* means a personal conviction in the veracity of a proposition. Returning to Champal ji's characterization of deities as like mountains, rocks, and trees, I realized that *manana* did not suggest *belief* in Eller's first sense of the term. Rather, *manana* means *acknowledging* some feature of the world that existed independently of our subjective perceptions. Like mountains and rivers, the reality of deities constitutes one of the objective conditions of human existence.

Moreover, *manana* involves *entering into relation* with deities: it is about creating, maintaining, and repairing mutually transformative relationships with divinities. It implies practices of ritual reciprocity, of contact and exchange between deities and devotees. Finally, *manana* is not an "inward state," as Rappaport understands it, nor is it a one-way act. Rather, it is an intersubjective, relational *process*. In this worldview, *manana* is coconstructed—by both deity and devotee—through time, care, and relation.

Eller's third sense of "belief" resonates with *manana*, which can also mean "to value" or "to honor."[4] In fact, in my fieldnotes, I found that my interlocutors used *manana* synonymously with the verbal constructions *man rakhana* and *man karana*,[5] which relate more closely to "honor" and "respect" than Eller's first sense of "belief."

Gods in the World has explored how human-divine relationality is a key factor in interpersonal, social, moral, and political life in Uttarakhand. For example, the ritual performer Ram Lal was exposed to the reality of deities when he experienced his first jagar rituals as a child: "Before we learn to walk, we learn the ways of the lineage [*kul*] and village [*gram*] deities," he said in his poetic, pithy style. At a broad level, *manana* entails becoming aware of, attuned to, and familiar with the presence of deities. *Manana* refers to an embodied knowledge that you are born into and something you cultivate over the course of your life. As we have seen throughout the book, relations between deities and devotees can deepen, transform, and sometimes sour, transforming their devotees' lives and trajectories.

Ram's mention of "lineage" and "village" deities indicates that attuning to the reality of deities is tied to both social and material place. The worship of lineage deities can go back several generations within a single family, while village deities also share deep, intimate relationships with not just individual families but entire villages and groups of villages. His broader point was that human-divine relationships are always *in place*—which makes it difficult for non-Pahari outsiders, such as myself, to fully comprehend or "honor" (*manana*) them.

For example, I once asked a jagari if I could become "possessed" while attending a jagar. I was curious about how random members of the audience could have the deity "come over" them. He shook his head and assured me there was little likelihood of that happening. I now understand that he meant that I am excluded from certain ritual relations with Pahari deities because I am not a Pahari person who has been sensitized or attuned to their presence over a lifetime. Through these conversations, I began to understand *manana* as a mode of *attunement* to Pahari deities, an ability to ritually affect and be affected by them. Rather than translate *manana* as belief, I correct my translation of what the woman at the wedding party said to me: The deities are only real for those they are *in relation with, who ritually acknowledge and honor them*.

In Pahari Hinduism, people have embodied, textured, and highly contextual ways of relating—*manana*—to the supernatural agents who populate their world. "Belief," I learned, is not an unchanging, undifferentiated, or one-way phenomenon, as in, "I believe in X." Rather, it is historically dynamic, relational, and multifarious. In Uttarakhand, people relate to their deities in a variety of ways, such as through divine embodiment in jagar rituals as well as Brahminically-mediated temple worship, and in each of those spaces, the deities present differently. At the same time, "belief" is not something we can always choose, nor is it something we can always control. Sometimes, gods and goddesses choose us.

A key aspect of *manana* is its fluidity and historical specificity. Relationships change. Neither humans nor deities are particularly easy to get along with, and, as we have seen, the dynamics of their relating can be tumultuous and uneven. Deities can intervene in the lives of their devotees, in family affairs, and in village politics, not always with the goal of restoring peace and order. In some cases, they aggravate tensions and political and economic inequities and divides. However nonnegotiable their presence, for caste-oppressed Pahari communities in particular, they can also be complexly configured and ambiguous beings.

Throughout our time together, Ram Lal challenged me to consider how local deities tangibly affect and are affected by the human-social world. Over the years, I have approached writing this book as responding to his challenge. However, there are also many aspects of his religious knowledge that Ram did not share with me. He insisted, "Only those who have received [or "been initiated into"] this knowledge [*gyan*] can talk of it." He added that, even if he were permitted to speak with me about this knowledge, it was not something he could talk about, as *manana* does not consist of intellectual propositions but, rather, has to be "realized within oneself."

On hearing this, my disappointment must have been palpable because Ram's teacher, Dhanvir ji, in whose home we were sitting, laughed mischievously and urged Ram to share some part of "his great, big secret" [*rahasya*] with me. To placate Dhanvir ji while avoiding answering directly, Ram regaled us with a short, humorous story:

> One day, long ago, Mirabai [a medieval, high-caste Rajput princess, saint of the *bhakti* movement, and devotee of Krishna] broke her slipper.
>
> When this happened, she exclaimed: "Oh no [*hai re*]! As a lover of love, no one can know my pain!"
>
> To fix her slipper, she went to a cobbler named Ravidas [a medieval saint of the bhakti movement who was born into a Dalit community]. Hanging next to the cobbler's worktable was a "photo" [Eng.] of Krishna, which fell to the floor when Mirabai entered the workshop.
>
> "Oh no! My Giridhar [Krishna] has fallen; no one can know my pain!"
>
> When she said this, Ravidas responded: "This cannot be your Giridhar; this is only your fancy [*kalpana*]. But if you really want to know [*janana*] him, then come to my house at midnight."
>
> Now, this was a test [*pariksha*], as it was not permissible for her to visit the home of a cobbler in the middle of the night. But because Mirabai was a true devotee of god [*bhagavan*], she went against the wishes of her family and went to his home. She passed the test, facing great adversity along the way.
>
> After this, Ravidas became her teacher [*guru*]. . . . Ravidas was actually the *sadguru* [the highest teacher]; he was a *paigambar* [a person beyond all worldly concerns who served as a messenger of God] of that time. He taught her that the pursuit of truth/reality [*satya*] is a painful thing.
>
> The essence of this story is that a guru can appear in any form, even in the form of a lowly cobbler.

The story concluded abruptly. I was sure Ram had more to say about the "essence" of this story, but he wanted to know what Dhanvir ji and I thought. As we discussed the story, we laughed about Princess Mirabai's exaggerated reaction at breaking her slipper and witnessing her beloved Krishna fall to the floor. Her hyperbolic exclamations suggested that she was lost in a world of fantasy and confusion. Dhanvir ji pointed out that, unlike the privileged princess, the cobbler Ravidas was unfazed when the image of Krishna fell to the floor. The story was also about caste politics, turning privilege on its head.

According to Dhanvir ji, the story reveals that Ravidas could distinguish between *satya* and *asatya*, or reality and nonreality. In contrast to the high-caste, melodramatic princess, the Dalit cobbler was more grounded, discerning, and possessed a privileged access or connection to *satya*. As a low-caste cobbler, he had dealt with hardship and adversity all his life, unlike Mirabai, who had led a sheltered existence. Ram's story implied that Ravidas's greatness as a guru and his experiences as a member of a socially and economically marginalized community were tied together. Ram and Dhanvir ji—as gurus themselves—identified closely with Ravidas, a figure who is beloved in Dalit communities and known for his anticaste message and emphasis on a *nirgun*, that is, "attribute-less" conception of divinity.[6]

In the story, Mirabai is not merely the butt of the joke, however. She is someone who needs—and can be—educated about the proper distinctions between reality and unreality. To check her motivations, the wise Ravidas presents her with an impossible demand: to break with caste and gendered norms by visiting the home of a low-caste cobbler in the middle of the night. In other words, Ravidas tests her by forcing her to break with her privilege and social norms (the "superficial" reality). To her credit, Mirabai did what Ravidas asked: "In her pursuit of knowledge, she went against all of society," Ram said.

I could not help but identify with Mirabai in the story, and perhaps this was Ram's cheeky purpose in telling it. In writing this book, I have become keenly aware of the limits of a non-Pahari ethnographic engagement with the life worlds of my Pahari interlocutors, their gods and goddesses, and, more generally, with any scholarly undertaking of this subject at all. Sometimes, I experienced these limits through language and the translatability of ideas, but more often, they had to do with the theory of knowledge that Ram and others shared with me. As Ram said, knowledge about the true nature of reality cannot be verbalized; it has to be "realized within oneself." Merely gaining scholarly, abstract, or conceptual knowledge is just "fancy" (*kalpana*).

The story ends with Mirabai arriving at Ravidas's doorstep to unlearn her superficial understanding of the world. She is ready to become a devotee. Mirabai's journey mirrored my own choreography, I realized. As my fieldwork was coming to an end, I reflected on the last sixteen months of my life that I, too, had spent among gurus, sitting in their courtyards, sipping tea with them. I could only hope that my own journey of *kalpana* was coming to an end and a new *gyan* was rising within.

Indian-Language Words with Diacritics

achhut	⟶	*achūt*
adhikar	⟶	*adhikār*
adikavi	⟶	*ādikavi*
ahamkara	⟶	*ahaṁkār*
akhara	⟶	*akhāṛā*
andha vishvas	⟶	*andha viśvās*
anpadh	⟶	*anpaḍh*
astha	⟶	*āsthā*
astra	⟶	*astra*
atma	⟶	*ātmā*
auji	⟶	*aujī*
avatar lena	⟶	*avatār lenā*
avtarit hona	⟶	*avatarit honā*
bahar ke log	⟶	*bāhar ke log*
bahu	⟶	*bahū*
bak bolana	⟶	*bāk bolanā*
bakkya	⟶	*bakkyā/bākya*
bali	⟶	*bali*
bauksari vidya	⟶	*bauksaṛī vidyā*
ber	⟶	*ber*
bhag	⟶	*bhāg*
bhagavan	⟶	*bhagavān*
bhakta	⟶	*bhakta*

bhakti	⟶	bhakti
bhot desh	⟶	bhoṭ deś
bhumi	⟶	bhūmi
bhut	⟶	bhūt
bhut-pret	⟶	bhūt-pret
brit barma	⟶	bṛt barmā
bulana	⟶	bulānā
chahara	⟶	cahara
chandi ka chanda	⟶	cāndī kā candā
chandi ka dhol	⟶	cāndī ka dhol
chhal	⟶	chaḷ
chhattar	⟶	chattar
chot	⟶	coṭ
dakait	⟶	ḍakait
dag	⟶	dāg
daku	⟶	ḍākū
dangariya	⟶	ḍaṅgariyā
darbar	⟶	darbār
darshan	⟶	darśan
das	⟶	dās
daur-thali	⟶	ḍaur-thālī
dham	⟶	dhām
dhami	⟶	dhāmī
dharamshala	⟶	dharamaśālā
dharma	⟶	dharma
dhol	⟶	ḍhol
dhuni	⟶	dhūnī
dhup	⟶	dhūp
dev bhumi	⟶	dev-bhūmi
devi-devata	⟶	devī-devatā
devata	⟶	devatā
dip	⟶	dīp
diyad	⟶	dīyāḍ
dosh	⟶	doṣ
dudha-dhari nag	⟶	dūdha-dhārī nāg
dvaraka-pati	⟶	dvārakā-pati
ekagrat	⟶	ekāgrat

INDIAN-LANGUAGE WORDS WITH DIACRITICS   193

gaddi	→	gaddī
gatha	→	gāthā
garbha grha	→	garbha gṛha
ghamand	→	ghamaṇḍ
ghamandi	→	ghamaṇḍī
ghata	→	ghāṭā
ghat lagana	→	ghāt lagānā
ghora	→	ghoṛā
git	→	gīt
gram	→	grām
guru	→	guru
guru dakshina	→	guru dakṣiṇā
gyan	→	gyān
hankar-jankar	→	haṇkār-jaṇkār
hantya	→	hantyā
harami nach	→	harāmī nāc
hava	→	havā
isht devata	→	iṣṭa-devatā
ishvar	→	īśvar
itihas	→	itihās
ji	→	jī
jagah	→	jagah
jagar	→	jāgar
jagari	→	jāgarī
jagariya	→	jagariyā
jagrit karana	→	jāgrit karana
jajaman	→	jajamān
janamashatmi	→	janamāṣṭamī
janch	→	jāṇc
jat	→	jāt
jata	→	jaṭā
jati	→	jāti
jugalbandi	→	jugalabandī
julus	→	julūs
jogi	→	jogī
kaisa ghata	→	kaisā ghāṭā

kala	→	kalā
kalpana	→	kalpanā
kampana	→	kāmpanā
kan	→	kaṇ
kharoch	→	kharoc
khashya	→	khaśya
khasiya	→	khasiyā
khel	→	khel
kripa	→	kṛpā
kshetra	→	kṣetra
kul devata	→	kul devatā
kundali	→	kuṇḍalī
lila	→	līlā
mahatma	→	mahātmā
mahanata	→	mahānatā
mahapurush	→	mahāpuruṣ
mahaul	→	mahaul
maidan	→	maidān
maike	→	maike
mait	→	mait
mandir	→	mandir
mantra vigyan	→	mantra vigyān
man karana	→	mān karanā
man rakhana	→	mān rakhanā
manana	→	mānanā
manauti	→	manautī
mandap	→	maṇḍap
mara	→	marā
mishran	→	miśran
mistri	→	mistrī
moti	→	motī
mrityu lok	→	mṛtyu lok
mukhdi-hasli	→	mukhaḍī-hasaḷī
mul	→	mūl
murti	→	mūrti
nach	→	nāc
nachana	→	nacānā or nācanā

nag	→	nāg
nagadosh	→	nāgadoṣ
nagara	→	nagāṛā
nam lena	→	nām lenā
naresh	→	nareś
nar lok	→	nar lok
nak mastak	→	nāk mastak
nasha	→	naśā
neta	→	netā
netagiri	→	netāgirī
niti	→	nīti
nyaute bolana	→	nyaute bolanā
nyaya devata	→	nyāya devatā
pahari	→	pahāṛī
panchava dham	→	pañcavā dhām
panchamrit	→	pañcamṛt
panchayat	→	pañcāyat
pandit	→	paṇḍit
pandav-nrtya	→	pāṇḍav-nṛtya
panno	→	panno
pap	→	pāp
pareshani	→	pareśānī
pariksha	→	parīkṣā
pasva	→	pasvā
patal lok	→	pātāl lok
phant	→	phāṇṭ
phora-phunsi	→	phoṛā-phuṇsī
picchli dhansli	→	pichlī-dhaṇslī
pithai	→	piṭhāī
prachar	→	pracār
prakop	→	prakop
prasad	→	prasād
puja	→	pūjā
pujari	→	pujārī
rama	→	rāma
rup	→	rūp
sadhu	→	sādhu

sach bolana	→	sac bolanā
sachai	→	saccāī
sakar	→	sākār
samsara	→	saṃsāra
sar	→	sār
satya nibhana	→	satya nibhānā
sanatan dharma	→	sanātan dharma
sant	→	sant
sannyasi	→	sannyāsī
saptah	→	saptah
sasural	→	sasurāl
shakti	→	śakti
shaitan	→	śaitān
shant	→	śānt
sharir	→	śarīr
shila	→	śilā
shilpakar	→	śilpakār
shodh	→	śodh
seva	→	sevā
siddha pith	→	siddha pīṭh
sindur	→	sindūr
sthan	→	sthān
suchi	→	sūcī
suphal	→	suphal
tabiyat kharab hona	→	tabīyat kharāb honā
thal	→	thāl
than	→	thān
thakur	→	ṭhākur
tirth sthan	→	tīrth sthān
totali	→	totalī
ugra rup	→	ugra rūp
ulta ber ka kanta	→	ulṭā ber ka kāṇṭā
vesh	→	veś
vikas	→	vikās

Notes

Prelude: The Healing Room

1. In accordance with social science ethics protocols, I have anonymized the names of my interlocutors unless they were public figures or specifically requested to be named. I have also changed the names of villages, although I have kept district names and names of cities to convey geographic specificity.
2. The word *bakkya* (pronounced *bakkyā* or *bākya*) in Garhwali is related to the Sanskrit-language word *vach* (speech). The activity a bakkya engages in is referred to as *bak bolana* (literally, "to speak/utter speech"). Such ritual specialists are called by other names as well, such as *puch*, related to the Hindi word *puchana*, "to ask." See William Sax, "Healing Rituals," *Anthropology & Medicine* 11, no. 3 (2004): 294.
3. Embodied deities in oracular rituals sometimes serve as go-betweens between human beings and other, more remote, detached, or elevated divinities such as Shiva or Nirakar, who are thought to be less inclined to involve themselves in the mundane affairs of their devotees, such as finding suitable employment or resolving disputes with relatives or neighbors. This is partly because some of these deities are thought to have once lived as ordinary human beings who subsequently joined the ranks of divinity by dint of their martial valor, sacrificial actions, yogic austerities, or by the boons of "higher" Hindu deities, such as Shiva. Despite their divinization, they remain closely tied to the human-social world and, as such, are able to intervene directly in the lives of their worshipers.
4. Clients and audiences had elaborate techniques to "evaluate" the efficacy and work of oracles like Sohan, and these evaluations helped sustain ritual performances, including the one I was witnessing. For instance, next to Sohan was a tray filled with coals that burned throughout the oracle's interactions with clients. The oracle used these coals to light the lamps on his altar and heat his tongs and trident—two of the deity's "signs" (*nishan*) that he always kept beside him. During particular rituals, the deity heated the metal tongs over a coal fire until they were red hot. He then licked the tongs, or rather, "ate" the fire. "The deities enjoy this," Billu told me, "it satisfies their hunger." Deities lick these fiery instruments, in part, to demonstrate how

powerful they are. Spectators often remarked that this is a sign that the medium's embodiment is legitimate—and that the medium, because he is under the influence of a powerful deity—cannot be harmed. "The fire does not leave a mark on his [the oracle's] skin, even though we can see it burn. Because of the deity's power, he [the oracle] feels no pain. I, on the other, cry out if I get burned by a tiny match," Billu said, laughing.

5. The phrase "taking your name" (*nam lena*) means "to acknowledge" and "to honor." The deity's complaint was that Ramesh was not honoring the gods properly.
6. I was reminded here of the dynamics of what is called *dvesha-bhakti* in other Hindu contexts: a form of devotionalism wherein a devotee is sharply critical of the deity to whom they are dedicated. In these devotional contexts, powerful "negative" feelings toward a deity, such as anger or hate, are equally efficacious in establishing close deity-devotee relations as positive emotions such as love and gratitude. See David Shulman and V. Narayana Rao, *Classical Telugu Poetry: An Anthology* (Berkeley: University of California Press, 2002).

Introduction: Textures of Divine Presence

1. My fieldwork was conducted primarily in Hindi as well as Garhwali and Kumaoni. In the ritual contexts in which I worked, Garhwali and Kumaoni dialects were primarily used, which I was able to understand. However, I worked closely with ritual performers to translate ritual and performance texts, so they could also interpret them for me.
2. Tanya M. Luhrmann, "Anthropology as Spiritual Discipline," *American Ethnologist* (2023): 1–4. For Luhrmann, ethnographic research and writing is "not only a science-like comparative enterprise but also a spiritual discipline" (1).
3. Jeanne Favret-Saada, "Being Affected," *HAU Journal of Ethnographic Theory* 2, no.1 (2012): 435–45.
4. Robert A. Orsi, *The Madonna of 115th Street: Faith and Community in Italian Harlem, 1880-1950*, 2nd ed. (New Haven, CT: Yale University Press, 2002), xxi.
5. Philip Lutgendorf, *The Life of a Text: Performing the Ramcaritmanas of Tulsidas* (Berkeley: University of California Press,1991), 250.
6. Diana Eck, *Darśan: Seeing the Divine Image in India* (New York: Columbia University Press, 1998), 38.
7. I understand the relationship between *sthan* (transliteration: *sthān*) and "presence" as a ritualized metonymy. Laurie Patton refers to metonymy as "a kind of mental mapping whereby we conceive of an entire person, object, or event by understanding a salient part of a person, object or event." See Laurie Patton, *Bringing the Gods to Mind: Mantra and Ritual in Early Indian Sacrifice* (Berkeley: University of California Press, 2005), 49. In this view, a "part" (*sthan*) is ritually operationalized as shorthand for the invocation of a greater, specific "whole," namely, divine presence.
8. Lucinda Ramberg, "Magical Hair as Dirt: Ecstatic Bodies and Postcolonial Reform in South India," *Culture, Medicine and Psychiatry* 33, no. 4 (2009): 501–22.
9. Discussing deities in Tamil Nadu, Soumhya Venkateshan observes that "embodied gods require care, but such care takes different forms depending on the type of deity, ranging from sustained and regular attention to respectful avoidance." See Soumhya Venkateshan, "Object, Subject, Thing: Tamil Hindu Priests' Material Practices and Practical Theories of Animation and Accommodation," *American Ethnologist* 47, no. 4 (2020): 454.

10. See Louis Dumont, *Homo Hierarchicus: An Essay on the Caste System*, trans. Richard Mark Sainsbury (Chicago, Illinois: University of Chicago Press, 1970); Joyce Burkhalter Flueckiger, *When the World Becomes Female: Guises of a South Indian Goddess* (Bloomington: Indiana University Press, 2013); C. J. Fuller, *The Camphor Flame: Popular Hinduism and Society in India* (New Delhi: Viking Penguin India 1992); Lucinda Ramberg, *Given to the Goddess: South Indian Devadasis and the Sexuality of Religion* (Durham, NC: Duke University Press, 2014); David Dean Shulman, *Tamil Temple Myths: Sacrifice and Divine Marriage in the South Indian Saiva Tradition* (Princeton, NJ: Princeton University Press, 1980).
11. Venkateshan, "Object, Subject, Thing," 448.
12. Matthew Engelke, *A Problem of Presence: Beyond Scripture in an African Church* (Berkeley: University of California Press, 2007).
13. See Matthew Engelke, "Material Religion," in *The Cambridge Companion to Religious Studies*, ed. Robert A. Orsi (New York: Cambridge University Press, 2012), 213. Engelke goes on to argue that focusing on the "materiality of religion allows us to explore crucial representational and communication aspects of religious thought and practice, not as free-floating signs that reveal meaning, but as indices, identities, and other markers that are inextricably linked to, dependent upon, and subject to the contingencies of the material world" (214).
14. Place and movement are not only particular to deities in north India, but rather, central to religious practice in general. As Tweed notes: "religions enable and constrain terrestrial, corporeal, and cosmic crossings . . . dwelling is as much an active process as crossing." See Thomas Tweed, *Crossing and Dwelling a Theory of Religion* (Cambridge, MA: Harvard University Press, 2006), 75–83.
15. For analyses of how *dosh* is understood and treated in South India, please see Amy Allocco, "Fear Reverence and Ambivalence," *Religions of South Asia* 7, nos. 1–3 (2013): 230–48; "The Blemish of 'Modern Times': Snakes Planets and the Kaliyugam," *Nidan: International Journal for Indian Studies* 26, no. 1 (2014): 1–21; "Snakes, Goddesses, and Anthills: Modern Challenges and Women's Ritual Responses in Contemporary South India" (PhD diss., Emory University, 2009).
16. There are nonhumans in Garhwal, other than gods and goddesses, who can also cause misfortune and disease if they are not given sthan. One example of such beings are *hantyas*, who are described as humans, generally women and small children, who have died traumatic and/or untimely deaths. The spirits (*atma*) of such beings are said to be unable or unwilling to leave the places and people whom they were close to in life. As a result, they exist in an existential limbo, an in-between realm between this world and the next. In this state, they are considered harmful; their attachment to the world of the living produces misfortune in the communities to which they belonged. Such spirits of the untimely dead are comparable to those written about by Amy Allocco, "Bringing the Dead Home: Hindu Invitation Rituals in Tamil South India," *Journal of the American Academy of Religion* 89, no.1 (2021): 103–42; William Sax, *God of Justice: Ritual Healing and Social Justice in the Central Himalayas* (Oxford: Oxford University Press, 2009): 165–99; Isabelle Nabokov, *Religion Against the Self: An Ethnography of Tamil Rituals* (Oxford: Oxford University Press, 2000); Bruce Kapferer, *A Celebration of Demons: Exorcism and the Aesthetics of Healing in Sri Lanka* (Bloomington: Indiana University Press, 1983), among others. *Hantya* need to be ritually placated to stop them from causing harm. One of the ways this is done is by offering them sthan through the performance of rituals wherein hantya are given dwelling places within family homes and/or shrines to inhabit.
17. I use *narrative* as a gloss for a wide variety of performances distinguished by the inhabitants of Uttarakhand themselves between long ballads and epics (*gathas*) and shorter folk songs (*git*),

such as *mangal-git*, or wedding songs, even though gathas are also, for the most part, sung. See Andrew Alter, *Dancing with Devtās: Drums, Power and Possession in the Music of Garhwal, North India* (Aldershot: Ashgate, 2008), 47. I refer to these gathas simply as "narratives," though the term *epic* is also appropriate in many cases, referring to sung narratives of considerable length that recount the heroic lives, deeds, and exploits of gods and/or extraordinary humans.

18. Transliteration: *jāgar*
19. Transliteration: *nāc*
20. The term *jagar* is polysemic: on the one hand, *jagar* refers to a ritual in which a designated deity or deities is/are induced by ritual drumming and the performance of narrative song to "possess" an oracle/medium of the spirit. See Allen Fanger, "The Jagar: Spirit Possession Seance Among the Rajputs and Silpakars of Kumaon," in *Himalaya: Past and Present*, ed. M. P. Joshi, C.W. Brown, A. C. Fanger (Almora: Shree Almora Book Depot 1990): 173–91. On the other hand, *jagar* refers solely to the oral, sung narratives performed in the process of "awakening" (*jagrit karana*) a divinity to both themselves and their worshipers. In other words, *jagar* refers to the ritual occasion as well as the god's story that is sung during the ritual.
21. As Stefan Fiol observes: "In most *jagar* rituals there are six distinct types of participants: the medium, or *paswa* (lit. "beast," also called the *mali* or *dangariya* [lit. "little horse"] in some areas); the ceremonial specialist, or guru (also called the *jagariya*); one or more vocal and instrumental accompanists; the host; the gods and goddesses (*devi-devtao*); and the invited attendees." See Stefan Fiol, *Recasting Folk in the Himalayas: Indian Music Media and Social Mobility* (Urbana: University of Illinois Press, 2017), 169
22. Andrew Alter, *Mountainous Sound Spaces* (Delhi: Cambridge University Press, 2014), 151–62; Fiol, *Recasting Folk in the Himalayas*; John Leavitt, "Oracular Therapy in the Kumaon Hills: A Question of Rationality," *Indian Anthropologist* 16, no. 1 (1986): 71–79; Aditya Malik, *Tales of Justice and Rituals of Divine Embodiment: Oral Narratives from the Central Himalayas* (New York: Oxford University Press, 2016); Sax, *God of Justice*.
23. David Haberman, *River of Love in an Age of Pollution: The Yamuna River of Northern India*, 1st ed. (Ewing: University of California Press, 2006); James Lochtefeld, *God's Gateway: Identity and Meaning in a Hindu Pilgrimage Place* (New York: Oxford University Press, 2010); Andrea Marion Pinkney, "Prasāda, the Gracious Gift, in Contemporary and Classical South Asia," *Journal of the American Academy of Religion* 81, no. 3 (2013): 734–56; Karin Polit, "The Making of Persons and Ancestors: Rituals of Birth and Death Among Dalits in the Garhwal Himalayas," in *Childbirth and Its Accompanying Rituals in South and South East Asia*, ed. Karin M. Polit and Gabriele Alex, (Heidelberg: Draupadi Verlag, 2016), 59–86; Luke Whitmore, *Mountain, Water, Rock, God: Understanding Kedarnath in the Twenty-First Century* (Berkeley: University of California Press, 2018).
24. For devotees of Nagaraja, a unique practice in Sem Mukhem temple is to release two snakes made of silver—a male and female—into the nearby river to remedy a condition known as *nagadosh* (literally, "fault of the serpent" or "serpent affliction"). A common way to incur nagadosh is to injure or kill a snake while one is engaged in agricultural labor. Nagadosh has negative consequences for the wellbeing of the individual transgressor as well as their family and community. To cure nagadosh, the transgressor might abandon the plot of land (to Nagaraja) where the incident happened as a form of penance, undertake a pilgrimage to Sem Mukhem or some other Nagaraja temple, or sponsor a jagar in which Nagaraja is ritually "danced" (*nachana*).
25. See Valentine E. Daniel, *Fluid Signs: Being a Person the Tamil Way* (Berkeley: University of California Press, 1984); A. K. Ramanujan, *Poems of Love and War: From the Eight Anthologies and the Ten Long Poems of Classical Tamil* (New York: Columbia University Press, 1985).

26. Ramanujan, *Poems of Love and War*, 232. Quoted in Diane P. Mines, "Waiting for Veḷḷāḷakaṇṭaṉ: Narrative, Movement, and Making Place in a Tamil Village," in *Tamil Geographies: Cultural Constructions of Space and Place in South India*, ed. Martha Ann Selby and Indira Viswanathan Peterson (Albany: State University of New York Press, 2008), 203.
27. As Edward Casey writes: "Places gather: this I take to be a second essential trait . . . revealed by a phenomenological topo-analysis. Minimally, places gather things in their midst—where "things" connote various animate and inanimate entities. Places also gather experiences and histories, even languages and thoughts. . . . What else is capable of this massively diversified holding action?" See Edward S. Casey, "How to Get from Space to Place in a Fairly Short Stretch of Time," in *Senses of Place*, ed. Steven Feld and Keith H. Basso (Santa Fe, NM: School of American Research Press, 1996), 24.
28. Tim Cresswell, *Place: A Short Introduction* (Hoboken: Wiley, 2004), 51.
29. Phenomenological and social constructionist theorists of place have generally examined placemaking as "the conscious and unconscious way[s] in which we invest places with meaning through our ongoing activities and rituals, contributing to them in ways that express the dreams, passions, needs and values of those in them with the physical features of the environment surrounding them." See Jennifer Abe, "Sacred Place: An Interdisciplinary Approach for the Social Science," in *Communities, Neighborhoods, and Health: Expanding the Boundaries of Place*, ed. Erlinda M Burton (New York: Springer Science+Business Media, 2011), 153. See also Keith H. Basso, *Wisdom Sits in Places: Landscape and Language Among the Western Apache* (Albuquerque: University of New Mexico Press, 1996) and E. C. Relph, *Place and Placelessness* (London: Pion, 1976).
30. As Michel de Certeau observes, citing the Vedic hymn Ṛig Veda 1.154 and George Dumézil's analysis of it: "In the Vedas, Vishnu, 'by his footsteps, opens the zone of space in which Indra's military action must take place.' The . . . ritual is a foundation. It 'provides space' for the actions that will be undertaken; it 'creates a field' which serves as their 'base' and their 'theater.'" See Michel de Certeau, *The Practice of Everyday Life*, trans. Steven Rendall (Berkeley: University of California Press, 1984), 124; Georges Dumezil, *Idées romaines* (Paris: Gallimard, 1969), 61–78.
31. Following Joyce Flueckiger, I translate *ugra* as "excess." As Flueckiger notes, *ugra* is often translated as "anger," "ferocity," and "malevolence." However, this term has a much wider range of meanings, including "huge," "strong," "powerful," "formidable," "passionate," and so on. See Flueckiger, *When the World Becomes Female*, 29.
32. Comparing deities to "winds" is common in many parts of South Asia, especially in the context of "spirit possession." See, for instance, Kathleen M. Erndl, *Victory to the Mother: The Hindu Goddess of Northwest India in Myth, Ritual, and Symbol* (New York: Oxford University Press, 1993). Erndl discusses how the goddess "plays" with her devotees in the form of a "wind" (*pavan*), in the greater Panjab region of north India where she conducted fieldwork.
33. Mines, "Waiting for Veḷḷāḷakaṇṭaṉ," 204.
34. Thomas A. Tweed, *Crossing and Dwelling: A Theory of Religion* (Cambridge, MA: Harvard University Press, 2006), 97.
35. Tweed, *Crossing and Dwelling*, 105.
36. Elaborating on Henri Lefebvre and Pierre Bourdieu's ideas, Nancy Munn continues: "Lefebvre's 'field of action' can also be viewed as the 'mobile spatial field' of the actor in contrast to a determinate region or locale; the latter is the concrete 'basis of action,' which lends itself at any given moment to the actor's moving field. . . . Since a spatial field extends from the actor, *it can also be understood as a culturally defined, corporeal-sensual field of significant distances stretching out from the body* in a particular stance or action at a given locale or as it moves through locales.

This field can be plotted along a hypothetical trajectory centered in the situated body with its expansive movements and immediate tactile reach, and extendable beyond this center in vision, vocal reach, and hearing (and further where relevant). *The body is thus understood as a spatial field (and the spatial field as a bodily field)*" [emphases mine'. See Nancy Munn, "Excluded Spaces: The Figure in the Australian Aboriginal Landscape," *Critical Inquiry* 22, no. 3 (1996): 450.

37. See Frederick Smith, *The Self Possessed: Deity and Spirit Possession in South Asian Literature and Civilization* (New York: Columbia University Press, 2006) and Shulman, *Tamil Temple Myths*. In theorizing ritual placemaking, I draw upon Frederick Smith and David Shulman's ideas regarding the localization of divinity in Tamil Nadu. Smith cites Shulman to argue that the localization, immanence, and the transportability of divinity "provides a background metaphysic" for the phenomenon of possession in South Asia. Smith writes:

> Thus [sacred presence] is the substantial and immanent means through which divinity, or any other power, is localized, whether it occurs in objects, places, or persons.... This extensiveness and localization of divinity, though not a concept actively enunciated in the early Tamil texts, was an assumed part of south Indian religion and much more of a force in central and north India than Shulman recognized.... The acceptance of the multilocality of divinity must surely have contributed to the notion that the divine, or any other less benign force, could penetrate and divinize any receptive individual. *In this way, the individual—the person in the form of the body—became a sacred site, confirming the Toda conception of sacred space noted by Murray Emeneau in 1938: "the "sacred place" and the "god" are the same thing"* [emphasis mine] (73).

38. See Sarah Caldwell, *Oh Terrifying Mother: Sexuality, Violence, and Worship of the Goddess Kali* (New Delhi: Oxford University Press, 1999); Erndl, *Victory to the Mother*; Nabokov, *Religion Against the Self*; Gananath Obeyesekere, *The Work of Culture: Symbolic Transformation in Psychoanalysis and Anthropology* (Chicago: University of Chicago Press, 2000); Kalpana Ram, *Fertile Disorder: Spirit Possession and Its Provocation of the Modern* (Honolulu: University of Hawaii Press, 2013); William Sturman Sax, *Dancing the Self: Personhood and Performance in the Pandav Lila of Garhwal* (Oxford: Oxford University Press, 2002).

39. I. M. Lewis is one of earliest and most influential proponents of the power-resistance paradigm within possession studies. In his foundational work, *Ecstatic Religion: A Study of Shamanism and Spirit Possession* (London: Routledge, 2005), Lewis distinguishes between two forms of spirit possession—namely, "peripheral" and "central"—on the basis of their relationship to the dominant social order where they occur. He argues that, unlike in "central" possession cults, where possession effectively endorses normative social hierarchies, possession practices in "peripheral" cults are an indirect expression of sociopolitical resistance by marginalized groups, such as women and so-called low-caste communities. According to Frederick Smith, in South Asian contexts, in addition to being examined as an autonomous category of behavior, possession has been studied as a form of shamanism, a psychological phenomenon, a mode of social resistance, and an ontological or existential reality. Commenting on these approaches to possession, Janice Boddy observes that scholarly attention was directed to the instrumental, strategic uses of consensual beliefs by socially disadvantaged (so-called status-deprived) individuals who, in claiming to be seized by spirits, indirectly brought public attention to their plight and potentially achieved some redress. See Janice Boddy, "Spirit Possession Revisited: Beyond Instrumentality," *Annual Review of Anthropology* 23 (1994): 410.

40. Isabelle Nabokov, *Religion Against the Self*.

41. Smith, *The Self Possessed*, 57.
42. Sax, *Dancing the Self*. In this excellent study of the Pandav Lila tradition, which dramatizes episodes from the Mahabharata epic in Garhwal, William Sax reveals how social prestige and political power are contested through narrative and ritual performance. Combining anthropological, religious studies, and performance studies approaches, Sax examines public rituals as powerful means for creating persons, relationships, and communities for Rajputs. *Gods in the World* also draws from Sax' other ethnographies in Uttarakhand, including *God of Justice*, which thematizes experiences of affliction and healing, and *Mountain Goddess: Gender and Politics in a Himalayan Pilgrimage* (New York: Oxford University Press, 1991), which discusses the royal pilgrimage tradition of the Goddess Nanda Devi. In each of these works, Sax illuminates the performative and psychosocial dynamics of religious practice in Uttarakhand. While there exist important theoretical, methodological, and thematic overlaps between Sax's work and my own—such as a shared focus on nonhuman agency, ritual "efficacy," and illness, health, and healing—*Gods in the World* also departs from the former in some key ways. For instance, whereas in each of his aforementioned books, Sax works with members of a single caste group—either Brahmins, Rajputs, or Dalits—*Gods in the World* is concerned with how relations between caste groups (and especially their religious specialists) are negotiated in people's everyday lives and narrative and ritual practices. In addition to focusing on the complexities of inter-caste and gender relations and dis/articulations of Pahari Hindu contexts of practice, *Gods in the World* also attends to how the rise of neoliberalism and Hindu nationalism across India since the 1990s has transformed Uttarakhand's social, political, and material landscapes—and the ways in which differently positioned Pahari actors are responding to these shifting historical realities, including the "Hindu-ization" of their deities, sacred sites, and narrative and ritual practices.
43. See Valentine E. Daniel and Judy F. Pugh, eds. *South Asian Systems of Healing* (Leiden: E. J. Brill, 1984).
44. Edith Turner, "The Reality of Spirits: A Tabooed or Permitted Field of Study," *Anthropology of Consciousness* 4, no.1 (1993): 9–12.
45. Joyce B. Flueckiger, "When the Goddess Speaks Her Mind: Possession, Presence, and Narrative Theology in the Gaṅgamma Tradition of Tirupati, South India," *International Journal of Hindu Studies* 21, no. 2 (2017): 165–85.
46. See also Ramberg, "Magical Hair as Dirt," 515.
47. Stephen Alter, *Sacred Waters: A Pilgrimage Up the Ganges River to the Source of Hindu Culture* (New York: Harcourt, 2001); Knut Aukland, "Pilgrimage Expansion Through Tourism in Contemporary India: The Development and Promotion of a Hindu Pilgrimage Circuit," *Journal of Contemporary Religion* 32, no. 2 (2017): 283–98.
48. Kumar M. Tiku, "In Uttarakhand, Young Women Lead an Exodus from Mountain Villages," *The Wire*, April 10, 2019, https://thewire.in/rights/uttarakhand-outmigration-crisis-villages.
49. Bhagirath, "Rural Migration May Alter Uttarakhand's Political Geography," *DownToEarth*, February 28, 2020, https://www.downtoearth.org.in/news/governance/rural-migration-may-alter-uttarakhand-s-political-geography-69510.
50. Vinod C. Tewari, "Himalayan Tsunami: Devastating Natural Disaster in the Uttarakhand Himalaya," accessed December 6, 2022, https://bibliographie.uni-tuebingen.de/xmlui/bitstream/handle/10900/50071/pdf/Tewari2_168.pdf?sequence=1.
51. Mujib Mashal and Hari Kumar, "Before Himalayan Flood, India Ignored Warnings of Development Risks," *New York Times*, February 8, 2021, https://www.nytimes.com/2021/02/08/world/asia/india-flood-ignored-warnings.html.

52. Tewari, "Himalayan Tsunami: Devastating Natural Disaster in the Uttarakhand Himalaya."
53. G. Sampath, "Don't Blame Nature for the Uttarakhand Flood Disaster," *Mint*, June 27, 2013, https://www.livemint.com/Opinion/hzKmWekwYOOtYKv8N6dZlN/Dont-blame-nature-for-the-Uttarakhand-flood-disaster.html.
54. Mukul Sharma, "Passages from Nature to Nationalism: Sunderlal Bahuguna and Tehri Dam Opposition in Garhwal," *Economic and Political Weekly* 44, no. 8 (2009): 35–42.
55. Sam Campbell and Laura Gurney, "Mapping and Navigating Ontologies in Water Governance: The Case of the Ganges," *Water International* 45, nos. 7–8 (2020): 847–64.
56. Vandana Shiva and J. Bandyopadhyay, "The Evolution Structure and Impact of the Chipko Movement," *Mountain Research and Development 1986*, 133–42.
57. India Today Web Desk, "PM Narendra Modi in Kedarnath: 5 Things He Said About Temple Shrine in Past," *India Today*, May 18, 2019, https://www.indiatoday.in/india/story/pm-narendra-modi-in-kedarnath-5-things-he-said-about-temple-shrine-in-past-1528054-2019-05-18.
58. Apoorvanand, "Modi in Kedarnath—After the Deluge, the Delusion," *The Wire*, October 23, 2017, https://thewire.in/politics/narendra-modi-kedarnath-uttarakhand.
59. Aukland, "Pilgrimage Expansion Through Tourism in Contemporary India," 283–98.
60. Joel Lee, *Deceptive Majority: Hinduism, Untouchability, and Underground Religion* (Cambridge: Cambridge University Press, 2021), 14.
61. Uttarakhand also has a 14 percent Muslim population while OBC/STs are less than 5 percent. See Ashutosh Bhardwaj, "Uttarakhand Elections: Across the Border; Next to UP, New Caste Calculus," *Indian Express*, February 15, 2017, https://indianexpress.com/elections/uttarakhand-assembly-elections-2017/uttarakhand-elections-across-the-border-next-door-to-up-new-caste-calculus-4525289/. Political commentators often contrast the Dalit-Muslim politics of Uttar Pradesh with the "Thakur-Brahmin" political dominance in Uttarakhand.
62. See Gerald D. Berreman, *Hindus of the Himalayas: Ethnography and Change*, 2nd ed., rev. and enl. (Delhi: Oxford University Press, 1993 [1963]). While the socioeconomic status of Brahmin and Rajput communities is roughly the same across Uttarakhand, some Pahari journalists and intellectuals told me that, for various historical reasons, Brahmins were dominant in the Kumaon region, while the same was true for Rajputs in Garhwal.
63. "Census Of India 2011 Release Of Primary Census Abstract Data Highlights," Indian Ministry of Home Affairs, April 30, 2013, https://idsn.org/wp-content/uploads/user_folder/pdf/New_files/India/2013/INDIA_CENSUS_ABSTRACT-2011-Data_on_SC-STs.pdf.
64. See Chinnaiah Jangam, Ramnarayan S. Rawat, Anupama Rao, and Gopal Guru, "A Dalit Paradigm: A New Narrative in South Asian Historiography," *Modern Asian Studies* 50, no. 1 (2016): 399–414. Chinnaiah Jangam writes: "Dalit, meaning a broken people, defines their self-perception, defies the humiliating Brahmanical Hindu past, and articulates a self-assertive agency in the public sphere" (406).
65. C. S. Adcock, "Debating Conversion, Silencing Caste: The Limited Scope of Religious Freedom," *Journal of Law and Religion* 29, no. 3 (2014): 369
66. Adcock, "Debating Conversion, Silencing Caste," 369.
67. As Jangam et al. write: "Untouchability has been institutionalized as a form of social practice in India for centuries, enforced by Hindu Brahmanical ideology which sanctioned violence, exclusion, and humiliation as punishments for those who questioned it." Jangam et al., "A Dalit Paradigm," 409.
68. See Karin Polit, "The Effects of Inequality and Relative Marginality on the Well-Being of Low Caste People in Central Uttaranchal," *Anthropology and Medicine* 12, no. 3 (2005): 225–37. See also Sax, *God of Justice*.

69. See Fiol, *Recasting Folk in the Himalayas*, 12; Peter Claus Zoller, "A Little Known Form of Untouchability in the Central Himalayas," in *Reading Slowly: A Festschrift for Jens E. Braarvig*, 1st ed., ed. Lutz Edzard, Jens W. Borgland, and Ute Hüsken (Wiesbaden: Harrassowitz Verlag, 2018), 485.
70. Ramnarayan S. Rawat, *Reconsidering Untouchability: Chamars and Dalit History in North India* (Bloomington: Indiana University Press, 2011).
71. See Kushal Choudhary and Govind Sharma, "Dalit Majority Village in Uttarakhand Plagued by Untouchability," *NewsClick*, June 24, 2022, https://www.newsclick.in/Dalit-Majority-Village-Uttarakhand-Plagued-Untouchability.
72. Jangam, et al., "A Dalit Paradigm," 413.
73. Choudhary and Sharma, "Dalit Majority Village."
74. See Anil K. Joshi, "Dalit Reform Movement in British Kumaon," *Proceedings of the Indian History Congress* 61 (2000): 978; Fiol, *Recasting Folk in the Himalayas*. Fiol writes:

    > Members of so-called Dom castes generally followed strict social codes whose violation was punishable by death.... They had to carry palanquins and lead ponies during the wedding ceremonies of their high-caste patrons, but they could not use palanquins or ponies in their own weddings; they had to live on the outside and lower end of a village, with their own access path, water source, cremation sites, and defecation sites.... They were sometimes sold as slave property between village proprietors; and they had to bury dead cows, the flesh of which they consumed, to the detriment of their social position. (38–39)

75. While the term *Dom* is no longer as prevalent as it once was, it is still employed by caste-privileged persons as a dehumanizing slur—a term of disparagement designed to "put Dalits in their place."
76. See C. S. Adcock, *The Limits of Tolerance: Indian Secularism and the Politics of Religious Freedom* (New York: Oxford University Press, 2014). Citing Adcock, Joel Lee observes that, in the early twentieth century, *shuddhi* served as a "mode of 'ritual-political assertion' through which untouchable groups ... collaborated with Munshi Ram's radical faction of the Arya Samaj to secure long-desired rights and respite from the long-hated rituals of humiliation enforced by the agrarian caste order." Lee, *Deceptive Majority*, 88. See also Susan Bayly, *Caste Society and Politics in India from the Eighteenth Century to the Modern Age* (New York: Cambridge University Press, 1999).
77. Chad M. Bauman, "Hindu-Christian Conflict in India: Globalization, Conversion, and the Coterminal Castes and Tribes," *Journal of Asian Studies* 72, no. 3 (2013): 639.
78. See J. M. Sebring, "The Formation of New Castes: A Probable Case from North India," *American Anthropologist* 74, no. 3 (1972): 587–600.
79. Fiol, *Recasting Folk in the Himalayas*, 12.
80. Fiol, *Recasting Folk in the Himalayas*, 40.
81. Jangam et al., "A Dalit Paradigm," 403.
82. See Fiol, *Recasting Folk in the Himalayas*, 40; Joshi, "Dalit Reform Movement," 976–85.
83. Fiol, *Recasting Folk in the Himalayas*, 40.
84. Jangam, et al. "A Dalit Paradigm," 405.
85. Jangam et al., "A Dalit Paradigm," 405. Jangam goes on to write that "the reconstruction of new self-identities was a quintessential part of [Dalit] political imagination. Therefore the identities of untouchables have moved away from stigmatized Brahmanical identities such as *Panchamas*, *Asprusya*, and been distanced from the patronizing *Harijan* identity bestowed by M. K. Gandhi. They have envisioned radical, self-assertive identities like Adi-Hindu, Adi-Andhra, and finally settled on the radical, rebellious identity of Dalits in contemporary India" (405–406).

86. See Stuart H. Blackburn, Peter J. Claus, Joyce B. Flueckiger, and Susan S. Wadley, eds., *Oral Epics in India* (Berkeley: University of California Press, 1989); Ramberg, *Given to the Goddess*; Zoller, "A Little-Known Form of Untouchability."
87. See also Aftab Singh Jassal, "Awakening the Serpent King: Ritual and Textual Ontologies in Garhwal, Uttarakhand," *Journal of Hindu Studies* 13, no. 2 (2020): 101–21.
88. In 2021, Pushkar Singh Dhami was elected as the chief minister of Uttarakhand. He has been a long-time, dedicated member of the Rashtriya Swayamsevak Sangh (RSS), a Hindu nationalist organization that has promoted violence against Uttarakhand's Muslim population, which constitutes 14 percent of the state's total population. See Harsh Mander, "How State-Backed Hindutva Rhetoric Is Fueling the Ethnic Cleansing of Uttarakhand," *Scroll.in*, November 3, 2023, https://scroll.in/article/1057843/how-state-backed-hindutva-rhetoric-is-fuelling-the-ethnic-cleansing-of-uttarakhand.
89. Fiol, *Recasting Folk in the Himalayas*, 23.
90. Historically, Dalits have "converted' (to Buddhism, Christianity, Islam, and other religions to resist what they perceive to be the religiously-sanctioned violence of casteism in Hinduism. See Lee, *Deceptive Majority*; Owen M. Lynch, *The Politics of Untouchability: Social Mobility and Social Change in a City of India* (New York: Columbia University Press, 1969); Gail Omvedt, *Seeking Begumpura: The Social Vision of Anticaste Intellectuals* (New Delhi: Navayana: Distributed by IPD Alternatives, 2008). See also Robert J. Stephens, "Sites of Conflict in the Indian Secular State: Secularism, Caste and Religious Conversion," *Journal of Church and State* 49, no. 2 (2007): 251–76. Robert Stephens notes that many modern Indian thinkers, such as B. R. Ambedkar, Dayanand Saraswati, and Sarvepalli Radhakrishnan "affirm the centrality of caste to 'Hinduism.' Indeed, the problem of the relationship between caste and 'Hinduism' has engaged a variety of thinkers from both religious and legal disciplines on a number of levels. Even prior to independence from the British, an important discussion focused on issue of religious conversion to 'non-Hindu' traditions, especially Christianity and Islam, and what changes the social event of conversion might entail regarding the new convert's caste status and legal identity" (269). Although statistics for religious conversions in India are notoriously hard to come by, approximately 7.3 million Dalits (also called "Ambedkarites" after the Dalit leader, B. R. Ambedkar) are now registered as Buddhists. See Krithika Varagur, "Converting to Buddhism as a Form of Social Protest," *The Atlantic*, April 11, 2018, https://www.theatlantic.com/international/archive/2018/04/dalit-buddhism-conversion-india-modi/557570/.
91. Ronki Ram, "Beyond Conversion and Sanskritisation: Articulating an Alternative Dalit Agenda in East Punjab," *Modern Asian Studies* 46, no. 3 (2012): 643. Also see Eliza Kent, "'Mass Movements' in South India, 1877–1936," in *Converting Cultures: Religion, Ideology and Transformations of Modernity*, ed. Dennis Washburn and Kevin Reinhart (Leiden: Brill, 2007). Eliza Kent observes that, in "mass conversions . . . large numbers of people connected by bonds constructed on the basis of caste and family *publicly* transfer their loyalties from one set of religious texts, institutions and leaders to another" (italics mine; 367). The public nature of conversion sets it apart from the emergence of "crypto-religion," wherein one's true religious affiliation, for various reasons, is not publicly declaimed.
92. Pierre Beaucage, Deirdre Meintel, and Géraldine Mossière, "Introduction: Social and Political Dimensions of Religious Conversion," *Anthropologica* 49, no. 1 (2007): 15.
93. Omvedt, *Seeking Begumpura*, 91–109. John Stratton Hawley and Mark Juergensmeyer, *Songs of the Saints of India*, rev. ed. (New Delhi: Oxford University Press, 2004). For information about the Sant Nirankari Mission and related movements, also see Mark Juergensmeyer, *Radhasoami Reality: The Logic of a Modern Faith* (Princeton, NJ: Princeton University Press, 1991); Harjot

Oberoi, *The Construction of Religious Boundaries: Culture Identity and Diversity in the Sikh Tradition* (Chicago: University of Chicago Press, 1994).
94. Ram, "Beyond Conversion and Sanskritisation," 641. In Ronki Ram's formulation, Dalit "homecoming" operates in sharp contrast to coercive Hindu nationalist projects of "homecoming," or *ghar vapasi*, aimed at "reconverting" or reincorporating religious minorities into the Hindu fold.
95. Fiol, *Recasting Folk in the Himalayas*, 10.
96. Jassal, "Awakening the Serpent King," 101–21.
97. Aftab S. Jassal, "Making God Present: Placemaking and Ritual Healing in North India," *International Journal of Hindu Studies* 21, no. 2 (2017): 141–64.
98. Flueckiger, *When the World Becomes Female*.

1. Making "Dev-bhumi," the Land of the Gods

1. *Avatar lena* ("to take incarnation") and *avatarit hona* ("to become incarnated") were phrases many of my local interlocutors employed in describing a deity's embodied manifestation in jagar rituals.
2. Anne Feldhaus, *Connected Places: Region, Pilgrimage, and Geographical Imagination in India* (New York: Palgrave Macmillan, 2003). In *Connected Places*, Feldhaus defines *region* as:

    a set of places that are connected with one another and that taken together contrast with some other set of places (another region). A region in this sense is not the concern of an "objective" geography. . . . Rather, [a] region . . . is one that is thought of as such by its residents and perhaps also by some others, [as] an area with a distinct identity and significance for people who live in it and for others who think and care about it. In this sense, a region is a kind of place (8).

3. Edward Casey, *Getting Back into Place: Toward a Renewed Understanding of the Place-World*. (Bloomington: Indiana University Press, 1993), 53.
4. Feldhaus, *Connected Places*, 13.
5. Diana L. Eck, *India: A Sacred Geography* (Westminster: Harmony, 2012).
6. See Pralay Kanungo and Satyakam Joshi, "Carving Out a White Marble Deity from a Rugged Black Stone? Hindutva Rehabilitates Ramayan's Shabari in a Temple," *International Journal of Hindu Studies* 13, no. 3 (2009): 279–99; Deepa S. Reddy, "Hindutva: Formative Assertions," *Religion Compass* 5, no. 8 (2011): 439–51.
7. "Kedarnath Will Become a Model Pilgrimage Site: PM Modi," *Times of India*, October 20, 2017, https://timesofindia.indiatimes.com/india/kedarnath-will-become-a-model-pilgrimage-site-pm-modi/articleshow/61150280.cms?from=mdr.
8. Kalyan Das, "PM Modi Visits Kedarnath, Says Decade Belongs to Uttarakhand," *Hindustan Times*, November 6, 2021, https://www.hindustantimes.com/india-news/more-pilgrims-to-visit-char-dham-shrines-in-10-yrs-than-over-last-century-modi-101636114454610.html.
9. Apoorvanand, "Modi in Kedarnath-After the Deluge, the Delusion," *The Wire*, October 23, 2017, https://thewire.in/politics/narendra-modi-kedarnath-uttarakhand.
10. Tusha Mittal and Alishan Jagri, "The Movement to Expel Muslims and Create a Hindu Holy Land," *Coda*, November 2, 2023, https://www.codastory.com/rewriting-history/the-movement-to-expel-muslims-and-create-a-hindu-holy-land/.

11. Jayati Ghosh, "Hindutva Economic Neoliberalism and the Abuse of Economic Statistics in India," December 14, 2020, https://doi.org/10.4000/samaj.6882.
12. Luke Whitmore, *Mountain, Water, Rock, God: Understanding Kedarnath in the Twenty-First Century* (Oakland: University of California Press, 2018).
13. See Brian Pennington, "Hinduism in North India," in *Hinduism in the Modern World*, ed. Brian A. Hatcher (New York: Routledge, 2016), 31–47. Also see Pennington's forthcoming book, *God's Fifth Abode: Entrepreneurial Hinduism in the Indian Himalayas*, which analyzes the relationship between processes of economic development and religious transformation in the pilgrimage city of Uttarkashi, Uttarakhand.
14. The concept of a "fifth abode" is analogous to that of the "fifth Veda," which was used to expand the Vedic canon and confer authority and stature on later, post-Vedic traditions such as the Mahabharata. Similarly, the "fifth abode" draws on the historical success and prestige of other well-known pilgrimage destinations while at the same time forging a new path for itself. Please see Alf Hiltebeitel, Vishwa Adluri, and Joydeep Bagchee, *Reading the Fifth Veda: Studies on the Mahabharata: Essays* (Leiden: Brill, 2011).
15. In South Asian languages, the word *prachar* has a number of meanings, including "publicity," "propaganda," "pervasion," "dissemination," and "expansion." Lexically, *prachar* can be analyzed as *pra+char*, where the prefix *pra* connotes "outward," and *char*, "movement." Thus, *prachar* can be translated as "outward movement."
16. The temple is ritually overseen by two families of temple priests (*pujaris*), both from the same village. Each controls the temple for half the year.
17. The story does not distinguish between the serpent and its statue, or *murti*. According to Hindu mythology, as a child, Krishna was particularly fond of milk products like butter and curd. Since snakes, too, are believed to like milk, this connects pan-Indian stories about Krishna to his serpentine appearance in Danda Nagaraja.
18. For example, one interlocutor, Jagat Lal Chamoli, who was a Brahmin, former headperson of Rin village, and veteran member of the Danda Nagaraja temple committee, alleged that Danda had originally been a temple dedicated to the god Shiva. "In the past, Danda was a Shiva temple, with the mark [*linga*] of Shiva in its inner sanctum. But then they [the pujaris] twisted and distorted the truth of this place, as pujaris tend to do, and it was turned it into a Nagaraja temple." He was angry about this: "My paternal grandparents used to come here every day, and they taught me everything there is to know about this temple when I was a child, so I know." Yet, even though Jagat ji was critical of the temple authorities, he admitted that they had done an excellent job "spreading awareness" [*prachar*] about Danda Nagaraja: "Not only do pilgrims come to the temple from all over Uttarakhand, they also come from Delhi, Mumbai, and Kolkata," he said.
19. Edwin T. Atkinson, *The Himalayan Gazetteer* (Delhi: Cosmo Publications, 1973), 3.
20. Richard Gombrich, *Theravāda Buddhism: A Social History from Ancient Benares to Modern Colombo*, 2nd ed. (New York: Routledge Taylor & Francis Group, 2006), 37.
21. Narendra Modi, "BJP Will Protect the Divinity of Devbhoomi Uttarakhand: PM Modi," Narendra Modi YouTube Channel, YouTube video, February 12, 2022, https://www.youtube.com/watch?v=X5m6GuwGqQI.I.
22. Arguments that Uttarakhand is *dev-bhumi* have also been used to block certain kinds of development, most notably the Tehri Dam. Hindu nationalists have also been part of the antidam agitations. For example, Swami Chidananda, the head of the Parmath Niketan Ashram in Rishikesh, writes: "India is a holy land; and holiest of the holy and greatest of the great is the

Himalaya especially its Uttarakhand region. All our scriptures support this view. Uttarakhand is *Dev-bhumi* (a place sanctified by the gods) and *Tapobhumi* (a sacred land where yogic 'inner heating' is practiced).... A land of gods, it is called. It makes its dwellers god-like." See Swami Chidananda, "Save The Himalaya" in *Bhagirathi ki Pukar* 7, no. 2, (1997): 1. As Mukul Sharma notes, "To oppose the Tehri dam, certain environmentalists have increasingly resorted to using Hindu myths about the Ganga. These myths together integrate the identity of a river and a 'Hindu' country." See Mukul Sharma, "Saffronising Green," *Seminar Magazine*, 2002, https://www.india-seminar.com/2002/516/516%20mukul%20sharma.htm.

23. Following the invasion of the subcontinent by the Ghurid dynasty, five dynasties ruled over the Delhi sultanate—the Mamluk dynasty (1206–1290), the Khalji dynasty (1290–1320), the Tughlaq dynasty (1320–1414), the Sayyid dynasty (1414–1451), and the Lodi dynasty (1451–1526).
24. As he put it, "Slowly, things are changing here, too. In the past, in Chandrabadani [Temple], we used to sacrifice many buffaloes and goats. But then a religious leader [swami] ended the tradition.... These practices [of animal sacrifice] are dying out."
25. As William Sax explains, "*Khashya* or *khasiya* refers to non-Sanskritic, 'tribal' indigenes of the central (and eastern) Himalayas." Many of those who today call themselves "Rajputs" are indeed descended from these communities. However, by the 1970s, the term had become a derogatory term of abuse and used only in private. See William S. Sax, *Mountain Goddess: Gender and Politics in a Himalayan Pilgrimage* (New York: Oxford University Press, 1991), 65n26.
26. Gerald Duane Berreman, *Hindus of the Himalayas: Ethnography and Change* (Berkeley: University of California Press 1972), 20.
27. Allen C. Fanger, "The Jagar: Spirit Possession Seance Among the Rajputs and Silpakars of Kumaon," in *Himalaya: Past and Present*, ed. M. P. Joshi, C. W. Brown, A. C. Fanger (Almora: Shree Almora Book Depot, 1990), 173.
28. Whereas Mr. Pant defined the term *sidhha pith* as a sacred place that facilitated the realization (*siddha*) of one's spiritual and material goals, Giridhar ji said it was a place where "realized beings" that is, *siddhas*, congregated to meditate upon Brahman and achieve release from the cycle of birth and death.
29. Some notable works that are widely available in bookstores and libraries across Garhwal include: Govind Chatak, *Garhwali Lokagathayen* (New Delhi: Takshila Prakashan,1996); Urbadatta Upadhyay, *Kumaun ki Lokagathaon ka Sahityak aur Sanskritik Adhyyan* (Bareli: Prakash Book Depot, 1979); and Shivanand Nautiyal *Uttarakhand ki Lokagathayen* (Almora: Shree Almora Book Depot, 1997), to name a few. In addition to colonial-era texts, such as those by Atkinson, *The Himalayan Gazetteer* and, E. S. (E. Sherman) Oakley, Tara Dutt Gairola, and Gangā Datt Upreti, *Himalayan Folklore* (Allahabad: Superintendent, Printing and Stationery, U. P., 1935), the bookshelves of many of my literate, middle-class interlocutors also included many contemporary works by Garhwali scholars.
30. *Dvaraka-pati* is an epithet for the god Krishna, who is said to have founded the legendary city of Dvaraka, located in present-day Gujarat.
31. Shiv Prasad Naithani, *Uttarakhand Gathoan ke Rahasya* (Almora: Shree Almora Book Depot, 2010).
32. Naithani, *Uttarakhand Gathoan ke Rahasya*, 185.
33. Naithani, *Uttarakhand Gathoan ke Rahasya*, 169.
34. Naithani, *Uttarakhand Gathoan ke Rahasya*, 194.
35. Naithani, *Uttarakhand Gathoan ke Rahasya*, 194.
36. Naithani, *Uttarakhand Gathoan ke Rahasya*, 199.

37. Naithani, *Uttarakhand Gathoan ke Rahasya*, 146.
38. Mysore Narasimhachar Srinivas, *Religion and Society Among the Coorgs of South India* (Oxford: Clarendon Press, 1952).

2. Affliction and Healing

1. These events occurred in the spring of 2010, soon after I began my doctoral dissertation research.
2. Michel de Certeau, *The Practice of Everyday Life*, trans. Steven Rendall (Berkeley: University of California Press, 1984), 115.
3. Lal is a common surname in Garhwal, especially within Dalit communities.
4. In this chapter, I will use the nomenclature "Nagaraja" to refer to Krishna after he settled in Garhwal and will refer to him as "Krishna" before he came to Garhwal, as I heard Garhwalis oscillate between these names.
5. In a famous essay, Ramanujan writes: "In India and Southeast Asia, no one ever reads the Ramayana or the Mahabharata for the first time. The stories are there, 'always already.'" A. K. Ramanujan, "Three Hundred Ramayanas: Five Examples and Three Thoughts on Translation," in *Many Ramayanas: The Diversity of a Narrative Tradition in South Asia*, ed. Paula Richman (University of California Press, 1991), 22.
6. While *dosh* is literally a "fault," "failing," "offense," or "accusation," in relation to Pahari deities, *dosh* manifests as forms of personal and collective "affliction." A *dosh* is thus an "affliction" with supernatural causation that negatively affects the bodies, minds, and social and physical environments of Pahari people.
7. In 2010–2011, I witnessed multiple jagaris, including Ram Lal, Ram's teacher Dhanvir ji, Champal ji, and Chander Singh Rahi perform the jagar narrative (*gatha*) of Krishna's arrival in Garhwal. In this chapter, I draw on their interpretations and insights as well as those of other religious practitioners and authorities, such as a ritual medium (*pasva*) of Nagaraja named Maheshu.
8. Extending Weil's understanding, Veena Das describes affliction as experiences or forces—such as impoverishment, structural violence, misfortune, or sickness—that corrode people's "capacities to engage life." See Veena Das, *Affliction: Health, Disease, Poverty* (New York: Fordham University Press, 2015), 2; Simone Weil, *The Simone Weil Reader*, ed. George A. Panichas (New York: McKay, 1977), 441.
9. The word *gantua* is etymologically related to *ganit* (lit., "mathematics"). *Gantuas* are known to "calculate," or diagnose, maladies and afflictions by studying a client's birth chart, among other things.
10. The verb "to attach" (*lagana*), in Hindi and Pahari dialects, is used in conjunction with nouns like "hurt" (*chot*) or "fault" (*dosh*), in phrases like "to be hurt" (*chot lagana*).
11. The spatial logic I am referring to animates the oft-told narrative of Nagaraja-Krishna and Gangu Ramola, but it is also present in ritual practices and everyday understandings of affliction and healing. This spatial logic has four interrelated dimensions. First, Pahari deities are motivated by a powerful desire to obtain "place," understood both literally and figuratively. Place refers both to a material site of presence, such as a body, home, or temple, as well as to a deity's recognition by their devotees. Second, because devotees are said to serve as a deity's "carriers"

or "vehicles" (*vahan*), devotees facilitate a deity's movement from one place to another. Third, obstructing a deity's movement or desire for place creates conflict as well as affliction, or *dosh*. In the story, Gangu Ramola's arrogance or pride is his downfall. Finally, "making place" for a deity transforms them into a peaceful (*shant*), benevolent, healing presence.

12. Ram Lal told me that garudas serve as "Nagaraja's vehicle [*vahan*] just like the lion is [goddess] Durga's vehicle." The garuda "transports" Nagaraja to the jagar ritual, which is why human mediums (*pasva*) embody garudas in *nach* prior to the ritual "arrival" and embodiment of Nagaraja, he informed me.

13. The Brit Barma is a formal song genre that describes and praises a particular god, inviting them to become physically present in the ritual. Ram Lal explained that such phrases are like the indices (*suchi*) of books or like aphorisms for which the jagar narratives that follow serve as commentaries. Descriptors in the Brit Barma often reference particular episodes in the narrative that follow and with which audiences are already familiar. The Brit Barma is recited prior to the ritualized performance of the god's jagar narrative. The Brit Barma portion of a deity's jagar performance describes the god's attributes and actions in relation to his devotees and adversaries. *Brit* is related to the Hindi and Sanskrit term *vrtti*, which in this case denotes "description," "elaboration," as well as "manifestation," that is, a deity's mode of being or presence in the world. *Barma* is equivalent to "Brahma" or "Brahman," that is, god. In Brit Barma invocations, deities are addressed in the second person by jagar performers, who invite them to become present as embodied actors in the ritual. See Aftab S. Jassal, "Making God Present: Placemaking and Ritual Healing in North India," *International Journal of Hindu Studies* 21, no. 2 (2017): 149–153.

14. John Stratton Hawley, "Every Play a Play within a Play," in *The Gods at Play: Līlā in South Asia*, ed. William Sturman Sax (New York: Oxford University Press, 1995).

15. I was introduced to Chander Singh Rahi (1942–2016) by one of my Garhwali mentors, the Hindustani classical musician Uma Shankar Chandola. In 2010–2011, I had the privilege of meeting with Rahi ji and his family on multiple occasions. Among other things, I thank them for sharing Rahi ji's unpublished writings and recordings with me and introducing me to other accomplished Pahari intellectuals, artists, and ritual performers. Prior to achieving national recognition as a Garhwali musician and cultural ambassador, Rahi ji was trained by his father to carry forward their family traditions by serving as a jagari. In the 1960s, Rahi ji began introducing millions across India to Pahari performance traditions via television and radio performances that were broadcast on Doordarshan and All India Radio (AIR). Prior to his death in 2016, he received numerous national awards, including the prestigious Padma Shri award, for his immense contributions to Pahari art and culture.

16. As I mentioned previously, in some versions of this story that I recorded, Gangu Ramola was identified as a reincarnation of Kaliya Nag who, in his new life, had forgotten about his prior encounter with Krishna and his promise of devotion to the god.

17. The word *nag* has multiple meanings. It can mean "serpent" but also refers to a class of divine beings and an ethnic group frequently mentioned in Pahari oral traditions and Sanskrit- and regional-language texts such as the Puranas.

18. My interlocutors often reminded me of the connection between Nagaraja's affinity for dairy products and the child-god Krishna's well-known fondness for the same. Please see John Stratton Hawley, *Krishna the Butter Thief* (Princeton, NJ: Princeton University Press, 1983).

19. Shivani Pathak, "Uttarakhand Is Mapping Snakes and Training Local Communities to Reduce Conflict Between Them: The Nature of Human-Snake Conflict in the Mountains Is Different from

That in the Plains," *Scroll.in*, December 27, 2020, https://scroll.in/article/982107/uttarakhand-is-mapping-snakes-and-training-local-communities-to-reduce-conflict-between-them.
20. Murphy Halliburton, "The Importance of a Pleasant Process of Treatment: Lessons on Healing from South India," *Culture, Medicine, and Psychiatry* 27, no. 2 (2003): 167.
21. Halliburton, "Importance of a Pleasant Process of Treatment," 162.
22. For further analysis of the processual, interrelated character of affliction and healing, please see: Carla Bellamy, *The Powerful Ephemeral: Everyday Healing in an Ambiguously Islamic Place* (Berkeley: University of California Press, 2011); Joyce Flueckiger, *In Amma's Healing Room: Gender and Vernacular Islam in South India* (Bloomington: Indiana University Press, 2006).

3. Political Divinities in the Village Square

1. For an account of *pandav nrtya* and related performance traditions, please see William Sturman Sax, *Dancing the Self: Personhood and Performance in the Pāṇḍava Līlā of Garhwal* (Oxford: Oxford University Press, 2002).
2. In ritual contexts involving divine embodiment, deities are "caused to dance" (*nachana*) through the bodies of human mediums. See Andrew Alter, *Dancing with Devtās: Drums, Power and Possession in the Music of Garhwal, North India* (Aldershot: Ashgate, 2008); Allen C. Fanger, "The Jagar: Spirit Possession Seance Among the Rajputs and Silpakars of Kumaon," in *Himalaya: Past and Present*, vol. 2, ed. M. P. Joshi and C. W. Brown (Almora: Shree Almora Book Depot, 1992), 173; Stefan Patrick Fiol, *Recasting Folk in the Himalayas: Indian Music, Media, and Social Mobility* (Urbana: University of Illinois Press, 2017). Aditya Malik, *Tales of Justice and Rituals of Divine Embodiment: Oral Narrative from the Central Himalayas* (New York: Oxford University Press, 2015); William Sturman Sax, *God of Justice: Ritual Healing and Social Justice in the Central Himalayas* (Oxford: Oxford University Press, 2009).
3. For an historical analysis of Rajput identity in the Himalayas, please see Arik Moran, *Kingship and Polity on the Himalayan Borderland: Rajput Identity During the Early Colonial Encounter* (Amsterdam: Amsterdam University Press, 2019).
4. In many parts of Uttarakhand, auji are also known as Bajgi and, as Stefan Fiol notes, they serve as ritual musicians "at the local temple or at the homes of high-caste patrons during calendrical and life-cycle rituals. One result of this hereditary duty is that Bajgi musicians are geographically dispersed across the region. Nonetheless, their spatial mobility is mostly confined to particular seasons in which they lead processions of local deities or wedding parties." Fiol, *Recasting Folk in the Himalayas*,10.
5. Kasturi Das, "Climate Change Forces Uttarakhand Farmers to Migrate," The Third Pole, May 17, 2021, https://www.thethirdpole.net/en/climate/climate-change-forces-migration-uttarakhand-farmers/.
6. Swati Thapa, "Caste, Gender, Climate Change: Farmers in Uttarakhand Struggle for Survival," *India Development Review*, July 12, 2023, https://idronline.org/article/climate-emergency/caste-gender-climate-change-farmers-in-uttarakhand-struggle-for-survival/.
7. This was a direct result of the administrative reservation, or quota-based affirmative action, system for marginalized groups. She was not simply a figurehead to fit the reservations criteria but at the same time, her husband did wield considerable power in the village.
8. See, for example, Lata Mani, *Myriad Intimacies* (Durham, NC: Duke University Press, 2022). As Mani eloquently puts it, "To do battle with race or caste is to simultaneously hold in one's

consciousness a challenging amalgam of truth and falsehood, fact and fiction: lies about caste/race, facts regarding their brutal persistence, and the truth that these categories can never adequately express the rich actuality or fullness of who one is" (45).

9. See Chinnaiah Jangam, Ramnarayan S. Rawat, Anupama Rao, and Gopal Guru, "A Dalit Paradigm: A New Narrative in South Asian Historiography," *Modern Asian Studies* 50, no. 1 (2016): 399–414. As Jangam writes, missionary, sociological, and anthropological representations of Dalit experience "reinforce the idea of untouchables as the lowest social being performing condemned occupations, without any part to play on the power structure of the village. In other words, the untouchable becomes a mute spectator who has neither the power nor the will to alter the traditional social structure and his/her own fate.... Thus while historical narratives showed a complete apathy and did not acknowledge the role the untouchables played in the making of nation, for the sociologists and anthropologists they remained an exotic vestige of the pre-modern feudal caste system" (403).
10. A key difference between aujis and jagaris is that while the former group of specialists is also classified as a *jati*, or caste community, jagaris belong to different jatis; serving as a jagari is not a jati-specific occupation.
11. For an analysis of *Dhol Sagar* as an (oral-)textual tradition, see chapter 6 of Andrew Alter's study *Dancing with Devtās*, 83–93.
12. As Caleb Simmons and others have noted, this miracle of the goddess is also known to occur in other parts of India, especially during Navaratri celebrations. Caleb Simmons, *Nine Nights of the Goddess: The Navaratri Festival in South Asia* (Albany: State University of New York, 2018). For an excellent, finely-textured analysis of other goddess-related miracles and goddess festivals, please see Rachel Fell McDermott, *Revelry, Rivalry and Longing for the Goddesses of Bengal: The Fortunes of Hindu Festivals* (New York: Columbia University Press, 2011).
13. The word *neta* (politician) is etymologically related to the Sanskrit term *niti* (political ethics).
14. This form of "placemaking" is distinct from what occurs in temple settings (chapter 1), translocal pilgrimage (chapter 6), or small-scale jagar rituals (chapter 4) where "place" is made for deities in the homes of individual worshipers. In jagar, for instance, deities do not appear as political divinities but rather give advice during times of crisis, heal relational, physical, and psychological problems, and provide other kinds of assistance specific to the individual or family sponsoring the ritual.
15. In Dyongarh, Bhagavati Devi is identified as a form of goddess Parvati. In parts of Uttarakhand, Bhagavati Devi is also known as Raj Rajeshvari, Chandravati, or Nanda Devi. For an in-depth account of the Nanda Devi pilgrimage tradition, see William Sturman Sax, *Mountain Goddess: Gender and Politics in a Himalayan Pilgrimage* (New York: Oxford University Press, 1991).
16. Hildegard Diemberger, *When a Woman Becomes a Religious Dynasty: The Samding Dorje Phagmo of Tibet* (New York: Columbia University Press, 2007).
17. Diemberger, *When a Woman Becomes a Religious Dynasty*, 144.
18. It occurred to me at the time that the porousness of social boundaries could be seen as analogous to the permeability of human bodies in *nach*, wherein another being enters and inhabits a human medium for the duration of the ritual.
19. Among other things, explanations that foreground the agency of deities serve to complicate "instrumentalist" understandings of divine embodiment that see it as simply a vehicle or mechanism for marginalized groups, including women and Dalits, to draw attention to, question, and transform structures of domination that are harmful to them. See Janice Boddy, "Spirit Possession Revisited: Beyond Instrumentality," *Annual Review of Anthropology* 23 (1994): 407–34.

20. In *The King and the Clown in South Indian Myth and Poetry*, David Shulman explains the concept of ḍaṇḍa in the following way: "The king's contamination by evil must be seen as bound up with the very essence of his activity as a ruler, or in the language of royal symbols, with his exercise of force—ḍaṇḍa, the power of the staff, symbol of his right and duty to punish." David Dean Shulman, *The King and the Clown in South Indian Myth and Poetry* (Princeton, NJ: Princeton University Press, 1985), 28. See also Steven Parish, "Postscript: The Problem of Power," in *Hierarchy and Its Discontents: Culture and the Politics of Consciousness in Caste Society* (Philadelphia: University of Pennsylvania Press, 1996) 225–42.
21. The word *harami*, used adjectivally, also means "devilish." Initially, I thought the headman was characterizing the woman's dance as "devilish" because her movements were jerky and inelegant, possibly indicating that she was possessed by a dangerous, malevolent spirit. However, this was not the case; the headman was calling into question the authenticity of her *nach*, implying that the woman was feigning divine embodiment.
22. I came to learn during my fieldwork that judging the veracity of displays of divine embodiment is a speculative exercise in which local audiences regularly engage.
23. William Sturman Sax, *God of Justice: Ritual Healing and Social Justice in the Central Himalayas* (Oxford: Oxford University Press, 2008).
24. Sax, *God of Justice*, 78.
25. Thomas J. Csordas, "Embodiment as a Paradigm for Anthropology," *Ethos* 8, no. 1 (1993): 5–47.
26. Jonathan Z. Smith, *Imagining Religion: from Babylon to Jonestown* (Chicago: University of Chicago Press, 1982), 54.
27. In 2012–2013, the per capita GDP for the state of Uttarakhand was 75,000 rupees per year. In other words, the donation requested was 1 percent of a family's annual income. See Arun Prabhudesai, "Per Capita Income of Various Indian States [2016]," Trak.in, December 19, 2017, http://trak.in/2012/average-per-capita-income-indian-states/.
28. For a detailed account of this culturally significant story and its enactment in the context of the Pandav Lila performance tradition in Garhwal, see Sax, *Dancing the Self*, 4–93.
29. Unlike the mediums of Nagaraja and Bhagavati Devi who were Rajputs, Unishor's medium was Dalit. I was told at the time that this god had a "special relationship" with Nagaraja and would therefore travel from far away to "dance" alongside him. Sharad ji later said to me that public rituals like panno were not only sites where villagers from different social groups and walks of life congregated but also where deities had a chance to meet and interact with one another.
30. While the deities danced in the maidan, I sat beside Sharad ji and other village elders, on the steps leading up to the goddess temple. Sharad ji had called me to sit with him, as he wanted me to have a good view of what was occurring in the maidan; he told me repeatedly to take out my camera to film the dancing deities. While sitting with the elders, I overheard one of them say that Unishor's medium seemed very frail and that his deity was too strong for him—the human medium was being overwhelmed. Someone responded that this was to be expected since he was from a "poor" Dalit village and probably didn't have access to the nourishing food that was needed for such strenuous ritual work. Surprisingly, everyone agreed with this analysis. "Yes, a good diet is important, for if the vessel [body] is not strong enough to contain the god, the god's power will easily destroy it." It was interesting to hear them connect the social and economic background of the medium, his diet, and his "dance." Sharad ji had earlier mentioned that a medium needed to be emotionally, mentally, and physically pure so that the god, likened to a wind (*hava*), could enter into him. In this case, however, it seemed to be a question of the medium's solidity and resilience as a vessel. For this ritual purpose, professional mediums

needed to eat well in order to strengthen their bodies. The social and economic background of a medium was therefore important—part of an everyday calculus through which people evaluated and talked about divine embodiment.

4. Undoing Love

1. Extravillage patrilocal marriage is the most common form of marriage in Kumaon. See William Sturman Sax, *Mountain Goddess: Gender and Politics in a Himalayan Pilgrimage* (New York: Oxford University Press, 1991): 71–84. In the villages of Kumaon where I conducted fieldwork, patrilocal (or virilocal) and patrilineal marriage is the norm across caste groups. However, as Gerald Berreman has pointed out, "Throughout the . . . area, matrilocality is an alternative to patrilocality. It is disfavoured but not infrequently resorted to by land-owning families with daughters but no sons so that the son-in-law can assume work and responsibilities of the male head of the household." See Gerald D. Berreman, "Sanskritization as Female Oppression in India," in *Sex and Gender Hierarchies*, ed. Barbara Diane Miller, Naomi Quinn, and Daniel Fessler (Cambridge: Cambridge University Press, 1993), 373.
2. Isabelle Nabokov, *Religion Against the Self: An Ethnography of Tamil Rituals* (Oxford: Oxford University Press, 2000), 32.
3. William Sax translates *chhal* as "crafty demon," which beautifully captures the deceptive nature of these beings. See William Sturman Sax, *God of Justice: Ritual Healing and Social Justice in the Central Himalayas* (New York: Oxford University Press, 2009), 84.
4. Monier-Williams, *A Dictionary, English and Sanskrit* (England: W. H. Allen, 2002 [1851]), 760.
5. See Gloria Goodwin Raheja and Ann Gold, *Listen to the Heron's Words: Reimagining Gender and Kinship in North India* (Berkeley: University of California Press, 1994), which describes how women's songs and ritual and narrative traditions reflect continuing connections between women's natal and marital worlds, even though patrilocal norms across much of north India pressure married women to sever ties with their natal homes. In *Unearthing Gender: Folksongs of North India*, (Durham, NC: Duke University Press, 2012), Smita Tewari Jassal describes how women's songs in a Bhojpuri-speaking region of Uttar Pradesh grapple with experiences of dislocation and loss in relation to patrilocal marriage. Also see Paul B. Courtright and Lindsey Harlan, *From the Margins of Hindu Marriage: Essays on Gender Religion and Culture* (New York: Oxford University Press, 1995).
6. Historically, anthropologists have contrasted "positive" possession, the favorable embodiment of a divinity within and through the body of a human medium, with "negative" possession, a term that describes events such as the harmful takeover of a female person by a ghost in the context of chhal affliction in Uttarakhand. See Erika Bourguignon, *Possession* (Prospect Heights, NY: Waveland Press, 1991 [1976]); I. M. Lewis, *Ecstatic Religion: A Study of Shamanism and Spirit Possession* (London: Routledge, 2005 [1971]). Furthermore, in South Asia, possession in general, and negative possession in particular, has been viewed as an experience more likely to occur in women than men. See Frederick M. Smith, *The Self Possessed: Deity and Spirit Possession in South Asian Literature and Civilization* (New York: Columbia University Press, 2006), 68; and Kalpana Ram, *Fertile Disorder: Spirit Possession and Its Provocation of the Modern* (Honolulu: University of Hawai'i Press, 2013). Explanations for this disparity have commonly borrowed the language of psychiatry and had the effect of simultaneously pathologizing women and

medicalizing possession. As Adeline Masquelier points out, for early commentators intent on classifying the exotic and alien, "possession was a theatrical form of hysteria, a disease that, as its name indicates, prevailed among women." Adeline Marie Masquelier, *Prayer Has Spoiled Everything: Possession, Power, and Identity in an Islamic Town of Niger* (Durham, NC: Duke University Press, 2001), 11.
7. Ram, *Fertile Disorder*, 2.
8. Nabokov, *Religion Against the Self*, 30.
9. Nabokov, *Religion Against the Self*, 86.
10. Nabokov, *Religion Against the Self*, 112.
11. [Emphasis mine.] Nabokov, *Religion Against the Self*, 112.
12. [Italics mine.] Ram, *Fertile Disorder*, 205. See also Sarah Pinto, *Daughters of Parvati Women and Madness in Contemporary India* (Philadelphia: University of Pennsylvania Press, Inc. 2014).
13. Ram, *Fertile Disorder*, 80.
14. Sarah Pinto, "Rational Love, Relational Medicine: Psychiatry and the Accumulation of Precarious Kinship," *Culture, Medicine, and Psychiatry* 35, no. 3 (2011): 393.
15. Pinto, Rational Love, Relational Medicine, 377.
16. See also Sarah Pinto, "'The Tools of Your Chants and Spells': Stories of Madwomen and Indian Practical Healing," *Medical Anthropology* 35, no. 3 (2016): 263–77.
17. Sarah Pinto, *Daughters of Parvati: Women and Madness in Contemporary India* (Philadelphia: University of Pennsylvania Press, Inc. 2014), 393.
18. Pinto, *Daughters of Parvati*, 394.
19. Ram, *Daughters of Parvati*, 17.
20. Ram, *Fertile Disorder*, 86.
21. Smith, *The Self Possessed*, 79.
22. Aftab S. Jassal, "Divine Politicking: A Rhetorical Approach to Deity Possession in the Himalayas," *Religions* 7, no. 9 (2016): 117.
23. My research interests were well known to people in and around Bani, and they sometimes invited me to attend jagar rituals in their homes and participate in other religious events. Over time, I grew very close to Deepak and the Bisht family. While conducting fieldwork in the area, the Bisht family invited me to live in an uninhabited house they had recently built for Deepak's youngest brother to move into after his upcoming marriage.
24. At each jagar ritual, the god specifies when the next jagar is to be performed, usually after three or six months. During the ritual, the god marks the woman's forehead with sacred ash (*vibhuti*). This marking keeps the afflicted woman's symptoms as bay for a stipulated period of time until the next jagar. If the jagars are performed on time, the woman remains well; if not, she becomes unwell again, and it becomes harder to cure her, I was told. The final ritual requires the sacrifice of a goat, and sometimes other animals, to the chhal/bhut, to be offered at a temporary shrine constructed for this purpose. The ghost is thought to consume the goat's blood, and the meat is cooked and eaten by those participating in the ritual. The ghost is also given other offerings, including a lock of hair and nail clippings from the afflicted woman's body, as well her clothes, bangles, and some other objects. The participants in this ceremony are forbidden from setting foot in the home of the sponsor for a certain period of time, such as for three, five, or seven days.
25. Bani was a predominantly Rajput (*thakur*) village, with very few Brahmin and Dalit families, the other two major caste groups in the region.
26. In November 2000, the new state of Uttarakhand was carved out of northern Uttar Pradesh, the most populous state in India. One of driving forces for the creation of this new state was the

widespread desire among its inhabitants for more economic development and governmental representation. Supporters of the statehood movement argued that statehood would stem the large-scale flow of Pahari outmigration to other parts of India. However, since statehood, rates of rural unemployment have remained high, especially in mountain districts, and outmigration has not decreased, but rather *increased*.

27. Elisabeth J. Croll, "The Intergenerational Contract in the Changing Asian Family," *Oxford Development Studies* 34, no. 4 (2010): 473–91; Premilla D'Cruz and Shalini Bharat, "Beyond Joint and Nuclear: The Indian Family Revisited," *Journal of Comparative Family Studies* 32, no. 2 (2001): 167–94.
28. Aidan Seale-Feldman, "Relational Affliction: Reconceptualizing "Mass Hysteria,'" *Ethos* 47, no. 3 (2019): 316.
29. See also Andrew Willford, "'Do You Hear Voices, or Do You Think You Hear Voices?' Malevolence and Modernity in the Psychiatric Clinic," *South Asia: Journal of South Asian Studies* 45, no. 1 (2022): 164–82.
30. Through jagar and consultations with family deities, some of these ghosts were identified as the troubled spirits of forgotten female ancestors. In other cases, chhal/bhut were also identified as deceased members of afflicted women's natal villages, with only a tenuous link to their families, as well as the spirits of people who had died violent deaths in the vicinity of their villages but were otherwise unknown to their families. In other cases, it was determined that the women had been attacked by a ghost immediately after they had married, often while making the physical journey from natal to marital home.
31. To exorcise these beings, ritual experts conducted a ritual wherein a substitute bride was presented to the chhal/bhut, such as in the form of a vegetable like a squash (*lauki*). In their attraction to young women, these ghosts share similarities with the *pey* demons described by Isabelle Nabokov (Clark-Decès).
32. For an excellent, in-depth account of the relationship between Pahari deities and conceptions of justice (*nyaya*) in Uttarakhand, please see Sax, *God of Justice*.
33. Gangnath is a temperamental, trickster-like divinity with a tendency for seducing women; he is an ancient, mysterious, and sometimes terrifying being who is said to have arrived in Kumaon from Nepal.
34. An historical designation for a subregion of Kumaon of which Bani is a part.
35. Saim Devata is sometimes described as a deaf, mute, and immobile deity whose primary abode is in Jhakar Saim, an ancient pilgrimage center in Kumaon, which I discuss at length in chapter 6. He is known as the maternal uncle (*mama*) of not just Golu Devata but also other deities in the region.
36. A powder that married women wear in the parting of their hair and on their foreheads.
37. This kind of "transfer" shares similarities with what Christopher Fuller describes in "The Renovation Ritual in a South Indian Temple: The 1995 Kumbhābhiṣeka in the Mīnākṣī Temple, Madurai," *Bulletin of the School of Oriental and African Studies, University of London* 67, no. 1 (2004): 40–63. Fuller describes a series of temple renovation rituals in Tamil Nadu, wherein "the Temple's towers and its images are emptied of divine power, which is transferred to waterpots, so that they can be renovated and in particular so that the images can be repaired and refastened; at the same time, the power in the pots is augmented by a series of sacrifice-worship rituals, and it flows back into the towers and images when the water is poured at the end" (59). This moment in the ritual in Bani also constituted a "transfer of power" that was designed to relocate the ghost. Fuller, "Renovation Ritual in a South Indian Temple," 61.

38. Brian Smith and Wendy Doniger write, "The operation of the ritual of sacrifice, it seems, depends on a sleight of hand... a shell game of displacement and replacement." Brian K. Smith and Wendy Doniger, "Sacrifice and Substitution: Ritual Mystification and Mythical Demystification," *Numen* 36, no. 2 (1989): 189. They go on to note that "the victim"—in this case, the goat—"represents or "becomes" (and thus substitutes for)... the human being who makes the offering," that is, Kiran—but also the Bisht family as a whole (190).
39. Lawrence Cohen, *No Aging in India: Alzheimer's the Bad Family and Other Modern Things* (Berkeley: University of California Press, 1998).
40. Sarah Lamb, *White Saris and Sweet Mangoes: Aging, Gender, and Body in North India* (Berkeley: University of California Press, 2000).
41. Ram, *Fertile Disorder*, 80.
42. In *Religion Against the Self*, Isabelle Nabokov (Clark-Decès) describes a similarly violent ritual procedure. For example, she writes: "I have watched others in the temple grabbing 'possessed' women by the hair and pulling them to the ground so they could have the demons whipped out of them with braided leather straps. Although these women sobbed and wailed, they made no attempt to avoid the blows or fight back, perhaps because they knew that any show of resistance by their *pey* would only prolong the beating" (100).
43. Pinto, *Daughters of Parvati*.
44. The younger men rarely pitched in, but Deepak's father—and men of his generation, in their fifties, sixties, and seventies—did help. "The boys don't do anything; they've become spoilt," he explained. In other parts of Uttarakhand, this labor inequality has for decades been tied to growing rates of alcoholism among men, leading to women organizing and calling for a ban on the sale of liquor in the state. See Seema Sharma, "Uttarakhand's Women Remain Vigilant Against Liquor Shops and Alcoholism," *Times of India*, August 23, 2015; Shekhar Pathak, "Fighting Alcohol in Uttarakhand," *Himal Southasian*, July 1, 1988, https://www.himalmag.com/fighting-alcohol-in-uttarakhand/.
45. Veena Das, *Affliction: Health, Disease, Poverty* (New York: Fordham University Press, 2015), 1.
46. Marilyn Strathern, *Partial Connections* (Lanham, MD: AltaMira Press, 2005).
47. By "dancing," she was referring to the act of embodying supernatural agents, specifically chhal/bhut, during jagar rituals. By this statement, she was implicitly contrasting her experiences with those of Kiran, who had, on occasion, displayed such behavior.
48. The phrase *"puja jana"*—literally, "to send ritual worship'—in this case, referred to the sacrifice of a goat, which marks the end of a cycle of jagar rituals for the treatment of ghost affliction.
49. I realized later that Sona ji was drawing a distinction between ghost affliction that affects the daughter-in-law directly and that which affects her family, specifically her children. In Sona ji's case, her children had been attacked, but, unlike Kiran, she had not "danced," which is perhaps why she was claiming that her condition had been less severe.
50. See Cohen, *No Aging in India*; Lamb, *White Saris and Sweet Mangoes*.

5. Out of Place: Lives of Oracles and Priests

1. By means of oral narrative performance, drumming, and other practices, jagaris ritually "call" or "invite" divinities to appear in/on the bodies of human mediums. Jagaris are also called *jagariyas*, *gurus*, and *dhamis*.

2. For jagaris and bakkyas, the "place" to which they are called often takes literal form, such as a woven mat on which they sit while performing jagar or meeting with clients in their healing rooms. To be called is also figurative, as it means dedicating one's life and professional practice to the ritual service of deities and their worshipers.
3. This chapter centers ritual performers' own narrative constructions of social identity and, in so doing, builds on the work of Joyce Flueckiger, *In Amma's Healing Room: Gender and Vernacular Islam in South India* (Bloomington: Indiana University Press, 2006); Kirin Narayan, *Storytellers, Saints, and Scoundrels: Folk Narrative in Hindu Religious Teaching* (Philadelphia: University of Pennsylvania Press, 1989); and Leela Prasad, *Poetics of Conduct: Oral Narrative and Moral Being in a South Indian Town* (New York: Columbia University Press, 2007), among others.
4. The term Scheduled Caste is a legal designation adopted in 1935 when the British colonial authorities listed the lowest-ranking Hindu castes in a schedule appended to the Government of India Act for purposes of statutory safeguards and other benefits. For decades, Indian national policy has sought to legislatively benefit Scheduled Caste and Scheduled Tribe populations (including the Reservation in Admission Act 2006 and the Protection of Civil Rights Act 1955), but despite such measures, and even *after* controlling for socioeconomic status (years of schooling, housing quality, and indebtedness), members of SC and ST groups in Uttarakhand had more than twice the risk of depression compared to the general population. Here, depression is conceptualized as an indicator of social inequality and vulnerability. Kaaren Mathias et al., "Cross-Sectional Study of Depression and Help-Seeking in Uttarakhand, North India," *BMJ Open* 5, no. 11 (2015): e008992.
5. In Uttarakhand, some of the artisan communities designated as Scheduled Caste include: *tamta, lohar, mistri, deval, chamar*, and *kolta*, among others. see Peter Claus Zoller, "A Little-Known Form of Untouchability in the Central Himalayas," in *Reading Slowly: A Festschrift for Jens E. Braarvig*, 1st ed., ed. Lutz Edzard, Jens W Borgland, and Ute Hüsken (Wiesbaden: Harrassowitz Verlag, 2018), 475.
6. Many caste-privileged people with whom I interacted saw Dalits not only as morally corrupt and dangerous but also as vectors of ritual impurity, which is also why the activities of Dalits are closely monitored. While the practice of "untouchability" is illegal according to the Indian Constitution, traditional, anti-Dalit discourses and practices continue to structure interactions between castes in Uttarakhand, as they do in other parts of India.
7. This had been his second overnight trip in a week, in addition to the two or three jagars he had been asked to perform in his own village. In the busiest months for jagar performers, usually around October to November, Champal ji performed up to ten jagars a week, with multiple performances in a single night.
8. Mukul Kumar, "Relationship of Caste and Crime in Colonial India: A Discourse Analysis," *Economic and Political Weekly* 39, no. 10 (2004): 1078–87.
9. Kavita Upadhyay, "Dalit Killed for Entering Flour Mill in Uttarakhand," *The Hindu*, October 8, 2016, https://www.thehindu.com/news/national/other-states/Dalit-killed-for-entering-flour-mill-in-Uttarakhand/article15432538.ece.
10. Prithviraj Singh, "Uttarakhand Dalits Demand Entry into Temples, Spark Fears of Conflict," *Hindustan Times*, May 18, 2016, https://www.hindustantimes.com/india/uttarakhand-dalits-demand-entry-into-temples-spark-fears-of-conflict/story-HXr6kxW0izxrZFzDs4TGXN.html.
11. Rajeev Khanna, "Why Uttarakhand HC Order on Temple Entry for Dalits Is a Landmark Judgment," *Catch News*, July, 14 2018, http://www.catchnews.com/india-news/why-uttarakhand-hc-order-on-temple-entry-for-dalits-is-a-landmark-judgment-122628.html.

12. Some of my interlocutors in Uttarakhand used the term *tantra* as a pejorative gloss to describe the practices of some jagaris and oracles, connecting divine embodiment to the ritual uses of magical incantations (*mantra*), diagrams (*yantra*), animal sacrifice, and offerings, such as alcohol and meat (see prelude). While on the one hand, tantra is sometimes seen as dangerous, secretive, and "polluting," on the other, it is woven into the fabric of everyday life and religion across the region. In Uttarakhand, jagaris and bakkyas are associated with what we might call "vernacular tantra"—an immense, heterogeneous body of knowledge and practice concerned with achieving pragmatic gains and benefits for practitioners, including psychophysical healing, material prosperity—and the ability to inflict harm upon one's enemies. For an excellent analysis of the many meanings and forms of tantra, please see Rachel Fell McDermott and Jeffrey J Kripal, *Encountering Kali: In the Margins at the Center in the West* (Berkeley: University of California Press, 2003); Hugh Urban, *The Power of Tantra: Religion, Sexuality, and the Politics of South Asian Studies* (New York: I. B. Tauris; distributed in the USA by Palgrave Macmillan, 2010); David Gordon White, *Tantra in Practice* (Princeton, NJ; Princeton University Press, 2000).
13. In *Deceptive Majority: Dalits, Hinduism, and Underground Religion* (Cambridge: Cambridge University Press, 2021), Joel Lee observes that Valmiki also appears as a robber or criminal in the oral traditions of the Lal Begi community in Uttar Pradesh. However, in those traditions, Valmiki—or rather Bal Mik—is not identified as the composer of the Ramayana. Instead, Lee notes, "The same name is grafted on the ancient Buddhist trope of the contrite highway brigand, earlier associated with the name Anguli Mala" (59). In contrast, in Champal's account, the daku Valmiki is clearly depicted as the composer of the Ramayana.
14. Aftab S. Jassal, "Divine Politicking: A Rhetorical Approach to Deity Possession in the Himalayas," *Religions* 7, no. 9 (2017): 117.
15. See Ishwar Awasthi and Balwant Singh Mehta, "Forced Out-Migration from Hill Regions and Return Migration During the Pandemic: Evidence from Uttarakhand," *Indian Journal of Labour Economics* 63, no. 4 (2020): 1107–24; B. P. Maithani, "Towards Sustainable Hill Area Development, Himalaya," *Man, Nature and Culture* 16, no. 2 (1996): 4–7; International Centre for Integrated Mountain Development (ICIMOD), *Labour Migration and Remittances in Uttarakhand. Case Study Report*. Kathmandu: ICIMOD, 2011.
16. Awasthi and Mehta, "Forced Out-Migration," 1111.
17. Rajendra P. Mamgain and D. N. Reddy, *Final Report Outmigration from Hill Region of Uttarakhand: Magnitude, Challenges and Policy Options* (Hyderabad, India: National Institute of Rural Development & Panchayati Raj, accessed December 6, 2022), http://nirdpr.org.in/nird_docs/srsc/srscrr261016-3.pdf.
18. For a detailed study of the god Mahasu, please see Asaf Sharabi, *The Biography of a God: Mahasu in the Himalayas* (Amsterdam: Amsterdam University Press, 2023).
19. In Pauri Garhwal where Ujval lived and practiced, it is not uncommon for large families to have a kin member ritually embody particular deities on a regular basis during jagar and other ritual events. Designated mediums are often chosen by the logic of patrilineal succession as well as by family and village deities themselves.
20. Bhairavnath was the main deity who acted through Jaipal, but there were also others who visited him on occasion.
21. Jaipal added that, while he was still in recovery in Patiala, the presence of the deity in/on Jaipal's body was accompanied by the ability to hear the deity's voice. In the beginning, "the voice was like a whisper," and he strained to make sense of what the deity was saying. Over time, however, the voice became louder until it was too much to bear, and this is when the deity started to enter and inhabit him fully, Jaipal explained.

22. Initially, when the deity began "coming over" him, Jaipal would lose all awareness of himself and his surroundings. Jaipal added, "I could not remember anything [what the deity had said and done through Jaipal]. . . . When Baba ji would leave me, it was as if I were waking from a deep sleep. People around me would tell me, 'Baba ji said this, or Baba ji said that,' but I had no recollection of it. But after serving Baba ji for a long time, I can now remember things, so I can repeat them for those who ask, such as yourself." During a separate conversation, Jaipal told me that on leaving his body, Baba ji would leave him with a parting gift: a clear memory of everything that had occurred while Jaipal had been "away." I received a similar report from another medium (*pasva*) who regularly embodied the god Nagaraja. This medium also described his memory of ritual events as a parting gift from his possessing deity.
23. This understanding is resonant across many non-Western cultures. For example, in Byron Good's classic essay on heart distress in Iran, he notes how while the brain is the seat of the rational faculty, "the vital or animal faculty resides in the heart; it provides the 'innate heat' and 'vital breath' (*pneuma* or *nafs*) to the body and is the seat of emotions." Byron J. Good, "The Heart of What's the Matter: The Semantics of Illness in Iran," *Culture, Medicine and Psychiatry* 1, no. 1 (1977): 36.
24. Yohanan Grinshpon, *Silence Unheard: Deathly Otherness in Pātañjala-Yoga* (Albany: State University of New York Press, 2002).
25. Some jagaris with whom I worked used the terms *chal* and *tal*—which is a more common word for "rhythm" in Indian music—interchangeably. They identified numerous different *chal/tal* that are employed in jagar, such as *nag chal*, *chauras*, *ganesh tal*, *ramola tal*, *artali*, *gharbhut*, and so on.
26. Townsend Middleton and Jason Cons, "Coming to Terms: Reinserting Research Assistants into Ethnography's Past and Present," *Ethnography* 15, no. 3 (2014): 279–90.

6. Playing in the Rain: Scenes from a Himalayan Pilgrimage

1. Bonnie Wheeler, "Models of Pilgrimage: From Communitas to Confluence," *Journal of Ritual Studies* 13, no. 2 (1999): 34.
2. Wheeler proposes a similar model of pilgrimage and pilgrimage sites built on the principle of "confluence," which "affirms difference in the common space without foreclosing otherness." Wheeler, "Models of Pilgrimage," 29. Confluency enables "competing discourses . . . [to] mingle in the fragile but intense space of pilgrimage . . . flowing together through space as well as time" (28–29).
3. In a similar example of placemaking in Tamil Nadu, Diane P. Mines shows how local temple organizations "make" the village by employing different processional routes during certain religious festivals. See Diane P. Mines, "Waiting for Veḷḷāḷakaṇṭaṉ: Narrative, Movement, and Making Place in a Tamil Village," in *Tamil Geographies: Cultural Constructions of Space and Place in South India*, ed. Martha Ann Selby and Indira Viswanathan Peterson (Albany: State University of New York Press, 2008), 199–220.
4. In 2021, Gairsain was announced as a third administrative division of the state.
5. Governmental bodies called Garhwal Mandal Vikas Nigam (GMVN) and Kumaon Mandal Vikas Nigam (KMVN) manage tourism in the two regions.
6. Anne Feldhaus, *Connected Places: Region, Pilgrimage, and Geographical Imagination in India* (New York: Palgrave Macmillan, 2003).

7. Doreen Massey, "The Responsibilities of Place," *Local Economy* 19, no. 2 (2004): 97–101. For Thomas Tweed in *Crossing and Dwelling: A Theory of Religion* (Cambridge, MA.: Harvard University Press, 2006), the "flows" that constitute place are "organic-cultural" in nature and include non/material and non/human dimensions (4). In "The Responsibilities of Place," Massey thematizes the "fact of global flows—of economic transactions and trade, of cultural influences, of populations, and of political ideologies" (97).
8. Massey, "Responsibilities of Place," 97.
9. Doreen Massey, *For Space* (London: Sage, 2005), 141.
10. Massey, *For Space*, 151. [Italics mine.]
11. Karen Pechilis, "To Pilgrimage It," *Journal of Ritual Studies* 6, no. 2 (1992): 59–91.
12. Wheeler, "Models of Pilgrimage," 26–41.
13. Thomas A. Tweed argues that religions are best understood as "confluences of organic-cultural flows that intensify joy and confront suffering by drawing on human and suprahuman forces to make homes and *cross boundaries*" [italics mine], *Crossing and Dwelling*, 4. During the pilgrimage to Jhakar Saim, pilgrims "cross" between different forms/scales of "place," including domestic spaces, villages, and temples, as well as between specialized contexts of practice and authority within Hinduism, namely, the religious domain of jagar priests and divine embodiment, on the one hand, and Brahmanically-mediated temple worship, on the other.
14. See chapter 4 for more information about patrilocal marriage in Uttarakhand.
15. William Sturman Sax, *Mountain Goddess: Gender and Politics in a Himalayan Pilgrimage* (New York: Oxford University Press, 1991). For analyses of pilgrimage practices in Uttarakhand, also see: Stephen Alter, *Sacred Waters: A Pilgrimage Up the Ganges River to the Source of Hindu Culture* (New York: Harcourt, 2001); David Haberman, *River of Love in an Age of Pollution: The Yamuna River of Northern India* (Berkeley: University of California Press, 2006); James G. Lochtefeld, *God's Gateway: Identity and Meaning in a Hindu Pilgrimage Place* (Oxford: Oxford University Press, 2010); Luke Whitmore, *Mountain, Water, Rock, God: Understanding Kedarnath in the Twenty-First Century* (University of California Press, 2018).
16. Aditya Malik, *Tales of Justice and Rituals of Divine Embodiment: Oral Narrative from the Central Himalayas* (New York: Oxford University Press, 2016).
17. See Andrea Marion Pinkney, "Prasāda, the Gracious Gift, in Contemporary and Classical South Asia," *Journal of the American Academy of Religion* 81, no. 3 (2013): 734–56; Vasudha Narayanan, "Water, Wood, and Wisdom: Ecological Perspectives from the Hindu Traditions," *Daedalus* 130, no. 4 (2001): 189.
18. As Bonnie Wheeler observes: "Pilgrimages are profoundly somatic activities: one moves physically through space to seek the physical presence of, if not contact with, the sacred. Touch is surprisingly essential, but visual and even olfactory proximity is also valued at the sacred site. The sacred and the bodily mingle in a complicated tension. Body yearns for body, contact feeds contact, and the corporeal yearns for contact beyond mortality." Wheeler, *Models of Pilgrimage*, 31.
19. Diana L. Eck, *Darsan: Seeing the Divine Image in India* (New York: Columbia University Press, 1998). See also Christopher Pinney, "The Indian Work of Art in the Age of Mechanical Reproduction: Or, What Happens When Peasants 'Get Hold' of Images," in *Media Worlds: Anthropology on New Terrain*, ed. Faye D. Ginsburg, Lila Abu-Lughod, and Brian Larkin (Berkeley: University of California Press, 2002), 355–69. Pinney characterizes darshan as "a physical relationship of visual intermingling" (39).
20. Matthew Engelke, "Material Religion," in *The Cambridge Companion to Religious Studies*, ed. Robert A. Orsi (Cambridge: Cambridge University Press, 2011), 223–27. See also Anandi Leela

Devaki Knuppel, "Beyond Seeing: Embodied Multisensory Performance, Experience, and Practice in Contemporary Transnational Gaudiya Vaishnavism" (PhD diss., Emory University, 2019), https://etd.library.emory.edu/concern/etds/gh93h053g.
21. To protect my Dalit interlocutors, I have decided not to name the akhara or the "great soul" who was invoked by the sannyasis.
22. Abhishek Dey, "Religion, Politics, Power, and Rage Against Muslims: Heady World of Seers at Haridwar's Akharas," *The Prin*, December 28, 2021, https://theprint.in/india/religion-politics-power-rage-against-muslims-heady-world-of-seers-at-haridwars-akharas/789821/.
23. Joel Lee, *Deceptive Majority: Dalits, Hinduism, and Underground Religion* (Cambridge: Cambridge University Press, 2021), 11.
24. Joel Lee, "Odor and Order: How Caste Is Inscribed in Space and Sensoria," *Comparative Studies of South Asia, Africa and the Middle East* 37, no. 3 (December 1, 2017): 470–90. Lee writes: "Caste functions, among other things, as a spatial-sensory order. It is experienced as an inscription into the environment—indeed, into the chemical and olfactory content of the air we breathe—of the Brahmanical ideological premise that every caste has its own distinctive, hierarchically ranked 'place' in the world, and that the places inhabited by subordinate castes should not only be set apart but should look, smell, and feel differently from those of the rest of society" (470).
25. Aftab S. Jassal, "Awakening the Serpent King: Ritual and Textual Ontologies in Garhwal, Uttarakhand." *Journal of Hindu Studies* 13, no. 2 (2020):101–21.

Epilogue: Beyond Belief

1. Transliteration: *mānanā*
2. Roy A. Rappaport, *Ritual and Religion in the Making of Humanity* (Cambridge: Cambridge University Press, 1999), 454.
3. Jack David Eller, *Introducing Anthropology of Religion: Culture to the Ultimate*, 3rd ed. (Abingdon, Oxon: Routledge, 2022), 32–33.
4. *Manana* is etymologically related to the antomyns *samman* and *apman*, which indicate "respect" and "disrespect," respectively.
5. Transliterations: *mān rakhanā* and *mān karanā*.
6. See Gail Omvedt, *Seeking Begumpura: The Social Vision of Anticaste Intellectuals* (New Delhi: Navayana Pub.: Distributed by IPD Alternatives, 2008); John Stratton Hawley and Mark Juergensmeyer. *Songs of the Saints of India* (New York: Oxford University Press, 2004).

Bibliography

Abe, Jennifer. "Sacred Place: An Interdisciplinary Approach for Social Science." In *Communities, Neighborhoods, and Health: Expanding the Boundaries of Place*. Ed. Erlinda M. Burton, 145–62. New York: Springer, Science Business Media, 2011.
Adcock, C. S. "Debating Conversion, Silencing Caste: The Limited Scope of Religious Freedom." *Journal of Law and Religion* 29, no. 3 (2014): 363–77.
———. *The Limits of Tolerance: Indian Secularism and the Politics of Religious Freedom*. New York: Oxford University Press, 2014.
Allocco, Amy L. "The Blemish of 'Modern Times': Snakes Planets and the Kaliyugam." *Nidan: International Journal for Indian Studies* 26 no. 1 (2014): 1–21
———. "Bringing the Dead Home: Hindu Invitation Rituals in Tamil South India." *Journal of the American Academy of Religion* 89, no. 1 (2021): 103–42.
———. "Fear, Reverence and Ambivalence: Divine Snakes in Contemporary South India." *Religions of South Asia* 7, nos. 1–3 (2013): 230–48.
———. "Snakes, Goddesses, and Anthills: Modern Challenges and Women's Ritual Responses in Contemporary South India." PhD diss., Emory University, 2009.
Alter, Andrew. *Dancing with Devtās: Drums, Power, and Possession in the Music of Garhwal, North India*. Aldershot: Ashgate, 2008.
———. "Epilogue: Listening to an Uttarakhandi Himalayan Space." In *Mountainous Sound Spaces*, 151–62, Delhi: Cambridge University Press, 2014.
———. *Mountainous Sound Spaces*. Delhi: Cambridge University Press, 2014.
Alter, Stephen. *Sacred Waters: A Pilgrimage Up the Ganges River to the Source of Hindu Culture*. New York: Harcourt, 2001.
Apoorvanand. "Modi in Kedarnath—After the Deluge, the Delusion." *The Wire*, October 23, 2017. https://thewire.in/politics/narendra-modi-kedarnath-uttarakhand.
Atkinson, Edwin T. *The Himalayan Gazetteer*. Delhi: Cosmo Publications, 1973.
Aukland, Alter Knut. "Pilgrimage Expansion Through Tourism in Contemporary India: The Development and Promotion of a Hindu Pilgrimage Circuit." *Journal of Contemporary Religion* 32, no. 2 (2017): 283–98.

Awasthi, Ishwar and Balwant Singh Mehta. "Forced Out-Migration from Hill Regions and Return Migration During the Pandemic: Evidence from Uttarakhand." *Indian Journal of Labour Economics* 63, no. 4 (2020): 1107–24.
Basso, Keith H. *Wisdom Sits in Places: Landscape and Language Among the Western Apache*. Albuquerque: University of New Mexico Press, 1996.
Bauman, Chad M. "Hindu-Christian Conflict in India: Globalization, Conversion, and the Coterminal Castes and Tribes." *Journal of Asian Studies* 72, no. 3 (2013): 633–53.
Bayly, Susan. *Caste Society and Politics in India from the Eighteenth Century to the Modern Age*. New York: Cambridge University Press, 1999.
Beaucage, Pierre, Deirdre Meintel, and Géraldine Mossière. "Introduction: Social and Political Dimensions of Religious Conversion." *Anthropologica* 49, no. 1 (2007): 3–9.
Bellamy, Carla. *The Powerful Ephemeral: Everyday Healing in an Ambiguously Islamic Place*. Berkeley: University of California Press, 2011.
Berreman, Gerald D. *Hindus of the Himalayas: Ethnography and Change*. 2nd ed. Delhi: Oxford University Press, 1993.
———. "Sanskritization as Female Oppression in India." In *Sex and Gender Hierarchies*, ed. Barbara Diane Miller, Naomi Quinn, and Daniel Fessler, 366–92. Cambridge: Cambridge University Press, 1993.
Bhagirath. "Rural Migration Aay Alter Uttarakhand's Political Geography." *Down-To-Earth*, February 28, 2020. https://www.downtoearth.org.in/news/governance/rural-migration-may-alter-uttarakhand-s-political-geography-69510.
Bhardwaj, Ashutosh. "Uttarakhand Elections: Across the Border; Next to UP, New Caste Calculus." *Indian Express*, February 15, 2017. https://indianexpress.com/elections/uttarakhand-assembly-elections-2017/uttarakhand-elections-across-the-border-next-door-to-up-new-caste-calculus-4525289/.
Blackburn, Stuart H. *Singing of Birth and Death: Texts in Performance*. Philadelphia: University of Pennsylvania Press, 1988.
Blackburn, Stuart H., Peter J. Claus, Joyce B. Flueckiger, and Susan S. Wadley, eds. *Oral Epics in India*. Berkeley: University of California Press, 1989.
Boddy, Janice. "Spirit Possession Revisited: Beyond Instrumentality." *Annual Review of Anthropology* 23 (1994): 407–34.
Bourguignon, Erika. *Possession*. Prospect Heights, NY: Waveland Press, 1991.
Caldwell, Sarah. *Oh Terrifying Mother: Sexuality, Violence, and Worship of the Goddess Kali*. New Delhi: Oxford University Press, 1999.
Campbell, Sam, and Laura Gurney. "Mapping and Navigating Ontologies in Water Governance: The Case of the Ganges." *Water International* 45, nos. 7–8 (2020): 847–64.
Casey, Edward S. *Getting Back into Place: Toward a Renewed Understanding of the Place-World*. Bloomington: Indiana University Press, 1993.
———. "How to Get from Space to Place in a Fairly Short Stretch of Time." In *Senses of Place*, ed. Steven Feld and Keith H. Basso, 13. Santa Fe: School of American Research Press, 1996.
Chatak, Govind. *Garhwali Lokagathayen*. New Delhi: Takshila Prakashan, 1996.
Choudhary Kushal, and Govind Sharma. "Dalit Majority Village in Uttarakhand Plagued by Untouchability." *NewsClick*, June 24, 2022. https://www.newsclick.in/Dalit-Majority-Village-Uttarakhand-Plagued-Untouchability.
Cohen, Lawrence. *No Aging in India: Alzheimer's, the Bad Family and Other Modern Things*. Berkeley: University of California Press, 1998.

Copeman, Jacob. *Veins of Devotion: Blood Donation and Religious Experience in North India*. New Brunswick, NJ: Rutgers University Press, 2009.

Courtright, Paul B., and Lindsey Harlan. *From the Margins of Hindu Marriage: Essays on Gender Religion and Culture*. New York: Oxford University Press, 1995.

Cresswell, Tim. *Place: A Short Introduction*. Hoboken, NJ: Wiley, 2004.

Croll, Elisabeth J. "The Intergenerational Contract in the Changing Asian Family." *Oxford Development Studies* 34, no. 4 (2010): 473–91.

Csordas Thomas J. "Embodiment as a Paradigm for Anthropology." *Ethos* 8, no. 1 (1993): 5–47.

Daniel, E. Valentine. *Fluid Signs: Being a Person the Tamil Way*. Berkeley: University of California Press, 1984.

Daniel, E. Valentine, and Judy F. Pugh, eds. *South Asian Systems of Healing*. Leiden: E. J. Brill, 1984.

Das, Kalyan. "PM Modi Visits Kedarnath, Says Decade Belongs to Uttarakhand." *Hindustan Times*, November 6, 2021. https://www.hindustantimes.com/india-news/more-pilgrims-to-visit-char-dham-shrines-in-10-yrs-than-over-last-century-modi-101636114454610.html.

Das, Kasturi. "Climate Change Forces Uttarakhand Farmers to Migrate." The Third Pole, May 17, 2021. https://www.thethirdpole.net/en/climate/climate-change-forces-migration-uttarakhand-farmers/.

Das, Veena. *Affliction: Health, Disease, Poverty*. New York: Fordham University Press, 2015.

D'Cruz, Premilla, and Shalini Bharat. "Beyond Joint and Nuclear: The Indian Family Revisited." *Journal of Comparative Family Studies* 32, no. 2 (2001): 167–94.

De Certeau, Michel, and Steven Rendall. *The Practice of Everyday Life*. Trans. Steven Rendall. Berkeley: University of California Press, 1984.

Dey, Abhishek. "Religion, Politics, Power, and Rage Against Muslims: Heady World of Seers at Haridwar's Akharas." *The Print*, December 28, 2021. https://theprint.in/india/religion-politics-power-rage-against-muslims-heady-world-of-seers-at-haridwars-akharas/789821/.

"Dhan Nirankar Ji." Sant Nirankari Mission, accessed January 18, 2024. https://dhannirankarji.org/snm/1/Sant-Nirankari-Mission.

Diemberger, Hildegard. *When a Woman Becomes a Religious Dynasty: The Samding Dorje Phagmo of Tibet*. New York: Columbia University Press, 2007.

Dumezil, Georges. *Idées Romaines*. Paris: Gallimard (1969): 61–78.

Dumont, Louis, and R. M. Sainsbury. *Homo Hierarchicus: An Essay on the Caste System*. Trans. Richard Mark Sainsbury. Chicago: University of Chicago Press, 1970.

Eck, Diana L. *Darsan: Seeing the Divine Image in India*. New York: Columbia University Press, 1998.

———. *India: A Sacred Geography*. Westminster: Potter/Ten Speed/Harmony/Rodale, 2012.

Eller, Jack David. *Introducing Anthropology of Religion: Culture to the Ultimate*. 3rd ed. Abingdon, Oxon: Routledge, 2022.

Engelke, Matthew. "Material Religion." In *The Cambridge Companion to Religious Studies*, ed. Robert A. Orsi. Cambridge: Cambridge University Press, 2011.

———. *A Problem of Presence: Beyond Scripture in an African Church*. Berkeley: University of California Press, 2007.

Erndl, Kathleen M. *Victory to the Mother: The Hindu Goddess of Northwest India in Myth, Ritual, and Symbol*. New York: Oxford University Press, 1993.

Fanger, Allen C. "The Jagar: Spirit Possession Seance Among the Rajputs and Silpakars of Kumaon." In *Himalaya: Past and Present*, ed. M. P. Joshi, C.W. Brown, A. C. Fanger, 173–91. Almora: Shree Almora Book Depot, 1990.

Favret-Saada, Jeanne. "Being Affected." *HAU Journal of Ethnographic Theory* 2, no. 1 (2012): 435–45.

Feldhaus, Anne. *Connected Places: Region, Pilgrimage, and Geographical Imagination in India*. New York: Palgrave Macmillan, 2003.

Fiol, Stefan Patrick. *Recasting Folk in the Himalayas: Indian Music, Media, and Social Mobility*. Urbana: University of Illinois Press, 2017.

Flueckiger, Joyce Burkhalter. *In Amma's Healing Room: Gender and Vernacular Islam in South India*. Bloomington: Indiana University Press, 2006.

———. "When the Goddess Speaks Her Mind: Possession, Presence, and Narrative Theology in the Gaṅgamma Tradition of Tirupati, South India." *International Journal of Hindu Studies* 21, no. 2 (2017): 165–85.

———. *When the World Becomes Female: Guises of a South Indian Goddess*. Bloomington: Indiana University Press, 2013.

Fuller, Christopher, J. *The Camphor Flame: Popular Hinduism and Society in India*. New Delhi: Viking Penguin India, 1992.

———. "The Renovation Ritual in a South Indian Temple: The 1995 Kumbhābhiṣeka in the Mīnākṣī Temple, Madurai." *Bulletin of the School of Oriental and African Studies* (University of London) 67, no. 1 (2004): 40–63.

Ghosh, Jayati. "Hindutva, Economic Neoliberalism and the Abuse of Economic Statistics in India." *South Asia Multidisciplinary Academic Journal*, nos. 24/25 (December 2020): http://journals.openedition.org/samaj/6882.

Gold, Ann and Gloria Goodwin Raheja. *Listen to the Heron's Words: Reimagining Gender and Kinship in North India*. Berkeley: University of California Press, 1994.

Gombrich, Richard. *Theravāda Buddhism: A Social History from Ancient Benares to Modern Colombo*. 2nd ed. New York: Routledge, 2006.

Good, Byron J. "The Heart of What's the Matter: The Semantics of Illness in Iran." *Culture, Medicine and Psychiatry* 1, no. 1 (1977): 25–58.

Grinshpon, Yohanan. *Silence Unheard: Deathly Otherness in Pātañjala-Yoga*. Albany: State University of New York Press, 2002.

Haberman, David. *River of Love in an Age of Pollution: The Yamuna River of Northern India*. 1st ed. Ewing, Berkeley: University of California Press, 2006.

Halliburton, Murphy. "The Importance of a Pleasant Process of Treatment: Lessons on Healing from South India." *Culture, Medicine and Psychiatry* 27, no. 2 (2003): 161–86.

Hawley, John Stratton, "Every Play a Play Within a Play." In *The Gods at Play: Līlā in South Asia*, ed. William Sturman Sax, 115–30. New York: Oxford University Press, 1995.

———. *Krishna the Butter Thief*. Princeton, NJ: Princeton University Press, 1983.

Hawley, John Stratton, and Mark Juergensmeyer. *Songs of the Saints of India*. New Delhi: Oxford University Press, 2004.

Hiltebeitel, Alf, Vishwa Adluri, and Joydeep Bagchee. *Reading the Fifth Veda: Studies on the Mahabharata: Essays*. Leiden: Brill, 2011.

India Today Web Desk. "PM Narendra Modi in Kedarnath: 5 Things He Said About Temple Shrine in Past." *India Today*, May 18, 2019. https://www.indiatoday.in/india/story/pm-narendra-modi-in-kedarnath-5-things-he-said-about-temple-shrine-in-past-1528054-2019-05-18.

Indian Ministry of Home Affairs. "Census Of India 2011 Release of Primary Census Abstract Data Highlights." April 30, 2013. https://idsn.org/wp-content/uploads/user_folder/pdf/New_files/India/2013/INDIA_CENSUS_ABSTRACT-2011-Data_on_SC-STs.pdf.

International Centre for Integrated Mountain Development (ICIMOD). *Labour Migration and Remittances in Uttarakhand. Case Study Report*. Kathmandu: ICIMOD, 2011.

Jangam Chinnaiah, Ramnarayan S. Rawat, Anupama Rao, and Gopal Guru. "A Dalit Paradigm: A New Narrative in South Asian Historiography." *Modern Asian Studies* 50, no. 1 (2016): 399–414.
Jassal, Aftab. "Awakening the Serpent King: Ritual and Textual Ontologies in Garhwal, Uttarakhand." *Journal of Hindu Studies* 13, no. 2 (2020): 101–21.
———. "Divine Politicking: A Rhetorical Approach to Deity Possession in the Himalayas." *Religions* 7, no. 9 (2016): 117. https://doi.org/10.3390/rel7090117.
———. "Making God Present: Placemaking and Ritual Healing in North India." *International Journal of Hindu Studies* 21, no. 2 (2017): 141–64.
Jassal, Smita Tewari. *Unearthing Gender: Folksongs of North India*. Durham, NC: Duke University Press, 2012.
Joshi, Anil. K. "Dalit Reform Movement in British Kumaon." *Proceedings of the Indian History Congress* 61 (2000): 976–85.
Joshi, Maheshwar P. "The Silpakaras (artisans) of Central Himalaya: A Diachronic Study." In *Himalaya: Past and Present*, ed. Allen C. Fanger, Maheshwar P. Joshi, and Charles W. Brown, 301–33. Almora, India: Shree Almora Book Depot no. 3, 1994.
Juergensmeyer, Mark. *Radhasoami Reality: The Logic of a Modern Faith*. Princeton, NJ; Princeton University Press, 1991.
Kanungo, Pralay, and Joshi, Satyakam. "Carving Out a White Marble Deity from Rugged Black Stone: Hindutva Rehabilitates Ramayan's Shabari in a Temple." *International Journal of Hindu Studies* 13, no.3 (2009): 279–99.
Kapferer, Bruce. *A Celebration of Demons: Exorcism and the Aesthetics of Healing in Sri Lanka*. Bloomington: Indiana University Press, 1983.
"Kedarnath Will Become a Model Pilgrimage Site: PM Modi." *Times of India*, October 20, 2017. https://timesofindia.indiatimes.com/india/kedarnath-will-become-a-model-pilgrimage-site-pm-modi/articleshow/61150280.cms?from=mdr.
Kent, Eliza. "'Mass Movements' in South India, 1877–1936." In *Converting Cultures: Religion, Ideology and Transformations of Modernity*, ed. Dennis Washburn and Kevin Reinhart. Leiden: Brill, 2007.
———. "Secret Christians of Sivakasi: Gender, Syncretism, and Crypto-Religion in Early Twentieth-Century South India." *Journal of the American Academy of Religion* 79, no. 3 (2011): 676–705.
Khanna, Rajeev. "Why Uttarakhand HC Order on Temple Entry for Dalits Is a Landmark Judgment." *Catch News*, July 14, 2018. http://www.catchnews.com/india-news/why-uttarakhand-hc-order-on-temple-entry-for-dalits-is-a-landmark-judgment-122628.html.
Knuppel, Anandi Leela Devaki. "Beyond Seeing: Embodied Multisensory Performance, Experience, and Practice in Contemporary Transnational Gaudiya Vaishnavism." PhD diss., Emory University, 2019. https://etd.library.emory.edu/concern/etds/gh93h053g.
Kumar, Mukul. "Relationship of Caste and Crime in Colonial India: A Discourse Analysis." *Economic and Political Weekly* 39, no. 10 (2004): 1078–87.
Lamb, Sarah. *White Saris and Sweet Mangoes: Aging, Gender, and Body in North India*. Berkeley: University of California Press, 2000.
Leavitt, John. "Oracular Therapy in the Kumaon Hills: A Question of Rationality." *Indian Anthropologist* 16, no.1 (1986): 71–79.
Lee, Joel. *Deceptive Majority: Dalits, Hinduism, and Underground Religion*. Cambridge: Cambridge University Press, 2021.
———. "Odor and Order: How Caste Is Inscribed in Space and Sensoria." *Comparative Studies of South Asia, Africa, and the Middle East* 37 no. 3 (December 1, 2017): 470–90.
Lewis, Ioan M. *Ecstatic Religion: A Study of Shamanism and Spirit Possession*. London: Routledge, 2005.

Lochtefeld, James. *God's Gateway: Identity and Meaning in a Hindu Pilgrimage Place*. New York: Oxford University Press, 2010.

Luhrmann, Tanya M. "Anthropology as Spiritual Discipline." *American Ethnologist* (2023): 1–4.

Lutgendorf, Philip. *The Life of a Text: Performing the Ramcaritmanas of Tulsidas*. Berkeley: University of California Press, 1991.

Lynch, Owen M. *The Politics of Untouchability: Social Mobility and Social Change in a City of India*. New York: Columbia University Press, 1969.

Maithani, B. P. "Towards Sustainable Hill Area Development, Himalaya." *Man, Nature and Culture* 16, no. 2 (1996): 4–7.

Malik, Aditya. *Tales of Justice and Rituals of Divine Embodiment: Oral Narratives from the Central Himalayas*. New York: Oxford University Press, 2016.

Mamgain, Rajendra P., and D. N. Reddy. *Final Report on Outmigration from Hill Region of Uttarakhand: Magnitude, Challenges and Policy Options*. Hyderabad, India: National Institute of Rural Development & Panchayati Raj, accessed December 6, 2022. http://nirdpr.org.in/nird_docs/srsc/srscrr261016-3.pdf.

Mander, Harsh. "How State-Backed Hindutva Rhetoric Is Fueling the Ethnic Cleansing of Uttarakhand." *Scroll.in*, November 3, 2023. https://scroll.in/article/1057843/how-state-backed-hindutva-rhetoric-is-fuelling-the-ethnic-cleansing-of-uttarakhand.

Mani, Lata. *Myriad Intimacies*. Durham, NC: Duke University Press, 2022.

Mashal, Mujib, and Hari Kumar. "Before Himalayan Flood, India Ignored Warnings of Development Risks." *New York Times*, February 8, 2021. https://www.nytimes.com/2021/02/08/world/asia/india-flood-ignored-warnings.html.

Masquelier, Adeline Marie. *Prayer Has Spoiled Everything: Possession, Power, and Identity in an Islamic Town of Niger*. Durham, NC: Duke University Press, 2001.

Massey, Doreen. *For Space*. London: Sage, 2005.

———. "The Responsibilities of Place." *Local Economy* 19, no 2 (2004): 97–101.

Mathias, Kaaren, Isabel Goicolea, Michelle Kermode, Lawrence Singh, Rahul Shidhaye, and Miguel San Sebastian. "Cross-Sectional Study of Depression and Help-Seeking in Uttarakhand, North India." *BMJ Open* 5, no. 11 (2015): e008992.

McDermott, Rachel Fell. *Revelry, Rivalry and Longing for the Goddesses of Bengal: The Fortunes of Hindu Festivals*. New York: Columbia University Press, 2011.

McDermott, Rachel Fell, and Jeffrey J. Kripal. *Encountering Kali: In the Margins at the Center in the West*. Berkeley: University of California Press, 2003.

Middleton, Townsend, and Jason Cons. "Coming to Terms: Reinserting Research Assistants into Ethnography's Past and Present." *Ethnography* 15, no. 3 (2014): 279–90.

Miller, Barbara Diane, Naomi Quinn, and Daniel Fessler. *Sex and Gender Hierarchies*. Cambridge University Press, 1993.

Mines, Diane P. *Fierce Gods: Inequality, Ritual, and the Politics of Dignity in a South Indian Village*. Bloomington: Indiana University Press, 2005.

———. "Waiting for Veḷḷāḷakaṇṭaṉ: Narrative, Movement, and Making Place in a Tamil Village." In *Tamil Geographies: Cultural Constructions of Space and Place in South India*, ed. Martha Ann Selby and Indira Viswanathan Peterson, 199–220. Albany: State University of New York Press, 2008.

Mittal, Tusha and Alishan Jagri. "The Movement to Expel Muslims and Create a Hindu Holy Land." *Coda*, November 2, 2023. https:/www.codastory.com/rewriting-history/the-movement-to-expel-muslims-and-create-a-hindu-holy-land/.

Modi, Narendra. "BJP Will Protect the Divinity of Devbhoomi Uttarakhand: PM Modi." Narendra Modi YouTube Channel. YouTube video. February 12, 2022. https://www.youtube.com/watch?v=X5m6GuwGqQI.
Monier-Williams. *A Dictionary, English and Sanskrit.* England: W. H. Allen, 2002 [1851]): 760.
Moran, Arik. *Kingship and Polity on the Himalayan Borderland: Rajput Identity During the Early Colonial Encounter.* Amsterdam: Amsterdam University Press, 2019.
Munn, Nancy D. "Excluded Spaces: The Figure in the Australian Aboriginal Landscape." *Critical Inquiry* 22, no. 3 (1996): 446–65.
Nabokov, Isabelle (Clark-Decès). *Religion Against the Self: An Ethnography of Tamil Rituals.* Oxford: Oxford University Press, 2000.
Naithani, Shiv Prasad. *Uttarakhand Gathaon ke Rahasya.* Almora: Shree Almora Book Depot, 2010.
Narayan, Kirin. *Storytellers Saints and Scoundrels: Folk Narrative in Hindu Religious Teaching.* Philadelphia: University of Pennsylvania Press, 1989.
Narayanan, Vasudha. "Water, Wood, and Wisdom: Ecological Perspectives from the Hindu Traditions." *Daedalus* 130, no. 4 (2001): 179–206.
Nautiyal, Shivanand. *Uttarakhand ki Lokagathayen.* Almora: Shree Almora Book Depot, 1997.
Oakley, E. S, and Lucy Wood Sullivan. *Holy Himalaya; the Religion, Traditions, and Scenery of Himalayan Province (Kumaon and Garwhal).* London: Oliphant Anderson & Ferrier, 1905.
Oakley, E. S. (E. Sherman), Tara Dutt Gairola, and Gangā Datt Upreti. *Himalayan Folklore.* Allahabad: Superintendent, Printing and Stationery, U. P., 1935.
Oberoi, Harjot. *The Construction of Religious Boundaries: Culture Identity and Diversity in the Sikh Tradition.* Chicago: University of Chicago Press, 1994.
Obeyesekere, Gananath. *The Work of Culture: Symbolic Transformation in Psychoanalysis and Anthropology.* Chicago: University of Chicago Press, 2000.
Omvedt, Gail. *Seeking Begumpura: The Social Vision of Anticaste Intellectuals.* New Delhi: Navayana: Distributed by IPD Alternatives, 2008.
Orsi, Robert A. *The Madonna of 115th Street: Faith and Community in Italian Harlem, 1880–1950.* 2nd edition. New Haven: Yale University Press, 2002.
Parish, Steven. "Postscript: The Problem of Power." In *Hierarchy and Its Discontents: Culture and the Politics of Consciousness in Caste Society.* Philadelphia: University of Pennsylvania Press (1996): 225–42.
Pathak, Shekhar. "Fighting Alcohol in Uttarakhand." *Himal Southasian,* July 1, 1988. https://www.himalmag.com/fighting-alcohol-in-uttarakhand/.
Pathak, Shivani. "Uttarakhand Is Mapping Snakes and Training Local Communities to Reduce Conflict Between Them: The Nature of Human-Snake Conflict in the Mountains Is Different from That in the Plains." *Scroll.in,* December 27, 2020. https://scroll.in/article/982107/uttarakhand-is-mapping-snakes-and-training-local-communities-to-reduce-conflict-between-them.
Patton, Laurie. *Bringing the Gods to Mind: Mantra and Ritual in Early Indian Sacrifice.* Berkeley: University of California Press, 2005.
Pechilis, Karen. "To Pilgrimage It." *Journal of Ritual Studies* 6, no. 2 (1992): 59–91.
Pennington, Brian. Forthcoming. *God's Fifth Abode: Entrepreneurial Hinduism in the Indian Himalayas.*
———. "Hinduism in North India," In *Hinduism in the Modern World,* ed. Brian A. Hatcher, 31–47, New York: Routledge, 2016.
Pinkney, Andrea Marion. "Prasāda, the Gracious Gift, in Contemporary and Classical South Asia." *Journal of the American Academy of Religion* 81, no. 3 (2013): 734–56.

Pinney, Christopher. "The Indian Work of Art in the Age of Mechanical Reproduction: Or, What Happens When Peasants 'Get Hold' of Images." In *Media Worlds: Anthropology on New Terrain*, ed. Faye D. Ginsburg, Lila Abu-Lughod, and Brian Larkin, 355–69. Berkeley: University of California Press, 2002.

Pinto, Sarah. *Daughters of Parvati: Women and Madness in Contemporary India*. Philadelphia: University of Pennsylvania Press, 2014.

———. "Rational Love, Relational Medicine: Psychiatry and the Accumulation of Precarious Kinship." *Culture, Medicine and Psychiatry* 35, no. 3 (2011): 376–95.

———. "'The Tools of Your Chants and Spells': Stories of Madwomen and Indian Practical Healing." *Medical Anthropology* 35, no. 3 (2016): 263–77.

Polit, Karin. "The Effects of Inequality and Relative Marginality on the Well-Being of Low Caste People in Central Uttaranchal." *Anthropology and Medicine* 12, no. 3 (2005): 225–37.

———. "The Making of Persons and Ancestors: Rituals of Birth and Death Among Dalits in the Garhwal Himalayas." In *Childbirth and Its Accompanying Rituals: An Anthropological Analysis of Birth and Childhood Rituals in South and South East Asia*, ed. Karin M. Polit and Gabriele Alex, 59–86. Heidelberg: Draupadi Verlag, 2016.

Prabhudesai, Arun. "Per Capita Income of Various Indian States [2016]." Trak.in, December 19, 2017. http://trak.in/2012/average-per-capita-income-indian-states/.

Prasad, Leela. *Poetics of Conduct: Oral Narrative and Moral Being in a South Indian Town*. New York: Columbia University Press, 2007.

Raheja, Gloria Goodwin, and Ann Grodzins Gold. *Listen to the Heron's Words: Reimagining Gender and Kinship in North India*. Berkeley: University of California Press, 1994.

Ram, Kalpana. *Fertile Disorder: Spirit Possession and Its Provocation of the Modern*. Honolulu: University of Hawai'i Press, 2013.

Ram, Ronki. "Beyond Conversion and Sanskritisation: Articulating an Alternative Dalit Agenda in East Punjab." *Modern Asian Studies* 46, no. 3 (2012): 639–702.

Ramanujan, A. K. *Poems of Love and War: From the Eight Anthologies and the Ten Long Poems of Classical Tamil*. New York: Columbia University Press, 1985.

———. "Three Hundred Ramayanas: Five Examples and Three Thoughts on Translation." In *Many Ramayanas: The Diversity of a Narrative Tradition in South Asia*, ed. Paula Richman, 22–48. Berkeley: University of California Press, 1991.

Ramberg, Lucinda. *Given to the Goddess: South Indian Devadasis and the Sexuality of Religion*. Durham, NC: Duke University Press, 2014.

———. "Magical Hair as Dirt: Ecstatic Bodies and Postcolonial Reform in South India." *Culture, Medicine and Psychiatry* 33, no.4 (2009): 501–22.

Rao, Velcheru Narayana and Shulman, David. Ed and Trans. *Classical Telugu Poetry: An Anthology*. Berkeley: University of California Press, 2002.

Rappaport, Roy A. *Ritual and Religion in the Making of Humanity*. Cambridge: Cambridge University Press, 1999.

Rawat, Ramnarayan S. *Reconsidering Untouchability: Chamars and Dalit History in North India*. Bloomington: Indiana University Press, 2011.

Reddy, Deepa S. "Hindutva: Formative Assertions." *Religion Compass* 5, no. 8 (2011): 439–51.

Relph, E. C. *Place and Placelessness*. London: Pion, 1976.

Sampath, G. "Don't Blame Nature for the Uttarakhand Flood Disaster." *Mint*, June 27, 2013. https://www.livemint.com/Opinion/hzKmWekwY0OtYKv8N6dZlN/Dont-blame-nature-for-the-Uttarakhand-flood-disaster.html.

Sax, William Sturman. *Dancing the Self: Personhood and Performance in the Pāṇḍava Līlā of Garhwal.* Oxford: Oxford University Press, 2002.
———. *God of Justice: Ritual Healing and Social Justice in the Central Himalayas.* Oxford: Oxford University Press, 2009.
———. "Healing Rituals." *Anthropology & Medicine* 11, no. 3 (2004): 293–306
———. *Mountain Goddess: Gender and Politics in a Himalayan Pilgrimage.* New York: Oxford University Press, 1991.
Seale-Feldman, Aidan. "Relational Affliction: Reconceptualizing 'Mass Hysteria.'" *Ethos* 47, no. 3 (2019): 307–25.
Sebring, J. M. "The Formation of New Castes: A Probable Case from North India. *American Anthropologist* 74, no. 3 (1972): 587–600
Sharabi, Asaf. *The Biography of a God: Mahasu in the Himalayas.* Amsterdam: Amsterdam University Press, 2023.
Sharma, Mukul. "Passages from Nature to Nationalism: Sunderlal Bahuguna and Tehri Dam Opposition in Garhwal." *Economic and Political Weekly* 44, no. 8 (2009): 35–42.
Sharma, Seema. "Uttarakhand's Women Remain Vigilant Against Liquor Shops and Alcoholism." *Times of India*, August 23, 2015.
Shiva, Vandana, and J. Bandyopadhyay. "The Evolution Structure and Impact of the Chipko Movement." *Mountain Research and Development* 6, no. 2 (1986): 133–42.
Shulman, David Dean. *The King and the Clown in South Indian Myth and Poetry.* Princeton, NJ: Princeton University Press, 1985.
———. *Tamil Temple Myths: Sacrifice and Divine Marriage in the South Indian Śaiva Tradition.* Princeton, NJ: Princeton University Press, 1980.
Shulman, David Dean, and V. Narayana Rao. *Classical Telugu Poetry: An Anthology.* Berkeley: University of California Press, 2002.
Simmons, Caleb. *Nine Nights of the Goddess: The Navaratri Festival in South Asia.* Albany: State University of New York, 2018.
Singh, Prithviraj. "Uttarakhand Dalits Demand Entry into Temples, Spark Fears of Conflict." *Hindustan Times*, May 18, 2016. https://www.hindustantimes.com/india/uttarakhand-dalits-demand-entry-into-temples-spark-fears-of-conflict/story-HXr6kxW0izxrZFzDs4TGXN.html.
Smith, Brian K. and Wendy Doniger. "Sacrifice and Substitution: Ritual Mystification and Mythical Demystification." *Numen* 36, no. 2 (1989): 189–224.
Smith, Frederick M. *The Self Possessed: Deity and Spirit Possession in South Asian Literature and Civilization.* New York: Columbia University Press, 2006.
Smith, Jonathan Z. *Imagining Religion: From Babylon to Jonestown.* Chicago: University of Chicago Press, 1982.
Srinivas, Mysore N. *Religion and Society Among the Coorgs of South India.* Oxford: Clarendon Press, 1952.
Stephens, Robert. "Sites of Conflict in the Indian Secular State: Secularism, Caste and Religious Conversion." *Journal of Church and State* 49, no. 2 (2007): 251–76.
Strathern, Marilyn. *Partial Connections.* Lanham, MD: AltaMira Press, 2005.
Swami Chidananda. "Save The Himalaya." *Bhagirathi ki Pukar* 7, no. 2 (February 7, 1997): 1.
Tewari, Vinod C. 2013. "Himalayan Tsunami: Devastating Natural Disaster in the Uttarakhand Himalaya." Eberhard Karls Universitat Tubingen, accessed December 6, 2022. https://bibliographie.uni-tuebingen.de/xmlui/bitstream/handle/10900/50071/pdf/Tewari2_168.pdf?sequence=1.
Thapa, Swati. "Caste, Gender, Climate Change: Farmers in Uttarakhand Struggle for Survival." *India Development Review*, July 12, 2023. https://idronline.org/article/climate-emergency/caste-gender-climate-change-farmers-in-uttarakhand-struggle-for-survival/.

Tiku, Kumar M. "In Uttarakhand, Young Women Lead an Exodus from Mountain Villages." *The Wire*, April 10, 2019. https://thewire.in/rights/uttarakhand-outmigration-crisis-villages.

Turner, Edith L. B. "The Reality of Spirits: A Tabooed or Permitted Field of Study." *Anthropology of Consciousness* 4, no. 1 (1993): 9–12.

Tweed, Thomas A. *Crossing and Dwelling: A Theory of Religion*. Cambridge, MA: Harvard University Press, 2006.

Upadhyay, Kavita. "Dalit Killed for Entering Flour Mill in Uttarakhand." *The Hindu*, October 8, 2016. https://www.thehindu.com/news/national/other-states/Dalit-killed-for-entering-flour-mill-in-Uttarakhand/article15432538.ece.

Upadhyay, Urbadatta. *Kumaun ki Lokagathaon ka Sahityak aur Sanskritik Adhyyan*. Bareli: Prakash Book Depot, 1979.

Urban, Hugh. *The Power of Tantra: Religion Sexuality and the Politics of South Asian Studies*. New York: I. B. Tauris and Palgrave Macmillan, 2010.

Varagur, Krithika. "Converting to Buddhism as a Form of Social Protest." *The Atlantic*, April 11, 2018. https://www.theatlantic.com/international/archive/2018/04/dalit-buddhism-conversion-india-modi/557570/.

Venkateshan, Soumhya. "Object, Subject, Thing: Tamil Hindu Priests' Material Practices and Practical Theories of Animation and Accommodation." *American Ethnologist* 47, no. 4 (2020): 447–460.

Weil, Simone, and George A. Panichas. *The Simone Weil Reader*. Ed. George A. Panichas. New York: McKay (1977): 441.

Wheeler, Bonnie. "Models of Pilgrimage: From Communitas to Confluence." *Journal of Ritual Studies* 13, no. 2 (1999): 26–41.

White, David Gordon. *Tantra in Practice*. Princeton, NJ: Princeton University Press, 2000.

Whitmore, Luke. *Mountain, Water, Rock, God: Understanding Kedarnath in the Twenty-First Century*. Oakland: University of California Press, 2018.

Willford, Andrew. " 'Do You Hear Voices, or Do You Think You Hear Voices?' Malevolence and Modernity in the Psychiatric Clinic." *South Asia: Journal of South Asian Studies* 45, no. 1 (2022): 164–82.

Zoller, Claus Peter. "A Little-Known Form of Untouchability in the Central Himalayas." In *Reading Slowly: A Festschrift for Jens E. Braarvig*, 1st ed., ed. Edzard Lutz, Jens W. Borgland and Ute Hüsken, 475. Wiesbaden: Harrassowitz, 2018.

Index

abode of the gods. *See dev-bhumi*
achhut. *See* untouchables
acknowledge and to honor (*nam lena*), 198n5
acknowledgement (*manana*), 25, 185–187
actions (*karma*), 59, 73, 131–132
Adcock, C. S., 205n76
adesh (command me), 147
adhikar (rights), 121
adhuri (inferior and partial), 182
Advaita Vedanta, 40
Advani, L. K., 28–29
affinal home (*saras/sasural*), 97
affliction (*dosh*), 5, 131, 210n6, 210n10; arrogance and, 62–65; astrology and, 55–56, 73; of *chhal*, 97–126; in dreams, 69–70; of ghosts, 97–126; as harmful attachment, 56; healing and, 71–74; *jagaris* and, 55, 60; of Krishna, 66–67; Nagaraja and Gangu Ramola and, 52–74; oracles and, 56; at *panno*, 88; *pasva* and, 55; Ramesh and, xvii; sources and origins of, 55–56; *sthan* and, 70–72. *See also nagadosh*
ahamkara (I-doing), 64, 65
akhara, 172–173
Allocco, Amy, 199n16
Ambedkar Mahasabha, 16
andha-vishvas (superstition), 35

aniconic images of the god Shiva (Shiva-*lingas*), xiv, 208n18
animal sacrifice (*bali*), 35; by Brahmins, 39; for ghosts in women, 110; at *jagar*, 216n24; by Muslims, 37, 38; for *nagadosh*, 72; *puja jana* and, 218n48
anpadh (unlettered), 182, 183
Arjuna, 81, 88
arrogance (*ghamandi*), 61–65
artisan (*shilpakar*), 16–17
Arya Samaj, 205n76
ashta-bali (multiday sacrificial ritual), xvi
Ashwatthaman, 57
ask (*puchana*), 197n2
astrological birth chart (*kundali*), 56; of Gangu Ramola, 43
astrology: affliction and, 73; *dosh* and, 55–56
Atkinson, E. T., 35
atma (spirits), 199n16
attachment (*lagana*), 56, 72, 106, 210n10
aujis: *bol* and, 80; castes and, 78; *jagaris* and, 79–80, 213n10; *jati* and, 76; Pandava brothers and, 78; as untouchables, 84
authoritative knowledge (*shastrik*), 35
avatarit hona (becoming incarnated), 207n1
avatar lena (taking incarnation), 207n1
avatars (incarnations), 6, 168; Nagaraja as, 27
awakened (*jagrit*), 61
Ayurveda, 56

Babri Masjid, 29
bagpipes (*mashakbaja*), 79
bahu (daughter-in-law), 99–126, 218n49
bak bolana (deities speak), 7, 197n2
bakkyas. *See* oracles
balance (*santulan*), 70
bali. *See* animal sacrifice
Barabar, 82, 86
bass drum (*dhol*), 77, 79, 104
beast. *See pasva*
become incarnated (*avatarit hona*), 207n1
belief (*manana*), 25, 185–187
bell (*ghanta*), xvii
ber (jujube tree), 60, 74
Berreman, Gerald, 39
bhag (direction), 106
Bhagavad Gita, 13
bhagavan, 32, 136
Bhagavata Purana, 32, 35
Bhagavati Devi, 80, 81, 83, 88, 91, 135, 164, 213n15, 214n29
Bhairavnath, 5–6, 7, 106, 135, 138–139, 141
bhajans (devotional songs), 35
bhaktas (devotees), 140
bhakti (devotion), 113, 188, 198n6
bhandara, 79
Bharatiya Janata Party (BJP), 13; castes and, 129; *dev-bhumi* and, 29, 36; Muslims and, 28–29, 38; *rath yatra* of, 28–29
Bhairavnath, 220n20
bhram (delusions), 182
bhut. *See* ghosts
bhut nach (ghost worship), 35
Billu, xiv–xvii, 197n4
bimari (disease), 58
birthplace of Ram (Rama-janama-bhumi), 28–29
Bisht, Deepak, 101–114, 118, 180
Bisht, Nitin, 101–103, 107, 118
BJP. *See* Bharatiya Janata Party
black magic (*hankar-jankar*), 57
black magic (*jadu-tona*), 35
body (*sharir*), 68, 145
bol (speech), 80, 145
Bourdieu, Pierre, 201n36
Brahman, 40, 182, 209n28, 211n13
Brahmanism, 35
Brahmaputra River, 12

Brahminical religion, 35, 38, 50, 205n85
Brahmins, 14–18, 30, 129–130, 204n62; animal sacrifice by, 39; at Danda Nagaraja, 27, 34–35, 208n18; Giridhar ji on, 50; *jagaris* and oracles and, 128; Krishna as, 46–47; on pilgrimages, 159–160, 165; pilgrimages and, 25; in village, 75–76
Brit Barma, 59, 211n13
Buddhism, 50, 206n90
bulana (call), 130
burtiya (ritual performer), 80
buy (*kharidana*), 180

Casey, Edward, 201n27
castes, 14–18, 219n6; BJP and, 129; Fiol on, 205n74; ghosts and, 99; *jagaris* and, 24, 127–153; Lee on, 223n24; oracles and, 127–153; possession and, 202n39; Sikhism and, 21; in village, 76–79, 84–85. *See also aujis*; Brahmins; *jati*; untouchables; upper-caste
Certeau, Michel de, 201n30
chahara (face), 59
chal (rhythm), 146, 221n25
chamar, 15, 219n5
chamatkar (miracles), 137
Chamoli, Jagat Lal, 208n18
Champal Mistri, 128–132, 185–186, 210n7
Chandola, Uma Shankar, 63, 211n15
Chandola, Vikrant, 19
chot lagana (being hurt), 210n10
chhal (crafty demon), 23–24, 215n3; affliction of, 97–126; in *jagar*, 218n47
Chhota Char Dham (small four abodes/seats), 30
Chipko movement, 13
chosen deity. *See isht dev*
chot (hurt), 210n10
Christianity, 206n90
chua-chut (untouchability), 15, 76
Clark-Decès, Isabelle. *See* Nabokov, Isabelle
collection (*phant*), 89
color (*varna*), 14–15
command me (*adesh*), 147
community (*samaj*), 177
compassion (*kripa/daya*), 86
concentration and effort (*dhyan aur parishram*), 173
Connected Places (Feldhaus), 207n2
contemplation (*samadhi*), 181
courts (*darbar*), 107

COVID-19 pandemic, 36
crafty demon. *See chhal*
Criminal Tribes Act of 1871, 129
crooked (*ulta*), 59
curses (*ghat lagana*), 57, 130

daku (gangsters), 128–129
Dalits. *See specific topics*
damaun (kettledrum), 77, 79, 104
dance. *See nach*
dance of the Pandavas. *See panno*
dancing. *See nachana*
Dancing the Self (Sax), 203n42
Danda Nagaraja, 22, 26–28, 166, 183; Brahmins at, 27, 34–35, 208n18; as fifth abode, 30, 32; fractious identities in, 34–36; *jagar* and, 35; Krishna in, 32–33, 42–44, 45; *pujaris* at, 34–35, 36; technologies of development in, 30–33
dangariya (small horse), 7, 200n21
darbar (courts), 107
darshan (seeing a deity), 4, 45, 167, 170
darshan dena, 45
darshan karana, 27
darshan lena, 44
das (servant), 76, 85–86, 164
Das, Veena, 210n8
daughter-in-law (*bahu*), 99–126, 218n49
daur (small double-headed drum), 79, 142
Deceptive Majority (Lee), 220n13
dedicate (*samarpit*), 72
deities speak (*bak bolana*), 7, 197n2
deity (*devata*), xvi. *See also specific topics*
deity's form (*rup*), 61
deity's power (*shakti*), xv, 9, 56–57, 113
delusions (*bhram*), 182
deodar tree (*diyad*), 171
description (*vritti*), 211n13
desire (*manauti*), 71, 166–167
deval, 219n5
devata (deity), xvi. *See also specific topics*
dev-bhumi (abode/land of the gods, sacred landscape), 6, 13, 22, 26–51, 208n22; BJP and, 29, 36; *lilas* and, 61; Muslims and, 37–39; mytho-histories of interregional conflict in, 46–49; Nagaraja and, 26–28; origin myths on, 36–39; technologies of development in, 30–33. *See also* Danda Nagaraja
devi ka sthan (place of the goddess), 160–161

devilish (*harami*), 214n21
Devi-Mayya, 40
devotees (*bhaktas*), 140
devotion (*bhakti*), 113, 188, 198n6
devotional songs (*bhajans*), 35
Dhami, Pushkar Singh, 206n88
dhamis, 7, 218n1
Dhanvir ji, 61, 62, 65, 67, 74, 143, 187–189, 210n7
dharamashala (rest houses), 18, 172
dharma (normative order), 64
dharma-sutra, 14
Dhaulagudiyar, 58
dhol (bass drum), 77, 79, 104
Dhol Sagar ("Ocean of Drumming"), 80
dhuni (ritual fire), 81, 156, 161, 164
dhyan aur parishram (concentration and effort), 173
direction (*bhag*), 106
disease (*bimari*), 58
divine embodiment. *See* embodiment
diyad (deodar tree), 171
dola-palkis (palanquins), 16, 205n74
Dom, 16, 205nn74–75
Doniger, Wendy, 218n38i
dosh. See affliction
doshas (humors), 56, 73
Draupadi, 38, 80, 90
dreams: affliction in, 69–70; of *sadhus*, 52; of serpents, 1–2
Dumézil, George, 201n30
dupattas (scarves), 156, 173–174
dvar (gateway), 147
dvaraka-pati, 47–49, 209n30
dvesha-bhakti, 198n6
Dyongarh, 75–96, 213n15

earthly activities. *See* lilas
Eck, Diana, 3
elaboration (*vrtti*), 211n13
Eller, Jack, 185, 186
embodiment, 6, 197n3; *jagaris* and, 127; in *maidan*, 87; on pilgrimages, 164; placemaking and, 9–10; in Tamil Nadu, 198n9; in villages, 83–84, 93–96
Engelke, Matthew, 4, 199n13
politics (*rajaniti*), 102
epic performances (*gatha lagana*), 77
excess (*ugra*), 9, 72, 201n31

face (*chahara*), 59
faith (*vishvas*), xvii
fancy (*kalpana*), 189
fault. *See* affliction
Feldhaus, Anne, 28, 207n2
fifth abode (*panchava dham*), 30, 32, 208nn13–14
Fiol, Stefan, 16, 200n21, 205n74
Flueckiger, Joyce, 10–11, 24–25, 201n31, 218n3
folk songs (*git*), 199n17
forbidden dancing (*harami nach*), 86
Fuller, Christopher, 217n37
fundamental aspects of Hindu gods (*vigrah*), 3

Gandhi, M. K., 16–17, 76, 128, 205n85
Ganganth, 107
Ganga River, 11, 12, 76
Gangnath, 107, 158, 178, 217n33
gangster (*daku*), 128–129
Gangu Ramola, 23, 28; affliction and, 52–74; astrological birth chart of, 43; *ghamand* of, 62–65; Giridhar ji on, 46, 47–48; Kaliya Nag and, 62, 211n16; Krishna and, 36, 40, 42–45, 48, 50, 54, 62–65, 210n11, 211n16; milk and, 63–64; *nagadosh* and, 62, 73; Nagaraja (serpent king) and, 54
ganit (mathematics), 210n9
gantua, 56, 210n9
garami (heat), 67
garbha-griha (inner chamber), 160
Garhwal. *See specific topics*
Garhwal Mandal Vikas Nigam (GMVN), 20, 221n5
garudas (mythical winged beings), 57–58
garv, 64
gateway (*dvar*), 147
gatha lagana (epic performances), 77
gathas (oral narratives), 6, 28, 199n17, 210nn6–7; Nagaraja and, 22–23
geometrical ritual diagrams (*yantras*), xiv–xv
ghamand (arrogance), 61–65
ghanta (bell), xvii
ghat lagana (curses), 57, 130
ghora (horse), 7
ghosts (*bhut*), 218n47; affliction of, 97–126; attachment and, 106; castes and, 99; exorcism of, 98–124, 217n31; at *jagar*, 24, 98–124, 216n24, 217n30; *jagaris* and, 107; Muslims and, 105; in Nepal, 105; troubles by, 98; women and, 23–24, 97–126, 217n31, 218n49
ghost worship (*bhut nach*), 35
ghouls (*pret*), 83
Ghurid dynasty, 37, 209n23
Giridhar ji, 40–42, 44, 45, 46, 209n28; on Brahmins, 50; on Gangu Ramola, 46; on *jagar*, 47; on Krishna, 50–51
git (folk songs), 199n17
Gita-Bhagavat, 35
give place (*sthan dena*), 67–68
GMVN. *See* Garhwal Mandal Vikas Nigam
God (*bhagavan*), 32, 136
god of justice (*nyaya devata*), 106–107
God's Fifth Abode (Pennington), 208n13
Golu Devata, 106–115, 122, 135; at Jhakar Saim, 154, 158, 165–168, 174, 175
Gombrich, Richard, 35
Good, Byron, 221n23
Goril. *See* Golu Devata
grace (*kripa*), 73, 74
gram. *See* village
gram sabha (village association), 83
Grinshpon, Yohanan, 145
guru (*jagariya*), 7, 42, 46, 115, 200n21, 218n1; on pilgrimages, 160, 161, 176. *See also jagaris*
guru dakshina (offering to guru), 136
Guru Gorakhnath, 164
gyan (knowledge), 187, 189

hakikat (objective reality), 185
Halliburton, Murphy, 73
hankar-jankar (black magic), 57
hantyas, 199n16
Hanuman, 40
harami (devilish), 214n21
harami nach (forbidden dancing), 86
Harijan (people of God), 16–17, 128, 205n85
Harjyu, 156–157, 158
Haru-Harit, 122
hava (like the wind), 9, 214n30
healing room, xiii–xviii
heart (*hriday*), 145
heat (*garami*), 67
highest god (*parameshvar*), 144–145
Hinduism. *See specific topics*
Hindutva, 150
holy persons (*sadhu-sant*), 144

horse (*ghora*), 7
hriday (heart), 145
humors (*doshas*), 56, 73
hurka, 79
hurt (*chot*), 210n10

identity (*pahchan*), 59
I-doing (*ahamkara*), 64, 65
ilaj karana, 58
ill-health (*tabiyat kharab hona*), 118
In Amma's Healing Room (Flueckinger), 218n3
incantations (*mantras*), xiv, 220n12
incarnations. *See* avatars
Indian Congress Party, 129
indices (*suchi*), 211n13
inferior and partial (*adhuri*), 182
In Amma's Healing Room (Flueckiger), 218n3
inner chamber (*garbha-griha*), 160
intoxication (*nasha*), 144
invitation (*nyauta*), 146
isht dev (chosen deity), 8, 26, 27, 106; Katyuris and, 49; Nagaraja as, 27
ishvar, 136
Ishvar ji, 78, 79–80
Islam. *See* Muslims

jadu-tona (black magic), 35
jagah (small place), 37, 43
jagar, 7–8, 19–20, 200n20; animal sacrifice at, 216n24; *bhut* in, 218n47; Brahminical religion and, 50; *chhal* in, 218n47; at Danda Nagaraja, 27; Danda Nagaraja and, 35; ghosts at, 24, 98–124, 216n24, 217n30; Giridhar ji on, 47; by *gurus*, 7, 46; at Jhakar Saim, 155; Krishna and, 37; Nagaraja and, 22–23, 32, 36, 40; participants in, 200n21; on pilgrimages, 25; placemaking and, 213n14; possession at, 186–187; women at, 216n24
jagaris, 7, 21, 210n7, 218n1, 219n2; on affliction, 60; *aujis* and, 79–80, 213n10; Brit Barma by, 59; calls by, 130; castes and, 24, 127–153; *chal* and *tal* and, 221n25; *dosh* and, 55; embodiment and, 127; ghosts and, 107; lives of, 127–153; migration and marginalization of, 133–137; pilgrimages with, 24–25; tantra and, 220n12; in village, 79–80
jagariya. *See* guru
jagirdar (powerful ruler), 42

jagrit (awakened), 61
jaharile (poisonous), 59
Jaipal, 220nn20–21, 221n22
jajaman (ritual sponsors), 77, 106, 109–111, 114
Jangam, Chinnaiah, 204n67, 205n85, 213n9
Jassal, Smita Tewari, 215n5
jat. *See* pilgrimage
jati (species): *aujis* and, 76; castes and, 14–16; in villages, 85
Jhakar Saim, 24–25, 154–183
jogi (wandering mendicant), 62–65, 71–72
joyful play (*khel*), 155
jugalbandi (musical dialogue), 158
jujube tree (*ber*), 60, 74
justice (*nyaya*), 166, 217n32

Kaliya Nag, 41–42, 61–62, 65, 73, 211n16
Kaliyavan, 59, 60
kalpana (fancy), 189
kampan (trembling), 145–146
kamzor (weakness), 121
Kansa, 58
kapha, 56
karma (actions), 59, 73, 131–132
karobar (profession), 155
katha (recitation of Bhagavata Purana), 32, 35
Kauravas, 38, 41, 57, 80
Kayuris, 48–49
Keshwan, Lalit, 62–65, 66, 71
kettledrum (*damaun*), 77, 79, 104
Khalji dynasty, 209n23
kharidana (buy), 180
khasiya, 39, 46, 209n25
khas sambandh (special relationship), 172–173
khel (joyful play), 155
King and the Clown in South Indian Myth and Poetry, The (Shulman), 214n20
KMVN. *See* Kumaon Mandal Vikas Nigam
knowledge (*gyan*), 187, 189
kolta, 219n5
kripa (grace), 73, 74
kripa/daya (compassion), 86
Krishna, 165, 188; affliction of, 66–67; birth of, 33; Brahman as, 40; as Brahmin, 46–47; in Danda Nagaraja, 32–33, 42–44, 45; *dvaraka-pati* and, 47–48, 209n30; Gangu Ramola and, 36, 40, 42–45, 48, 50, 54, 62–65, 210n11, 211n16; *garudas* and, 57–58; *gathas*

Krishna (*continued*)
 on, 210n7; Giridhar ji on, 50–51; *jagar* and, 37; *jogi* of, 62–65, 71–72; Kaliya Nag and, 41–42, 61–62; Kurmanchal and, 48–49; in Mahabharata, 23, 56, 60, 63–64; milk and, 208n17; Nagaraja and, 8, 22, 23, 27, 32, 35, 48, 51, 52, 210n4, 211n18; as *sadhu*, 53; *sanatan dharma* and, 47; as *sannyasi*, 46–47; Sem Mukhem and, 32, 42–45, 49; *sthan* of, 49, 64; Vishnu and, 50; at Yamuna River, 61

Kshatriyas, 14, 15
kshetra (region), 28, 158–159
kul (lineage), 186
kul devatas (lineage deities), 3
Kumaon Mandal Vikas Nigam (KMVN), 221n5
kundali. *See* astrological birth chart
Kurmanchal, 48–49

lagana (attachment), 56, 72, 106, 210n10
land of the gods. *See* dev-bhumi
large stone. *See* shila
Lee, Joel, 205n76, 220n13, 223n24
Lefebvre, Henri, 201n36
Lewis, I. M., 202n39
lilas (plays, earthly activities), 3, 26, 32, 61
lineage (*kul*), 186
lineage deities (*kul devatas*), 3
linga, 136; Shiva-*lingas*, xiv, 208n18
list (*parchi*), 111
Lodi dynasty, 209n23
lohar, 15, 219n5
love (*pyar se*), 60
Luhrmann, Tanya M., 198n2
Lutgendorf, Philip, 3

Mahabharata, 3; Krishna in, 23, 56, 60, 63–64; in *maidan*, 23; Sax on, 203n42. *See also panno*
Mahadev. *See* Shiva
Mahadevi. *See* Parvati
mahaul (atmosphere), 158
Maheshu Dhami, 64, 67–73, 210n7
maidan (village grounds): crisis in, 87–90; Mahabharata in, 23; women and, 86–87
maike. *See* natal village
mait. *See* natal village
majbut (strong), 121
make place (*sthan banav*), 72
mama (maternal uncle), 4, 58, 154–155, 162–163, 217n35

Mamluk dynasty, 209n23
manana (acknowledgement, belief), 25, 185–187
manauti (desire, wish), 71, 166–167
mandap, 174
mangal-git (wedding songs), 199n17
Mani, Lata, 212n8
manifestation (*prakop*), 69
manifestation (*vrtti*), 211n13
mannad, 79
mantras (incantations), xiv, 220n12
marriage, patrilocal, 97–126, 215n1
mashakbaja (bagpipes), 79
Massey, Doreen, 159
Mata ji, 26–27, 45
material manifestation of divinity (*prasad*), 169
maternal uncle (*mama*), 4, 58, 154–155, 162–163, 217n35
mathematics (*ganit*), 210n9
Mayya-Devi, 122
Meena, 38–39
Menavati, 71–72
metonymy, 198n7
milk: Gangu Ramola and, 63–64; Krishna and, 208n17; Nagaraja and, 211n18
Mina ji, 157–160
Mines, Diane, 8, 221n3
Mirabai, 188–189
miracles (*chamatkar*), 137
mishran (mixing/mingling), 157–160
mobile spatial field, 9, 201n36
Modi, Narendra, 13, 29, 129
Mori Lal, 54
mrityu lok (world of the dead), 98
multiday sacrificial ritual (*ashta-bali*), xvi
Munn, Nancy, 9, 201n36
Munshi Ram, 16, 205n76
murti (statue, temple image), 27, 43; of Golu Devata, 168; Nagaraja as, 33; of serpent, 208n17
mushkilein (troubles), 102
Mushkunda, 59
musical dialogue (*jugalbandi*), 158
Muslims/Islam, 204n61; animal sacrifice by, 37, 38; BJP and, 28–29, 38; conversion to, 206n90; *dev-bhumi* and, 37–39; ghosts and, 105; RSS and, 206n88
mythical winged beings (*garudas*), 57–58

Nabokov (Clark-Decès), Isabelle, 10, 99–100, 218n42
nach (dance), 7, 111, 214nn29–30; on pilgrimage, 155. *See also panno*
nachana (dancing), 61, 67, 68, 80, 200n24; by Ganganth, 107; ghosts and, 123–124; on pilgrimages, 161, 171–172
nag. See serpent
nagadosh (serpent affliction), 2, 45, 67; animal sacrifice for, 72; by Gangu Ramola, 62, 73; Katyuris and, 49; by Nagaraja, 54, 68, 200n24; at Sem Mukhem, 200n24; troubles and, 68–69
nagara, 79, 134
Nagaraja (serpent king): affliction and, 52–74; as *avatar*, 27; Brahmin as, 40; as chosen deity, 8; *darshan dena* of, 45; *dev-bhumi* and, 26–28; Gangu Ramola and, 54; *gathas* and, 22–23; Gita-Bhagavat and, 35; as *isht dev*, 27; *jagar* and, 22–23, 32, 36, 40; Krishna and, 8, 22, 23, 27, 32, 35, 48, 51, 52, 210n4, 211n18; as maternal uncle, 4; milk and, 211n18; *as murti*, 33; *nagadosh* by, 54, 68, 200n24; *pasva* of, 210n7; Sem Mukhem and, 39–44, 49; *sthan* of, 44; *vahan* of, 211n11. *See also* Danda Nagaraja
nag devata (serpent deities), 2
Naithani, Shivprasad, 48–49, 50, 51
nam lena (acknowledge and to honor), 198n5
Nanda Baba, 41
Nanda Devi, 4, 162–163
Narad, 63
Narayan, 63–64
Narayan Astra, 57
naresh, 45
nar lok (world of the living), 98, 155
nasha (intoxication), 144
natal village (*mait, maike*), 86, 97, 106, 110, 119, 121, 177
National Institute of Rural Development (NIRD), 134
Navaratri, 213n12
Nepal, 105
neta (politician), 82, 213n13
netagiri (politicking), 82, 90–93
Nirakar, xiv, 4
NIRD. *See* National Institute of Rural Development
nishan (sign), 197n4
niti (political ethics), 213n13
Nonresident Indian (NRI), 21

normative order (*dharma*), 64
NRI. *See* Nonresident Indian
nyaute, 146
nyaya (justice), 166, 217n32
nyaya devata (justice god), 106–107

Oakley, E. S., 35
objective reality (*hakikat*), 185
obstructions (*vighan-badha*), 102
"Ocean of Drumming" (*Dhol Sagar*), 80
offering to guru (*guru dakshina*), 136
oracles (*bakkyas*, ones who speak), xiii, 7, 197n4; castes and, 127–153; *dosh* and, 56; lives of, 127–153; migration and marginalization of, 133–137; tantra and, 220n12; *vach* and, 197n2
oral narratives. *See gathas*
Orsi, Robert, 3
outbreak (*prakop*), 69

Pahari *log* (people "of the mountains"). *See specific topics*
pahchan (identity), 59
palanquins (*dola-palkis*), 16, 205n74
panchamrit, 91
panchava dham (fifth abodes), 30, 32, 208nn13–14
panchayat (village council), 83, 102
Pandavas, 57; *aujis* and, 78; dance of, 75–77
panno (*pandav nrtya*, dance of the Pandavas), 75–95, 214n29; ambiguous exclusions in, 86–87; ambiguous inclusions in, 84–86; *maidan* crisis during, 87–90; performance of, 80–84
pap (sin), 60
parameshvar (highest god), 144–145
parchi (list), 111
pareshani (troubles), 65, 118; by ghosts, 98; *nagadosh* and, 68–69
Parvati, 80, 213n15
pasva (beast), 7, 200n21; *dosh* and, 55; of Nagaraja, 210n7
patrilocal marriage, 97–126, 215n1
Patton, Laurie, 198n7
pavitra (pure), 35
peaceful (*shant*), 6, 57, 87
Pechilis, Karen, 159
Pennington, Brian, 208n13
people of God (*Harijan*), 16–17, 128, 205n85

people "of the mountains" (Pahari *log*).
  See specific topics
phant (collection), 89
phenomenology, 201n27, 201n29
pilgrimage (*jat*), 7–8, 144; boundaries on, 163–165; to *Chhota Char Dham*, 30; confluence in, 221n2; embodiment on, 164; enclosure and courtyard on, 165–168; fifth abode and, 208n14; with *jagaris*, 24–25; *jagar* on, 25; to Jhakar Saim, 154–183; mingling on, 157–160; *nach* on, 155; placemaking on, 159–160; region and, 28; to Sem Mukhem, 45, 200n24; Wheeler on, 222n18; women on, 156, 160–163
pilgrimage on a chariot (*rath yatra*), 28–29
pilgrimage site (*tirth kshetra*), 13
pithai (sacred red powder), 170
pitta, 56
place. *See sthan*
placemaking, 5–6; embodiment and, 9–10; *jagar* and, 213n14; *manana* and, 25; on pilgrimages, 159–160; politics and precarity of, 11–14; possession and, 68; practices of, 6–11; in Tamil Nadu, 221n3; in villages, 23
place of realization (*siddha pith*), 32, 33, 144, 209n28
place of the goddess (*devi ka sthan*), 160–161
plate (*thali*), 79, 114, 147
plays. *See lilas*
poisonous (*jaharile*), 59
political ethics (*niti*), 213n13
politician (*neta*), 82, 213n13
politicking (*netagiri*), 82, 90–93
possession, 10; at *jagar*, 186–187; in *pandav nrtya*, 81; placemaking and, 68; positive and negative, 215n6; of women, 202n39, 215n6, 218n42. *See also* ghosts
power-resistance paradigm, 202n39
prachar (spread awareness), 31, 208n15
prakop (outbreak, manifestation), 69
pranam (salutations), 53
prasad (material manifestation of divinity), 169
prayer (*puja-path*), 181
pret (ghouls), 83
puchana (ask), 197n2
puja (ritual worship), 32, 35, 109–110, 122; on pilgrimages, 160
puja jana (send ritual worship), 218n48

puja-path (prayer), 181
pujaris (temple priests), 27, 33–34, 75, 208n16; at Danda Nagaraja, 31–32, 34–35, 36; on Krishna, 36–37; on pilgrimage, 174–182; at Sem Mukhem, 40, 45
pulse reading, 1–2
Puranas, 3
pure (*pavitra*), 35
purify (*shuddhi*), 16
pyar se, 60

Ramanujan, A. K., 54
Radha Soami Satsang Beas (RSSB), 18
rahasya (secret), 188
Rahi, Chander Singh, 62, 63, 210n7, 211n15
rajaniti (entered politics), 102
Rama-janama-bhumi (birthplace of Ram), 28–29
Ramanujan, A. K., 54, 210n5
Ramayana, 3, 65, 165, 172, 182–183; recitations of, 35
Ramesh, xvii–xviii
Ram Lal, 19, 56–61, 73, 74, 141–154, 184–189, 210n7, 211n12; dream and, 53–5
Ramoligarh. *See* Gangu Ramola
Rappaport, Roy, 185
Rashtriya Swayamsevak Sangh (RSS), 206n88
rath yatra (pilgrimage on a chariot), 28–29
Ravana, 65
Ravidas, 188–189
realized beings (*siddhas*), 209n28
recitation of Bhagavata Purana (*katha*), 32, 35
region (*kshetra*), 28, 158–159
Religion Against the Self (Clark-Decès), 100, 218n42
religious mendicants (*sadhus*), 53
rest houses (*dharamashala*), 18, 172
reverence (*shraddha*), 177
rhinoceros, 87–88
rhythm (*chal*), 146, 221n25
rights (*adhikar*), 121
Rig Veda: castes in, 14; Vishnu in, 201n30
ritual fire (*dhuni*), 81, 156, 161, 164
ritual sponsors (*jajaman*), 77, 106, 109–111, 114
ritual worship (*puja*), 32, 35, 109–110, 122
RSS. *See* Rashtriya Swayamsevak Sangh
RSSB. *See* Radha Soami Satsang Beas
rup (deity's form), 61

sachhai (truth), 144
sacred ash (*vibhuti*), 216n24
sacred lanscape. *See dev-bhumi*
sacred red powder (*pithai*), 170
sadhus (religious mendicants), 53
sadhu-sant (holy persons), 144
Saim Devata, 108, 122, 164, 217n35; at Jhakar Saim, 154–155; as maternal uncle, 4
Saint Nirankari Mission, 18
saints (*sants*), 140
samadhi (contemplation), 181
Samaj, Arya, 16
samarpit (dedicate), 72
sambandh (relations), 146
sanatan dharma, 47
sannyasi (renunciant), 46–47, 67, 172, 174–175, 180, 182–183
sants (saints), 140
santulan (balance), 70
saras (affinal home), 97
Satyaram ji, 104–108
Sax, William, 39, 203n42, 209n25, 215n3
Sayyid dynasty, 209n23
scarves (*dupattas*), 156, 173–174
Scheduled Castes (SC), 15, 17, 128, 133, 134, 219n4
Seale-Feldman, Aidan, 105
Sebring, J. M., 16
secret (*rahasya*), 188
seeing a deity (*darshan*), 4, 45, 167, 170
Sem Mukhem, 8, 27, 28, 166, 183; Brahman and, 40; *darshan* at, 45; as fifth abode, 30; Krishna and, 32, 42–45, 49; *nagadosh* at, 200n24; Nagaraja and, 39–44, 49; pilgrimage on a chariot to, 200n24; pilgrimages to, 45; *pujaris* at, 40, 45; serpents at, 45; *shila* and, 43–44
Sem Nagaraja, 43, 46, 47
Sem Ravals, 45
send ritual worship (*puja jana*), 218n48
serpent (*nag*), 211n17; dreams of, 1–2; *murti* of, 208n17; at Sem Mukhem, 45
serpent affliction. *See nagadosh*
serpent deities (*nag devata*), 2
serpent king. *See* Nagaraja
servants (*das*), 76, 85–86, 164
seva (service), 40, 166
shakti (deity's power), xv, 9, 56–57, 113

shame (*sharam*), 124
Shankara, 50
shant (peaceful), 6, 57, 87
Sharad ji, 75, 77, 78, 81–82, 214nn29–30
sharam (shame), 124
sharir (body), 68, 145
Sharma, Mukul, 208n22
shastra (textual traditions), 182
shastrik (authoritative knowledge), 35
Shesh Nag, 43
shila (large stone): Sem Mukhem and, 43–44; Sem Nagaraja and, 43, 46, 47
shilpakar (artisan), 16–17
Shilpakar Sabha, 16
Shiva, 165; *Dhol Sagar* and, 80; Gangu Ramola and, 50; in healing room, xiv
Shiva-*lingas* (aniconic images of the god Shiva), xiv, 208n18
shodh (research), 148–153
shraddha (reverence), 177
shuddhi (purify), 16
Shudras, 14
Shulman, David, 202n37, 214n20
siddha pith (place of realization), 32, 33, 144, 209n28
siddhas (realized beings), 209n28
signs (*nishan*), 197n4
Sikhism, 20; castes and, 21; Saint Nirankari Mission and, 18
Simmons, Caleb, 213n12
sin (*pap*), 60
sindur, 174
Singh, Karan, 75–77
Sita-Ram, 40
small four abodes/seats (*Chhota Char Dham*), 30
small horse (*dangariya*), 7, 200n21
small place (*jagah*), 37, 43
Smith, Brian, 218n38i
Smith, Frederick, 202n37
Smith, J. Z., 87
social constructionist theory, 201n29
social order and hierarchy, 86, 214n20
Sohan, xiii–xviii, 197n4
special relationship (*khas sambandh*), 172–173
species. *See jati*
speech (*bol*), 80, 145
speech (*vach*), 197n2
spirits (*atma*), 199n16

spread awareness (*prachar*), 31, 208n15
statue. *See murti*
sthan (place), xvi, 3; affliction and, 70–72; of Krishna, 49, 64; metonymy and, 198n7; of Nagaraja, 44; region and, 28
sthan banav (make place), 72
sthan dena (given place), 67–68
strong (*majbut*), 121
suchi (index), 211n13
superstition (*andha-vishvas*), 35
Swami Chidananda, 208n22
Swami Nigamanand, 12

tabiyat kharab hona (ill-health), 118
taking incarnation (*avatar lena*), 207n1
tal, 221n25
Tamil Nadu, 8, 198n9, 202n37; ghosts and women and, 98, 100; placemaking in, 221n3; temple renovation rituals in, 217n37
tamta, 15, 219n5
tantra, 220n12
Tehri Dam, 12–13, 208n22
temple image. *See murti*
temple priests. *See pujaris*
textual traditions (*shastra*), 182
thali (plate), 79, 114, 147
tirth kshetra (pilgrimage site), 13
Tirupati, 10
trembling (*kampan*), 145–146
troubles (*mushkilein*), 102
troubles (*pareshani*), 65, 118
truth (*sachhai*), 144
Tughlaq dynasty, 209n23
Tweed, Thomas, 9, 199n14, 222n13

uch jati (upper-caste), 15, 16, 20, 37–38, 76–79, 128–129
ugra (excess), 9, 72, 201n31
Ujval Das, 133–137
ulta (crooked), 59
Unishor, 90–91, 214n29
unlettered (*anpadh*), 182, 183
untouchables (*achhut*), 213n9; *aujis as*, 84; as impure, 85; Krishna as, 64
untouchability (*chua-chut*), 76
upper-caste (*uch jati*), 15, 16, 20, 37–38, 76–79, 128–129

Uttarakhand. *See specific topics*
Uttarakhand Gathoan ke Rahasya (Naithani), 48

vach (speech), 197n2
vahan (vehicles), 68, 210nn11–12
Vaishyas, 14
Valmiki, 131–132, 165, 172, 220n13
varna (color), 14–15
vata, 56
vehicles (*vahan*), 68, 210nn11–12
Venkateshan, Soumhya, 198n9
vernacular tantra, 220n12
VHP. *See* Vishwa Hindu Parishad
vibhuti (sacred ash), 216n24
vighan-badha (obstructions), 102
vigrah (fundamental aspects of Hindu gods), 3
village (*gram*), 186; castes in, 76–79, 84–85; embodiment in, 83–84, 93–96; *jagaris* in, 79–80; natal, 86, 97, 106, 110, 119, 121, 177; *pandav nrtya* in, 75–95, 214n29; placemaking in, 23; political divinities in, 75–97
village association (*gram sabha*), 83
village council (*panchayat*), 83, 102
village grounds. *See maidan*
Vishnu, 63; Kayuris and, 49; Krishna and, 50; in Rig Veda, 201n30; on Shesh Nag, 43
vishvas (faith), xvii
Vishwa Hindu Parishad (VHP), 12
vrtti (description, elaboration, manifestation), 211n13

wandering mendicant (*jogi*), 62–65, 71–72
weakness (*kamzor*), 121
wedding songs (*mangal-git*), 199n17
Weil, Simone, 55, 210n8
Wheeler, Bonnie, 154, 155, 159, 221n2, 222n18
wind (*hava*), 9, 214n30
wish (*manauti*), 71, 166–167
women, 21; Gangnath and, 217n33; ghosts and, 23–24, 97–126, 217n31, 218n49; as *hantyas*, 199n16; at *jagar*, 216n24; *maidan* and, 86–87; on pilgrimages, 156, 160–163; possession of, 202n39, 215n6, 218n42; songs of, 215n5
world of the dead (*mrityu lok*), 98
world of the living (*nar lok*), 98, 155

Yamuna River, 11, 41–42, 61
yantras (geometrical ritual diagrams), xiv–xv

GPSR Authorized Representative: Easy Access System Europe, Mustamäe tee
50, 10621 Tallinn, Estonia, gpsr.requests@easproject.com

www.ingramcontent.com/pod-product-compliance
Lightning Source LLC
Chambersburg PA
CBHW022044290426
44109CB00014B/973